THE HANDBOOK OF
GROUP PLAY THERAPY

THE HANDBOOK OF GROUP PLAY THERAPY

How to Do It
How It Works
Whom It's Best For

Daniel S. Sweeney and Linda E. Homeyer, Editors

Foreword by Garry L. Landreth

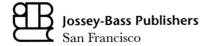

Jossey-Bass Publishers
San Francisco

Jossey-Bass books and products are available through most bookstores. To contact Jossey-Bass directly, call (888) 378-2537, fax to (800) 605-2665, or visit our website at www.josseybass.com.

Substantial discounts on bulk quantities of Jossey-Bass books are available to corporations, professional associations, and other organizations. For details and discount information, contact the special sales department at Jossey-Bass.

 This paper is acid-free and 100 percent totally chlorine-free.

Library of Congress Cataloging-in-Publication Data

Group play therapy : how to do it, how it works, whom it's best for
  / Daniel S. Sweeney and Linda E. Homeyer, editors; foreword by
  Garry Landreth. — 1st ed.
      p. cm.
    Includes bibliographical references and index.
    ISBN 0-7879-4807-1 (cloth : acid-free paper)
    1. Group play therapy.   I. Sweeney, Daniel S.   II. Homeyer, Linda.
  RH505.P6 G76 1999
  618.92'89165—dc21

                                                    98-40229

FIRST EDITION
PB Printing 10 9 8 7 6 5 4 3 2 1

CONTENTS

PART THREE: GROUP PLAY THERAPY ISSUES AND TECHNIQUES   177

To Garry Landreth, whose mentoring and friendship
has meant so very much to us, and whose vision and mission has
meant so much to the world of play therapy and to children.

FOREWORD

Although the field of play therapy has made great strides since the ground-breaking work of pioneers in the early 1900s, little has been done to facilitate the development of group play therapy. There has been to my knowledge only one group play therapy text published in the past seventy-five years.

In the broad field of counseling, the efficiency of saving counselor time has often been considered a major attraction of group counseling. Research has shown, however, that the use of groups provides advantages other than expediency. Group counseling can provide individuals with the kinds of experiences that help them learn to function effectively, to develop tolerance to stress and anxiety, and to find satisfaction in working and living with others. Developments in the use of groups in therapy have largely taken place in work with adolescents and adults. There seems to be no clear answer as to why it has taken over thirty years for a second book on play therapy to appear on the scene. Play therapists and what they do in the playroom will be changed by this book.

Individuals function most of their lives within some sort of group. Against this background of interaction with others, one's self-concept is formed and many times distorted. This distorted perception of self, and self in relation to others, occurs in the dynamics of the family group relationship. Seemingly then, the most effective place for dealing with adjustment difficulties is within a relationship that incorporates the basic structure which originally contributed to the difficulty.

Group play therapy is a dynamic approach which holds great promise for improving, expanding, and enhancing the play therapy relationship to meet the existing needs of children. In this relationship, children learn from each other, encourage each other, support each other, work out difficulties, share in pain and joy, discover what it is like to help each other, and discover that they are capable of giving as well as receiving help. In this unique relationship children discover their own uniqueness and at the same time begin to realize that other children are like them in that they, too, have fears, problems, concerns, and deeply hidden issues. That other children, too, have experienced hurt, pain, frustration, anger, and wounded spirits. That other children, too, want to escape, hide, run away, and lose themselves from parts of life that cannot be controlled. That other children, too, experience the exhilaration that freedom and creative expression can bring. This is the essence of group play therapy.

Children in group play therapy learn from each other about themselves and about each other. They also learn important lessons about social interaction and develop the communication and interactive skills necessary for living satisfying and rewarding lives. Children cannot live in isolation. Therefore, we must provide them with opportunities to maximize the interpersonal skills necessary for living life effectively in interactions with other people. Group play therapy can become a reality testing laboratory for children, a place to redefine self.

A play therapy group represents immediate social reality and enables children to test their behavior. The group can serve as a practice field in which children can become aware of their own feelings, how they feel about and act toward others, and how others perceive and act toward them. In the larger society, children encounter rather rigid and fixed structural demands, which are inhibiting factors in their striving for self-discovery and change. The flexibility and acceptance experienced in the play therapy group is a liberating agent for children, providing an opportunity for them to experiment in their own way with reality as they perceive it.

This book provides an integration of theory and practice in group therapy. It presents the reader with much needed information about issues and techniques necessary for implementing a play therapy group with specific populations of children. This is insightful and inspiring reading about children's needs and how the play therapy relationship in a group setting can meet those needs in a uniquely natural and spontaneous way. With this book now available to play therapy practitioners, there should be no reason for confusion about what group play therapy is or hesitancy in bringing several children into the play therapy room. How, why, when, and for whom to organize play therapy groups is made crystal clear in this book. Careful and detailed information along with examples of what happens in play therapy groups is described from the first-hand experiences of the authors. This book is must reading for all play therapists.

GARRY L. LANDRETH
Regents Professor
Director, Center for Play Therapy
University of North Texas

PREFACE

We are delighted and honored to have prepared the book you now hold in your hands. Both of us are committed to the continued expansion of the use of play therapy as the primary medium of intervention for children. If children are to have access to effective mental health services, then increased numbers of counselors, psychologists, social workers, nurses, psychiatrists, and other appropriate professionals must learn to enter the child's world of play.

There has been a marked increase in professional literature on play therapy. This continually growing body of work includes books and professional journal articles on play therapy theory, practice, and research. However, very little has been written about group play therapy.

The beginnings of group play therapy can be found in the original work of Haim Ginott and S. R. Slavson. We have included a classic article from each of these individuals in Part One of this book. Part Two contains the application of major play therapy theories to the group process. We believe it is imperative for effective therapy to have a congruent approach with which to conceptualize individuals and their issues. Part Three, on group play therapy issues and techniques, provides you with a look at a variety of techniques that you can add to your work with children. The ability to select techniques with purpose and intention when working with children is key to treating the individual child as well as the "personality" of the group. Part Four is rich with applications of group play therapy to special populations. Each chapter provides insight into working with particular needs or in particular settings.

We trust this book will assist you in skill development and in your increased understanding of working with children in a group play therapy setting. We challenge you—as we continuously challenge ourselves—to advocate for, learn from, and enjoy being with the children.

Acknowledgments

There are so many people involved in the production of a text, particularly an edited one. We must first and foremost thank our chapter authors, whose contributions not only reflect their expertise but also their dedication to the field and love for children. We also acknowledge and appreciate those who have given permission to reprint previously published material.

We would also like to thank Garry Landreth, Jason Aronson, and the editorial staff at Jossey-Bass for their encouragement and support.

Professionally, we need to acknowledge our respective universities: George Fox University (D.S.S.) and Southwest Texas State University (L.E.H.) for their support of our writing and research.

Personally, we need to express our acknowledgment and love for our families: Marla, Jessica, Michele, Renata, and Josiah (D.S.S.) and Dan (L.E.H.). These caring people listen supportively when we talk at length over long periods of time regarding our projects and graciously tolerate the many hours at our desks. These people are a significant and vital part of our worlds.

Newberg, Oregon　　　　　　　　　　　　　　　　　　　　DANIEL S. SWEENEY
March 1999　　　　　　　　　　　　　　　　　　　　　　LINDA E. HOMEYER

THE HANDBOOK OF
GROUP PLAY THERAPY

PART ONE

INTRODUCTION TO GROUP PLAY THERAPY

CHAPTER ONE

GROUP PLAY THERAPY

Daniel S. Sweeney and Linda E. Homeyer

Group play therapy is a natural union of two effective therapeutic modalities. Play therapists and group therapists share several important traits. Both are committed to a therapeutic process that is creative and dynamic. Both are centered on the development and maintenance of safe and therapeutic relationships. Both are focused on facilitation of an unfolding process as opposed to the application of an immediate solution. Both are engaged in efforts requiring prerequisite training and supervision. The marriage of play therapy and group process is a natural and intuitive response to the needs of emotionally hurting children.

Children can and do benefit from the relationships and interactions with other children within the context of a group play setting. In the same way that group counseling works with adults, group play therapy provides for children a psychosocial process through which they grow and learn about themselves and others:

> In group counseling relationships, children experience the therapeutic releasing qualities of discovering that their peers have problems too, and a diminishing of the barriers of feeling all alone. A feeling of belonging develops, and new interpersonal skills are attempted in a "real life" encounter where children learn more effective ways of relating to people through the process of trial and error. The group then is a microcosm of children's everyday world. In this setting children are afforded the opportunity for immediate reactions from peers as well as the opportunity for vicarious learning. Children also develop a

sensitivity to others and receive a tremendous boost to their self-concept through being helpful to someone else. For abused children who have poor self-concepts and a life history of experiencing failure, discovering they can be helpful to someone else may be the most profound therapeutic quality possible. In the counseling group, children also discover they are worthy of respect and that their worth is not dependent on what they do or what they produce but rather on who they are [Berg & Landreth, 1998, p. 258].

Children learn about themselves in group play therapy. They learn because they are permitted to communicate in their own language—play—and they learn as they hear and observe the perceptions of the therapist and the other children toward them. Children learn that is not just acceptable to be unique, it is valued. Cooperation is important in a group, and compliance sometimes imperative. At the same time, creativity and originality is honored. A therapeutic play group may provide the closest thing to the structure and acceptance of a family as is possible for some children. Van der Kolk (1985) listed several elements of the play therapy group that contribute to these benefits:

- Accepting the child totally
- Extending a simple invitation to play without explanations, goals, reasons, questions, or expectations
- Helping the child learn self-expression and enjoy respect
- Permitting but not encouraging regressive behavior early in therapy
- Permitting all "symbolic behavior" while limiting destructive behavior
- Prohibiting children from physically attacking each other
- Enforcing limits calmly, noncritically, and briefly; mentioning limits only as necessary
- Feeling and expressing empathy

The chapters that follow will bring greater focus to the theory and process of group play therapy. This chapter provides a brief introduction to the subject in general, offering a brief look at play therapy and therapeutic play groups to serve as foundational material for the balance of the book.

Play Therapy

Most readers will have a basic familiarity with the theory and process of play therapy. The following summary is provided as context for the discussion of using play therapy in groups. Landreth (1991) provides a succinct and comprehensive definition of play therapy:

Play therapy is defined as a dynamic interpersonal relationship between a child and a therapist trained in play therapy procedures who provides selected play materials and facilitates the development of a safe relationship for the child to fully express and explore self (feelings, thoughts, experiences, and behaviors) through the child's natural medium of communication, play [p. 14].

The premise upon which play therapy is based is spelled out in the last few words of this definition. Therapists who understand the importance of play in the lives of children, and that children naturally communicate through play, are well on their way to understanding the world of children. Conversely, the therapist who employs traditional adult-style counseling with children sends a very clear message to child clients: "I am unwilling to enter your world of communication; therefore, if this process is going to work, you have to leave that world and come into my adult world, which includes my level of thinking and communication."

The recognition of the importance of children's play is paramount. Its value to children and its subsequent value to the therapeutic process with children is crucial. Caplan and Caplan (1974) summarize several unique attributes about child's play:

- Play is a voluntary activity by nature. In a world full of requirements and rules, play is refreshing and provides a respite from everyday tension.
- Play is free from evaluation and judgment by adults. Children are safe to make mistakes without failure and adult ridicule.
- Play encourages fantasy and the use of imagination. In a make-believe world, children can exercise the need for control without competition.
- Play increases interest and involvement. Children often have short attention spans and are reluctant to participate in a lower interest, less attractive activity.
- Play encourages the development of the physical and mental self (pp. xii–xvii).

The group play therapy process would do well to recognize these imperatives about the play of children. Landreth (1991) suggests: "Children's play can be more fully appreciated when recognized as their natural medium of communication. Children express themselves more fully and more directly through self-initiated spontaneous play than they do verbally because they are more comfortable with play. For children to 'play out' their experiences and feelings is the most natural dynamic and self-healing process in which children can engage" (p. 10).

Sweeney (1997) discussed the fundamentally preoperational nature of play and play therapy. Adult talk therapy is essentially characterized by the formal operations of Piagetian development. Adult communication is by its nature abstract and sophisticated, whereas children are by their nature concrete and simple. Play and language are essentially relative opposites, as they are contrasting forms of representation. When compelled to cognitively verbalize, children must translate thoughts into the accepted medium (talk). The inherent limitation is that children must fit their world into this existing medium. Play and fantasy, however, do not carry this limitation. Children can create without the restriction of making their creation verbally understandable. Play and children, therefore, do not lend themselves to operationalism—they are in fact *pre*operational.

The diagnostic criteria for many of the childhood disorders in the DSM-IV (American Psychiatric Association, 1994) are essentially sensory based. This makes sense, because children themselves are so sensory focused. It would seem, therefore, that a treatment approach for children should also be sensory based. Talk therapy approaches do not meet this criterion. Play therapy does.

It is crucial to remember that the lives of children are so often outside their own control and are often intruded upon, sometimes in very traumatic ways. Therapeutic interventions, therefore, should not only be nonintrusive but provide high levels of safety for children. Play therapy does this. Play therapy provides children a safe place and safe relationship in which to abreact. It works through the use of metaphors and symbols, where toys and play may represent an abuser or an abusive situation; through the use of projection, where intense and frightening emotions may be projected onto the play media and activity; and through sublimation, where negative emotions toward people may be displaced onto toys. Additionally, play therapy allows the child to experience in fantasy what is not allowed in reality: mastery and control over people and situations.

Group play therapy combines the advantages of the play therapy event with the benefits of group process. In the safety and growth-promoting setting of the play therapy experience and the natural course of interaction with other children in the group experience, children learn about themselves, others, and life.

Group Play Therapy in Practice

When children are experiencing interpersonal and intrapersonal difficulties, group play therapy can be a dynamic intervention. In addition to learning about themselves and others, children benefit from the reciprocal encouragement of the group process. Before discussing some technical considerations of group work with children, it is helpful to explore some of the benefits and rationale for group play therapy with children. Sweeney (1997) summarized nine basic advantages of therapeutic play groups:

- Groups tend to promote spontaneity in children and may therefore increase their level of participation in the play. The therapist's attempt to communicate permissiveness is enhanced by the group dynamics, thus freeing children to risk engagement in various play behaviors.
- The affective life of children is dealt with at two levels—the intrapsychic issues of individual group members and the interpersonal issues between the therapist and group members.
- Vicarious learning and catharsis take place in any group setting. Children observe the emotional and behavior expressions of other group members and learn coping behaviors, problem-solving skills, and alternative avenues of self-expression. As children see other group members engage in activities that they may initially feel cautious or apprehensive about, they gain the courage to explore.
- Children experience the opportunity for self-growth and self-exploration in group play therapy. This process is facilitated by the responses and reactions of group members to a child's emotional and behavioral expression. Children have the opportunity to reflect on and achieve insight into self as they learn to evaluate and reevaluate themselves in light of peer feedback.
- Groups provide significant opportunities to anchor children to the world of reality. Limit setting and reality testing occur not only between the therapist and individual group member but also among the children themselves. Because the group serves as a tangible microcosm of society, the group play therapy experience is tangibly tied to reality.
- Because play therapy groups serve as a microcosm of society, the therapist has the opportunity to gain substantial insight into the children's presentation in their everyday lives. This real-life perspective may be seen in the microcosm evident in the playroom.
- The group play setting may decrease a child's need or tendency to be repetitious or to retreat into fantasy play. While these behaviors may be necessary for some children in the processing of their issues, the group play therapy setting can bring children stuck in repetition or fantasy into the here-and-now.
- Children have the opportunity to practice for everyday life. The therapeutic play group provides the opportunity for children to develop interpersonal skills, master new behaviors, offer and receive assistance, and experiment with alternative expressions of emotions and behavior.
- The presence of more than one child in the play therapy setting may assist in the development of the therapeutic relationship for some children. As withdrawn children observe the therapist building trust with other children, they are often drawn in. This helps reduce the anxiety of children unsure about the playroom and the person of the therapist.

Ethical and Legal Considerations

It is appropriate to reiterate the need and ethical responsibility for a group play therapist to have proper training and supervised experience in the field. Additionally, child therapists must be familiar with the laws of the state in which they practice. Counselors should also be aware of the ethical guidelines of the corresponding professional organizations, as well as the policies and procedures for any employing institution. For therapists who focus on group work, the Ethical Guidelines for Group Counselors established by the Association for Specialists in Group Work (1990) are also a useful resource.

Parental permission must be obtained prior to providing group therapy for children, just as with individual counseling. Since parents are legally responsible for their children, they must be made aware of the purpose of the group, and appropriate consent secured. Bear in mind that child custody is frequently an issue, so it is crucial for the therapist to ensure that it is the legal guardian who is providing the consent, and that it is informed consent. Planned exercises should be explained to the parents—and to the children. In some situations, namely a school counseling setting, additional authorization may not be necessary.

Just as with any group, children cannot be given an absolute promise of confidentiality when in group play therapy. Confidentiality may need to be broken by the therapist in a reportable situation, as when it is essential to report abuse to authorities or to pass information on to school or agency administrators per policy.

Some states have strengthened parental rights laws. These laws may provide, in part, that no school employee may "encourage or coerce a child to withhold information from the child's parents" (Texas Education Code, 1995). Consequently, school counselors have been informed that they may not request that the children in a counseling group maintain the confidentiality of what is shared by others in the group sessions. Even though the law may have been intended to be sure school personnel do not impose secrecy between any particular child and his or her parents, this expanded application has been made. Clearly, being well informed of one's own state and professional laws and ethical codes is important.

Screening and preparation for the play groups is also an ethical issue. Children are rarely self-referred, so it is the therapist's responsibility to ensure appropriate group placement. Just as with adult groups, children should have the opportunity to participate or leave the group.

Group Selection and Size

The success of a play therapy group may well be related to the selection of group members and the size of the group. Ginott asserts that the basic requirement for selection to a group is the presence of and capacity for "social hunger" (1975).

This refers to children's need to be accepted by their peers and a desire to attain and maintain status in the group.

Some children will not respond well to group play therapy. These children should generally be seen on an individual basis. While this is generally a case-by-case decision, Ginott (1961) suggested some contraindications:

- Siblings who exhibit intense rivalry
- Extremely aggressive children
- Sexually acting-out children
- Children experiencing difficulty due to poor infant-mother attachment
- Sociopathic children (that is, children intending to inflict harm or revenge)
- Children with an extremely poor self-image

The chapters that follow will discuss various criteria for group selection. It is generally recommended to use individual play therapy as part of the process of screening for potential group play therapy members. Even a single play session may reveal the indication or contraindication for inclusion in a group. Other screening methods may also be appropriate, including parent report, teacher report, behavioral assessment, and child interviews.

Another consideration in group work with children is the size of the group. Generally, the younger the children, the smaller the group. Very young children are usually just beginning to learn how to function in groups of any kind outside of their immediate family. An associated issue may be the level of structure that is provided in the group, and whether this should be related to the age of the children. This will generally vary according to the group theory and the group population, as will be discussed in later chapters. It is important to remember that it is challenging to attend to too many children, and most facilities cannot accommodate a large group. Remember that two children make a group, and even this small a group can be very beneficial.

It may be helpful to keep the group balanced. For example, whereas it is often helpful to run groups on particular topics and for particular populations, it may be appropriate to avoid composing a group of children who have experienced the same trauma. This may be necessary to prevent an escalation of traumatic behaviors or emotions.

If a group has two girls, it may be helpful to balance it out with two boys. It is generally suggested that a group not have a majority of one gender. If a group has two withdrawn children, it may be helpful to balance it with two outgoing or assertive children.

Although this varies with sibling group play therapy and other cases, the age range of children in group play therapy should generally not exceed twelve months. The difference between a three-year-old and a five-year-old is simply too great for most therapeutic purposes. Unless developmental delays are an issue, this is an appropriate rule of thumb to follow. In terms of gender, children generally do not need to be separated by gender until middle school or junior high school age. Finally, physical size of the children also needs to be taken into consideration. Given the variety of growth patterns of individual children, a single larger or smaller child is not recommended. As with other dynamics, balance is the key.

Group Setting and Materials

A crucial initial consideration should be the facility and materials to be used for the therapeutic play group. A regular counseling office may not be appropriate because of the necessity to set too many limits. Whereas many group rooms are equipped with carpeting, chairs, and soft pillows, a play group room will often have different needs. Ideally, a group room that is set aside for play therapy groups is best, floored with tile and equipped with sturdy toys and furniture. An adequately sized room that is not devoted to play therapy will work, however, as long as the therapist recognizes the need for appropriate limits.

The room should not be too small or too large. A room that is at least twelve by fifteen feet is suggested. A playroom that is too small can lead to frustration and aggression between group members. A room that is too large not only creates the possibility of uncontrolled behavior but also enables the withdrawn child to avoid interaction. The potential for high levels of noise and messiness should also be noted, making the location of the group room in a counseling facility an important consideration.

The play materials may vary according to theory and purpose. Landreth (1991, p. 116) suggests that in general, the play media should be selected to support the following purposes:

- Facilitate a wide range of creative expression
- Facilitate a wide range of emotional expression
- Engage children's interests
- Facilitate expressive and exploratory play
- Allow exploration and expression without verbalization
- Allow success without prescribed structure
- Allow for noncommittal play

Another consideration may also be suggested. It may not be appropriate to provide enough toys of any one type so that each group member can have one. Whereas this may seem to promote fairness, it deprives children of the opportunity to learn to share and resolve conflict with limited play materials.

With older children and adolescents, an activity group setting of some kind is recommended. One of the primary benefits of activity groups is that group members enjoy the continued opportunity for nonverbal expression that play therapy provides, with the accompanied advantage of group activities and discussion.

Length and Frequency of Sessions

The length of each group session must be considered. It is generally recommended to relate the length of the group session to the age of the child members. Simply, the younger the children are—generally, the shorter the session. The group facilitator must consider the attention span of the children, taking note to consider psychological age over chronological age. For preschool children and early elementary-aged children, a play therapy group may run for twenty to forty minutes. For children approaching middle or junior high school, the groups may run well over an hour.

The duration of the group will also vary. Gumaer (1984) noted that most research indicates that for group counseling to be effective with children, a minimum of ten sessions is necessary. Again, this will vary for play groups meeting in different settings (schools, hospitals, and so on) and for different populations (sexually abused, grieving, and so on).

Frequency of group meetings is another issue to deliberate. This will relate to the purpose of the group and the severity of presenting problems. Intensive short-term groups meeting two to five times per week may be very effective. Kot's (1995) research reported positive results on the efficacy of short-term, intensive child-centered play therapy with children who had witnessed domestic violence and were temporarily residing in family shelters. Although this research involved individual play therapy, it points to the significant potential for short-term, intensive therapeutic play groups.

Therapeutic Responses

While the responses of the group play therapist may again vary according to theory and setting, a few basics should be considered. The therapeutic role of the counselor in group play therapy is similar to that in individual play therapy. However, the group play therapist must have a high tolerance for messiness and noise and must be able to handle frequent chaos. It is imperative that the therapist keep responses balanced between group members and avoid placing the focus on children who are more active or needy. This is an easy trap to fall into but sends messages of nonacceptance to children who are less verbal and less active. These messages generally reinforce an already present—and negative—view of self.

As with any client, therapeutic responses should not be intrusive, and with group play therapy should include the child's name. If a response is made without the child's name, the group members may not know to whom the response is directed. Additionally, it is helpful to avoid using the third person when interacting with the children. For example, when simply tracking behavior, it is best to replace statements like "Randy is playing in the sand" with those in the form "Randy, you're playing in the sand." Children, not unlike adults, are honored when talked to rather than talked about.

Limit-Setting in Groups

The appropriate setting of therapeutic limits in play therapy is one of the most curative and growth-promoting aspects of the counseling process. The pace of group play therapy is magnified considerably over that of individual sessions, and the attending and responsive skills of the therapist may be greatly challenged. The group play therapist must be an expert limit-setter.

A reminder of the basic rationale for setting limits in the playroom may be helpful. Landreth and Sweeney (1997) summarized the following:

> (1) Limits define the boundaries of the therapeutic relationship; (2) limits provide security and safety for the child, both physically and emotionally; (3) limits demonstrate the therapist's intent to provide safety for the child; (4) limits anchor the session to reality; (5) limits allow the therapist to maintain a positive and accepting attitude toward the child; (6) limits allow the child to express negative feelings without causing harm, and the subsequent fear of retaliation; (7) limits offer stability and consistency; (8) limits promote and enhance the child's sense of self-responsibility and self-control; (9) limits protect the play therapy room; and (10) limits provide for the maintenance of legal, ethical, and professional standards [p. 34].

Limits and limit setting are unique in the therapeutic play group. Group members experience limits set not only by the therapist but also by the other group members. As suggested earlier, this serves a key function. The group play therapist also must be keen in anticipating limits and resolved to set limits. Clear and total (not conditional) limits are also imperative when working with groups. Because the activity level may be so high, it can be a temptation to constantly set limits so as to maintain control. The group play therapist should be patient and allow children to work things out for themselves, while setting appropriate limits.

Conclusion

Haim Ginott (1961) suggested that group play therapy is based on the assumption that children will modify their behavior in exchange for acceptance. This premise, combined with the capacity and tendency of children to seek out and establish relationships, underlies the therapeutic advantage for using group play therapy. Ginott posited that the primary goal for group play therapy, like all therapy, is enduring personality change (a strengthened ego and enhanced self-image). To this end, Ginott proposes several questions, from which we can summarize the primary therapeutic goals of group play therapy:

- Does the method facilitate or hinder the establishment of a therapeutic relationship?
- Does it accelerate or retard evocation of catharsis?
- Does it aid or obstruct attainment of insight?
- Does it augment or diminish opportunities for reality testing?
- Does it open or block channels for sublimation? (p. 2)

The answers to these questions bring focus to the goals of therapeutic play groups. Group play therapy should facilitate the establishment of a therapeutic relationship, the expression of emotions, and the development of insight, and it should provide opportunities for reality testing and for expressing feelings and needs in more acceptable ways.

The opportunity for children to connect with each other in reciprocal ways leads to an increased capacity to redirect behaviors into a more self-enhancing and interpersonally appropriate manner. Group play therapy experiences foster insight, which leads to a greater degree of self-control and correspondingly helps to decrease externalizing (acting-out or aggressive) and internalizing (acting-in or regressive) behaviors. Through the opportunity to communicate in their natural medium of communication, children also have increased opportunities to express feelings, desires, and needs in the group play therapy setting.

Although group play therapy has been successfully employed with children for some time, its use has been somewhat limited. Group play therapy successfully blends the benefits of play therapy and group process, and may well serve to optimize the limited resources of both therapists and children. Children grow and heal in a process that helps them translate their learning into life outside the play setting. Group play therapy provides this setting.

References

American Psychiatric Association. (1994). *Diagnostic and statistical manual of mental disorders* (4th ed.). Washington, DC: Author.

Association for Specialists in Group Work. (1990). ASGW ethical guidelines for group counselors. *Journal for Specialists in Group Work, 15*(2), 119–126.

Berg, R., & Landreth, G. (1998). *Group counseling: Concepts and procedures* (3rd ed.). Muncie, IN: Accelerated Development.

Caplan, F., & Caplan, T. (1974). *The power of play.* New York: Anchor Books.

Ginott, H. (1961). *Group psychotherapy with children: The theory and practice of play therapy.* New York: McGraw-Hill.

Ginott, H. (1975). Group play therapy with children. In G. Gazda (Ed.), *Basic approaches to group psychotherapy and group counseling* (2nd ed., pp. 327–341). Springfield, IL: Thomas.

Gumaer, J. (1984). *Counseling and therapy for children.* New York: Free Press.

Kot, S. (1995). *Intensive play therapy with child witnesses of domestic violence.* Unpublished doctoral dissertation, University of North Texas, Denton.

Landreth, G. (1991). *Play therapy: The art of the relationship.* Muncie, IN: Accelerated Development.

Landreth, G., & Sweeney, D. (1997). Child-centered play therapy. In K. O'Connor & L. Braverman (Eds.), *Play therapy: Theory and practice* (pp. 17–45). New York: Wiley.

Sweeney, D. (1997). *Counseling children through the world of play.* Wheaton, IL: Tyndale House.

Texas Education Code, Section 26.009, a (1995).

Van der Kolk, C. (1985). *Introduction to group counseling and psychotherapy.* Columbus, OH: Merrill.

CHAPTER TWO

PLAY GROUP THERAPY

A Theoretical Framework

Haim G. Ginott

The tendency to regard group therapy as "superficial" has abated consider-ably during the last decade, but it has not completely disappeared. The belief is still expressed that group therapy is a superficial form of treatment suited for people who lack either the money or the patience required in individual therapy. However, on a national and international scale, group therapy has been gaining acceptance both by individual clinicians and by treatment agencies.

Two factors account for the change in attitude toward group therapy: (1) Group therapy has evolved a systematic theory with principles and processes that can be tested by the scientific method. (2) Necessity, "the mother of inven-tion," has compelled many therapists to try group therapy in an effort to meet more realistically the growing demands for service. In the course of trial and error, many have found group therapy to be not just individual therapy extended to sev-eral participants simultaneously but a qualitatively different experience with rich potentialities of its own.

Nicholas Hobbs (1951) expressed the thoughts of many group therapists when he wrote: "It is one thing to be understood and accepted by a therapist, it

Originally published in *International Journal of Group Psychotherapy, 8*(4), 410–418. Copyright © 1958 by American Group Psychotherapy Association, Inc. Reprinted by permission.

is considerably a more potent experience to be understood and accepted by several people who are also honestly sharing their feelings in a joint search for a more satisfying way of life" (p. 281).

The aim of group therapy, as of all therapy, is to effect basic changes in the intrapsychic equilibrium of each patient. Through relationship, catharsis, insight, reality testing, and sublimation,[1] therapy brings about a new balance in the structure of the personality, with a strengthened ego, modified superego, and improved self-image. The inner experience responsible for the curative effects in maladjusted persons is the same in all therapies, just as the repair value of certain medications is the same, whether administered orally, intramuscularly, or intravenously. Every therapeutic system must explain its effectiveness and justify its existence in terms of the effects on the identifiable variables of the inner processes that constitute therapy. In evaluating a particular therapy approach, the following questions must be answered:

1. Does the method facilitate or hinder the establishment of a therapeutic relationship?
2. Does it accelerate or retard the evoking of catharsis?
3. Does it aid or obstruct the derivation of insight?
4. Does it augment or diminish the opportunities for reality testing?
5. Does it open or block channels for sublimation?

The variations in the intensity and the richness of these elements account, to a large degree, for the differences in therapy results. These criteria will be used in evaluating play group therapy.

Does Play Group Therapy Facilitate or Hinder the Establishment of a Therapeutic Relationship?

The presence of several children seems to facilitate the establishment of a desired relationship between the therapist and each child. The group setting proves helpful, especially during the initial meeting. The first encounter with the therapist is frequently frightening to the small child. He is reluctant to separate from his mother and to follow a strange person to an unfamiliar room. It is less threatening to him to enter the new situation in the company of two or three children of the same age. It is also easier for the mother to separate from her child in the company of two or three waiting and wailing mothers.

---

[1]These five elements were first introduced by S. R. Slavson.

In individual therapy, it is not unusual for a child at his first session to feel ill at ease, to withdraw completely, and to spend the whole session without daring to utter a word or touch a toy. In play group therapy the presence of other children seems to relax the atmosphere, diminish the tension, and stimulate activity and participation. The group "induces" spontaneity and the children relate to the therapist and develop a feeling of trust in him more readily than in individual therapy. This is illustrated by the following play therapy sequence:

Seven-year-old Edna refused to enter the playroom for her first session. She sat in the waiting room, her face buried in mother's lap and her arms around mother's waist. In an emphatic voice, she proclaimed, "I ain't going in without my mother." In spite of her loud protests, the therapist led Edna into the play-room. She looked like a lamb going to slaughter. She stood in the corner of the room crying bitterly, "I want my mamma." The two other girls observed Edna with curiosity. "Why is she crying?" asked Betty. Ruth, who only ten sessions ago went through a similar experience, answered, "She's afraid of the doctor. That's why she's crying." Ruth turned to Edna and said sympathetically, "You're scared, aren't you?" Edna did not reply, but she stopped crying. "I know you're scared," Ruth went on, "I felt just the same when I first came here." "You did?" said Edna, turning her face away from the wall. She took one step forward and said to Ruth, "You was afraid too? I'm scared of doctors 'cause they hurt you." "Not this one," assured Ruth. A few minutes later Edna and her newly acquired friends were busily engaged in digging a moat and building a castle in the sandbox.

The group provides opportunities for multilateral relationships unavailable in individual play therapy. Besides an accepting and respecting parent surrogate, the group offers the patients a plethora of identification models and ego ideals. Children identify themselves not only with the therapist but with the other members of the group. An effeminate boy, for example, may derive ego strength from associating with an accepting masculine playmate, and an overprotected child may become more independent by identifying himself with more autonomous group members. Schizoid children who live too great a part of their lives in fantasy are drawn to reality by more outgoing members. Hyperkinetic children, on the other hand, may become less active and more introspective under the neutralizing influence of calmer groupmates. The result is that both the withdrawn and the overactive achieve a healthier balance between the inner world of fantasy and outer world of reality.

The focus of treatment in play group therapy is always the individual child. No group goals are set and no group cohesion is looked for. Each child may engage in activities unrelated to other members. Subgroups form and disband spontaneously according to the ever-changing interests of the participants. Yet intrapatient relations are an important element in group treatment. The therapeutic process is enhanced by the fact that every group member can be a giver and not only a receiver of help. As Hobbs (1951) summarized it: "In group therapy a person may achieve mature balance between giving and receiving, between dependence on self and realistic self-sustaining dependence on others" (p. 293).

There are also risks in play group therapy. For example, a child who is ostracized by the group may relive the original trauma too vividly and with damaging results. However, such dangers are not inherent in the group but are a result of faulty grouping. Just as in adult group therapy, patients in play therapy should be grouped for the therapeutic impact they have on each other.

Does Play Group Therapy Accelerate or Retard the Evocation of Catharsis?

Children differ greatly in their use of cathartic media, and in their preferences for "playing out" or "saying out" their problems. The therapeutic medium best suited for young children is play. The term *play therapy* is frequently misinterpreted by teachers and parents. As one teacher commented about children in therapy: "What they need is less play, not more play." In therapy, the term *play* does not connote its usual recreational meaning, but is equivalent to freedom to act and react, suppress and express, suspect and respect.

In a secure atmosphere, play is the child's most natural language of self-expression. Through play, he can state how he feels about himself and the significant people and events in his life. When the therapist comprehends the child's play language and is able to communicate his understanding, the child usually proceeds with new and deeper expression of feelings. The sequence of the child's play activities and the therapist's responses become then a psychologically conducted conversation in a language well understood and appreciated by the child.

It is very important in working with small children not to be too verbal and too "textbookish." It is not always necessary even for older children to verbalize all their feelings in therapy. The symbolic language of toys is quite vivid and meaningful to most children and often it is sufficient for them to "talk out" the problems in their own play language. Many serious mistakes in child therapy are committed by adults who try to give verbal insight to children whose symbolic language is play. Forcing children to verbalize is like compelling them to converse in a foreign language.

Play group therapy provides two media of catharsis, play and verbalization, so that each child can utilize the symbolic means of expression which best meets his need. Symbolic catharsis is always more therapeutic than direct acting out. It is more helpful for all concerned if the child kicks the mother doll rather than the mother, shoots the baby doll rather than the baby, and stabs the father doll rather than the father.

In individual therapy, catharsis is mostly free-associative. It consists of the child moving freely from activity to activity and from play to play. The seemingly unrelated activities, like the verbal free association of adults, can lead to the emergence of themes related to the patient's core problems.

Play group therapy has an advantage over individual treatment in regard to catharsis. Besides "free associative catharsis," it provides also "vicarious" and "induced" catharsis (Slavson, 1954). Many children, especially the more fearful ones, participate covertly as spectators in activities they crave but fear. The group accelerates the child's feelings of the permissiveness of the setting. When one child comes forth with a "daring activity," others in the group find it easier to do the same. Children who are afraid to initiate any activity on their own gain the courage to do so in the company of others. It is as if the children help each other realize that the playroom is a "safety zone" amid life's heavy traffic, where they can rest or roam without fear of authority figures and careless drivers.

It is dramatic to observe a child who stands in the corner of the room, not daring to make a step and yet following with eager eyes the activities in which he would like to indulge, how his eyes open when another boy spanks the baby doll or shoots the mother doll. It is noticeable how children move from passive observation to occasional involvement to initiating activities, and finally to cooperating with others.

Ten-year-old Jim held a rubber snake in his hand and said with great venom, "I like this snake better than my brother. I hate my brother. He's not just a nuisance, he's a pest." Nine-year-old Todd, who was standing in the corner of the room, withdrawn and quiet, came over to Jim and said, "My brother's a pest too." The eyes of the two boys lit up with a strange glitter as they helped each other express their negative feelings toward their siblings.

Jim: I can't stand my brother.
Todd: My brother is no good.
Jim: Mine is more than no good.
Todd: Mine's the worst.
Jim: I wish I didn't have a brother.
Todd: I wish my brother would disappear.
Jim: I wish my brother was never born.
Todd: I wish my brother was never thought to be born.

Every time the therapist mirrored their statements, both of the boys raised their hands, exclaiming, "We vote for it." This was Todd's third session. The first two sessions he spent in complete silence.

It must be stressed that catharsis is always grounded in relationship. It occurs only when there is trust between the child and the therapist. Only in a secure atmosphere do children feel free to regress to earlier stages of emotional arrest and relive them in a more health-conducive milieu.

Does Play Group Therapy Augment or Retard the Derivation of Insight?

There is no direct relationship between insight and adjustment. There are many psychotics who have an uncanny grasp of the dynamics of their personality, while the bulk of the so-called normal people have relatively little insight into the motivation of their behavior.

This remark is not made to devaluate insight, but to point out its limitations as a change-catalyzer in therapy. Frequently insight is a result rather than a cause of therapy, attained by people who have grown emotionally ready to get acquainted with their unconscious. This pertains both to adults and children. Through emotional growth in inner security, children acquire a keener awareness of themselves and of their relations to the significant people in their lives. This insight is frequently derivative and achieved without the aid of interpretations and explanations. As Slavson (1952) points out: "In activity groups in which no interpretation is given, children become aware of the change within themselves and of their former motives and reactions" (p. 192). In play therapy, insight is both direct and derivative, both verbal and nonverbal.

Some leading therapists feel that for adults individual therapy provides a better setting for derivation of insight than group therapy. They believe that only the deep transference relationship of individual treatment can give patients the security and the courage to face their unconscious. This may be true in adult therapy. However, experience with groups of young children has indicated that mutual stimulation of ideas and feelings and the reciprocal emotional activation bring to the surface profound insights, as the following excerpt from a group session will illustrate:

Six-year-old Victor was in therapy with three other boys. For sessions on end he tried to "boss" the other children. He yelled at them, threatened them, threw sand and splashed paint on them. During one of these skirmishes, he suddenly stopped his attack and said to the therapist, "I wonder why I like to hurt other kids?" Victor was silent for a moment and then he added, "I guess it's 'cause I hate them." "You hate some kids bad?" said the therapist. "Yes," he replied angrily, "and I hate my brother most."

It seems that the group crystallized the situation for Victor. It made him aware of his problems so that he could face them and reflect upon them in the very situation that ordinarily provoked the difficulties. In individual therapy it would have taken much longer for the child even to be confronted with the problem.

Does Play Group Therapy Augment or Diminish Opportunities for Reality Testing?

Unlike individual treatment, play group therapy provides a tangible social setting for discovering and experimenting with new and more satisfying modes of relating to peers. The group constitutes a social milieu where new insights can be tested in terms of reality mastery and interindividual relationships.

The presence of several children in the playroom serves to anchor the therapy experience to the world of reality. Infantile feelings of omnipotence and magic that interfere with good adjustment are unmasked and modified by the group. The children help each other to become aware of their responsibilities in interpersonal relationships. The following excerpt will illustrate the point.

Nine-year-old George resented bitterly the few limitations set in the playroom as part of his individual therapy. He claimed to be "superman" and seemed intent on destroying the toys, damaging the room, and attacking the therapist. When George was transferred from individual therapy into a group of older boys, he tried to continue his aggressive pattern. However, in the group George met some rival "supermen."

When George threw a wooden block at ten-year-old David, the boy looked at him with surprise and, in a very convincing voice, he echoed one of the playroom limitations. "This is not for throwing," he said, "only rubber toys are for throwing." When George deliberately shot a dart at his face, David became angry. He took hold of George, shook him and said, "Look, the playroom is for playing, not for hurting. This is the law in here."

"I'm above the law," said George, "I'm superman." "Shake," said David, extending his hand. "I'm superman, too." "I'm super-superman," answered George. "And I'm super, super, superman," retorted David. The boys burst out in a loud laughter. The therapist said, "Both of you are supermen and above the law?" "No," answered George, "nobody here is superman and nobody's above the law."

The group as a miniature society offers motivation and support for change as well as a safe arena for testing new patterns of behavior. In the group a child learns not only what aspects of his behavior are socially unacceptable but also what elicits peer approval. He can observe and experience that sharing of toys or ideas is acclaimed by "society" and also that his contributions are expected and welcome.

A decided advantage of the group is that it allows the children to experience the external reality as satisfying and helpful. To many children, reality has become charged with massive negative expectations. They perceive the world as hostile and depriving and expect from it nothing but doom. These children find the conditioned reality of the therapy an emotionally moving experience. They have had previous group experiences, but in those groups they had to be most unlike themselves and constantly on guard. It was in groups that they had to conceal more than reveal, and where the barrier between them and the other persons was the highest. The following excerpt from a play group therapy session will serve as an illustration.

Garrulous Gracie, age ten, was in therapy with two very quiet and withdrawn girls. For many sessions Gracie dominated the scene with her ceaseless jabber, and she could really talk a "blue streak" about everything and about nothing.

One day Linda, aged eleven, turned to Gracie and said in a very soft and sympathetic voice, "Why do you always talk so fast, Gracie?" The question caught Gracie by surprise. She mumbled unintelligibly for a moment and then blurted out in seething anger, "Because nobody listens to me, that's why. The minute I open my mouth my mother says, 'Here she goes again.' And my father yells 'Shut up!' so I have to talk fast."

"Oh," said Linda, "that's too bad. But we're not your family. We'll listen to you. Just take it easy."

In therapy groups children are exposed to a new quality of intimate relations. They learn that they can shed defenses and yet stay protected, that they can get close to contemporaries and to an adult and not get hurt. In the security of the therapeutic atmosphere the children can face each other squarely and honestly and achieve, perhaps for the first time in their lives, emotional closeness instead of physical proximity to other beings.

Does Play Group Therapy Open or Block Channels for Sublimation?

One of the aims of psychotherapy with children is to help them develop sublimations that are compatible with society's demands and mores. The capacity to accept some, repress few, and sublimate many primitive urges is the mark of a mature person.

Unlike adult therapy, play therapy offers many sublimatory activities in the therapy situation. Some of the toys and materials in the playroom are introduced for this purpose. For example, children may sublimate anal interest by playing with mud and clay, oral interest by "cooking" and "serving meals," and sexual interest by dressing and undressing dolls. Also, some of the limits in play group therapy are planned to encourage sublimation. Direct physical attacks at each other are prohibited. Such attacks merely serve to displace aggression from original sibling to substitute sibling. It is more therapeutic to channel aggressive impulses into symbolic acting out against inflated clowns and life-sized dolls and into sublimatory competitive games.

One of the indices of progress in play group therapy is the movement from displacement to sublimation. In the initial stage of therapy, children tend to displace hostility onto groupmates and onto the therapist. They attack group members, grab their toys, and interfere with others' activities. As therapy progresses, sublimations replace displacements. Instead of attacking each other, children engage in rivalrous shooting at a target and in competitive games; instead of squirting water at one another, they feed dolls; instead of splashing paint, they color pictures; instead of throwing blocks, they build "homes."

Summary

The basic assumptions of this article are that the inner experience responsible for the healing process in maladjusted persons is the same in all therapies, and that every therapy system must explain its effectiveness in terms of its contributions to the identifiable variables common to all therapy. The unique contributions of play group therapy to the establishing of a therapeutic relation, to the evocation of catharsis, to the derivation of insight, to the testing of reality, and to the finding of sublimations, were pointed out and evaluated.

References

Hobbs, N. (1951). Group-centered therapy. In C. R. Rogers (Ed.), *Client-centered therapy: Its current practice.* Boston: Houghton Mifflin.

Slavson, S. R. (1952). *Child psychotherapy.* New York: Columbia University Press.

Slavson, S. R. (1954). A contribution to a systematic theory of group psychotherapy. *This Journal, 4,* 3–29.

CHAPTER THREE

PLAY GROUP THERAPY FOR YOUNG CHILDREN

Samuel R. Slavson

In the application of group therapy to various personality problems we have found that the accepted techniques of either activity or interview therapy (or group analysis) are not suitable for very young children. In the case of activity groups, unrestrained acting out without the necessary inner controls that are ordinarily present in the more mature person leads to chaos beyond the group's tolerance. The ability of any given group, as well as individuals, to withstand or absorb hostility and aggression has definite limits. Each individual and each aggregate of people has its own capacity to tolerate aggression or hostility density. When these limits are exceeded in groups, tension and anxiety set in, which are expressed in hyperactivity, rowdyism, or wanton destructiveness. Unless restraints are applied by some outer agency such as parent, teacher, leader, or therapist, the group becomes severely disorganized and uncontrollable. This is true of all groups whether children, adolescents, or adults and is the primary reason why grouping is so important and the choice of children suitable for group therapy has been repeatedly emphasized.

It has also been observed that different members of groups are affected differently by overt boisterous behavior or by repressed hostility. The endurance for these emotions varies in individuals and is conditioned by character structure and

Originally published in *Nervous Child,* 1948, 7(2), 318–327.

early experiences with aggression and hostility in the family. The superego in the young child is still unformed and the executive functions of the ego are less effectual during the pre-oedipal and early latency stages than during later development. The young child is, therefore, still devoid of the controls that emanate from the repressions and inhibitions which have been only partially evolved or not at all. In view of these circumstances the function of the therapist (parent and teacher, as well) is in fundamental respects unlike that with older children. He needs to be more active and more fully in control of the group's activities as well as of the behavior of each member in it.

In group play, patterns of behavior and problems emerge that are not present in the play of one child. Interstimulation and the various types of interaction inevitably arise from the concurrent activity of several children, which is referred to as the catalytic effect—positive and negative—they have on one another. The anxiety stimulated by the presence of other children and the support they give one another in their hostility toward the adult induce hyperactivity and destructiveness seldom encountered in the play of one child. It is, therefore, necessary for the therapist to be more vigilant as to the trends and possible developments in a group than in the treatment of one child, and employ strategies and techniques to prevent disorganization, emotional tension, and anxiety. Since the young child's unconscious is near the surface, it is not difficult to stimulate its flow in play activity, which may have no meaning to him in terms of his specific personality problems and needs, or may be even detrimental to him at a given stage in treatment.

Acting out has value only when it is an outcome of, and related to, the unconscious of the child and his emotional conflicts. Diffuse hyperactivity, which may express hostility toward the environment, including the therapist, is in itself not therapeutic. The value of acting out lies in the relation that it has to the conflicts of the patient. Acting out of hostility by an older child, an adolescent, or adult makes him aware of the true intent and significance of his actions. This is shown in various forms of guilt manifestations such as confession, placation, submission, and restitution—all of which indicate the presence of superego formation which is still not present in the very young child.

Acting out by the young child does not bring about awareness of or insight into the meaning of behavior. It therefore has little or no therapeutic value beyond release. Because of this absence of superego formation, low degree of guilt, weak ego structure, and basic narcissism, acting out alone does not meet the treatment conditions of group psychotherapy.

For this reason, acting out has to be limited, restrained, and directed with young children. At the same time, it is necessary that the therapist call attention to the latent meaning of behavior. This form of interpretation has several therapeutic values. In the first place, a relationship is established akin to transference, because the child feels he is understood by the therapist. Secondly, it makes him aware of his real problems and the meaning of hostile intent of his behavior. He becomes vaguely aware of the fact that his aggressive behavior in the group is only a substitute for aggressions he feels toward other persons. In a more neurotic child, interpretation serves to bring forward repressed impulses, conflicts, and anxieties, and makes the young patient aware of his real difficulties.

When using play therapy, whether in group or in individual psychotherapy, the therapist must be aware of the significance and meaning of play in its many facets. He must recognize that play to a child is what serious, productive work is to an older person. Through play the child carries out the tasks of his life, and he uses play for many other ends as well. To review the many theories of play, such as experimentation with reality, discharge of excess energy, recapitulation of the phylogenetic experience of the race, a form of mastery, an effort to attenuate reality, would take us far afield.

Play in education and in child development has been evaluated and described in an extensive and rich literature and need not be repeated here. It is necessary to call attention to the fact, however, that to the therapist play has additional meaning, as well as the developmental. He is interested in the fact that through play the child expresses traumatic fixations, conflicts, and hostilities and that he employs it as a means of communication and abreaction. The child also uses play to disguise genuine conflicts and difficulties, or he may use play to relax tension and anxiety. Of greatest importance, particularly to the group therapist, is the fact that as the young patient discharges aggression and seeks to overcome traumatic anxieties through play, it serves as a regulative mechanism. The therapist also sees group play as a possibility for overcoming narcissistic and autistic fixations and for discharging libido centrifugally through relationships with others in the group. The child discovers the advantages of such relationships, and his ego-libido drives are redirected outwardly toward his playmates and the objects he uses in his play, which are usually cathected.

The play therapist is also aware of the importance of play as a sublimation of primary instinctual drives, which in their primitive form are socially not acceptable. The service of play in finding permissible and acceptable outlets for primary impulses is of considerable value with which one must reckon. The catalytic effect of the others in a group greatly helps in this.

The specific advantage of the group in play therapy lies in the catalytic effect that each patient has upon the other, which makes it easier for them to act out and to bring forth in behavior fantasies and ideas. Another value of the group is that it reduces the tendency to repetition. The young child, particularly, tends to repeat the same activity. This is largely due to the limited scope of his capacities and experiences and the security that a known situation gives him. He is either afraid or unable to evolve variety in the use of play materials. While he is full of phantasy his imagination is comparatively limited. When several children play together, their interaction and mutual support help to employ the materials progressively, rather than to become fixed at one level of self-expression. This has been observed in educational and in therapy groups and constitutes what is often referred to as a "growth-producing environment."

In play groups—and this is to a great extent also true of other groups—children assign to themselves roles which are reflections or extensions of their basic problems. In such roles one either plays out the awareness of what he is or a hopeful phantasy of what he would like to be. Thus a child playing the role of a dog may feel himself being treated with the same indifference and impersonality as is the dog; he may seek to get the loving acceptance and protection which a pet receives in the home, or he may attribute to himself the oral strength that is usually associated with dogs. In a group such fantasies are reinforced and find easy and natural means of coming through in a variety of play forms and activity channels.

As in all psychotherapy, the fundamental dynamics are present in such groups. These are (1) relationship, (2) catharsis, (3) insight and/or ego strengthening, (4) reality testing, and (5) sublimation.

In group psychotherapy there are multilateral relations among the members, in addition to the attitudes they may have toward the therapist. These relationships serve to neutralize the transference toward the therapist and aid the cathartic process. The anxiety created by hitherto unacceptable behavior is lessened by the acceptance and support the children give one another. Under these circumstances it is easy for them to express hostility toward the therapist and reveal themselves in the light of their difficulties.

In activity group therapy, as in psychoanalysis, the relation between therapist and patients is unilateral. Feelings are directed from the patient to the therapist, the therapist remaining neutral and to a large extent also passive. In play therapy for young children, however, the therapist reacts to the behavior and feelings of the children, in a manner similar to case work. In the latter, as in group play therapy, the relationship is bilateral. Thus group play therapy, in its essentials, resembles individual psychotherapy, though largely modified in some secondary aspects. In both the transference is a bilateral one and the role the therapist plays in other respects is also similar.

The functions and equipment of an activity group therapist with children in latency are in many essentials different from those of a group play therapist. Though the activity group therapist must understand the hidden meanings in behavior (as does also the group play therapist) he remains largely passive and overtly unresponsive. The group play therapist, on the other hand, responds to the acts and utterances of the patients to help them acquire insight. The element of insight is the essential difference between activity groups for children in latency and play groups for younger children.

Catharsis is an essential factor in all psychotherapy. Through it the patient is able to divest himself of conflicts and emotions fixed through traumatic experiences in early childhood that form the root of personality disturbances. Thus, through play and language layers of repressed feelings are unfolded. Play is only one means, and the most suitable means for children, for communicating the content of the unconscious and the distress that pressures of environment create, that is, catharsis. Play under specially set conditions and in the presence of a permissive, understanding adult is a form of communication as well as catharsis.

Concerning the factor of reality testing, tangible objects, relationships with others, and actual situations constitute true reality to the child. They are more real to him than are ideas and words. Here he has an opportunity not only to experience but also to test himself as to his powers and mastery. He has things and materials with which to work and play. He either fails or succeeds, and as a result evolves perceptions concerning his own powers and abilities. He tests himself against others in submission-domination, anaclitic, or symbiotic relationships. Through the new relationships he evolves new patterns and new attitudes. During this period he begins to realize himself as a person, evaluates his powers, measures them against the realities of his environment, and eventually adjusts his behavior in accordance with his feelings of weakness or strength, as the case may be. Thus play activity becomes a measure of the self in relation to reality. This is the element of ego strengthening as well as reality testing.

Ego strengthening, which is so important in the psychotherapy of children, occurs in play groups through the same dynamic situations as in activity therapy groups and in all psychotherapy, for that matter. The acceptance of the child by the other children and the therapist begets the conviction that he is loved, and—what is more important—that he is worthy of love. The result of this new awareness is a more wholesome self-image and perception of his worth, which in turn help integrate powers and bring impulse under control. Thus the executive function of the ego as a control of impulses and the mediator between the self and outer realities is strengthened.

In psychotherapy of older persons, especially in psychoanalysis, the factor of insight is of paramount importance in this connection. Insight acquired through release of emotional tensions and overcoming resistances to unlocking the gates of the unconscious further strengthens the ego, as well as being a source of new values and more wholesome understanding. The degrees and levels of insight that a small child can acquire, however, are subject to speculation. Through our own observation in this regard, we are inclined to believe that children are capable of a high degree of insight, though it may manifest itself in forms other than those to which we are accustomed in adolescents and adults. Theirs is a more perceptive type and less verbalized or cognitive, but frequently one is impressed with the uncannily penetrating remarks children make about situations, themselves, and others.

One of the important values of all play therapy, especially in a group, is the fact that sublimations are ready at hand. Whatever the stage of the child's libido organization may be, as he finds sublimation for it in group situations, his primitive drives are transformed into controlled, socially approved patterns of behavior and more adequate adaptations to reality. Anal-urethral cravings, for example, are expressed in play with water, paints, and clay. Genital interests are worked through symbolically in occupations such as drawing and painting, fire-setting (which should be permitted), pyrography with an electrically heated stylus, squirting of water, shooting of guns, throwing rubber-cupped darts, play with family dolls, toy furniture, and doll house—especially toilet equipment. Some of these toys also serve to discharge as well as sublimate aggressive drives, sibling rivalry, and hostile feelings. In the group each member works out attitudes toward siblings and other members of the family. Thus catharsis, reality testing, and sublimation—though each having a distinct function—fuse in the play of very young children in groups, and perhaps also in all therapy groups.

Anger and aggression find numerous means for sublimation and displacement in play groups. A child may bang against things in the room or he may hammer a toy. To redirect hostile feelings he may destroy toys, tools, and materials or he may hammer boards together with a view of making some useful object. Instead of directly attacking the therapist, as a substitute for a parent, he may paint or deface the walls and furniture. In the young child displacement and sublimation often go hand in hand, as do transference and substitutions. They may often be confused.

◆ ◆ ◆

To illustrate some of the general principles in the preceding pages, we submit an abstract of a record of a group play session with three boys, five to six years old. Brief comments on some of the major dynamics of the events that took place in the group are also included.

John is the first to arrive and seems a little more friendly than during the past few weeks.

John: Where's everybody?

Therapist: They'll be along soon. *[John seems to have considerable hesitation in coming to the playroom where the group meets, but he finally does when the therapist says that the others are coming soon.]*

John: *[immediately going over to get paper]* I want a lot of colored paper. Who was here last week?

Therapist: Judah and Mike.

> *John:* *[angrily]* My mother said that nobody was here last week. Where is Mike?
>
> *Therapist:* Mike will be coming.
>
> *John:* *[seeming very restless]* I am going to my mother. Mike isn't here.
>
> *Therapist:* Why are you going to your mother, John?
>
> *John:* I am going to get a nickel. My mother said nobody was here last week and now she has to give me a nickel.
>
> *Therapist:* John, you can go to your mother after our meeting but I think you should stay here now.

John seems to hesitate and wanders around the room. He looks at the paper. He comes over to the therapist and puts his paper down.

> *John:* I'm not going to stay because Mike isn't here.
>
> *Therapist:* John, are you afraid to be here in the meeting room alone with me? *[John does not answer but seems to get relief from the therapist's saying this. He relaxes immediately.]*
>
> *John:* I am going to work on my plane. *[He begins to saw, which he does very well. Speaking proudly and boastfully]* Look at the thirty cents that I got from my grandfather. My girlfriend, Janet, also gives me money. *[He shows the therapist the thirty cents.]*

John feels uncomfortable being alone with the therapist. This discomfort is partly due to his displaced hostility from his mother on the therapist and partly because of his sexual preoccupations in regard to the former. He substitutes the therapist for his mother and the same anxieties that are associated with her come to the surface now.

John is disappointed that the therapist, like his own mother, has not given him siblings (playmates). She disappoints him and he is angry at her, he wants to punish her by leaving her and going to his mother, whom he plans to victimize for lying to him, which is probably his fantasy.

When the therapist interprets to John his feelings toward her, he at once relaxes and settles down to work. The therapist understood him and since she understands him she is less of a threat. To be understood also means to be accepted, and his negative transference is at once changed into positive feelings. As a result of this rapport, John feels secure and boasts: he is liked by others as well. Even his girlfriend gives him money. In this is implied a defense against his sexual impulses as well as hostile feelings toward the therapist: she is not the only one in his affections, there are others, that is, the basic transference is a negative one.

Mike is the strongest member of the group, on whom John relies and whom he fears.

Mike arrives and appears to be angry.

Mike: [*to the therapist*] I was waiting for you downstairs.

Judah arrives wearing a mask.

Judah: We put paint all around your office because you weren't there.
Therapist: I waited until our time to go upstairs. If you were angry, you boys could have told me rather than painted my office.
Judah: [*enthusiastically*] My uncle gave me this mask. He just got back from overseas and, boy, you should see the souvenirs he brought for me.

Mike finds some candy that was left from the last session and grabs it.

John: [*trying to grab the candy from Mike*] That candy belongs to me. Give it to me.

Mike and John start running around the room while John keeps trying to get the candy from Mike.

Mike: It does not belong to you and you can't have any candy.
John: The candy is so mine.
Mike: [*throws a piece of candy across the room*] There you are. Run and get it.
John: [*picks up the candy*] Come on, give me some more. The rest is really mine.
Mike: [*throws another piece, which John runs after*] And you're not getting any more.
John: I'm going to run out and tell my mother.
Therapist: Why are you going to tell your mother?
John: I'll tell Mike's mother.
Therapist: Why don't you tell Mike?

John ignores the suggestion of the therapist. Mike stops fighting him.

Mike: [*to Judah*] Why don't we go out and get water for the painting.

Mike and Judah go out to get water for the finger painting. John begins to work with the paper, cutting out a design on orange paper which he had crayoned black. Judah and Mike come running back into the room.

Judah: I am going to make a witch picture.
Mike: I am making a Halloween picture, too.

The boys work for a while. Then Mike tries to put paint from his hand on John. Judah follows and tries to do this also.

Therapist: *[to Judah and Mike]* Why are you boys angry at John?
    Mike: Because John got here early.
Therapist: But John got here at the time he was brought. Mike, maybe you just don't like the idea that someone else is here alone with me.
    Mike: You're right.

Mike then pretends to dab paint in John's direction without really doing so.

Therapist: Mike, you just feel like acting silly now.
    Mike: Gee, you're right again. You're becoming a mind reader!

Both Mike and Judah are angry. It is easy to guess the cause of their anger. They act out their anger against the therapist by messing up her office, which is in another part of the building, and by depriving John of candy. Later Mike, the most disturbed of the three boys, reveals the reason for his hostility toward John. He acts out his sibling rivalry, and as the therapist helps him to understand that he is jealous of John for being alone with her, his anger abates. He pretends to throw paint at John but does not actually do it. The therapist is somewhat defensive about John: she seems to justify, or at least explain, his being alone with her. This can be interpreted that she prefers John, which is both bad and untrue. The interpretation of Mike's feelings alone would have been sufficient. When the therapist says that Mike is just being silly, she expresses her disapproval and exercises control over him, which is necessary with very young children.

All three boys go on working. Judah finishes his painting.

    Judah: Well that's done. I guess I'll work on an airplane now. *[to the therapist]* Would you help me?

Mike had started several "war paintings," all at the same time. He finishes them all at the same time after working diligently. The therapist sees no design in them, although she believes that Mike is using his hands more freely and is actually finger painting rather than working the way he did last week, which was just piling paint.

    Judah: *[draws an airplane on wood and comes over to the therapist]* Will you saw this for me? Gee, I'm glad you got the saw you promised me.
    John: *[moving closer to the therapist]* Would you make me something, too?

Therapist: Of course I would. *[John seems very pleased at this.]*

Judah: Gee, I have an idea. Let's all make pumpkins out of wood. This is how we could do it. All we have to do is to nail pieces of wood together into a square.

John: *[to the therapist]* Could you help me saw this piece of heavy wood?

Judah then starts to nail the two pieces together but has to hunt for the nails. John goes over to him and hands him a nail that he has found.

Judah: Thanks a lot. *[John seems pleased by this.]* John, come on and help me with this work. You could even start one for yourself.

The hostility felt by Mike and Judah is now sublimated in activity: aeroplanes and war paintings. The therapist, however, notes that Mike is much freer in his work, which is very important for this boy. Judah is pleased that the therapist got the saw he wanted and because of this warm feeling toward her wants her to work with him. This in turn makes John jealous and he, too, wants her help—an expression of sibling rivalry. When John gives Judah the nails and Judah in turn invites him to work with him, there is personality growth beyond narcissistic preoccupations and an expanded capacity for object relationships. John's act can be seen, however, as a placation because of his own fear of the hostile feelings he harbors toward Judah, but as Judah accepts him, that is, forgives him, he feels relieved.

Mike: Let's all go now.

Judah: I want to finish. *[He leaves his wood and takes some of the paint with which he starts to paint a picture on the wall.]*

Therapist: *[to Judah]* You know we are not allowed to paint on the walls of the room.

Judah: Oh don't worry. It will be okay because no one will know I did it.

Therapist: That doesn't matter. We are still not permitted to paint the walls.

Judah: *[continuing to paint]* I think it will be all right. Look at the paint that other people put on the wall.

Therapist: Maybe you are angry because other people use this room.

Judah: That's right.

Mike: *[chiming in]* You're right.

Therapist: You see, the toy cars are ours and so is the bulletin board. . . . If you want to leave, I think we should go now. *[They all wanted to go.]* I think you should all go outside and wash.

They follow the suggestion. This is the first time that any of them have gone to wash their hands before going to eat. Because someone is in the wash room there is some delay. Mike starts banging on the door. Judah runs for a hammer and starts banging. John also participates: he kicks the door and bangs on it. They are finally able to get inside.

> *Judah:* *[to the therapist]* Would you get paper for me? I want you to lift me up so that I can get the paper for myself.
> *Mike:* I want paper, too.
> *John:* Me, too.

Judah and John are with the therapist. This disturbs Mike and he suggests terminating the session. Judah does not want to go, and because the therapist did not counter Mike's suggestion, he attacks her by painting the wall. When she remonstrates with him he finds every plausible means for justifying his act and finally he and Mike admit that they are angry because others, as well, use the room, that is, the therapist loves other children as well as them. Judah's choice to paint a house and an owl is in itself significant.

The fact that John, a frightened and withdrawn boy, can participate in an act of such direct aggression as banging and kicking the door is very valuable to him. He could not possibly have done it when alone. The example (catalysis) of the others gave him the courage to do it.

> *Judah:* Let's go down through the back stairway.

The group follows Judah's suggestion. There is no running ahead. All three walk alongside the therapist. Judah and Mike take her hand and John takes Judah's hand.

> *Judah:* Let's stop at the stationery store.
> *Mike:* Yes. I see something I want.
> *John:* That's a good idea. I see something, too.
> *Judah:* I want a collection of books but all the things cost too much. I only have a dime. *[He gives up the idea with some difficulty.]*
> *Mike:* Let's go now. I think we should stop and eat first, though.

Judah and John agree and they all choose vanilla ice cream sodas and eat without playing with the ice cream the way they formerly did.

> *Therapist:* *[while the boys are eating]* What would you like to eat next week?
> *Judah:* Frankfurters.

Mike: Yes, frankfurters.

John: That's right, frankfurters.

Judah: And please have plates, and forks and knives and mustard and flowers—daffodils—and then we'll all sing: "Here comes the bride."

Therapist: Who is going to be the bride?

Judah does not answer.

The back stairway is dark and has special significance for these boys as it also had for the children in other groups. They are afraid and keep together and cling to the therapist. Note that John, because of his timidity and fear of contact with the therapist, holds another boy's hand both in this instance and later on. In the discussion of refreshments, Judah brings forth the idea of a bride. Did he see himself marrying the therapist (his mother)? One can only speculate on this. When asked by the therapist who the bride would be he does not answer, he represses it.

On the way to the five-and-ten-cent store, John tries to put chalk on the therapist and Mike sort of hits her with a gun. This really takes the form of pushing the therapist from the back. Mike and Judah then take the therapist's hand and John takes Judah's hand again. John keeps taking out his thirty cents to show how much money he has. In the store they hesitate a great deal about choosing what to buy. They look at all the various objects and Mike finally decides.

Mike: I'm going to buy stickers and tags for Christmas packages.

Judah: I want tags and stickers, too. *[He decides this although he had been handling something else.]*

John: I'm getting them, too. *[John also buys crayons that Judah had picked up but didn't have the money to pay for.]*

The group walks back to the office.

Judah: I would like to have a hundred thousand dollars and buy a big store.

Mike: I would, too.

John: So would I.

PART TWO

MAJOR APPROACHES TO GROUP PLAY THERAPY

CHAPTER FOUR

THE FREEDOM TO BE

Child-Centered Group Play Therapy

Garry L. Landreth and Daniel S. Sweeney

Just like childhood itself, child therapy is a journey—a process of exploration that the therapist has the special privilege of partnering in. It is within this partnership, or relationship, that hurting children find healing and a sense of self. For some children this journey comes within an individual relationship with a play therapist; for some children it includes a relationship with other children as well as the therapist.

Child-centered group play therapy is indeed a journey of exploration, as children find within themselves the resources to solve problems and heal. The counseling model, developed by Carl Rogers (1951) and adapted by Virginia Axline to counseling with children, focuses on providing a permissive and growth-promoting atmosphere in which children can reach their full potential. The play therapist is interested not in the child's problem but in the child. The play therapist is not therapeutically prescriptive but prescriptively therapeutic. The play therapist is not focused on directing the therapeutic process but on facilitating a process that will unfold as the therapist trusts the inner person of the child. It is a journey of self-exploration and self-discovery.

The child-centered group play therapist should be a person trained in play therapy and group therapy. These skills, however, remain secondary to the play therapist's attitude, as Landreth and Sweeney (1997) point out: "Child-centered play therapy is not a cloak the play therapist puts on when entering the playroom and takes off when leaving; rather it is a philosophy resulting in attitudes and behaviors for living one's life in relationships with children. It is both a basic philosophy of the innate human capacity of the child to strive toward growth and maturity and an attitude of deep and abiding belief in the child's ability to be constructively self-directing. Child-centered play therapy is a complete therapeutic system, not just the application of a few rapport-building techniques" (p. 17).

Child-Centered Theory

Child-centered play therapy is based on the theoretical constructs of client-centered therapy developed by Carl Rogers (1951). These constructs were applied to working with children through play therapy by Virginia Axline (1947), a student and colleague of Rogers. The child-centered approach to play therapy, like client-centered therapy, is based on a process of being with children as opposed to a procedure of application. It is not so much a process of reparation as it is a process of becoming. Rogers (1986) summarized the essence of the approach: "The person-centered approach, then, is primarily a way of being that finds its expression in attitudes and behaviors that create a growth-producing climate. It is a basic philosophy rather than simply a technique or a method. When this philosophy is lived, it helps the person expand the development of his or her own capacities. When it is lived, it also stimulates constructive change in others. It empowers the individual, and when this personal power is sensed, experience shows that it tends to be used for personal and social transformation" (p. 199).

It is this *formative tendency* that all persons—indeed, all of nature—possess that forms the foundation for the child-centered approach to working with children. The child-centered theory of personality structure is based on three central constructs: the organism or person, the phenomenal field, and the self (Rogers, 1951).

The Organism

The organism is all that a child is, consisting of the child's self-perceptions including thoughts, feelings, and behaviors as well as the child's physical constitution. Because the person is always in the process of developing, the child is "a total organized system in which alteration of any part may produce changes in any other part" (Rogers, 1951, p. 487). This developmental process in children is emphasized, as every child "exists in a continually changing world of experience of which he is the center" (p. 483). Children interact with and respond to this personal and continually changing world of experience.

Therefore, a continuous dynamic intrapersonal interaction occurs in which every child (organism), as a total system, is striving toward actualizing the self.

Landreth and Sweeney (1997) posit that this dynamic and animated process is an internally directed movement toward becoming a more positively functioning person, toward positive growth, toward improvement, independence, maturity, and enhancement of self as a person. The child's behavior in this process is goal-directed in an effort to satisfy personal needs as experienced in the unique phenomenal field that for that child constitutes reality (Landreth, 1991).

Phenomenal Field

The phenomenal field consists of everything that is experienced by the child. These experiences include everything happening within an organism at a given time—whether or not at a conscious level, internal as well as external—including perceptions, thoughts, feelings, and behaviors. Essentially, the phenomenal field is the internal reference that is the basis for viewing life; that is, whatever the child perceives to be occurring is reality for the child. This points to a fundamental rule of thumb in child-centered play therapy, which is that the child's perception of reality is what must be understood if the child and behaviors exhibited by the child are to be understood.

Whatever the child perceives in the phenomenal field, therefore, assumes primary importance as opposed to the actual reality of events. The magnitude of emotion that a child experiences corresponds to the perceived significance of the behavior, which is focused on maintaining and enhancing the organism. Rogers (1951) proposed that "behavior is basically the goal-directed attempt of the organism to satisfy its needs as experienced in the field as perceived" (p. 491). Reality is therefore determined individually and subjectively. This concept is central to child-centered play therapy.

The behavior of any child or group of children must always be understood by looking through the eyes of a child. Thus the therapist intentionally avoids judging or evaluating even the simplest of the child's behaviors (a picture, a stack of blocks, a scene in the sand) and works hard to try to understand the internal frame of reference of each child in the group (Landreth & Sweeney, 1997). If the therapist makes contact with the person of the child, the child's phenomenal world must be the point of focus and must be understood. Children are not expected to meet predetermined criteria or fit a set of preconceived categories (Landreth, 1991).

Self

The third central construct of the child-centered theory of personality structure is the self. Self is the differentiated aspect of the phenomenal field that develops from the child's "evaluational interactions with others" (Rogers, 1951, p. 498).

The consequence of how others perceive a child's emotional and behavioral activity and accordingly react involves the formation of the concept of "me." The self is formulated as an "organized picture, existing in awareness as figure . . . or ground . . . of the self and the self-in-relationship . . . , together with the positive or negative values which are associated with those qualities and relationships, as they are perceived as existing in the past, present, or future" (p. 501).

According to Rogers (1951), even very young infants engage in a process of "direct organismic valuing" beginning with such simple experiences as "This taste bad, and I don't like it," even though they may lack descriptive words or symbols that match the experience. This is the beginning of a natural and continuous process in which children positively value those experiences that are perceived as self-enhancing and place a negative value on those that threaten or do not maintain or enhance the self.

This process of evaluation—by parents, others, and self—points to one of the key benefits in child-centered group play therapy. As children develop, they experience parents and others and symbolize themselves as good or bad dependent on these evaluations. To preserve a positive self-concept, the child may distort such experiences and deny to awareness the satisfaction of the experience (Rogers, 1951). "It is in this way . . . that parental attitudes are not only introjected, but . . . are experienced . . . in distorted fashion, as if based on the evidence of one's own sensory and visceral equipment. Thus, through distorted symbolization, expression of anger comes to be 'experienced' as bad, even though the more accurate symbolization would be that the expression of anger is often experienced as satisfying or enhancing" (Rogers, 1951, p. 500). The group play therapy experience provides the opportunity for the child to be viewed by the child-centered therapist as a positive and growing self, while also experiencing the evaluation of the other group members within an atmosphere of permissiveness and acceptance.

Rogers (1951) hypothesized that the self grows and changes as a result of continuing interaction with the phenomenal field. In the child-centered group play therapy process, the *group itself is the phenomenal field*. The group fosters a growth-producing climate, and the child's interactions with it facilitate the child's concept of self. Rogers described the structure of the self-concept as "an organized configuration of perceptions of the self which are admissible to awareness. It is composed of such elements as the perceptions of one's characteristics and abilities; the percepts and concepts of the self in relation to others and to the environment; the value qualities which are perceived as associated with experiences and objects; and the goals and ideals which are perceived as having positive or negative valence" (p. 501). This not only speaks to the child's behavior being consistent with the child's concept of self, but also the ability of the group to facilitate positive change in self-concept.

An understanding of Rogers's (1951) propositions regarding personality and behavior is key to understanding the child-centered approach to treatment. Boy and Pine (1982) provided a paraphrase and synopsis of Rogers's propositions, which furnishes a summary for viewing each child as

- Being the best determiner of a personal reality
- Behaving as an organized whole
- Desiring to enhance self
- Goal-directed in satisfying needs
- Being behaviorally influenced by feelings that affect rationality
- Best able to perceive the self
- Being able to be aware of the self
- Valuing
- Interested in maintaining a positive self-concept
- Behaving in ways that are consistent with the self-concept
- Not owning behavior that is inconsistent with the self
- Producing psychological freedom or tension by admitting or not admitting certain experiences into the self-concept
- Responding to threat by becoming behaviorally rigid
- Admitting into awareness experiences that are inconsistent with the self if the self is free from threat
- Being more understanding of others if a well-integrated self-concept exists
- Moving from self-defeating values toward self-sustaining values (p. 47)

Child-Centered Group Play Therapy

Child-centered group play therapy combines the distinct advantages of child-centered play therapy with the recognized benefits of group process. An understanding of the child-centered play therapy process is important, as is an understanding of the basic premises of child-centered group theory. Landreth (1991) provides a definition of play therapy that adapts well for the group play therapy process: "Play therapy is defined as a dynamic interpersonal relationship between a child and a therapist trained in play therapy procedures who provides selected play materials and facilitates the development of a safe relationship for the child to fully express and explore self (feelings, thoughts, experiences, and behaviors) through the child's natural medium of communication, play" (p. 14).

The group play therapy process must be dynamic and interpersonal, focused on relationships (between the therapist and group members and between the group members themselves). The child-centered group play therapy process focuses on the healing power of the relationship as opposed to technique and prescription. The therapist should be someone who is trained in play therapy and group therapy procedures. It is not appropriate to meet with a group of children and provide some toys, yet maintain an adult therapy posture and do individual therapy with each child in a group setting. The play materials must be selected, as opposed to providing a random collection of toys. This selection should be purposed and intentional. The child-centered group play therapist should be a facilitator of safe relationships rather than a director of group activities and exercises. Exploration and expression of self can not occur where there is no safety. Obviously, the group process with children should honor their natural medium of communication, play.

Person-Centered Group Theory

A person-centered approach to group therapy follows Rogers's (1951) premise that there is a basic trust in the client's ability to move forward in a positive and constructive manner if the conditions that foster this growth are present. Similarly, child-centered group play therapy is based on an abiding trust in the group's ability to develop its own potential through its movement in a positive and constructive direction. Hobbs (1951) wrote about "group-centered psychotherapy," emphasizing the importance of the group leader's understanding and acceptance of all individuals in the group. In later writings, Hobbs (1964) underscores the significance of this commitment to the group member as "putting aside tendencies to evaluate what is good and right for other people. It requires a respect for their integrity as individuals, for their right to the strength-giving act of making and living by their own choices. And it requires, perhaps above all, a confidence in the tremendous capacities of individuals to makes choices that are both maturely satisfying to them and ultimately satisfactory to society" (p. 158). This has significant implications for children, who are so often evaluated and so rarely given choices. The facilitator of a children's group should be very careful to help each child to feel safe enough to grow (or not to grow) and make choices.

The group-centered leader does not accept responsibility for the group but encourages the group members to assume this responsibility, while providing the basic therapeutic conditions of empathy, acceptance, warmth, and positive regard. With such a climate, group members come to rely on their own abundant internal resources for self-direction, self-evaluation, and improved self-concept (Rogers, 1980). Person-centered therapy asserts that positive change occurs within the context of a therapeutic relationship—and a group provides multiple relationships through which members can move toward positive change. Rogers (1967) suggested several hypotheses common to person-centered groups:

- Defenses are gradually dropped as the client begins to feel safe through the freedom of the group.
- Relationships will develop more often if they are built on a feeling level.
- Self-understanding and relationship to others will become more accurate.
- Personal attitudes and personal behaviors will change.
- Group members will relate to others more effectively in daily life interactions.
- Trust will develop in the group following confusion and fractionation.

The facilitator of a person-centered group does not apply techniques to promote group growth. The leader and emerging therapeutic relationships are the instruments for change. Rogers (1970) discourages use of techniques that tend to empower the leader rather than the group: "I try to avoid using any procedure that is planned; I have a real 'thing' about artificiality. If any planned procedure is tried, the group members should be as fully in on it as the facilitator, and should make the choice themselves as to whether they want to use that approach" (p. 56).

The very use of the term *facilitator* is instructive about the way in which groups should be approached. The skills of the group therapist, while important, are secondary to the personhood of the therapist; as when this personhood facilitates a climate of interpersonal relationship, group members become more affectively involved in the group process (Boy, 1990). This reflects the priority that is placed on the group interaction rather than any leader. Bozarth (1981) identified several major attributes for the person-centered group facilitator:

- Facilitators are willing to participate as group members.
- Facilitators demonstrate acceptance and a willingness to understand each group member.
- Facilitators are willing to appropriately self-disclose personal struggles.
- Facilitators are willing to give up power, control, and the image of expertise; they look rather for ways to have personal influence.
- Facilitators trust in the ability of the group and group members to move in positive directions without their input.

As noted, the therapist does not take a person-centered approach as much as he lives a person-centered way of life in therapy. Bozarth and Brodley (1986) asserted that this person-centered lifestyle leads to a process that is less focused on skills, techniques, and leadership strategies and more on self-development and self-exploration. The group-centered therapist, therefore, like the person-centered therapist with an individual client, views techniques and games as potential impediments to the group's process and natural growth. Likewise, the child-centered play therapist takes this position. Methods and prescription advance the agenda of the therapist and take the focus off of the child group members, whose so-called problems have often seen more than enough focus by so many adults.

Child-Centered Play Therapy

Virginia Axline (1947) concisely clarified the fundamental principles that provide guidelines for establishing and maintaining a therapeutic relationship and making contact with the inner person of the child in the play therapy experience. Landreth (1991) revised and extended Axline's eight basic principles as follows:

- The therapist is genuinely interested in the child and develops a warm, caring relationship.
- The therapist experiences unqualified acceptance of the child and does not wish that the child were different in some way.
- The therapist creates a feeling of safety and permissiveness in the relationship so the child feels free to explore and express self completely.
- The therapist is always sensitive to the child's feelings and gently reflects those feelings in such a manner that the child develops self-understanding.
- The therapist believes deeply in the child's capacity to act responsibly, unwaveringly respects the child's ability to solve personal problems, and allows the child to do so.
- The therapist trusts the child's inner direction, allows the child to lead in all areas of the relationship, and resists any urge to direct the child's play or conversation.
- The therapist appreciates the gradual nature of the therapeutic process and does not attempt to hurry things along.
- The therapist establishes only those therapeutic limits that help the child accept personal and appropriate relationship responsibility (pp. 77–78).

These principles all point to the development and maintenance of a strong therapeutic relationship. This therapeutic relationship is, in fact, so powerful that it is the central factor determining the success or failure of therapy. Moustakas (1959) believed that "through the process of self-expression and exploration within a significant relationship, through realization of the value within, the child comes to be a positive, self-determining, and self-actualizing individual" (p. 5).

In the child-centered approach to play therapy, the focus is on the child rather than on the presenting problem. It is assumed that the therapist who concentrates upon assessment and diagnosis has a greater likelihood of losing sight of the child. Symptoms may be important, but not as important as the child. Although interpretation of play behaviors is interesting, it generally serves the need of the therapist and not the child. This relationship is therefore focused upon a present, living experience (Landreth, 1991):

Person . . . . rather than . . . . problem

Present . . . . rather than . . . . past

Feelings . . . . rather than . . . . thoughts or acts

Understanding . . . . rather than . . . . explaining

Accepting . . . . rather than . . . . correcting

Child's direction . . . . rather than . . . . therapist's instruction

Child's wisdom . . . . rather than . . . . therapist's knowledge (p. 79)

This relationship develops as the therapist communicates understanding and acceptance. Children begin to recognize their inner value when the play therapist responds sensitively to the inner emotional part of their person by accepting and reflecting feelings, whether verbally or nonverbally expressed. The child-centered play therapist generally avoids asking questions, for several reasons. Questions tend to take children out of their world of affectivity and into the world of cognition, which defeats the developmental rationale for using play therapy. Questions also tend to structure the relationship in the direction of the therapist, placing the focus on the therapist rather than the child. This naturally interferes with the process of the child's play. The value of symbolic expression and the safety of therapeutic projection may be eliminated through the asking of too many questions.

Child-centered play therapy avoids any kind of evaluation. Children are encouraged but not praised, because praise establishes an evaluative pattern. It is important to note that evaluative statements deprive the child of inner motivation. Additionally, the child-centered play therapist avoids interfering with the child's play. This does not eliminate participation in the child's play, which can be done at the direction of the child, though it should be noted that the more the therapist becomes involved in the child's play, the more difficult it is to keep the child in the lead. Interference, however, may involve offering solutions or suggestions, or allowing the child to manipulate the therapist into becoming a teacher or doing things for the child. Assistance can be provided in the exceptional circumstances when the child has tried and truly cannot do something alone. Children do not learn self-direction, self-evaluation, and responsibility when the therapist evaluates or provides solutions.

Diagnosis and Treatment Planning

Although it may be considered important to discuss the issues of diagnosis and treatment planning because of the current climate of the mental health field, these are clearly not the central issues in child-centered play therapy. Person-centered therapy views diagnosis and evaluation as distracting and potentially detrimental to the client (Rogers, 1951). The focus of the child-centered play therapist is on the inner person of the child; it is on what the child is capable of becoming as opposed to the child's ways of being in the past. The children in the therapeutic play group are the focus; the problems for which they have been referred are not. Essentially, knowledge about problems is not at all necessary to establish a therapeutic relationship with children and may in fact be a substantial distraction.

"Maladjustment," therefore, should be viewed within the context of the developing relationship and as resulting from a state of incongruence between the self-concept of a child and the experiences of the child. Incongruence between a child's self-concept and a child's experience will naturally result in an incongruence of behavior, thus causing what would be labeled maladjustment. The play group therapy process for children provides the environment in which these incongruences can be processed, as children are given opportunity to experience affirmation of their needs of growth and self-realization.

Axline (1947) suggested that an "adjusted person seems to be an individual who does not encounter too many obstacles in his path—and who has been given the opportunity to become free and independent in his own right. The maladjusted person seems to be the one who, by some means or other, is denied the right to achieve this without a struggle" (p. 21). She further explained the differences between well-adjusted and maladjusted behavior:

> When the individual develops sufficient self-confidence . . . consciously and purposefully to direct his behavior by evaluation, selectivity, and application to achieve his ultimate goal in life—self-realization—then he seems to be well adjusted.
>
> On the other hand, when the individual lacks sufficient self-confidence to chart his course of actions openly, seems content to grow in self-realization vicariously rather than directly, and does little or nothing about channeling this drive in more constructive and productive directions, then he is said to be maladjusted. . . . The individual's behavior is not consistent with the inner concept of the self which the individual has created in his attempt to achieve complete self-realization. The further apart the behavior and the concept, the greater the degree of maladjustment [pp. 13–14].

The setting of treatment goals in the child-centered group play therapy process must take into consideration this perspective on maladjustment. Just as diagnosis is generally eschewed in the person-centered process, the setting of specific treatment goals is seen as antithetical to the natural and unfolding process of therapy. Children are in a state of constant change and continuous development, and are themselves considered to be the most appropriate determiner of change within self. Therefore, the therapy process is not an application of prescriptive goals and treatment but a discussion of growth and change that proceeds from the internal frame of reference of the developing individual. When this process is indeed child-centered, therapy and therapeutic growth are not dependent on the therapist but on the child. The child's self-concept and perception of others become less dependent on the attitudes of other people, and the child can build self-confidence and an ability for self-direction. The child is able to own his or her own feelings and behaviors and feels in greater control, more empowered, and more congruent.

The establishment of specific treatment goals, therefore, is not an aspect of child-centered group play therapy. Such establishment would be incongruent with the philosophy of child-centered theory, as described by Landreth and Sweeney (1997):

> The central hypothesis governing what the therapist does is an unwavering belief in the child's capacity for growth and self-direction. The establishment of specific treatment goals would be a contradiction of this belief. Goals or objectives of treatment imply that the therapist knows where the child should be and that there is a specific structure by which to get there. The play therapist is not wise enough to know where another person should be in his or her life or what that person should be working on or toward. Life is much too complex to be understood by diagnosis and controlled by a prescription for growth. Further, the child is the best determiner of what should be focused on in play therapy. How can children learn self-direction if even their play is directed? Diagnostically based treatment goals usually result in the therapist's being focused on the treatment goal. Such an approach would be much too structuring and would restrict the creative potential of the child and the relationship [p. 38].

Although specific and prescriptive treatment goals are not established for children in the child-centered group play therapy process, there are broadly defined therapeutic objectives that are considered congruent with the child-centered theoretical and philosophical approach. According to Landreth (1991):

The general objectives of child-centered play therapy are consistent with the child's inner self-directed striving toward self-actualization. An overriding premise is to provide the child with a positive growth experience in the presence of an understanding supportive adult so the child will be able to discover internal strengths. Since child-centered play therapy focuses on the person of the child rather than the child's problem, the emphasis is on facilitating the child's efforts to become more adequate, as a person, in coping with current and future problems which may impact the child's life. To that end, the objectives of child-centered play therapy are to help the child

1. Develop a more positive self-concept
2. Assume greater self-responsibility
3. Become more self-directing
4. Become more self-accepting
5. Become more self-reliant
6. Engage in self-determined decision making
7. Experience a feeling of control
8. Become sensitive to the process of coping
9. Develop an internal source of evaluation
10. Become more trusting of self [p. 80].

Within the framework of these general objectives, children in group therapy are free to work on specific problems, which is often the case. It is important to underscore that this is the child's choice and not a result of the therapist's direction, suggestion, or implication. The play group therapist believes in and trusts the child's capacity to set his or her own goals and direction: "In this view, no attempt is made to control a child, to have the child be a certain way, or to reach a conclusion the therapist has decided is important. The therapist is not the authority who decides what is best for the child, what the child should think, or how the child should feel. If this were to be the case, the child would be deprived of the opportunity to discover his/her own strengths" (Landreth, 1991, p. 81).

Therapeutic Limit Setting

The group play therapist must be an expert limit-setter. The presence of two or more children in the playroom magnifies (sometimes exponentially) the need for limits to be set. An exploration of the child-centered approach to group play therapy would be incomplete without a discussion of the role of therapeutic limit setting as a facilitative dimension in the process. As noted, children do not grow where they do not feel safe. And children do not feel safe, valued, or accepted in a completely permissive relationship. Moustakas (1959) summarized the importance of limits as a vital and necessary part of relationships:

> Limits exist in every relationship. The human organism is free to grow and develop within the limits of its own potentialities, talents, and structure. In psychotherapy, there must be an integration of freedom and order if the individuals involved are to actualize their potentialities. The limit is one aspect of an alive experience, the aspect which identifies, characterizes, and distinguishes the dimensions of a therapeutic relationship. The limit is the form or structure of an immediate relationship. It refers not only to a unique form but also to the possibility for life, growth and direction rather than merely to a limitation. . . . In a therapeutic relationship, limits provide the boundary or structure in which growth can occur [pp. 8–9].

The purpose for limits in the group play therapy process emphasizes the child-centered group play therapist's focus on the process rather than specific behaviors. Just as the focus of the group process is not on specific behaviors but on the relationship and the underlying affective element relative to the behaviors, the child's desire to break the limit in the group is always of greater importance than the actual breaking of a limit. The various purposes for setting limits can be summarized as follows (Axline, 1947; Bixler, 1949; Ginott, 1994; Landreth, 1991; Moustakas, 1959; Sweeney, 1997):

- Limits define the boundaries of the therapeutic relationship.
- Limits provide security and safety for the child, both physically and emotionally.
- Limits demonstrate the therapist's intent to provide safety for the child.
- Limits anchor the session to reality.
- Limits allow the therapist to maintain a positive and accepting attitude toward the child.
- Limits allow the child to express negative feelings without causing harm and experiencing the fear of retaliation.
- Limits offer stability and consistency.
- Limits promote and enhance the child's sense of self-responsibility and self-control.
- Limits promote catharsis through symbolic channels.
- Limits protect the play therapy room.
- Limits provide for the maintenance of legal, ethical, and professional standards.

Permissiveness is a crucial element of the group play therapy process. These are not, however, completely permissive relationships in the playroom. Children are not allowed to do just anything they may want to do. The group play therapist should establish a prescribed structure that provides boundaries for the relationship. Limits inherently need to be set on the following: (1) behavior that is harmful or dangerous to any children in the group or the therapist, (2) behavior that disrupts the therapeutic routine or process (continually leaving playroom, wanting to play after time is up), (3) destruction of room or materials, (4) taking toys from playroom, (5) socially unacceptable behavior, and (6) inappropriate displays of affection (Landreth & Sweeney, 1997).

These are typical limits in the play therapy relationship. As suggested, the need for these limits can be greatly magnified in the group setting. The potential for disruptive, harmful, and destructive behaviors increases as more children are added to the therapeutic process. Appropriate and balanced limits are essential, as children will quickly perceive the disequilibrium of a therapist who is imbalanced in the application of limits.

As important as therapeutic limits are, it is equally important that they should not be set until they are needed. Providing a long list of prohibited activities at the beginning of the first group play therapy session would definitely not encourage or facilitate exploration and expression by the children. When children are allowed to express themselves affectively, there is greater opportunity for significant learning and growth. This can certainly be hampered by a preliminary dissertation on restrictions.

When limits are needed in the group process, the therapist should take a matter-of-fact and firm approach. This is necessary so that the child will not feel chastised. The therapist's role is obviously not parental and authoritative but rather facilitative yet structured. While there are usually more limits set in group play therapy than individual, they should nevertheless be as minimal as possible. Limits should also be specific rather than general (generality makes for unclear boundaries), total rather than conditional (conditional limits are confusing and can lead to power struggles), and enforceable. As Landreth and Sweeney (1997) note, "Since boundaries have previously been determined, the play therapist can be consistent and thus predictable in setting limits. This consistency and predictability help the child to feel safe. It is within this structure that the feeling of permissiveness is more important than actual permissiveness. When limit setting becomes necessary, the child's desire to break the limit is always the primary focus of attention because the child-centered play therapist is dealing with intrinsic variables related to motivation, perception of self, independence, need for acceptance, and the working out of a relationship with a significant person" (p. 49).

Rationale for Using Group Play Therapy

Although efficiency in terms of saving therapist time has often been considered a major attraction of group play therapy, the placing of several children in a group provides advantages beyond expediency. Group play therapy can give children the kinds of experiences that help them learn to function effectively, to explore their behavior, to develop tolerance to stress and anxiety, and to find satisfaction in working and living with others. If a group play therapy approach is to be employed, it would seem logical to assume the play therapist should understand the rationale for placing children in groups before this approach is attempted.

The presence of another child or several children enhances the therapeutic relationship by facilitating the following dimensions of the play therapy experience (Axline, 1947; Ginott, 1994; Schiffer, 1969; Slavson, 1964):

- It is less threatening for the child to enter the new experience in the company of two or three other children.
- The presence of several children facilitates the establishment of a desired relationship between the therapist and each child.
- The presence of other children diminishes tension and stimulates activity and participation.
- The presence of other children increases spontaneity.
- The therapeutic process is enhanced by the fact that every child can be a giver and not only a receiver of help.
- The group accelerates the child's awareness of the permissiveness of the setting.
- Children are forced to reevaluate their behavior in the light of peer reactions.
- Group play therapy provides a tangible social setting for discovering and experimenting with new and more satisfying modes of relating to peers.
- The presence of several children serves to tie the therapy experience to the world of reality.
- The group provides opportunity for vicarious and direct learning (problem solving, alternative behaviors, and so on).
- The therapist is provided insight into how the child may be in the real world.

Group Structure and Logistics

The structure of a child-centered play therapy group is not based on the application of techniques. Thus the child-centered group play therapist does not enter the group with a specific agenda. Therapeutic change is a result of a therapeutic relationship, that is, the children in the group will change in response to the group participants and the environment created by the therapist. The considerations discussed in this section are important but cannot replace the curative value of the play therapy relationship. Many of the points raised here will be familiar from Chapter One, but it is useful to restate them in the course of covering the child-centered group play therapy approach in greater depth.

Group Selection and Size

Child-centered play therapy groups should be appropriately structured in terms of the selection of group members and the size of the group. A group that consists of the wrong mix of children or is too large will diminish the ability of the therapist to create a warm, accepting, and growth-promoting environment. The selection process, therefore, is a crucial element to the success of the group. Generally, since child-centered theory is focused on the child and not on the problem, groups are not specifically organized around a diagnosis.

However, there are general considerations for placing children in group play therapy. According to Ginott (1994), children generally recommended for group play therapy are withdrawn children, immature children, children with phobic reactions, children with "pseudo assets" (that is, children who are too good, obedient, and orderly, overgenerous, and too concerned with pleasing adults), children with habit disorders, and children with conduct disorders. Ginott also notes that children with intense sibling rivalries, sociopathic children, children with accelerated sexual drives, children who persistently steal, and extremely aggressive children are not recommended for group play therapy. These children's behaviors may have possible destructive effects on other children in the group. For example, sexually abused children should not be placed with non–sexually abused children because they may abuse such children. Another category of children not recommended for play therapy is children with gross stress and trauma reactions. Generally, children in categories not recommended for group play therapy have such intense personal needs that they need the complete and undivided attention and focus of the play therapist all to themselves. Therefore, they should be placed in individual play therapy.

Several issues related to group selection should be considered. Initially, it should be emphasized that the primary screening mechanism for group therapy membership is an individual play therapy session with each child. Children may be referred from individual therapy or placed immediately into a group following an initial session. Parent and teacher interviews are additionally helpful in group placement, although there may be a tendency for the referring parties (children rarely self-refer) to be problem-focused rather than child-focused.

An initial consideration in determining group membership will be the age of the children, who should generally be within one year of one another. The developmental differences between young children two or more years apart can be substantial. Developmental or psychological age is more important than chronological age, but the physical maturity of the child must also be considered. A developmentally delayed boy who is larger and stronger than younger boys at a similar level may be problematic.

When considering the gender mix of a play therapy group, it is generally not an issue of import until children reach nine years of age. As children enter the middle school years, psychosocial development, particularly in terms of relating to the other gender, becomes a matter of concern and genders should not be mixed. Prior to age nine, it is recommended that groups be generally gender balanced if both boys and girls are included. A group of four is better balanced with two boys and two girls than with three boys and one girl.

Another consideration in group play therapy is the size of the group. An initial rule of thumb is that the younger the children, the smaller the group. Play therapy groups may have only two or three children, depending on the needs and ages of the children and the size of the facility. Since child-centered group play therapy focuses on the creation of a therapeutic environment in which children can actualize their potential, the larger the group, the more challenging it will be for the therapist to create these conditions. Groups larger than five children are not recommended.

Group Playroom and Materials

The physical setting for group play therapy is also important. A designated playroom is recommended, but a designated section of a larger room (such as a classroom) may also be used. A major consideration is a setting that affords privacy and is large enough to afford a certain degree of freedom within the context of limitations on destructiveness. A room that is too small restricts children's expressions and may promote frustration. Likewise a room that is too large may encourage too much activity and inhibit the development of a relationship with the counselor or other children because too little contact and interaction occurs.

In play therapy, toys are considered to be children's words and play is their language, therefore careful attention should be paid to the selection of toys and materials that allow for children's self-directed activity and facilitate a wide range of feelings and play activity (Landreth, 1991). It should be recognized that not all play media encourage children's expression or exploration of their feelings, needs, and experiences. As noted, it is not play therapy to simply provide a random collection of toys coupled with an adult therapy approach. Additionally, play therapy is not used as a method for learning or for the child to get ready to do something else. The purpose is not to engage the child in some play behavior in preparation for trying to get the child to talk, tell about something that has happened, or describe something the child wants in life. This may naturally occur within the unfolding of the process, but is never a goal. The child's play is the message, and the toys are the tools. Landreth's chapter on playroom and materials in his book *Play Therapy: The Art of the Relationship* (1991) has an extensive listing of toys suitable for play therapy.

Play materials should be simple, generic, and safe. Toys that are too complicated or mechanical, involve complex structure, or that require the play therapist's assistance to manipulate are not appropriate because their potential to frustrate children may enable dependence in children who already feel helpless or inadequate. Therefore, as Landreth (1991, p. 116) notes, toys and materials should be selected that

- Facilitate a wide range of creative expression
- Facilitate a wide range of emotional expression
- Engage children's interests
- Facilitate expressive and exploratory play
- Allow exploration and expression without verbalization
- Allow success without prescribed structure
- Allow for noncommittal play

Length, Frequency, and Duration of Sessions

The length of child-centered group play therapy sessions should also be considered. This is variable and may relate to the setting of the groups—with groups being held in schools having a shorter time limit, groups held concurrently with parent sessions being limited to the therapeutic hour, and so on. The general rule of thumb is to establish the length of the group session based on the ages of the group members, noting that the younger the children, the shorter the session—reflecting the children's shorter attention span. The most effective time frame for preschool and primary grade children would be thirty- to forty-five-minute sessions. Some groups should perhaps meet twice a week.

In the process of child-centered group play therapy, the frequency and duration of therapy is established by the needs of the child and not the agenda of the therapist. As Axline (1947) pointed out, the child-centered play therapist does not hurry the process along: "If the therapist feels that the child has a problem and she wants to attack the problem as soon as possible, she must remember that what she feels is not important. If the child has a problem, he will bring it out when he is ready. The problem of maladjustment is so complex that one cannot draw a simple circle around some singular experience and say, 'This is it' " (p. 126).

Play therapy groups are generally held once or twice a week, although this structure is certainly flexible. The needs of the child group members should take precedence over any prescribed group schedule, which is admittedly for the professional convenience of the counseling setting or the therapist. It must be remembered that the developmental and emotional needs of children do not necessarily follow the prescribed structure of the adult service-providers. Additionally, it must be remembered that a week in a child's life is not equal to the same amount of time in an adult's life. A week in the young child's life can feel like a very long time, and this must be considered when scheduling children.

Also, the intense emotional needs of the child resulting from certain life experiences must be taken into account. The traumatized child may be seen two or three times a week in the first few weeks and then move to a schedule of once-a-week sessions, in addition to or prior to placement in a play therapy group. Intensive short-term groups, meeting two to five times per week, may be very effective. Kot's (1995) research reported positive results on the efficacy of short-term, intensive child-centered play therapy with children who had witnessed domestic violence and were temporarily residing in women's shelters. Although this research involved individual play therapy, it points to the significant potential for short-term intensive therapeutic play groups.

The duration of the group play therapy process will also vary. This may relate to play groups meeting in different settings (schools, hospitals, and so on) and to the severity of the presenting issues. Gumaer (1984) noted that most research indicates that for group counseling to be effective with children, a minimum of ten sessions is necessary. This points to the need for adequate time for a therapeutic rapport and environment to be established, adequate time for the natural growth process, and adequate time for termination. To reiterate, this timetable is best established by the needs of the children, although logistical constrictions must be considered.

Case Example

Any discussion of a specific case example of child-centered group play therapy would not include extensive information about individual group members. Background information about children in therapy groups tends to be problem focused. Moustakas (1959) correctly noted that most therapeutic relationships with children unfortunately involve problem-centered interactions. The development of therapeutic relationships should be, therefore, child-focused rather than problem-focused.

Child-centered play therapy views children within the framework of *emotionalized attitudes*, as discussed by Axline (1955):

> In psychotherapy, we are dealing with emotionalized attitudes that have developed out of the individual's past experiencing of himself in relation to others. These emotionalized attitudes influence his perception of himself as either adequate or inadequate, secure or insecure, worthy of respect or not worthy of respect, having personal worth or deficient in this basic feeling. His perception then, in turn, determines his behavior. The individual's behavior at the moment seems to be his best efforts to maintain and defend his selfhood and so maintain a psychological identity and a resistance to threats against his personality. Consequently, the child who is emotionally deprived and who has had experiences that seem to form and reinforce feelings of inadequacy and lack of personal worth learns the kind of behavior that protects his self-esteem and lessens the impact of threats against his personality. . . . He may refuse to behave certain ways that are expected or demanded by others in order to maintain a self with integrity [p. 619].

In the following case example, three children (Randy, age seven; Judi, age seven; and Steve, age eight) are meeting for the first time in a play therapy group at an elementary school. They have all been referred because of so-called socialization problems. Randy has been described as an anxious child who does not have any friends, Judi as an introverted child who relates more to adults than to children, and Steve as a somewhat hyper child who tends to annoy his peers.

Initial Session

Since it is difficult to describe child-centered group play therapy without giving specific examples, in keeping with the person-centered characteristic of illustrating principles through verbatim accounts (Raskin & Rogers, 1989), the following is a brief transcript of some of the therapeutic interactions with the children in the playroom.

Therapist: Randy, Judi, and Steve—this is our playroom, and you can play with the toys in a lot of the ways you would like to.

The child-centered group play therapy approach is permission-giving. The therapist uses each child's name, which honors each child, and establishes the egalitarian status of each group member.

Steve: [*rushing into the room toward the sandbox*] I want to play in the sand!

It is not unusual to have children of varying levels of emotional and sociable levels.

Therapist: Steve, it looks like you've got something in mind. [*Judi moves slowly into the room while looking at the toys.*] Judi, it looks like you're checking out the toys on that shelf.

In group play therapy, it becomes very important to use the child's name, so that each group member is aware of who is being addressed. Steve has an intentional plan, and the therapist needs to acknowledge this. At the same time, the other children need to be responded to. It can be a temptation to respond primarily to the most active and vocal children, but therapeutic responses should be spread out equally among the group members.

Judi: Yeah, I guess so. [*Judi has reached out tentatively to touch the cash register, but has pulled her hand back. Randy is still standing next to the door, furtively glancing around.*]

The initial session of group play therapy is often tentative and exploratory for the children. They are not just exploring the playroom but also checking out the therapist and the other children.

Therapist: Judi, it seems like you're wondering if it's OK to play with that. In here, you can choose what to play with. Randy, it looks like you're wondering about this place.

The therapist's voice tone should match the voice tone and activity level of the child. The response to Judi is warm and empathic but places the responsibility for making the choices on her. It might be tempting for the therapist to give Randy a specific invitation to play, because of his tentativeness. He should be allowed to make this choice himself.

Steve: [*Grabs the rubber snake and runs across the room, poking the snake at Randy's face. Randy cringes and tries to fend off the snake.*]
Therapist: Steve, it looks like you would like to scare Randy with that snake, but he is trying to tell you he doesn't like what you are doing. He wants you to stop.

Recognition of feelings is key to the child-centered approach. Verbalizing Randy's nonverbal message helps Steve to hear Randy's message and gives Randy the needed support that he is understood.

> Steve: [Leaves Randy and with great glee begins chasing Judi around the room.]
> Judi: [screaming] Quit that!
> Therapist: Steve, you're having lots of fun chasing Judi; but Judi, you are telling
>   him you don't like what he is doing.

Tracking of activity and responding to feelings is the same as in individual play therapy, just more so. It is important that both children be responded to equally. Both children need to know they have been heard and understood.

> Steve: [Drops the snake on the floor and goes back to the sandbox.]
> Judi: [Picks up some puppets and begins to make a puppet show.]
> Randy: [Plays with a toy in the corner behind the easel stand, out of sight.]
> Therapist: So, Steve, you decided to do something else; and Judi, you decided to
>   play with the puppets.

Recognizing that children have made a decision affirms their strength. No response is made to Randy because he seems to need to be left alone at the moment. The therapist is keenly sensitive to where Randy is and what he is doing but respects his choice to hide.

> Randy: [Sits on the floor under the easel looking out at the group.]
> Judi: [continues puppet story, saying to the therapist] Good morning. I'm the lion.
>   [gives a loud roar]
> Therapist: Good morning, lion. That's a big roar.

The therapist can interact without structuring. [Other interactions occur as Judi develops the puppet story.]

> Therapist: Randy, looks like you decided to sit right there.

Nonevaluative recognition communicates acceptance of his decision to sit and look.

> Steve: [has been digging in the sand, burying toy soldiers; says to no one in particular] I'm
>   going to bury all of these guys.
> Therapist: [to Steve] Yep, looks like you've buried a bunch of them.

Toys are not labeled until the child identifies the item.

Randy: [*Emerges from under the easel, joins Steve, and begins digging in the sand.*]

The activity of other children in group play therapy invites and entices shy, quiet children. Randy relaxes enough to begin playing.

Steve: [*to Randy*] Hey! Neat! You can dig the holes, and I'll bury these guys.

Steve's statement is encouraging to Randy and helps him feel included.

Therapist: Randy, you've decided to play in the sand with Steve—and Steve, sounds like you like that!

A simple tracking of the play activity provides affirmation of the choices made by the children, particularly Randy.

Steve: [*grabs the sand pail and yells*] This is going to be a bomb! [*holds bucket up high and drops it on the floor as Randy protests*]
Therapist: Steve, I know that was fun for you, but the sand is for staying in the sand box. You wanted the bucket—but Randy, you are telling Steve you want to play with it.

The therapist shows understanding of each child's behavioral and emotional message and sets an appropriate limit. The limit setting follows the A.C.T. model, proposed by Landreth (1991). This highly effective model provides for: *A*cknowledging the child's feelings (it is important to begin the setting of limits by continuing reflection and acceptance), *C*ommunicating the limit (in a neutral and nonpunitive manner), and *T*argeting an acceptable alternative (which recognizes that the child still has a need to express self and can do so within acceptable boundaries). A limit that is set objectively—with acceptance and without disapproval—is most often received and responded to by children with compliance.

Randy: [*picks up bucket and begins to fill it with sand again*] I'm going to build a castle.
Steve: These soldiers can guard the castle.

Steve's aggression has subsided because he has been allowed to act it out, and he joins in the play activity in a helpful way.

> *Judi:* *[stands watching the boys]* There needs to be a family living in the castle. *[retrieves the doll family from the doll house and adds them to the castle scene]*
>
> *Therapist:* You're all making that castle just the way you want it to be.

The therapist's comment empowers the children, recognizing their own decision making, effort, and creative ability. This comment also affirms their working together, while not providing praise and approval. The child-centered play therapist does not evaluate and focuses on the effort rather than the product. The difference between encouragement and praise is key in the child-centered group play therapy process. By focusing on the effort, the therapist can make self-esteem–building statements without creating the leading and approval-seeking dynamic that comes from statements of praise. It also models this important dynamic for the group members in their interaction with each other.

> *Judi, Randy, and Steve:* *[almost in unison]* Yeah!

General Comments

In an initial session, the child-centered group play therapist is focused on creating an environment of acceptance that promotes the inherent growth-producing tendencies of the children. The therapist is thus concerned with being sensitive to each child's feelings and perception, helping the child to feel safe, making emotional contact with the child, and returning responsibility for self to the child. "The building of a relationship begins with what the child sees and perceives in the therapist and is dependent on the therapist's sensitivity to the child's experiencing at the moment. Making contact with the child means responding with gentleness, kindness, and softness to the child's communication of self. Through the process of accepting the child's attitudes, feelings, and thoughts, the therapist enters the child's world. Once contact with the child has been made in this way, a trusting relationship can begin to develop" (Landreth, 1991, p. 157).

Each child in the case described here reacted differently to the therapist's communication of this message. Although this was an initial session, some of the previously stated benefits of child-centered group play therapy are already evident. Randy demonstrated movement from being generally anxious in the group to interacting with the other children. His physical movement from distance to closer proximity to the therapist and the other children was one example of the benefit of placing shy, anxious children in play therapy groups. Steve's aggressive behavior was ameliorated by the group, particularly by the therapist giving expression to the displeasure of the other children at some of his behaviors. He was given the opportunity to reevaluate his acting-out behaviors in the presence of Randy and Judi, as well as the therapist. Judi begins by playing alone and seeking to engage the therapist, which is typical of her introverted behavior outside the playroom, where she attempts to relate primarily with adults. She, too, is drawn into the play process.

Conclusion

In the child-centered group play therapy process, children experience an environment that is marked by warmth and acceptance and promotes safety and growth. This environment allows children the opportunity to discover that their peers may be struggling too, which helps to deconstruct the barriers that children have of feeling alone in their pain. A sense of belonging develops, and children learn appropriate ways to relate within and outside the playroom. Gumaer (1984) summarized the value of child-centered group counseling:

> Group counseling provides a lifelike representation of children's everyday world. The small group situation is a microcosm of the child's real world. Children interact in group therapy; share their lives and receive feedback from peers about their feelings, thoughts, and behavior. They relate interpersonally and learn to identify effective and ineffective social skills. Children learn about themselves by hearing other children's perceptions of them. They learn how they are similar and different, and that it is all right to be unique. Children learn they must conform and cooperate in some instances, but also that original and creative thinking is appreciated and supported [p. 213].

All children experience a need to feel understood and accepted. In the group-centered approach to play therapy, children experience a consistent and accepting response from the therapist, regardless of their presenting problem, degree of normality, or extent of personal adjustment. The play therapy experience allows children to communicate about these issues in their own natural medium. The group experience allows children to process these issues on both an intrapersonal and an interpersonal level. The child-centered therapy process takes the focus off the therapist and allows the children to experience self-exploration, self-discovery, and self-realization. It is the actualization of empowerment.

References

Axline, V. (1947). *Play therapy: The inner dynamics of childhood.* Boston: Houghton Mifflin.
Axline, V. (1955). Play therapy procedures and results. *American Journal of Orthopsychiatry, 25,* 618–626.

Bixler, R. (1949). Limits are therapy. *Journal of Consulting Psychology, 13,* 1–11.

Boy, A. (1990). The therapist in person-centered groups. *Person-Centered Review, 5*(3), 308–315.

Boy, A., & Pine, G. (1982). *Client-centered counseling: A renewal.* Boston: Allyn & Bacon.

Bozarth, J. (1981). The person-centered approach in the large community group. In G. Gazda (Ed.), *Innovations to group psychotherapy* (2nd ed.). Springfield, IL: Thomas.

Bozarth, J., & Brodley, B. (1986). Client-centered psychotherapy: A statement. *Person-Centered Review, 1*(3), 262–271.

Ginott, H. (1994). *Group psychotherapy with children: The theory and practice of play therapy.* Northvale, NJ: Aronson.

Gumaer, J. (1984). *Counseling and therapy for children.* New York: Free Press.

Hobbs, N. (1951). Group-centered psychotherapy. In C. R. Rogers (Ed.), *Client-centered therapy: Its current practice* (pp. 278–319). Boston: Houghton Mifflin.

Hobbs, N. (1964). Group-centered counseling. In C. Kemp (Ed.), *Perspectives on the group process.* Boston: Houghton Mifflin.

Kot, S. (1995). *Intensive play therapy with child witnesses of domestic violence.* Unpublished doctoral dissertation, University of North Texas, Denton.

Landreth, G. (1991). *Play therapy: The art of the relationship.* Muncie, IN: Accelerated Development.

Landreth, G., & Sweeney, D. (1997). Child-centered play therapy. In K. O'Connor & L. Braverman (Eds.), *Play therapy: Theory and practice* (pp. 17–45). New York: Wiley.

Moustakas, C. (1959). *Psychotherapy with children: The living relationship.* New York: HarperCollins.

Raskin, N., & Rogers, C. (1989). Person-centered therapy. In R. Corsini & D. Wedding (Eds.), *Current psychotherapies* (4th ed., pp. 155–194). Itasca, IL: Peacock.

Rogers, C. (1951). *Client-centered therapy.* Boston: Houghton Mifflin.

Rogers, C. (1967). The process of the basic encounter group. In J. Bugental (Ed.), *Challenges of humanistic psychology* (pp. 261–278). New York: McGraw-Hill.

Rogers, C. (1970). *Carl Rogers on encounter groups.* New York: HarperCollins.

Rogers, C. (1980). *A way of being.* Boston: Houghton Mifflin.

Rogers, C. (1986). Client-centered therapy. In I. Kutash & A. Wolf (Eds.), *Psychotherapist's casebook: Theory and techniques in the practice of modern therapies* (pp. 197–208). San Francisco: Jossey-Bass.

Schiffer, M. (1969). *The therapeutic play group.* New York: Grune & Stratton.

Slavson, S. R. (1964). *A textbook in analytic group psychotherapy.* New York: International Universities Press.

Sweeney, D. S. (1997). *Counseling children through the world of play.* Wheaton, IL: Tyndale House.

CHAPTER FIVE

GROUP APPLICATIONS
OF ADLERIAN PLAY THERAPY

Terry Kottman

In Adlerian play therapy (Kottman, 1993, 1994, 1995, 1997, 1998), the play therapist uses the materials and basic strategies of play therapy (such as tracking, restating content, limit setting, and so forth) to communicate with children, while conceptualizing issues and relationships and adapting interventions from the perspective of Individual Psychology (Adler, 1930/1963, 1931/1958; Dinkmeyer, Dinkmeyer, & Sperry, 1987). In Adlerian play therapy, there are four phases of the counseling process: building an egalitarian relationship, exploring the child's lifestyle, helping the child gain insight into that lifestyle, and reorienting and reeducating the child, helping the child learn new skills for relating to self, others, and the world (Kottman, 1995). These phases are not necessarily separate and discrete. For instance, the play therapist will continue to build a relationship with the child throughout their time together; the play therapist may quickly understand one aspect of the child's lifestyle and try to help him or her gain insight into that aspect at the same time that exploration of other aspects of the child's lifestyle continue. However, Adlerians believe that the therapy must proceed in an orderly fashion through all four steps, even when in truncated form necessitated by time-limited sessions.

In each phase of counseling, the play therapist tries to incorporate growth in the four "crucial necessities that each child must have in order to successfully meet life's challenges" (Lew & Bettner, 1998a, p. 5)—the "Crucial Cs" of connecting, feeling capable, feeling as if they count and are significant, and having courage (Lew & Bettner, 1998a, b). At the same time, the Adlerian play therapist is also consulting with parents (and sometimes teachers) on ways for them to help the child, themselves, and other family members make shifts in perceptions, attitudes, behaviors, and interactional patterns. With some children, the play therapist also consults with teachers about strategies for helping the child, the teacher, and the child's classmates.

When working with groups, the Adlerian play therapist must also consider group dynamics, stages of group development, and group intervention strategies as well. In some ways, a group approach is ideal for working with children using Adlerian play therapy—especially during the second (exploring the lifestyle), third (helping the child gain insight into the lifestyle), and fourth (reorientation and reeducation) phases.

Adlerians believe that it is inappropriate to conceptualize clients without considering their social context. During the second phase of play therapy, it is extremely important for the therapist to gather information about how clients interact with others. Group play therapy gives the therapist a milieu for observing individual children in a ready-made social context and noting patterns as clients act out their lifestyles—demonstrating their perceptions of themselves, others, and the world and revealing the attitudes and behaviors generated by those perceptions. This phase of a play therapy group can also provide a perfect setting for the play therapist to observe how each of the children demonstrates the extent to which he or she exhibits the Crucial Cs (Lew & Bettner, 1998a, b).

Based on a sense of the clients' lifestyles and their attainment of the Crucial Cs, the Adlerian play therapist can plan intervention strategies for the third and fourth phases of the play therapy. For example, with children who do not seem to connect with other children, it would be important in the third phase of therapy to point out missed connections with other children in the group and make gentle guesses about the origin and goal of this behavior. During the fourth phase of play therapy, the therapist would attempt to find ways to teach these children new skills for making interpersonal connections and provide practice in this area through the other members of the group.

To understand how Adlerians work with children in the process of group play therapy, it is necessary to have a grasp of the basic premises of Individual Psychology. If readers wish to pursue more information about Individual Psychology beyond that covered in this chapter, they should consult Ansbacher and Ansbacher (1956), Dinkmeyer, Dinkmeyer, and Sperry (1987), or Manaster and Corsini (1982) for definitive discussions of Adlerian theory.

Individual Psychology

The theory of Individual Psychology was originated by Alfred Adler in the early decades of the twentieth century (Adler, 1930/1963, 1931/1958) and further developed by Rudolph Dreikurs (1953; Dreikurs & Soltz, 1964). Adlerian theory of human personality is practical and optimistic. Adler believed that each person is special, unique, and has the potential for making a positive contribution. Adler coined the terms *social interest, feelings of inferiority,* and *lifestyle,* which are especially relevant to the practice of Adlerian play therapy.

- *Social interest.* According to Adlerian theory, all human beings are born with a predisposition to make connections with other human beings (Ansbacher & Ansbacher, 1956). This innate tendency for moving toward a sense of belongingness within the human community is called *social interest.* Children must learn how to operationalize this innate desire to make contact with others. However, if the adults in their lives do not foster this capacity, children may never develop the skills they need to successfully make connections with others.

- *Feelings of inferiority.* According to Adler, young children, because they are not as strong, capable, and knowledgeable about the world as older people, tend to have a sense of relative weakness and vulnerability (Ansbacher & Ansbacher, 1956). He believed that as children grow up this sense of relative powerlessness develops into feelings of inferiority that undergird the self-image of every human being (Ansbacher & Ansbacher, 1956). He also thought that people develop specific strategies (which ultimately affect many aspects of their lives) for dealing with these feelings (Dinkmeyer et al., 1987). Usually a person will manifest one of the three primary patterns of dealing with inferiority feelings: becoming completely discouraged, giving up, and acting incapable and incompetent; becoming discouraged, overcompensating, and acting as if omniscient and omnipowerful; and using the feelings of inferiority as a challenge and a spur to greater effort and positive striving.

- *Lifestyle.* Another important Adlerian concept is that of lifestyle, which is a person's characteristic pattern of operating in the world (Ansbacher & Ansbacher, 1956). Lifestyle is based on the person's subjective beliefs about self, others, and the world. As children grow up, they observe how people behave, how people react to them, how people treat one another. They observe attitudes and relationships. Young children are extremely observant, but they may make mistaken or faulty interpretations of what they observe and incorporate these mistaken beliefs about self, others, and the world into their lifestyles (Dreikurs & Soltz, 1964). These faulty beliefs are a major cause of discouragement and maladjustment. Because people act as if their subjective interpretations of events and interactions are true, they may behave in ways that are negative and self-destructive.

Adlerians base their conceptualization of clients and relationships on several theoretical assumptions about human development, human behavior, and human personality. According to Adlerian theory, people are constantly interpreting life from a subjective perspective, are creative and self-determining, and are purposefully moving toward goals (Adler, 1930/1963; Ansbacher & Ansbacher, 1956; Dinkmeyer et al., 1987). The following paragraphs offer a brief explanation of each of these concepts and describe how these ideas pertain to group Adlerian play therapy.

• *People are constantly interpreting life from a subjective perspective.* Adler suggested that how a person interprets what happens is much more important than what actually happens (Adler, 1930/1963; Ansbacher & Ansbacher, 1956; Dinkmeyer et al., 1987; Manaster & Corsini, 1982). This is a key idea in Adlerian play therapy, because it means that each person has a unique way of looking at experiences and interactions. It is the responsibility of the Adlerian play therapist to attempt to understand the child's life from the child's perspective, the parent's life from the parent's perspective, and the teacher's life from the teacher's perspective (Kottman, 1997). In group play therapy, the therapist's job becomes much more difficult, because each group member will have a unique, subjective interpretation of group interactions. The therapist must attempt to glean these perceptions by watching the play of individual members and the interactions between group members and by asking selected questions.

• *People are creative and self-determining.* Adlerians believe that human beings (both children and adults) are constantly recreating themselves by making decisions about how to apply the perceptions in their lifestyles (Ansbacher & Ansbacher, 1956; Dinkmeyer et al., 1987; Manaster & Corsini, 1982). Children under the age of six or eight also have the ability to change the convictions within their lifestyles—they are flexible enough in their interpretations and perceptions that they can create new ways of looking at themselves, others, and the world and learn completely new behaviors and attitudes (Ansbacher & Ansbacher, 1956; Dinkmeyer et al., 1987; Kottman, 1995).

This ability to make choices is essential to the process of Adlerian play therapy (Kottman, 1995, 1997) because it means that the therapist can have an impact on the formation of clients' lifestyles. The process of group play therapy can foster new input into a child's thoughts, feelings, and behavior from multiple individuals. By teaching the children in the group to be encouraging to one another, pointing out one another's assets and helping one another experiment with new attitudes and behaviors, the play therapist can enhance the process of change in group members. Many children will grow and blossom simply by providing support and encouragement for others.

　• *People are purposefully moving toward goals.* Adler believed that all behavior is goal-directed (Ansbacher & Ansbacher, 1956; Dinkmeyer et al., 1987; Manaster & Corsini, 1982). He said that people are motivated by movement toward specific purposes, rather than by trauma from the past or by instincts. Adlerians working with children who manifest negative behavior usually examine the children's actions, feelings, and reactions to correction, and also the feelings and actions of the adults who interact with them, to determine the goal of misbehavior—generally attention, power, revenge, and proving inadequacy (Dreikurs & Soltz, 1964; Kottman, 1995). When working with children whose goal is power, it is also important to understand whether they come from environments where they have too little power, too much power, or things are out of control.

In discussing the Crucial Cs, Lew and Bettner (1998a, b) suggested children may also be moving toward positive goals of cooperation, self-reliance, making a contribution, and being resilient. If adults begin to understand both the positive and negative goals of behavior, they can interact more effectively with children who are striving toward destructive ends, help children striving in negative directions better understand their own behavior, and help children explore ways they can work toward positive goals.

The Adlerian play therapist predicates most interactions with children on an understanding of their primary goal of behavior and the environment in which they live. For instance, with children whose goal is proving their own inadequacy, the play therapist focuses almost solely on assets, encouraging every possible effort inside the playroom. With children whose goal is power and who have too much control in their families, the play therapist focuses on sharing power with the child, rather than letting the child control every aspect of the interaction.

Group play therapy provides the therapist with much opportunity for observation of children's goals. Watching group members interact with one another, the play therapist has a window into their usual mode of operation, which can give valuable clues about goals of behavior. With children who are striving toward one of the four goals of misbehavior, the therapist can quickly begin to use tentative hypotheses about these goals. As children gain insight into their own motivation for self-defeating behaviors, the therapist can move them more toward the positive goals of behavior through brainstorming activities, modeling of positive goal striving by the higher-functioning members of the group, and feedback from other members about how negatively focused behavior affects others.

Group Considerations

In forming a play therapy group, the leaders must consider the need to achieve a balance of group member personalities and behaviors, and to involve parents and the teacher. It is also necessary to choose a format for the group.

Balancing Group Members

One of the key elements in successful groups for children is achieving a balance of personalities and behaviors among group members (Beyer, 1997; Siepker & Kandaras, 1985). To achieve group balance, if the leader has not previously worked with potential members, it is helpful to have a screening interview or play session for observation of the child as well as an initial session with the parents (and the teacher—or perhaps the teacher alone—if the problem is manifested at school) to discuss possible inclusion in the group. In these screening sessions, the leader must consider whether this particular child is appropriate for group play therapy and whether this particular child is appropriate for this specific group. If the child is appropriate, it is helpful to discuss goals for the therapy process with the parents and teacher.

In most Adlerian play therapy groups, the leader will want to mix children who are experiencing higher degrees of difficulty with children who are experiencing only minor difficulty. This provides the leader with potential members who are able and willing to provide encouragement and appropriate constructive feedback to other members. Children who exhibit positive behavior and attitudes can serve as models for the other children and as potential "cotherapists."

The Adlerian play therapy group leader will usually attempt to balance the various members along the following dimensions if possible: active versus passive, outgoing versus withdrawn, susceptible to peer pressure versus resistant to contagion, inhibited versus impulsive, high social interest versus low social interest, and primarily striving toward negative goals of behavior versus primarily striving toward positive goals of behavior. In a group of six to eight children, having representatives from different places on several of these continua can make the group a setting where children are more likely to learn from one another and be able to help one another grow and change.

Involvement of Parents and Teachers

In most children's groups, parents and teachers are not actively involved in the therapeutic process (Beyer, 1997; Siepker & Kandaras, 1985). However, in individual Adlerian play therapy, regular consultation with parents is an essential component, and the therapist frequently consults with teachers as well (Kottman, 1993, 1995, 1997). Adlerians believe that it is impossible to understand an individual without some exploration of his or her social context and that change is limited in children without accompanying change in the family system and sometimes the system in the classroom. Therefore, the optimal arrangement in group Adlerian play therapy would be some sort of ongoing parent consultation and teacher consultation as an adjunct to the play therapy. However, this is not feasible in many settings, so the group leader may wish to consider some adapted arrangement that provides some access to parents and teachers even if not every week.

The parent component usually consists of teaching parenting skills such as encouragement, logical consequences, and goals of behavior. Possible delivery formats for this component include inviting parents to attend group consultation meetings two or three times during the course of the play therapy group, holding individual parent consultations with the parents of one or two different group members every week on a rotating basis, arranging phone consultation with parents as needed, or including parents in Adlerian parenting classes before, after, or during the course of the play therapy group. Helpful references for designing parent consultation strategies include *Systematic Training for Effective Parenting: Parent's Handbook* (Dinkmeyer & McKay, 1989); *Children: The Challenge* (Dreikurs & Soltz, 1964); *A Parent's Guide to Understanding and Motivating Children* (Lew & Bettner, 1998a); and *Active Parenting Today* (Popkin, 1993).

Consulting with teachers usually takes place at intermittent intervals during the process of Adlerian play therapy—either over the telephone or in person depending on the situation. The therapist may make suggestions for new ways of perceiving or interacting with children in the classroom. This process usually involves training teachers in Adlerian concepts and skills such as goals of behavior, logical and natural consequences, social interest, and encouragement. Useful references for exploring teacher consultation strategies include *Responsibility in the Classroom: A Teacher's Guide to Understanding and Motivating Students* (Lew & Bettner, 1998b); *A Teacher's Guide to Cooperative Discipline: How to Manage Your Classroom and Promote Self-Esteem* (Albert, 1989); *Systematic Training for Effective Teaching* (Dinkmeyer, McKay, & Dinkmeyer, 1980); *Active Teaching* (Popkin, 1994); *Maintaining Sanity in the Classroom* (Dreikurs, Grunwald, & Pepper, 1982); and *Positive Discipline in the Classroom: How to Effectively Use Class Meetings* (Nelson, Lott, & Glenn, 1993).

Format of the Group

Group leaders must also make decisions about whether a play therapy group will be structured or unstructured, closed or open, and time-limited or ongoing (Beyer, 1997; Siepker & Kandaras, 1985). These issues tend to be rather intertwined. For example, with a time-limited play therapy group, leaders will tend more toward highly structured sessions in an effort to ensure the attainment of group and individual goals for the therapy. With an open play therapy group, the leader must use some structure to make sure new members understand group rules and establish some kind of relationship with other members.

Case Example

The case example is an application of group Adlerian play therapy. The first section will contain a description of group members and their presenting problems. In the second section, I will briefly explain my theoretical conceptualization of each member. The next section will contain a description of the process of Adlerian group play therapy, and the conclusion section will provide a description of outcomes of the therapy.

Group Members

There were six children in the self-named "Black Birds" group: Rachel (age six), Mike (age six), Jason (age seven), Sarah (age seven), Leah (age six), and Shelby (age seven). They were all in first grade in a local elementary school. I had volunteered to lead a group developed to help several children who had been identified by their teacher (Ms. Kline) as having low self-concept. As I discussed the formation of the group with the school counselor (Mrs. Barry), I focused on ways to achieve a balance of group members, work with the parents and teacher of the members, and format the group for maximum growth.

Because the children who were to be the Black Birds were all in the same class in school and I was not a regular staff member with access to them at regular intervals, I decided on several different activities to screen potential group members. I observed several times in their classroom and during their recess time on the playground and consulted with Ms. Kline and Mrs. Barry about specific children and group goals. I conducted individual play sessions with three of the candidates. During these sessions, I allowed them to free play, asked them to do several types of play interactions with me, and asked them questions.

For the Black Birds, I chose Rachel and Shelby as my high-functioning, "model" children. As I observed them on the playground and in the classroom, they were children who seemed to be having a great deal of fun. They were self-confident and independent—outgoing, active, and resistant to peer pressure.

Mike and Sarah were less adept, but still only experiencing minor problems in their relationships and in their attitudes and behavior in the classroom. Mike was mildly passive and withdrawn, occasionally making negative comments about himself and others. His teacher reported that he had a few good friends but was reluctant to work on new relationships. Although his progress in reading was excellent, Mike seemed to feel as though he was not particularly successful, especially in the area of math. Quite frequently, Ms. Kline had to remind him to keep on task during math. While he initially returned to the work at hand, he would eventually stop trying to solve the problems and look out the window, daydreaming.

Sarah, on the other hand, had confidence in her math ability but was struggling with reading. She frequently got into power struggles with Ms. Kline about whether she was doing her reading assignments at home. Her mother had reported to the teacher that she "just couldn't get Sarah to try at home and had given up the effort." According to Mrs. Barry, Sarah had "gone through" several sets of friends since the beginning of school. She seemed to make friends relatively easily, but when conflicts occurred she would generally stop all interaction with a specific friend or group and turn to the task of making new friends.

Jason and Leah had the most problems. While he performed very well on individual assignments, Jason exhibited an elevated need for interpersonal power and control that precluded his working in groups on classroom projects. He was frequently defiant and belligerent in school, getting into yelling matches with children and teachers. Jason had no friends and complained constantly that the other children in the class "picked on him." If anyone else had a problem in the class, Jason was usually involved—either in conflict with the other child or trying to blame one of his classmates for the difficulty. Ms. Kline and Mrs. Barry reported feeling frustrated with his parents, who tended to "let him do whatever he wanted" in fear of provoking an asthma attack if they thwarted him.

Leah was, in many ways, the opposite of Jason. She was extremely shy, with no friends and (when possible) little interaction with adults. Eye contact and normal conversation seemed almost painful to her. Leah was barely passing her academic subjects and cried whenever it was time go out to the playground for recess. Ms. Kline commented that Leah seemed to wish that "everyone would just forget that she is here." Mrs. Barry reported that Leah's mother said that this was typical of her behavior in every area of her life.

For the Black Birds, I had several phone conversations with the parents, especially those of Jason and Leah. Mrs. Barry offered Adlerian parenting classes using the *Systematic Training for Effective Parenting* curriculum during the semester, and parents of five of the group members attended. Although both Mrs. Barry and I asked Jason's parents to attend the parenting class, they declined, saying that they were "very busy people" who did not have problems handling Jason's behavior. They told Mrs. Barry that they believed Jason's difficulties in school were due to Ms. Kline's lack of experience.

Ms. Kline was eager to learn how to apply Adlerian principles in her classroom, so she used Mrs. Barry as an on-site consultant, and I met with her for forty-five minutes once a week for the duration of the group. She began to implement many of the suggestions from the resources listed in this chapter in her classroom and noticed many positive changes—in her own attitude and behaviors and in the members of the group and the other children in her class.

I prefer relatively structured, closed groups with the number of sessions agreed upon in advance. For the Black Birds group, I decided to do ten sessions, lasting for forty-five minutes once a week, with an option for two extra sessions if I felt that we had not yet attained our goals at the end of ten sessions.

Theoretical Conceptualization

A major part of the role of the Adlerian play therapist is developing hypotheses about the lifestyles of clients, including an assessment of levels of social interest, goals of behavior, attainment of the Crucial Cs, assets, and beliefs about self, others, and the world. The following is a brief description of my theoretical conceptualization of each of the members of the Black Birds group, based on the data that I gathered during the screening process and during the first and second phases of play therapy.

Rachel and Shelby, the model children, strongly exhibited the Crucial Cs, especially connecting with others and feeling capable. They had high levels of social interest and were striving toward positive goals of cooperation and making a contribution to their classmates and school. When they did exhibit any misbehavior, the goal was almost always to gain attention in constructive ways.

Rachel tended to strive for attention by being cute and trying to please other children and adults. Her behavior fit the pattern of oldest children from families with an atmosphere that encourages compliance and cooperation. Rachel's interpersonal assets were a genuine joy in building relationships, a desire to help others, and a willingness to cooperate. Rachel believed that she could be successful in most of her endeavors, especially those in the social area, but her confidence in this area was slightly tainted by her belief that she must please others and be compliant to gain acceptance. Her view of others was basically positive, but only somewhat trusting due to her belief that acceptance was conditional. She had the idea that the world was basically a safe and happy place where most people were kind and cooperative.

Shelby's goal of behavior was also attention, but he went about getting it by being quiet, cooperative, and studious. This mode seemed to be related to his role as the only child of older parents who used a democratic style of parenting and valued helping others and "doing your best at whatever you do." Shelby's belief that he could make a significant contribution to others and that others could gain their own significance if they were willing to work at cooperating and making a contribution was a valuable asset in a group. His faith that the world was a place where everyone could connect, feel capable, and be important and courageous helped make him a leader within the group who could encourage the other members.

Mike and Sarah had somewhat lower levels of social interest and more negative lifestyles than the model children. Mike's primary goal of behavior was gaining attention by being passive and self-defeating, but occasionally he seemed to be striving for power through passive-aggressive behaviors. Although making and keeping friends and being successful in reading were assets for Mike, he seemed to feel as though he was not really significant or capable. Mike apparently felt that he was not very important or special and that others would probably not like him very much. This rather negative worldview sometimes seemed to prevent him from taking risks or gaining confidence in his own abilities.

Sarah's feeling of being capable in math was frequently undermined by her belief that she would never learn to read. Rather than demonstrating the courage to continue trying at things that became difficult for her, she had a pattern of quitting—at both her academic endeavors and her friendships. This tendency to give up frequently offset Sarah's assets (having the ability to make new friends and be successful in math). This also seemed related to her striving to always be in control of herself, which is a form of the goal of power. I felt that this was related to her mother's tendency to give in to Sarah in an effort to "keep peace in the family."

Jason and Leah both had relatively self-defeating lifestyles. Jason was an only child whose parents blamed his asthma on "the pollution of the environment by people who just don't care about anything." They did not set any limits, allowing him to do whatever he wanted at home and suggesting that school personnel follow suit. Jason's lack of trust in others and his belief that he was not in control of his own life led him to believe that he must be in control of everything and everyone else in his world. Despite his obvious intelligence and grasp of academic subjects, Jason did not seem to know how to connect with others and the only way he seemed to feel that he could be special or important was by denigrating other people.

Leah also struggled with making connections and feeling significant. She seemed determined to prove to others that she was inadequate and unimportant. Leah's father had abandoned the family before Leah was a year old, and Leah may have transferred some of her beliefs about lack of worth relative to her father to a lack of worth in general. She seemed afraid of the world, and her inability to deal with this fear and corresponding lack of courage was preventing her from trying new experiences and making friends. Her performance in terms of academics was only a relative strength, and it was difficult to generate a list of other assets due to her limited willingness to enter into experiences and relationships.

Process of Group Adlerian Play Therapy

The phases of Adlerian play therapy groups have a parallel structure to the stages usually described in group counseling for children (Beyer, 1997; Siepker & Kandaras, 1985). In the initial sessions of the group, the leader works on building a relationship with each member and on facilitating the members' forming relationships with one another. During the transition stage of the group, the leader will ask questions and provide exercises for exploring the lifestyle of each group member. As the working stage develops, the leader, through interpretations and activities, will help the members gain insight into their own and one another's lifestyles. During the termination stage, members will learn new skills and practice these skills in the context of the group in preparation for application when the group ends.

Initial Stage: Building a Relationship. The initial stage of the Black Birds group lasted three sessions. I structured the first session around deciding on a group name and group rules and discussing group goals. During this time, Rachel suggested the name of "Black Birds" because everyone in the group happened to have some black article of clothing on that day. Although Jason complained that this was not the name he would have picked, all the group members agreed to the name. Jason and Sarah complained about some of the rules and group goals the others suggested, but they eventually agreed on lists for both rules and goals.

I wanted the group goals to be concrete and attainable—focused on enhancing the level of the Crucial Cs, helping the members increase their ability to catch themselves when they were engaging in self-defeating attitudes and behavior, and recognizing some of their assets. The list of group goals the members of the Black Birds developed included saying positive things to others, taking turns, saying positive things about themselves, and trying things that they would not usually try. Leah did not participate in the discussion at all, but she did smile at Shelby several times when he asked her opinions about various ideas.

The next two sessions each began with twenty minutes of unstructured play time so that I could observe the members' natural style of interacting with one another and the play media. Then I had twenty minutes of structured play activities designed to help the members begin to build relationships with one another. At the end of each session, we took five minutes to clean up the room together.

In Session 2, neither Leah nor Mike participated in the free play, despite the efforts of Shelby, Sarah, and Rachel to engage them. For the structured play, I emptied out the doll house and asked all of the members to play in the doll house, sharing the responsibility of placing the furniture and the dolls. Jason and Sarah had several power struggles about where things should go, but Rachel and Shelby suggested compromises that seemed satisfactory to both. Leah moved some of the furniture to different places, and Shelby, Sarah, and Rachel made encouraging comments about her "knowing where stuff should go."

During Session 3, while the other children played together, Leah and Mike each spent the free play time picking up toys and putting them down, not taking much time with any one toy and not talking with any of the other members. For the structured activity, I asked the members to divide into two subgroups and take turns putting on a puppet show using a relatively specific plot outlined by me about getting along with friends. In the subgroup consisting of Jason, Rachel, and Mike, Jason tried to take over the story but got stuck when he was trying to generate ways of resolving conflict. Rachel and Mike gave him several ideas of how to compromise, which they incorporated into the story. In the subgroup consisting of Shelby, Leah, and Sarah, Shelby and Sarah thought of most of the ideas, with an occasional smile from Leah. Shelby assigned Leah to be a shy turtle in the puppet show who was not sure of how to make friends or resolve conflict. Other animal puppets (acted by Shelby and Sarah) gave Leah's turtle suggestions on how to go about building relationships in (mostly) constructive ways. When Sarah's fox told the turtle that she should go into her shell if other people did not do what she wanted, Leah shook her head and would not do this. Shelby's dog puppet resolved this issue by making some other suggestions for the turtle.

Other Adlerian play therapy strategies that I used during the initial stage of the group were encouraging and setting limits. In addition, cleaning up the room together was not simple housekeeping; it was a specific activity designed to support the therapy (Kottman, 1993, 1995, 1997). I stressed modeling encouragement techniques because I wanted the members to learn to use this skill with one another. Encouragement involves giving positive feedback about progress, assets, and effort in a nonevaluative way. By using phrases like, "You really worked hard at that." "You have made a lot of progress in that area." "Wow, this entire group knows how to do that." I began to teach the children to value their own worth and to acknowledge the worth of others.

The process of limit setting started in the first session as the group members and I generated a list of group rules. I made sure that this list included not hurting one another or the leader (either by words or by deeds) and not damaging the playroom or the toys. I also explained the Adlerian play therapy approach (described in Kottman, 1995) to limit setting, which involves a four-step process:

1. *Set the limit in a nonjudgmental way that uses the rules of the playroom as a basis for the limit.* For example, "It's against the playroom rules to hit another person."
2. *Make a guess about the underlying feelings and goal of the behavior.* For example, "I am thinking that you are really angry at Shelby right now." Or "It seems like you want to see if you can get the other members to do what you want."

3. *Generate alternative, appropriate behaviors and come to an agreement on acceptable alternatives.* For example, "I bet you can think of something you can hit in here that wouldn't be against the playroom rules." And "That's right—it isn't against the playroom rules to hit the pillows." In a group situation, the other members of the group can help the leader and the target member think of acceptable possibilities.

4. *If the child does not abide by the agreement about acceptable alternatives, set up logical consequences.* For example, "You made the decision to hit Mike even though you know it is against the playroom rules and you agreed to just hit the pillows. Now we need to think of a consequence if you were to make that choice again."

The consequence should be somehow related to the original transgression if possible. Again, other members of the group can help think of consequences and help enforce them when appropriate. If the behavior might somehow endanger a child or permanently damage property, the leader may decide to link the third and fourth steps by generating the consequence for potential transgressions at the same time the members are generating alternatives. However, this implies that the leader does not have faith that the child will follow the agreement, so the fourth step is better left separate if that is possible with the specific group.

With this group, I seldom had to limit any of the members. Several times during the initial sessions, Jason tried to overpower other members by yelling at them or moving close to them but tended to stop when I set the limit and made guesses about his need to be in control.

He was also the only member who actively resisted cleaning the room together, although Leah initially did not help with this process. Like many clients, the others seemed to find that picking up the room together increased their sense of partnership. In the group, the members got to have input into what they were willing to pick up and what they thought that others should pick up. Since this negotiation process can take considerable time and I had only allotted five minutes for cleanup, I decided to assign one member per session as the designated person to decide on individual responsibility for cleaning up specific toys or specific areas of the room. I started with Jason the first week and Sarah the following week, since they were the two who had the most vested interest in telling others what to do. Jason gave Sarah a hard time when she was the one assigning what members had to pick up. When he saw that I was complying with Sarah's requests and I pointed out to him that people were more likely to cooperate with him the next time he was in charge if he cooperated when they were in charge, he began to be more compliant.

Transition Stage: Gathering Information About Lifestyles. In the transition stage (Sessions 4 through 6), I gathered information about each child's lifestyle, including data related to family atmosphere, family constellation, goals of behavior (Kottman, 1995, 1997), and the Crucial Cs (Lew & Bettner, 1998a, b). To do this, I observed the members during the twenty minutes of free play, asked lifestyle questions (discussed in Kottman, 1995), and talked to Mrs. Barry, Ms. Kline, and the parents of the group members. During the structured twenty minutes in Sessions 4 and 5, I asked the members to complete a Kinetic Family Drawing and a Kinetic School Drawing (Knoff & Prout, 1985) and used lifestyle questions to help us process what the children had drawn. All the drawings were interesting, but the most significant were Mike's, Jason's, and Sarah's. In Mike's drawings, all the figures were much larger than he was and seemed almost threatening. Jason's drawing of his family had a picture of him lying on a stretcher being carried to the hospital, with his parents watching and crying. There was a caption that said, "I hope he won't die." In Sarah's home drawing, everyone was smiling and happy, whereas in her school drawing, the figure that represented her was crying and had a caption that said, "I will never learn how to read."

In Session 6, I reduced the amount of free play to ten minutes and used the remaining thirty minutes for each of the children to do a five-minute show about "a family" with either the puppets or the animal figures. Rachel, Shelby, Sarah, and Jason all really seemed to enjoy doing this. Mike was somewhat reluctant but told a wonderful story about a family of snails who always drew into their shells whenever something happened that they did not like. Leah surprised the entire group when she chose a family of dinosaurs that communicated through growls. By this time, Rachel, Shelby, Sarah, Mike, and even Jason were all working hard to encourage Leah to participate, so she got a resounding round of applause for her show.

As I was gathering information during this stage of the group, I was formulating lifestyle hypotheses for each member. As in earlier work (Kottman, 1995), I conceptualized the clients by making a list of how they would complete the following statements:

- I am (or I must be) . . .
- Others are . . .
- The world is . . .
- Therefore, my behavior must . . .

It is also helpful to make a list of each client's assets, goals of behavior, and strategies for attaining the Crucial Cs. I have tried to summarize these hypotheses for each of the members in the Theoretical Conceptualization section earlier in this chapter.

Working Stage: Helping Clients Gain Insight into Lifestyles. During the working stage, it is the leader's responsibility to use information gathered during the previous stage to help the children in the group learn more about themselves and the others in the group. In Sessions 7 through 10, I used my lifestyle hypotheses to make guesses about each member's lifestyle, with the hope that gaining insight in this area would motivate the children to make changes in perceptions, attitudes, and behavior.

The interventions I used during this stage included tentative hypotheses, "spitting in their soup," encouragement, metaphors, and connecting the real world to the playroom. I shared tentative hypotheses about the members' play and their verbalizations with them. These guesses centered around the goals of behavior, the Crucial Cs, mistaken and self-defeating perceptions, and effects of family atmosphere and family constellations.

I also "spit in the soup" of members by pointing out when they were sabotaging themselves through their attitudes, perceptions, feelings, and behaviors. I believe that if clients can learn to recognize when they are thinking, feeling, and behaving in ways that are self-defeating, they can begin to change these patterns. For example, when I spit in Jason's soup about the fact that he was sabotaging his attempts to make friends with Shelby by always trying to tell him what to do, I was trying to help Jason learn to recognize and make adjustments in this self-defeating pattern.

I was also trying to "catch them being good," using encouragement to point out effort, progress, and assets being demonstrated in their interactions with others in the group. This was easy to do in this group because by Session 8 they had all made significant progress—becoming more cohesive and cooperative, taking risks with activities they would not have attempted in the initial sessions, and working at taking turns and being supportive of one another.

Since this is a skill that is very helpful for group members to learn to provide for one another, I decided to use part of Session 8 to play a board game that I had made up about encouragement, where they took turns drawing cards with one another's names. To get a token, they had to give positive feedback about assets, progress, or effort to that person. They enjoyed this game so much that they asked to play it again in subsequent sessions.

Several different approaches to metaphor are indispensable during the working stage of Adlerian play therapy. Applications I used included using members' metaphors to communicate, mutual storytelling, and designing therapeutic metaphors for individual members and for the entire group.

By using the members' metaphors presented in their play, the leader can communicate in indirect ways that are comfortable to many children. In this group, several of the children (Mike, Leah, and Jason) seemed to prefer to communicate through metaphors provided by puppets or animal figures. I tried to respectfully keep the metaphors intact without interpreting the metaphor or trying to get the children to confirm the underlying message. I took this path because in the past when I have broken a child's metaphor by asking for a more concrete meaning or interpreting what the metaphor means, the child has invariably refused to answer me and changed the course of the play.

In a play therapy approach to mutual storytelling, the therapist asks a child to use the puppets, dolls, animal figures, or other toys to tell a story with a beginning, a middle, and an end (Gardner, 1971, 1986; Kottman, 1995; Kottman & Stiles, 1990). As the child tells the story, I try to decide which of the characters represents the child and how the relationships and situations in the story parallel the child's life. I also listen for themes that indicate the child's lifestyle, mistaken perceptions, attainment of the Crucial Cs, goals of misbehavior, and assets. When the child is done, I retell the story using the same characters, setting, and beginning of the story, but with a new middle and ending. In the retelling, I attempt to suggest socially appropriate ways of striving toward goals and handling social situations and methods of attaining the Crucial Cs that are not self-destructive. I may spit in the soup of the characters if they are exhibiting mistaken perceptions or self-defeating thoughts or behaviors. If possible during the retelling, the assets of the child originally telling the story become an important component in the successful resolution of the problems encountered by the protagonist of the story.

With the Black Birds, during Sessions 9 and 10, I abandoned free play and used the entire forty minutes on an adaptation of this intervention that invited the other group members to provide input into the retelling. I had three members tell a story in Session 9 (Jason, Rachel, and Mike) and three in Session 10 (Shelby, Sarah, and Leah). After each story, I asked the other members to draw an illustration for the ending of the story, making alternative suggestions for constructive ways the protagonist could have handled relationships or situations. Then I used the ideas generated by the children to retell each story.

Although I could not design a metaphor for every child in the group, I did develop a metaphor for the entire group (Lankton & Lankton, 1989; Mills & Crowley, 1986). I made up a story about a group of animals who went on a journey together. I tried to describe each of the animals as subtly sharing something in common with one of the members of the group. For example, there was a dinosaur who wanted to be friends with the rest of the group but did not know how to speak the language of the other members. This character represented Leah and her desire to relate to the other children, which was being undermined by her lack of courage and social skills. Another character, the tiger, always wanted to tell everyone what to do because he was afraid if he did not that they would be attacked and killed somewhere along their journey. The tiger was to represent Jason and his fear that if he did not stay in control he would die of asthma. In my telling of the story, I suggested several solutions to various problems of the characters, and I also solicited suggestions from group members on how the characters in the story could work toward dealing with their situations. The children, including Leah and Mike, were very excited about coming up with recommendations for each of the characters.

For Shelby and Rachel, who both tended to be a bit perfectionistic, I used a story about how to relax and enjoy life from *More Annie Stories* (Brett, 1992), a book containing therapeutic metaphors. I also consulted the school's librarian to find some books about being a tyrant (for example, *Tyrone the Horrible,* Wilhelm, 1988) and being overly sensitive about getting your way and not trusting others (for example, *Spinky Sulks,* Steig, 1988). I asked Ms. Kline if she would use these books for her reading aloud and discussion time in the classroom.

In group Adlerian play therapy, one of the tasks of the working stage is helping children begin to generalize what they have learned in the playroom to the rest of the world. During Sessions 7 through 10, by making comments connecting progress and insights that had developed within the group with possible applications in the rest of the world, I tried to facilitate transfer of new ways of perceiving self, others, and the world and new skills in interacting with others. For example, when Jason told Shelby that it was his turn to have a ball next rather than just taking it away from him, I would say, "Maybe next time someone on the playground has a toy that you want, you could tell him that it is your turn rather than just taking it from him."

Termination Stage: Reorientation and Reeducation of Clients. In the stage of getting ready for termination by reorienting and reeducating clients (Sessions 10 through 12), I made plans for teaching new coping skills, interactional patterns, and appropriate behavior that members of the Black Birds needed to implement changes in attitude and perception they had made in the working stage. I also consulted with Ms. Kline about how she could extend these lessons in her classroom. Specifically, I wanted to have the group brainstorm alternative approaches to problem situations and difficult relationships for Mike, Sarah, and Jason. I also wanted those three members to learn and practice coping strategies such as problem-solving tactics and negotiation skills (how to get your way without being either aggressive or passive-aggressive). I hoped Mike, Leah, and Jason would improve their social skills (such as concrete ways to make friends) using the puppets, dolls, animal figures, role plays, and art exercises as training tools. Rachel and Shelby needed to learn to relax more easily, and Rachel needed to learn methods other than pleasing to gain her significance. It was also important for the group members to practice these skills (again using puppets, dolls, art projects, and role-plays) within the safety of the group and get encouragement from me and the other members acknowledging their own and one another's efforts and progress. With cooperation from Ms. Kline and their parents, even after the end of the group, the members could continue to consolidate the growth that they had made during the group.

Conclusion

Although there were no "miracle cures" among the members of the group, it was a beneficial experience for everyone, including me. Rachel and Shelby consolidated their already solidly positive beliefs about themselves, others, and the world. They gained added confidence about their ability to build and maintain constructive relationships with others, as well as specific skills for encouraging and supporting others and for relaxing. Mike had the opportunity to expand his circle of friends, gaining confidence in his capacity for taking risks and making friends. He also learned that he was a very special person whom other people could trust and appreciate. For Sarah, the experience of being forced to continue relationships with other children, even when there were conflicts, was a little bit frightening and very challenging. She learned that she did have the courage to stick with a situation even when things got tough. Jason made the most obvious shifts in his views of himself, others, and the world and in his behavior. By having to reach compromises, work out problems, and share control with me and the other members of the group, he gained a sense of safety and cooperation. He learned that he was not going to expire if he was not in control of every situation and began to feel a little more comfortable with the idea that there was a part of his life (his asthma) that he might not be able to control. As a result of this learning, his asthma actually seemed to improve and he had fewer asthma attacks and trips to the hospital. Leah gained confidence in her ability to communicate with others. She was still very shy, but she had made several friends in the group and seemed to feel more capable of mastering social interactions and new situations.

My own growth in this process was exciting to me. I tend to be a bit grandiose and assume that it is my responsibility to help all of my clients gain insight and effect changes single-handedly. Through the interactions among the members of this group, I learned and relearned that this is a mistaken belief that can sabotage my efforts at times. The Black Birds taught me that they were much better therapists than I could ever hope to be. In their encouragement of one another and in their gentle spitting in their own and one another's soup, they showed me that they could help themselves and help one another in amazing ways.

I also learned how easy it is to adapt strategies from individual application of Adlerian play therapy to a group situation. Many of the activities described in this chapter I invented or adapted specifically for this group, and I have thought of a myriad other ideas that would also work with future groups. The Black Birds, in their willingness to try new things, have shown me (once again) that I am only limited by my own mistaken beliefs. As long as I believe that I can connect with children, they will be willing to connect with me. When I go into a group believing that I am capable, I use my leadership skills effectively and the group almost always flows smoothly. If I believe that I can gain my significance, that I can "count," in positive ways, I can inspire others to believe that they are unique, special, and important. When I have the courage to try new things and act as if they will work, others will follow me, risking new situations and relationships.

References

Adler, A. (1958). *What life should mean to you.* New York: Putnam. (Original work published 1931)

Adler, A. (1963). *The problem child.* New York: Putnam. (Original work published 1930)

Albert, L. (1989). *A teacher's guide to cooperative discipline: How to manage your classroom and promote self-esteem.* Circle Pines, MN: American Guidance Service.

Ansbacher, H., & Ansbacher, R. (Eds.). (1956). *The individual psychology of Alfred Adler: A systematic presentation in selections from his writings.* San Francisco: Harper San Francisco.

Beyer, B. (1997, October). *Effective therapy groups.* Paper presented at the 14th Annual Association for Play Therapy International Conference, Orlando, FL.

Brett, D. (1992). *More Annie stories: Therapeutic storytelling techniques.* New York: Magination.

Dinkmeyer, D., Dinkmeyer, D., & Sperry, L. (1987). *Adlerian counseling and psychotherapy* (2nd ed.). Columbus, OH: Merrill.

Dinkmeyer, D., & McKay, G. (1989). *Systematic training for effective parenting: parent's handbook (STEP)* (3rd ed.). Circle Pines, MN: American Guidance Service.

Dinkmeyer, D., McKay, G., & Dinkmeyer, D. (1980). *Systematic training for effective teaching.* Circle Pines, MN: American Guidance Service.

Dreikurs, R. (1953). *Fundamentals of Adlerian psychology.* Chicago: Alfred Adler Institute.

Dreikurs, R., Grunwald, B., & Pepper, F. (1982). *Maintaining sanity in the classroom.* New York: HarperCollins.

Dreikurs, R., & Soltz, V. (1964). *Children: The challenge.* New York: Hawthorne/Dutton.

Gardner, R. A. (1971). *Therapeutic communication with children: The mutual storytelling technique.* Northvale, NJ: Aronson.

Gardner, R. A. (1986). *The psychotherapeutic technique of Richard A. Gardner.* Northvale, NJ: Aronson.

Knoff, H., & Prout, H. (1985). *Kinetic drawing system for family and school.* Los Angeles: Western Psychological Services.

Kottman, T. (1993). The king of rock and roll. In T. Kottman & C. Schaefer (Eds.), *Play therapy in action: A casebook for practitioners* (pp. 133–167). Northvale, NJ: Aronson.

Kottman, T. (1994). Adlerian play therapy. In K. O'Connor & C. Schaefer (Eds.), *Handbook of play therapy* (Vol. 2, pp. 3–26). New York: Wiley.

Kottman, T. (1995). *Partners in play: An Adlerian approach to play therapy.* Alexandria, VA: American Counseling Association.

Kottman, T. (1997). Adlerian play therapy. In K. O'Connor & L. Braverman (Eds.), *Play therapy: Theory and practice* (pp. 310–340). New York: Wiley.

Kottman, T. (1998). Billy, the teddy bear boy. In L. Golden (Ed.), *Case studies in child and adolescent counseling* (2nd ed., pp. 75–88). Old Tappan, NJ: Macmillan.

Kottman, T., & Stiles, K. (1990). The mutual storytelling technique: An Adlerian application in child therapy. *Journal of Individual Psychology, 48,* 148–156.

Lankton, C., & Lankton, S. (1989). *Tales of enchantment: Goal-oriented metaphors for adults and children in therapy.* New York: Brunner/Mazel.

Lew, A., & Bettner, B. L. (1998a). *A parent's guide to understanding and motivating children.* Newton Center, MA: Connexions.

Lew, A., & Bettner, B. L. (1998b). *Responsibility in the classroom: A teacher's guide to understanding and motivating students.* Newton Center, MA: Connexions.

Manaster, G., & Corsini, R. (1982). *Individual psychology: Theory and practice.* Itasca, IL: Peacock.

Mills, J., & Crowley, R. (1986). *Therapeutic metaphors for children and the child within.* New York: Brunner/Mazel.

Nelson, J., Lott, L., & Glenn, S. (1993). *Positive discipline in the classroom: How to effectively use class meetings.* Rocklin, CA: Prima.

Popkin, M. (1993). *Active parenting today.* Atlanta, GA: Active Parenting.

Popkin, M. (1994). *Active teaching.* Atlanta, GA: Active Parenting.

Siepker, B., & Kandaras, C. (1985). *Group therapy with children and adolescents.* New York: Human Sciences.

Steig, W. (1988). *Spinky sulks.* New York: Farrar, Straus, & Giroux.

Wilhelm, H. (1988). *Tyrone the horrible.* New York: Scholastic.

CHAPTER SIX

THE INVISIBLE VILLAGE

Jungian Group Play Therapy

Judi Bertoia

Jungian psychology has traditionally focused on the therapeutic dyad and is usually oriented toward adults. More recently, however, Jung's work has been extended to include both child development and a small body of literature on therapeutic work with groups. Jung (1971) believed that psyche creates everyday reality for children and adults and that creative activity unites our inner and outer worlds. Jung notes "the debt we owe to the play of the imagination is incalculable" (p. 63.).

This chapter addresses key theoretical constructs of a Jungian approach to play therapy with groups of children. Two case examples illustrate the power of Jungian therapy to facilitate an individual's development and healing through group work, while a third example demonstrates how Jungian group play therapy is used to improve the fundamental dynamics of the group itself.

Introduction to Jungian Theory

Carl Gustav Jung was a Swiss psychiatrist who continued to develop his ideas about the nature of the human psyche until his death in 1961 at the age of eighty-six. Initially part of Freud's inner circle, Jung disagreed with him on the nature of

Note: The author wishes to thank Clarissa Zammitt for her insightful commentary.

libido; by publishing his own views in 1912, Jung caused a split with Freud. Jung's was a broader concept of libido as pure life energy, a nonspecific psychic energy.

Following the split with Freud, Jung went through a period of isolation and rejection by his peers. During this time he underwent great psychological turmoil and experienced a flood of fantasies and emotional chaos. By writing, drawing, and entering a time of play with the same passion he had in childhood, Jung gave these experiences concrete form. He built an entire miniature village beside a lake, painted extensively, and sculpted images in stone. Jung writes that everything he developed and wrote about in subsequent years was based on the fantasies, dreams, and experiences of this period (1961, p. 192). Several key concepts such as the collective unconscious, individuation, and the transcendent function evolved from this difficult but fertile time.

Personal and Collective Unconscious

Prior to Jung's contributions, the unconscious was recognized as a psychic region with its own nature and rules. It was understood to be composed of repressed personal experiences inaccessible to the ego. Jung (1961) enriched this concept by differentiating between a personal and a collective unconscious. He describes the *personal unconscious* as containing subliminal impressions, forgotten psychic material, perceptions lacking the psychic energy to reach consciousness, and unconscious ideas too undeveloped to become conscious. The personal unconscious also contains those elements of an individual's life that are repressed because they are painful or because they were not adaptive to the particular childhood environment. Contents such as these are incompatible in some way with the conscious attitude of the individual. For example, traumatic separation from the primary caregiver or rejection of a potentially valuable talent by the family group could both be contained within the personal unconscious.

This repressed material constitutes one's *shadow*—the inferior, undeveloped, and unwanted parts of one's being. Jung (1954b) reminds us that in the personality's attempts to integrate the shadow, unconscious contents are invariably first projected out upon concrete persons and situations (p. 170). Primarily perceived as negative, the shadow also contains values and attributes that are needed by consciousness but may appear in forms that are difficult to accept or integrate (von Franz, 1964, p. 170). For Jungians, the therapeutic process involves integrating these shadow aspects into the conscious personality.

The *collective unconscious* consists of innate organizing patterns, called *archetypes*, that are reflected in universal and historical motifs. Archetypes link the body and psyche because they are experienced through affect and influence behavior. One's personal experiences are attracted to related archetypal cores much as iron filings are drawn to a magnet. Because they carry such a strong, potentially overpowering charge of psychic energy, archetypal influences are most evident when the ego is especially vulnerable such as at times of crisis, change, and chaos. "Archetypes arouse affect, blind one to realities, and take possession of will" (Samuels, Shorter, & Plaut, 1986, p. 26). For example, experiences related to the actual mother will attach to the image of the archetypal mother at one of its opposites of "good mother" or "bad mother," coloring future experiences of mothers.

Because archetypes are so numerous, they can be imagined as an inner village with some neighbors living closer, some further away, and others on the wrong side of the tracks. In this way, personal significance determines whether an archetype has been experienced and lived out in the world or strongly denied or repressed, becoming a less accessible part of one's shadow. Still other archetypes are so distant from individual experience that they are present as potentials but may never be known in one's life, remaining deep in the unconscious. Thus, by virtue of being human, everyone's "village"—their collective unconscious—has the archetypal potential for a divine child and a Hitler, an evil witch and a Mother Teresa. The village also includes archetypal processes such as birth, death, the journey, and marriage or union. One critically important archetype is the Self. Jungian group play therapy provides a setting for these villagers to be introduced to consciousness.

Self and Ego

Jung describes the Self as both the central archetype and as an all-encompassing circumference containing both the conscious and unconscious aspects of an individual. The Self is seen as the primary organizing and directing archetypal image of the fullest human potential. It is the seed containing all latent possibilities of the individual (von Franz, 1964, p. 161). The Self, a unifying principle that demands recognition and integration, is viewed as being akin to a God-image (Samuels et al., 1986, p. 135). It is important to recognize that the Self is not always benign to a temporal being, and so the ego must mediate psychic demands of achieving wholeness with the realities of day-to-day living.

Fordham (1985) views the totality of an undifferentiated self as being present from the beginning of life and comprising innate archetypal and ego potential. As the child interacts with the environment, beginning with the family group, this potential unfolds through intrapsychic and interpersonal processes. At birth, the initial unconscious unity deintegrates and through appropriate environmental contact (usually with the mother) the sense of well-being is reintegrated. The ongoing interactions between the child's potentials and the environment repeat this pattern of deintegration and reintegration. The fragments of awareness gradually coalesce into a more solid ego. This process continues over a lifetime. Once the ego is sufficiently developed in childhood, the personality is not as overwhelmed with challenges from life experience or from internal archetypal contents because it has developed defense mechanisms for coping with these adversities. Facilitating communication between the ego and the Self, conscious and unconscious, is the focus of Jungian play therapy with individuals and groups of children (Allan, 1988; Allan & Bertoia, 1992; Bertoia, 1993).

Complex

A complex is characterized by marked emotionality and contributes to behavior, although the individual may not be conscious of it (Samuels et al., 1986, p. 34). When a complex is constellated, it manifests in outer world difficulties as if saying to consciousness, "Look at me! I am here!" These difficulties appear symbolically in drawings, dreams, and play (Furth, 1988, p. 2). Jung (1960) indicates that when the material from a personal complex is reintegrated, the individual experiences an increase in energy and a feeling of release and healing.

The experience of a collective or group complex, however, creates feelings of strangeness and disorientation. While the experience may be fascinating, it is more likely to feel threatening. In group work, the amount of psychic energy attached to one or more archetypes by members of the group may become the group complex. Individuals may identify with one another's suffering through activation of the same archetype because they have experienced a similar crisis; such a connection facilitates greater empathy for another.

Individuals may also be overcome by shadow elements of a specific archetype and as a group demonstrate similar behavior and affect while they are within the archetype's grip. Group energy potentiates the power of the archetype, just as a crowd of sports fans, a church congregation, or a mob has greater power to influence behavior than any individual in a group of strangers could exercise over another. Jung (1960) comments that social, political, and religious groups influence the collective unconscious. At times of change within the community, intuitively gifted individuals sense the change and if a "translation of the unconscious into a communicable language proves successful, it has redeeming effects" (p. 315). Jungian group play therapy attends to personal and collective complexes through an exploration of emotions and behaviors, translating them into a language that consciousness can understand.

Image, Symbol, and the Transcendent Function

Depth psychology believes the unconscious communicates not through rational, linear language but rather through metaphor and myth, that is, through symbolic language. Image is the language of the unconscious. Psyche's speech is the mytho-poetic, often numinous, experience of an image arising from the unconscious. This imaginal communication between Self and ego is a key concept in Jungian psychology.

Jung argued with Freud's reductive view of symbols as simply signs or symptoms of the unconscious. Jung (1966) extended the definition to include the idea that a *true* symbol should be understood as an intuitive idea, one that cannot yet be formulated in any other or better way (p. 70). Jung's early work used symbol and image synonymously, but his later work distinguishes the image as containing emotions and affect as well as symbolic content. Additionally, while the image is a *container* of opposites, the symbol is a *mediator* of opposites (Samuels et al., 1986, p. 72).

The psyche essentially consists of images that are full of meaning and purpose and that "picture" vital activities (Jung, 1961, p. 325). The image is a totality that encompasses opposites. Jung (1971) writes,

> This autonomous activity of the psyche . . . is a continually creative act. The psyche creates reality every day. The only expression I can use for this activity is *fantasy*. Fantasy is just as much feeling as thinking; as much intuition as sensation. . . . Fantasy, therefore, seems to me the clearest expression of the specific activity of the psyche. It is, pre-eminently, the creative activity from which the answers to all answerable questions come; it is the mother of all possibilities, where, like all psychological opposites, the inner and outer world are joined together in living union. Fantasy it was and ever is which fashions the bridge between the irreconcilable claims of subject and object, introversion and extroversion [p. 52].

Hillman (1975) writes that, paradoxically, the image is inside us yet we also live in the midst of images (p. 23). Each of us carries an inner village and each of us exists within a group and culture that contains a multiplicity of invisible villagers from our past and present myths, history, religious teachings, and art. As the personal or collective psyche submits images to conscious awareness, the possibility for healing or further development is presented.

The *transcendent function* is the capacity of the unconscious to facilitate movement from a one-sided attitude toward unification with its opposite. Jung considered the transcendent function to be the most important factor in psychological processes because of its capacity to transcend the current difficulty, providing a perspective beyond the purely personal and offering a possible solution to the problem. The energy arising from unconscious tension between opposites bridges into consciousness through symbols that have both a personal meaning and also a broader cultural or group significance. Because of its multivalent quality, the image links the temporal and atemporal, rational and nonrational. "The symbol is an unconscious invention in answer to a conscious problem," whose function is to mediate opposites (Samuels et al., 1986, p. 146). The transcendent function then is a dialectic process where thesis and antithesis meet. The work of interpretation and amplification of the image becomes the synthesis, resulting in a new attitude consciously carried by the individual or group.

Jungians believe that psyche contains regenerative and self-healing capacities that can be activated by working through the images that psyche presents. In play therapy, Jungians trust that psyche will offer the required images and activity. A Jungian therapist does not "fix" the child but rather enters the metaphor offered by the unconscious and explores it with the child, all the while trusting that psyche's sense of timing, or *kairos*, will direct the activities. The healing potential of the symbol is activated by bringing it into consciousness. Through spending time with the image in such activities as play, sculpting, or drawing we invest energy into the flow of this imaginal language (Furth, 1988, p. 11). Because the natural language of children is fantasy and play, Jungian therapy speaks directly with the inhabitants of their imaginal worlds.

Individuation

Another key concept developed by Jung is individuation—the fullest possible realization of one's potential. Individuation refers to the development of one's wholeness not as a linear process but rather as a circumnabulation of the self (the ongoing circular movement around the essential core of one's being) in collaboration with the ego. By integrating into consciousness the energy flow from the unconscious, the individuation process progresses in its own circular manner, a spiral pattern where similar content may be reexperienced during a lifetime but at a deeper level each time. Stevens (1990) explains individuation both as normal development, a waking up into life, and as a deeper progressive integration of the unconscious, timeless self in the personality of the time-bound individual (p. 188). Greater wholeness supports participation in one's environment while simultaneously providing greater psychological maturity. Thus the therapeutic work of Jungian groups may bring unconscious material into consciousness for either developmental or reparative purposes.

Individual and Group Work

Jung (1954a) believed wholeness is the result of an intrapsychic process that depends essentially on the relationship of one individual with one other person. He also viewed this individuation process, if followed faithfully, as reaching our highest spiritual function for the well-being of society (1954b). Here Colman (1995), a pioneer in group relations theory, would argue that individuation in its fullest sense must also "include group consciousness or risk being synonymous with narcissistic individuation" (p. 32). Unlike Jung, Colman believes that society benefits not just from many individuals' achieving their fullest potential personally but also from individuals' achieving a higher level of conscious development *as a collective unit*. In recognizing the interconnected field of all life, Colman reasons that humanity now has the capacity for evolving into a more compassionate, integrated, responsible, and inclusive form.

Jung himself had a strong distrust of the group, seeing it as the opposite of the individual and the matrix out of which the individual must differentiate (1954a). He also saw the group as having a potential for gripping one in mass destructive behavior, believing group experience occurs on a lower level of consciousness more akin to herd animals (1954b). However, he did recognize the critical nature of the group in our development, indicating that before individuation can progress, each of us must develop some adaptation to collective norms. He also saw relationship as essential, especially for the benefits of working through the transference that invariably arises.

In Jungian group play therapy it is the interaction of these interpersonal relationships and intrapsychic process that promotes growth and healing. The interface between the two establishes an interconnected field where the child's inner village can be projected onto others so as to be seen and then re-collected. Within the group, multiple villagers become visible, experienced, and integrated as needed. Also within the group, the collective can explore its behaviors and attitudes, and so become more conscious and adaptive as psyche directs.

Group play therapy with children provides the container, a *temenos*, for the growth of both child and group. As children move from their primary family group into their peer group, new psychological adaptations are required of them. Using Jungian concepts, children can benefit from opportunities for personal development, reparation of trauma, and processing higher group consciousness.

Jungian Concepts Applied to Group Play Therapy

The following material is based on an assumption that a therapist engaging in group play therapy has training in both play therapy and group work. It is critical that a therapist have also done considerable personal analysis in order to differentiate between personal and client material, individual and group content. The general format in all Jungian group play therapy is to enter the work at a conscious level using clear, rational language in the here-and-now. Within the session work deepens into the nonrational or metaphoric language of the unconscious. The sessions conclude by returning to external reality and firmly anchoring children in the present. This process strengthens the energy flow between the ego and Self intrapsychically and also helps the children mediate between internal and external demands. Rather than having Alice tumble down the rabbit hole and stay there, the therapist acts as an elevator operator where descent to various depths, depending on the session, is always accompanied by ascent to ground level.

These group dynamics are demonstrated in the case material that follows. Unlike nondirected play therapy with individuals, group work requires a degree of direction. The therapist must still negotiate between the conscious and unconscious, but in groups this communication must be performed simultaneously on a personal level and also within the collective unconscious of the whole group. The therapist must work with the transference from the child and the group as a collective. By monitoring and appropriately expressing feelings and somatic experiences, the therapist gives audible expression to psyche's language. By straddling both conscious and unconscious and personal and collective realms the therapist mediates the language of the unconscious, translating or interpreting the images so the entire group begins to grasp the invisible but certainly present archetypes.

Three examples of group play therapy will be discussed in order to illustrate Jungian concepts and show how they are useful in a group setting. The first group presented is composed of first graders participating in fairy tale enactment, and the second is a group of bereaved children. These two examples demonstrate the value of individual work contained within the group context. The third case is a classroom of children with a history of scapegoating one child. This example demonstrates the recent extension of Jungian therapy to facilitate growth of consciousness within a larger group.

Case Example 1: Three Billy Goats Gruff

This first example involves a first-grade class where dramatization was a common activity. The referral of one child was made as plans were developing for the annual, introductory counselor visits to the classroom. Group work was easily adapted for therapeutic purposes when consultation was sought for this youngster, and the teacher and counselor planned interventions for the group as a whole.

Although living in a very supportive home, this child was extremely cautious in the world. This was a typical classroom in an affluent neighborhood, and while the community held very high standards for success, her large family seemed quite easy-going. Even though there was no apparent reason for her apprehension, she was strongly defended against interactions with others in the school setting. This child had developed a persona, or false self, of being quiet, compliant, and helpful. Her natural inquisitiveness and energy in early childhood had been discouraged during a series of family crises when she was a toddler. By consistent nonparticipation and silence she had adapted to her new world at school, observing rather than actively engaging it, stubbornly refusing to take part in group activities and often not speaking. Our therapeutic goal was to use dramatization to encourage her participation in class.

Theoretical Conceptualization. Fear of crossing into new territory was typical for this child; coming to school, interacting with peers, and facing the risks of new activities all frightened her. Although not experiencing any trauma personally, this child had internalized the dominant emotional tone of her family while she was very young. It seemed she viewed the world as a dangerous place and believed the less noticed one was, the less likely one was to have difficulty. While this is consistent with Fordham's (1985) view of the child's ability to adapt to the caretakers for survival purposes, the behavior pattern was no longer adaptive at home or in her expanded world beyond the family.

To cope with the anxiety of possible ego fragmentation, she used defenses of regressing into silence, repressing her fear and desire to participate, and projecting her primitive consuming and aggressive feelings onto a hostile world. The pictures she created as part of regular classroom activities revealed her fears and wish to hide; the images she drew initially were covered with dark red and black watercolor washes. Following some individual therapeutic work within the classroom, the initial images became farm animals hatching and children playing. These images suggested the transcendent function had been activated, and the child was preparing to enter a new phase of growth.

This work proceeded on multiple levels. The counselor responded to the drawings in the third person initially with comments such as, "I notice there's lots and lots of black and red covering the first part." To these the child nodded. Subsequent interpretations stayed with the imaginal world for a time, "The animals feel safe when they're hidden by the black and red." Later, as the washes became lighter or only partially covered the page, interpretations linking the child's imaginal and external worlds were offered, "I wonder if you sometimes feel scared at school and want to hide like these animals." This was met with vigorous nods, and "but sometimes you want to join in too," earned a soft "yes." To meet external goals of increased socialization and class participation, the interpersonal behaviors required by the system, while strengthening her intrapsychic processes, a series of fairy tale enactments was planned.

Process of Group Play Therapy. Because the class of twenty had been together for a term, group cohesion had been established. The counselor had been in the classroom interacting with most students individually over a period of two weeks, working with their drawings or other creative activities.

Because fairy tales were part of the usual curriculum, story time was readily adapted to group therapy. At first the teacher followed the usual pattern of reading a story and having children volunteer to enact it. Different children became the characters or audience, with everyone who wanted to having a chance to talk afterward. The referred child was a silent but intent witness to the developments in the first story enactment.

At this point the shy child's drawings indicated an internal readiness to attempt a new relationship with the group; no wash hid the newborn animals or young children as they played. Following the usual teaching pattern, "Three Billy Goats Gruff" was read and then enacted voluntarily. Faded yellow fabric became the old, dry grass and vibrant green was chosen for the new growth. Soft blankets became goatskins; a life-sized arched bridge became home to the curmudgeonly troll attired in a dark fuzzy bath mat.

The counselor now participated in these groups, interpreting the transference among the imaginal members. For example, "Mr. Troll, you are a scary person," or "Ms. Troll, you always threaten to hurt anyone who comes near you." or "Wow, Ms. Troll, you really feel powerful when you jump out and yell at the goats." At the end of the performances the therapist encouraged group discussion of similar experiences. Using exploration of thoughts, feelings, and behaviors the children were helped to understand the dynamics and plan alternate behaviors. Children were asked how many of them remembered a time of being frightened, feeling adventuresome, or acting territorial like a dog barking at newcomers. As the children were speaking, the referred child's body language confirmed an increasing willingness to participate. She agreed to do so when invited by the teacher.

It is important for the therapist to actually enter into the fantasy conceptually, envisioning the group members for who they have become. For example in this group, the shy child *became* the timid Littlest Billy Goat. As the timid little goat looked for a long time at the bridge and distant grass, I was aware of my own accelerated heart rate and sense of apprehension. By saying, "It's really scary to go to a new place," I articulated the fear we shared. Following a long pause and tracking her gaze I added, "especially when there's a troll waiting to eat you up." Again she nodded. Here the archetypal fears of the unknown and of being consumed were present.

Group members then spoke, expressing other possibilities. For example, "Ah, you're too little for the troll to eat." When she still hesitated another encouraged her, "The grass is *really* good over there." The Biggest Billy Goat was very support-ive, saying, "You can do it! And *I'm* right behind you." The collective support nur-tured her buried sense of the heroic. "The group can give the individual a courage, a bearing, and a dignity that may easily get lost in isolation" (Colman, 1995, p. 3). She crossed the bridge. When challenged by the troll, she stopped and softly said, "Please, Mr. Troll, I'm really hungry and want that grass [pointing to the other side]. I'm too little to eat, but my big brother is coming . . . he'll fill you up."

While it felt like a thunderous achievement to the adults, the group just non-chalantly accepted her behavior and watched for the next goat to cross. The group did one more enactment of the story that day and then as a large group discussed the experience. Several children noticed that the shy child had taken part and told her they liked her participation. One child said enthusiastically, "Next time you have to be the *Big* Billy Goat." Although she did not volunteer for more roles be-fore this unit was completed, she did participate more willingly within the class setting and with her peers.

The children were told we had two more sessions. In those we worked with the story of "Goldilocks and the Three Bears." The theme of going out into the world is the archetypal heroic journey in Jungian psychology. The associated feel-ings of fear and success were expressed through story and made visible in the group, enabling all members to consciously integrate aspects of the shadow and move forward in the individuation process.

Case Example 2: Bereavement

Children who had experienced the recent death of a significant adult were invited to join this bereavement group. The group included boys and girls from ages ten to twelve. Because it was a community group the children knew each other, but not well. The goal was twofold: on one level the program focused on providing information to the children about death, loss, and developing coping strategies in-tended to nurture ego strength. On a deeper level, the series was designed to pro-vide a container for the imaginal to be recognized, given voice, and embodied. There were six two-hour sessions, and arrangements were made subsequently for one child whose father had died suddenly to join siblings in family work.

Theoretical Conceptualization. This was a group of eight pre-adolescents who had been touched by the archetype of Death, or *Thanatos*. To develop a sense of cohesion and safety, limits and ground rules were discussed in the first session. Be-cause the therapist knew the children ranged from overtly expressive to silently stoic, the importance of respect for all content, whether verbal or other form of creative expression, was stressed. A child who was often overwhelmed and in tears was highly sensitive and initially carried some of the pain for another youngster who denied having any. Midway through the series each child drew an especially favored activity with the person who was now dead. The child who usually denied any sadness was especially vocal in saying that he didn't care. Here the transference within the group was crucial, for another boy said, "It's easy to be angry and shout that you don't care. It's too scary to cry and say how much you miss your grandma!" The resistant child burst into tears. The group's acceptance of his tears and pain, their quiet witnessing, allowed him to open the communication he had so desperately blocked. His expression of vulnerability, as the oldest "tough" male in the group, allowed the younger quiet boy to shift from using a puppet for speech to his own voice in the next session. While each loss was unique to each child, the commonalties of Death as an archetype linked them for these weeks in a shared human experience. Sorrow met its opposite in the playfulness of group collage; anger met laughter in the snowball fights of shredded phone books. The tension of opposites became less an internal anxiety and more a manageable life experience.

Process of Group Play Therapy. The basic outline of the sessions cognitively was to identify the loss and how it affected roles, support systems, and coping strategies. On an imaginal level drawings, collages, and journals initiated discussions. The children chose the music to be played during some sessions and frequently used cuddly body puppets to speak for them. Given this opportunity for the unconscious to offer appropriate images to each child—which could then be voluntarily shared within the group—the feelings, attitudes, and behaviors engendered by death were explored from many perspectives. Reactions were normalized and coping strategies from the peer group increased skills for managing the pain and dealing with a nonbereaved world.

Individual activities at the beginning of each session moved the children from the external world of daily activities into their interior landscapes. Although various generic modalities were used—such as a film, story, or piece of music—to explore a specific topic, the imaginal element of these methods invited quick descent to personal subterranean territory. While there was a specific topic for each session, the images determined how the session progressed. In the last few minutes group members shared a snack, nurturing the physical body after the expenditure of considerable emotional and psychic energy.

The following examples of the written responses that accompanied images indicate the powerful interior worlds of these children. These writings are the accompaniment to "The Rosebush," a projective technique of relaxation, imagery, and writing (Allan & Bertoia, 1992, p. 157). One child's expression of anger and defensiveness also reflects his age-appropriate interest in the more graphic details of death: *"I look like a rosebush. I am a thorny rosebush. I have no flowers. My leaves are blood Red. My branches and stems are the color of guts. I have thorns that are as sharp as a razor blade. I am a mean bush."*

This child's tension had been experienced in the group transference; one member articulated his unconscious state saying, "You're so squirmy, I feel like you aren't listening to me. That makes me mad." Although he was denying his anger and pain, the group and his physical body certainly experienced his tension.

Another child wrote, *"I'm a wild rose bush and I look like a four-headed monster. My flowers are feeling flowers. I scare however [sic] comes along."* The group first noticed that this drawing had shown a five-flowered rosebush, but one was scribbled out so strongly it nearly tore the page, like the change in the number of people in his family. The four heads left had facial expressions ranging from happy to OK. This child said the rosebush *was* his family, with Mom gone, but he could only cry inside, like the large tree crying as it touched the rainbow in his picture. The transference to the blank page was interpreted by the group.

An especially intuitive child first drew the group members whose emotions had most impact on her as angry and restless and then drew her own anger and impatience. Once the feelings were articulated, she drew her rosebush. *"I am a rosebush which is silver and has silver colored thorns. My flowers are baby blue. My roots don't show, they are imaginary and they are purple."* She interpreted the content herself, surprised by the drawing's significance. The ephemeral nature of the large silver rose, much higher than the other blue flowers, reflects her loss. The sensations of having a lump in my own throat and a strange feeling of disorientation prompted my comment, "Your family feels blue or sad since Nana's death. I wonder if you feel kind of uprooted or unsettled too?"

Two final examples from this session demonstrate the power of image to touch numinous elements of the soul and access the healing function of the unconscious.

"I was a rosebush that went around the solar system. I live everywhere and see everything. I look like nothing but a floating line."

"I have no thorns and my only protection is that if I am broken I can repair myself through time. I live near a large meadow with high grass near me. There are trees and only deceased ghosts and animated figures come now."

The power of the collective to invite Death into our presence brought its angry, painful nature. As an archetype, Death also graced us with its magnificent beauty and awe. Literal death brings sorrow. Imaginal Death carries the universal potential for rebirth.

Case Example 3: The Scapegoat

The power of archetypes to influence individual and group life is especially evident in scapegoating. Colman articulates this phenomenon very clearly in his book in relation to adults, yet it is also a commonly manifested archetype among groups of children (Allan & Bertoia, 1992). The following case study traces the history and interventions used with a fifth-grade class in an inner-city school. Once a working-class neighborhood, this locale was now in transition from a multiethnic community to a gentrified district. This particular class had a five-year history of scapegoating the same child, and various interventions had been tried in past years. This therapist worked with the group weekly over a three-month period.

Theoretical Conceptualization. By entering this situation the therapist encounters the transference from the group and the underlying chaotic dynamics. Jung (1954a) writes that this entry of therapist into a group "leads both of them to a direct confrontation with the daemonic forces lurking in the darkness" (p. 375). Hillman (1975) notes that "emotion is a gift that comes by surprise, a mythic statement rather than a human property. It announces a movement in soul, a statement of the process going on in a myth which we may perceive in the fantasy images that emotion accompanies" (p. 177). The process of scapegoating is an archetypal one, with an ancient history. The therapist was aware that she was going into a group with the potential to shift the scapegoat role from the individual currently carrying it to another child, the teacher, or the therapist.

Underlying scapegoating is an unwillingness to accept responsibility for one's behavior as well as feelings of anger and fear. Herein lies one key to working therapeutically with this archetype. While the archetype appears first in the behavior—the drive to activity stimulated by the feeling—it can also appear in images and in style of consciousness, such as a specific mind-set through which life is filtered (Montero, 1995). By recognizing the nonhuman or beyond-human aspect of archetypes and giving them a place in the world, the therapeutic relationship eases the burden for the individual carrying the archetype. Exploration within this relationship depotentiates the need for destructive possession and honors human life as it cares for soul. Thus the therapist needed to invite the archetypal images into the room, and then work with the group *as a collective* to interpret the dynamics and to create alternatives.

Both Hillman (1975, p. 33) and Colman (1995, p. 60) speak of the dangers of adhering only to the group's conscious awareness, since consciously denying psyche's partial figures creates a need to define at least one collectively, hence the unconscious creation of a scapegoat. The therapist must address the plurality of images within each child and the group. This allows both a greater understanding of the group's process and decreases the possibility of serial scapegoats being created.

Process of Group Play Therapy. What Hillman (1995) describes as opening the door to the imaginal realm by asking for a dream—without interpreting it—was accomplished with this class by the Rosebush activity. A combination of guided imagery, drawing, and writing, this material was used by the therapist to gain a sense of individual unconscious material; it was not interpreted with the children in any form. In the second session this class diverted the planned discussion on Responsibility to their pressing issue—a five-year history of scapegoating one child.

By working with this group's verbal images an underlying dynamic appeared. Anger, both generalized and toward authority, became evident. It is not surprising they had developed a reputation as a difficult class, one that was very hard on substitute teachers, or that this specific child was chosen as their scapegoat. Colman (1995) notes that to be helpful to a group the consultant must focus attention on how the need for a scapegoat and the choice of victim is a diversion from the deeper collective issue (p. 106), in this case blaming others or avoiding personal responsibility. In an unconscious attempt to avoid the discussion topic of Responsibility by shifting to scapegoating, the group revealed their own deeper issue. Their scapegoating behavior and its related emotions were the manifestation of their resistance to accepting responsibility. Inviting the images and dialogue around the scapegoating issue led to an understanding of this dynamic and to recognition of anger's power and the underlying fear and sense of powerlessness. Following a discussion where anger and fear were explored, a series of Anger Mountain activities (Bertoia, 1996) was created. These activities included imagery, drawing, writing, and sculpting.

In the second session, the target child's mannerisms and behavior were the identified source of collective rejection, but her frequently articulated thinking function, clear sense of rules and justice, and alliance with authority were an invisible part of the group dynamic. An earlier classroom attempt to manage the problem involved removing the child and discussing the situation, assuming she did not know. However, she had both knowledge of and distress over the lack of consultation with her. As this year progressed, she and the counselor had discussed her wish to have an open discussion with the class. Both her parents and the classroom teacher believed this would be valuable, although none of the adults had anticipated the collective's readiness to begin. When one child announced that they had discussed this before, the group was silent for a moment, then angrily reminded him that it was supposed to be a secret. As the group briefly but emphatically litanized the scapegoat's "disgusting" behaviors, interrupting each other to add yet another of her flaws, Fear surfaced in the room.

Having the counselor verbalize both its potency and visceral effect personally allowed the others in the room to acknowledge it also. Comparisons such as lynch mob and pack of wolves stirred even the apparent leaders. Of such powerful experiences Montero (1995) writes, "I have observed that if at the appropriate moment a group is alerted to this force—right as it happens—members are less likely to reject an interpretation, instead becoming receptive to an image that allows the central dynamic to emerge. The group is then moved forward as if by magic to a more egalitarian, inclusive, and satisfying resolution of conflict" (p. xii).

This collective fear was related to the obvious fear everyone held of becoming a scapegoat, but more deeply, it was related to the fears of accepting responsibility as they grew up and the profound fear of the changes in the community while being powerless to prevent them. The strongest leaders as a subgroup were the boys from nuclear working-class families—the young males in a changing cultural milieu, and the ones with the most to lose as society struggles with the chaos of new but undefined roles.

The remainder of this class discussion was unusually long, yet it stirred the children and counselor deeply. In hindsight, it is apparent this was liminal space. Montero says, "Periods of crossings in individuals and social systems are characterized by extremely rich, often horrific, and always dangerously absorbing imagery erupting from the death and rebirth archetype energized" (Montero, 1995, p. xi). Guggenbühl (1996) notes that collective aggression such as scapegoating can be overcome *with* the students but not imposed *against* them. He also indicates that a key element is identifying leaders who may sabotage or challenge new strategies. It is critical to bring the old power structure into the open, depotentiating the system through interpretation of the transference and exploring the meaning of the old myth. This session was the turning point.

Subsequent sessions used drawing and sculpting to further explore the students' feelings. Activities over the next weeks proved the monstrous did indeed require outlets. Video images in *Rainbow Warriors* helped unite the group through discussion and the play of sculpting and arranging squadrons. Group painting and other creative activities continued to provide outlets for the imaginal collectively.

Two critically important elements were the classroom teacher and the supports offered to him by an educational assistant and a consultant in behavior management. His assistant provided strong support for the physically disabled and behaviorally disordered children in the room, helping them undertake new behaviors determined by the group. This adult group member also engaged in processing each day's events with the teacher. Alternate strategies for classroom management from the behavior specialist were also invaluable. Most important however, was this gifted teacher himself, whose novel study units provided much deeper exploration of scapegoating dynamics in stories such as *Number the Stars*, about the Nazi era, and *The Giver* (Lowry, 1989, 1993). The latter is a powerful science fiction story of a truly conscious scapegoat, Jonas, whose task at age twelve is to bear the collective memories for an unconscious society where "Sameness" is the rule. These selections paralleled the classroom dynamics and although no overt links were made, the novel study amplified and deepened the children's understanding.

The insightful comments of ten-year-olds through this process were truly inspiring. The scapegoating—of anyone—stopped and most children became more responsible. The scapegoated child had her "best year ever," and the majority of the children were showing an unanticipated humor, wisdom, and maturity. Although they remained a challenging class, this child-adult collective learned a great deal and became more conscious of human dynamics as a group. While the dramatic changes in the children were diluted with subsequent regroupings in the following years, their current journal work indicates the impact of this experience. It is as strongly present with them as it is with the teacher and therapist.

Concluding Thoughts

Because of the multiplicity of intrapsychic images, even the typical therapeutic dyad constitutes a group, imaginally at least. However, play therapy is very successful with larger groups as well. With preselected issues such as bereavement, divorce, or social skill development, groups of six to eight whose members are no more than three years apart function best. The common experience and developmental level means a similar complex is quickly constellated and group cohesion develops rapidly. Movement from regressive behaviors usually progresses to reparation themes rather quickly. This was demonstrated to me quite graphically with an early group whose symbolic medical skills cured an "alien" (Allan & Bertoia, 1992, p. 197). Large groups of twenty to thirty are especially effective when working with preexisting composition and ongoing group dynamics. While play is not as varied as in a fully equipped playroom, the fantasy elements and therapist attitudes are consistent with traditional play therapy.

Perhaps the most critical element for success is the therapist—whose belief in the process must be absolute. The wounded healer archetype is constellated, and the unconscious transference from the therapist activates the healer within the children. "*We* will go where psyche must take us." The child is accompanied and the therapist is participant-observer in the fullest sense, for in a group much psychic content is constellated and transference comes from many sources. Children have ready access to vast imaginal stores and play invites many participants to enter. Jungian group play therapy invites the multitude to be present and to be heard. For it is through our voices, our embodiment, that the invisible Others have their needs met. Then they leave us to continue our daily lives less disturbed by their unconscious tugs. Like Axline (1947), who believed that the relationship between child and therapist is the deciding factor in therapeutic success or failure, I firmly believe that it is the therapist's ability for intrapsychic and interpersonal relationship to the personal and collective that determines the outcome.

Group play therapy has been most instructive to me, and several journals are filled with my reflections. Two insights color my work most consistently. First is the phrase "out of the mouths of babes." Individual play therapy reveals the depths of soul that children touch quite regularly. This leaves me in awe. In groups, however, the sophisticated insights children offer about the dynamics operating within themselves and the collective also astound me. I have come to realize that the elders live very close to consciousness in many children, and their wisdom speaks readily when the collective provides the right container. Jungian group play therapy can be such a vessel.

My other frequent thought, especially at the outset of group sessions, is that while I may plan an activity that will invite the imaginal work, I have absolutely no idea what I'm doing or where I'm going. This thought is most unsettling, and I really do not enjoy the sense of disorientation. Yet I now realize that it happens very frequently and in fact is a marker to the entrance of Psyche's realm. Since I trust we will be directed where we need to go and I fully believe in this process, I swallow hard and remind myself the children and I are in good hands.

Kerényi (Jung & Kerényi, 1949) describes the value of myth as being able to move an individual almost effortlessly to an immersion in the primordial concerns that open from a multiplicity of images streaming out of the ground (p. 4). In the same volume, Jung notes that unconscious images can be expressed only in part by the human figure, often requiring the use of the abstract, animal, vegetative, and inorganic material to express the depth and complexity contained within (p. 161). In these examples and in regular Jungian group play therapy, the mythic elements of the imaginal world stumble, float, and stomp across the bridge from unconscious to consciousness. Burly goats and cranky trolls, silver roses and erupting volcanoes, Ancient Death and Emerging Society: the transcendent richness of the inner village offers the just-right images to individuals and the collective for healing through play. I invited the invisible villagers in, and now I must accompany them.

References

Allan, J. (1988). *Inscapes of the child's world: Jungian counseling in schools and clinics.* Dallas, TX: Spring.

Allan, J., & Bertoia, J. (1992). *Written paths to healing: Education and Jungian child counseling.* Dallas, TX: Spring.

Axline, V. M. (1947). *Play therapy: The inner dynamics of childhood.* Boston: Houghton-Mifflin.

Bertoia, J. (1993). *Drawings from a dying child.* New York: Routledge.

Bertoia, J. (1996). *Anger mountain, anger personified.* Unpublished manuscript, Pacifica Graduate Institute, Carpinteria, CA.

Colman, A. D. (1995). *Up from scapegoating: Awakening consciousness in groups*. Wilmette, IL: Chiron.

Fordham, M. (1985). *Explorations into the self*. London: Karnac Books.

Furth, G. M. (1988). *The secret world of drawings: Healing through art*. Boston: Sigo Press.

Guggenbühl, A. (1996). *The incredible fascination of violence: Dealing with aggression and brutality among children*. (J. Hillman, Trans.). Woodstock, CT: Spring.

Hillman, J. (1975). *Re-visioning psychology*. New York: HarperCollins.

Hillman, J. (1995). *The thought of the heart and the soul of the world*. Woodstock, CT: Spring.

Jung, C. G. (1954a). *The psychology of the transference*. Princeton, NJ: Princeton University Press.

Jung, C. G. (1954b). *The practice of psychotherapy*. Princeton, NJ: Princeton University Press.

Jung, C. G. (1960). *The structure and dynamics of the psyche*. Princeton, NJ: Princeton University Press.

Jung, C. G. (1961). *Memories, dreams, and reflections*. New York: Random House.

Jung, C. G. (1966). *The spirit in man, art, and literature*. Princeton, NJ: Princeton University Press.

Jung, C. G. (1971). *Psychological types*. Princeton, NJ: Princeton University Press.

Jung, C. G., & Kerényi, C. (1949). *Essays on a science of mythology*. Princeton, NJ: Princeton University Press.

Lowry, L. (1989). *Number the stars*. Boston: Houghton Mifflin.

Lowry, L. (1993). *The giver*. Boston: Houghton Mifflin.

Montero, P. (1995). Foreword. In A. D. Colman, *Up from scapegoating: Awakening consciousness in groups* (pp. ix–xiii). Wilmette, IL: Chiron.

Samuels, A., Shorter, B., & Plaut, F. (1986). *A critical dictionary of Jungian analysis*. New York: Routledge.

Stevens, A. (1990). *On Jung*. New York: Penguin Books.

von Franz, M. L. (1964). The process of individuation. In C. G. Jung (Ed.), *Man and his symbols* (pp. 158– 229). New York: Doubleday.

CHAPTER SEVEN

CHILD, PROTECTOR, CONFIDANT

Structured Group Ecosystemic Play Therapy

Kevin O'Connor

The theoretical model upon which the type of group play therapy described in this chapter is based is a subset of the broader theoretical model of ecosystemic play therapy. The ecosystemic therapist views the child as being embedded in a series of nested systems including family, school, peer, culture, legal, medical, and others. Within this model, the play therapist considers the impact and interaction of each of these systems in developing and implementing any psychotherapeutic intervention. Structured group play therapy is simply one way of addressing problems children experience in their peer system. Both the ecosystemic play therapy and the structured group play therapy models have been thoroughly delineated in *The Play Therapy Primer* (O'Connor, 1991). Therefore, only a synopsis of the latter, which is the focus of this chapter, will be presented here.

Structured group play therapy includes components that address cognitive, behavioral, emotional, physical, and social aspects of the child's difficulties. This multimodal approach promotes rapid change and maximum generalization of the child's progress. The primary function of this type of group is improvement in the quality of the child's peer social interactions. Much of the time, play therapists place children in such groups because they are inappropriately aggressive or because they act out in the context of peer interactions. This chapter, however, focuses on the treatment of a child who was referred because his tendency to interact only with adults in an adult-like manner interfered with his developing peer friendships.

Components of Structured Group Play Therapy

The Cognitive Component: Problem-Solving Training and Interpretation

Two elements of structured group play therapy directly address the cognitive aspects of a child's interactions with peers. Problem-solving training and social skills training (Camp, Blom, Herbert, & Van Doornick, 1977; Goldfried and Davison, 1976; Meichenbaum, 1977; Meichenbaum and Goodman, 1971) were widely advocated in the clinical literature of the 1970s and are still widely used. The underlying assumption is that both problem solving and social interactions involve certain basic steps and skills that the therapist can directly teach to a child. Both types of training are widely used in public schools and in residential treatment centers. Both types are represented in packaged programs designed for institutional use. *Think Aloud* (Camp et al., 1977) is an example of a packaged problem-solving program. *Developing Understanding of Self and Others* [DUSO] (Dinkmeyer, 1973) is an example of a social skills training program. I have merged the essential features of both problem-solving and social skills training into a simple, easy to learn component of structured group play therapy. I use a four-step problem-solving strategy with children from the ages of four to twelve. I ask children in the group to go through the following steps whenever they are faced with an interpersonal problem (O'Connor, 1991).

Problem. Identify and operationally define the problem at hand. It is important that this phase of the process be done from the child's point of view. A child who is hitting another child may not see the hitting as a problem, though the victim certainly would. For the child doing the hitting, the problem is more likely to be the anger he or she is experiencing or the risk of consequences if the behavior continues.

Plan. Develop plans that resolve the problem as defined above. All plans are acceptable at this stage, even those that are impossible in reality or socially inappropriate. Ideally, plans developed should solve the current problem and decrease the likelihood of the problem recurring in the future. The plans should also avoid requesting help from an adult wherever and whenever possible. The goal here is to foster creative, flexible, and independent thinking.

Action. Evaluate the plans made above and determine which one to implement or put into action. At this stage, pragmatics and reality are key aspects of the process. The child should evaluate how the plan chosen will affect the problem as well as the impact it will have on his or her own feelings and the feelings of others involved.

Answer. Answer the question: "How did my plan work?" The child is to evaluate the effectiveness of the plan as implemented in the ACTION step according to those same criteria and adjust it as needed.

In the context of structured group play therapy, children primarily address interpersonal problems using this format. Hypothetical situations, events that the children report that occur outside of the session, and any problems that arise during group all provide excellent opportunities to apply the strategy. The goal is to have the children internalize the process to the point that it becomes automatic. This will only occur with near-continuous repetition and rehearsal. The use of situations other than those that occur in the group helps to promote generalization of the skills learned.

In addition to directly teaching the children a problem-solving strategy, it is important to facilitate their overall use of language in interpersonal contexts. One of the best tools for accomplishing this is the therapist's use of interpretation (O'Connor, 1991; O'Connor and Lee, 1991). First, the therapist models the use of language and may provide the children with additional vocabulary that they can use to convey the subtleties of their experience. Second, the therapist demonstrates the importance of emotions and motives in understanding intra- and interpersonal events. Third, the therapist can help children to understand both the continuity of their behavior over time and the complementarity of behavior between children. Last, the therapist can help the children see connections between their early experience and their current behavior, thereby helping them to break old patterns. The combination of interpretation and the problem-solving strategy can provide children with powerful tools for understanding and subsequently altering their behavior.

The Physical Component: Relaxation Training and Planned Activities

Prior to the onset of formal operations thinking at about age eleven, children tend to learn more from experience than from language. They are focused on their bodies and on their interaction with the physical world. For any intervention to be successful with children in this age range, it is imperative that the therapist incorporate a physical component. In structured group play therapy, this can be done in many ways, two of which will be described here. One is to incorporate general relaxation training into group sessions. The other is to plan both fine and gross motor activities consistent with the developmental level of the children. These exercises should expand on the cognitive aspects of the group. Alternatively, the play therapist might use dance, drama, music, martial arts, or exercise programs to accomplish the same ends.

The purpose of the relaxation training is twofold. Primarily, it focuses the children on their bodily states and helps adjust their level of arousal to one where optimal learning can take place. It fosters impulse control. Relaxation training also helps children learn a routine by using a predictable sequence of exercises and repetitive vocabulary.

Virtually any relaxation training program can be effectively employed in a group setting. Progressive deep muscle relaxation (Jacobson, 1938) is a standard and the play therapist can employ it with or without the alternate contracting and relaxing of the muscles. Generally, children under the age of eleven seem to do better when using the alternating contraction and relaxation of the muscles. Simply put, the therapist teaches them to repeatedly contract and relax large muscle groups in a consistent order (head to foot or vice versa), while focusing on the experience of muscle relaxation. The play therapist can increase the level of relaxation achieved by helping the children learn to control their breathing rates and through the use of guided imagery.

The structured group play therapist must make the application of the relaxation to social interaction explicit. The play therapist will do this by helping children in the group focus on their bodily experience during both pleasant and unpleasant interactions. The group should include a focus on the bodily experience of different emotions. The children can also be taught to use relaxation to enhance their ability to complete the problem-solving strategy.

Besides using relaxation training, it is important that any group for younger children include activities that facilitate appropriate social interaction and the development of interpersonal skills. High-interest activities that promote sharing, cooperation, turn taking, group problem solving, impulse control, and the like are all very valuable in the conduct of structured group play therapy. A cognitive understanding of the function and implementation of various social skills is imperative if children are to repeat and generalize functional behaviors, but such an understanding is not sufficient to produce behavior change. The play therapist must give children the opportunity to test their understanding and to integrate the information on a physical and/or experiential level. Each of us has had the experience of trying to follow written instructions for assembling some object and finding that there is often a significant difference in our cognitive understanding of what we have read and the reality of the task at hand. Helping the children in the group translate their cognitive understanding into practical application is an essential element of structured group play therapy.

The Behavioral Component: A Behavior Modification System

All organisms learn best and change most rapidly in an environment that provides rewards for success and consistent and logical consequences for failure. Children in structured group play therapy are certainly no exception. The type of behavior management implemented by the play therapist may range from one that is extremely detailed and structured in the case of severely disturbed or acting-out children to one that is so informal that it remains outside the conscious awareness of the children involved. In either case, it is important that the therapist consider the types of behavior to be reinforced, the types of behavior for which consequences will be imposed, the types of reinforcers and the types of consequences that will be imposed, the reinforcement schedule, and the strategy for fading the reinforcers over time before beginning the group.

The behaviors to be reinforced might include a list of developmentally appropriate social behaviors. The play therapist may or may not choose to explicitly verbalize these target behaviors to the children. The behaviors for which consequences will be imposed generally include, at least, the destruction of property, hurting others (verbally and/or physically), and hurting oneself.

The play therapist will determine the types of reinforcers used and the reinforcement schedule according to the developmental level of the group members. Children in the preoperational stage (ages two to six) often need primary reinforcers administered at very high frequency in order to maintain their behavior. For this age group, the play therapist must impose consequences immediately so that the children are able cognitively to connect the problem behavior and the consequence. Any consequence imposed should also be of very short duration. For example, it is recommended that a "time-out" for a child at this age last no more than one to two minutes per year of the child's age. Children in the concrete operations stage of development (ages six to eleven) respond to secondary reinforcers, but usually only if these can be redeemed for concrete reinforcers at some point in the future. These children usually respond well to point systems, but only when those points represent movement toward a specific reward such as a toy or a desired activity. During this stage, children also tolerate more delay between a target behavior and the administration of rewards or consequences. At all ages the liberal use of social rewards is important.

With older and less disturbed children, the play therapist may not need to develop a formal behavioral system so long as social rewards are liberally administered.

For all groups, however, it is imperative that the therapist has thought through the consequences that will follow severe acting out that poses a threat to self or others. Is the child to be excluded from group? If so, for how long? Is the child to lose privileges? If so, then the privileges lost must in some way be logically connected to the problem behavior. Is the child to be restrained or physically managed? Each of these questions leads to decisions that have a significant impact on the running of the group and should be made before a crisis occurs. Nothing is more destructive to a group's process than witnessing the severe acting out of one of its members being mishandled. The children may then experience the group as unsafe or punitive or both, resulting in significantly diminished participation or increased acting out.

Finally, it is important for the play therapist to decide how to fade the reinforcement system used over time as the children make developmental progress. For example, a group of severely acting out ten-year-olds may need concrete reinforcers administered at short intervals in order to maintain their behavior at the beginning of the group. However, if the group is successful, then the children should be able to move to secondary reinforcers administered at rather long and intermittent intervals as they progress. Ideally, they would be functioning at a level where social reinforcers were sufficient to maintain their behavior by the time the group ended. Many therapists settle into the use of a particular system and do not change it over time, either because they simply do not think about it or they are afraid the children will regress. Failure to move the children toward developmentally appropriate and socially common reinforcers over the course of the group significantly reduces the chance that behavior learned in the session will generalize to environments where the reinforcers are not present.

The Emotional Component: Guided Discussion and Interpretation

Children's ability to make and sustain peer friendships will benefit from the acquisition of specific social skills and a cognitive understanding of such interactions, but it is not likely to be successful or rewarding if they are unable to integrate their emotional experience into the process. Without emotional integration children will, at best, be going through the motions in their peer interactions. The play therapist accomplishes the goal of integrating emotion into all aspects of the group process by conducting guided discussions and actively interpreting children's experience as well as the group process.

Emotion should be a verbal and experiential part of every aspect of the group process. The consideration of one's own and others' emotions is an essential part of effective social problem solving. Emotions should be identified at the PROBLEM, ACTION, and ANSWER stages of the problem-solving process. Relaxation training is most effective when children understand its connection to, and impact upon, their emotional experience. Further, the play therapist can cue children to use a relaxation strategy to manage their behavior in the face of strong negative emotions, particularly anxiety. Lastly, activities that foster the functional expression of emotions facilitate the children developing a sense of control over their feelings and the ability to sublimate those that cannot be fully expressed in reality.

The play therapist may use guided discussions to focus the group on the role of emotion in social interactions. In these discussions the play therapist chooses a topic that is relevant to many of the group members and initiates a discussion that includes problem solving. For example, in a group where many of the children have experienced a parental divorce, the therapist might initiate a discussion about the types of feelings children have in the face of a divorce. One way to do this is by reading the group a story about divorce and then asking the group to compare and contrast their experiences with those portrayed in the story. Once some of the negative consequences of divorce have been owned by the children, the therapist then engages the group in problem solving.

Emotion should be the focus of most of the interpretive work done by the therapist while conducting the group. Children are not prone to processing their emotional experience, in part because doing so requires a certain capacity for abstraction that may go beyond their developmental level. They also tend to try to avoid negative emotions whenever possible. Therefore, it is useful for the therapist to use interpretation to:

1. Label emotions: "You seem very angry right now. I think being teased hurt your feelings." "The little boy in the story we just read was jealous of his new baby sister."
2. Help the child make the connections between emotions, experiences, and behavior: "Sometimes I think you hit me because you want me to hold you, but you are afraid to ask." "It seems like you get so excited you just can't hold it in so you start to hop around a lot."
3. Help the child incorporate the idea that emotions are a necessary element in guiding their interpersonal interactions: "When you get sad it seems like telling your mom about it works a lot better than going to your room and crying because then she knows you need a hug and kiss." "When you hit someone when you are angry you might feel better, but the other person feels bad and then you get in trouble."

While these examples should serve to get the play therapist started incorporating interpretation in group work, a thorough discussion of the development and delivery of interpretations is beyond the scope of this chapter. For a complete review of this topic see *The Play Therapy Primer* (O'Connor, 1991).

The Social Component: Structured Activities

The very nature of structured group play therapy tends to focus children on the social aspects of the experience. After all, they are in a room with other children. It is surprising, however, how often therapists do not make full use of the other children in the group and do not focus the children on one another. Instead, parallel interactions between each of the children and the therapist come to be the norm. The children never come to see the value of their peers in the group setting because they are too focused on the reward potential created by their interactions with the therapist.

Simple strategies for increasing the peer focus of the children include the reinforcement strategies used, interpretation, and structured activities. Directly rewarding developmentally appropriate peer interaction is a powerful tool, but still tends to focus the children on the adult dispensing the rewards rather than the antecedent behavior being reinforced. When the play therapist gives children the means to directly reinforce other group members for engaging in behavior the children experience as pleasurable, the learning is more powerful and more focused. Similarly, peer pressure to conform to a particular standard of behavior is generally more powerful than adult reinforcement. Simply having the entire group wait for one child who is not cooperating to join in can be a very effective form of limit setting if not overused. Also, the use of rewards provided to the group as a whole for a successful collective effort, rather than for individual responses, can increase the positive group focus of the members.

The therapist can use interpretation to focus the children on the reciprocal nature of their behavior and on the impact of their interactions on one another. During the problem-solving process, children can identify ways in which they can get their needs met by approaching peers directly rather than always approaching an adult first. Children can also learn the emotional value that peers have in their daily lives, particularly when focused on the pleasure they receive from positive peer feedback.

Lastly, the therapist can greatly enhance the social aspect of the group through the use of developmentally appropriate activities. As previously discussed, these activities provide the children with the opportunity to engage in safe and pleasurable interactions so as to practice their newfound skills. Such activities also become directly reinforcing, in and of themselves, pushing the children to seek out peer involvement more frequently. Such activities might include cooperative games like Frozen Tag or Red Rover, group art projects, or having the group plan a holiday party.

Basic Assumptions in the Conduct of Structured Group Play Therapy

Children's Developmental Level

Because the focus of structured group play therapy is on the peer socialization of the group members, each child should be at a developmental level where such a goal is appropriate. Children under the developmental age of two or three are not suitable candidates for this type of group. Their primary focus is on the development of a relationship with a caretaker and nothing should interfere with this. Children between the developmental ages of three and five are generally not appropriate candidates for this type of group. They continue to be predominantly focused on the development of relationships with adults in general. For this reason, many three- to five-year-olds will not have an interest in, or the energy available for, the development of peer relationships. This does not mean that group work is not possible at this age, only that it may be developmentally inappropriate or of low priority.

Once children reach the developmental age of five, then peer relationships become progressively more important, reaching a peak during adolescence. For children between the ages of five and young adulthood, therapeutic group involvement can be a very powerful intervention. The structured group play therapy model presented here seems to be most appropriate for children from the ages of five to twelve. As children move into formal operations thinking and adolescence, they tend to find the concrete structure somewhat inhibiting. Even some preadolescents do better in a more open-ended, process group.

Children's Pathology

Again, because the focus of structured group play therapy is on the improvement of children's social skills, the group members ought not to be experiencing a level of psychopathology so intense that it precludes any possibility of their effectively interacting with their peers. Three classes of children seem poorly suited to this type of group: (a) children who have significant problems with reality testing or pervasive developmental delays; (b) children who are exhibiting signs of character pathology, such as the ability to hurt others with no evidence of remorse or a preference for social isolation with no evidence of psychosis; and (c) children who have experienced a very recent trauma, as they often require a level of nurturance and support that is difficult for a play therapist to provide within the context of a group. With each of these groups, it is generally best to begin working on the essential features of the children's difficulties through individual play therapy and then to progress to structured group play therapy.

Group Composition

The general rules for the creation of a group are as follows:

1. There should be no more than four to six children in a group run by one adult and no more than six to ten children in a group with two adults.
2. There should be no more than a three-year age spread among the group members, especially among younger children.
3. The socioeconomic status and/or the children's ethnic background should be somewhat similar. This may be one of the least important variables unless the differences between the children are very dramatic, in which case the group may become focused on these issues and unable to address other content or behavioral areas.
4. The children should all be within fifteen IQ points of one another.
5. The ability to mix boys and girls within a group varies with the age of the children, the type of group, and the goals of the intervention. There is no fixed rule, but it is a dimension you should consider (O'Connor, 1991, p. 328).

While these general guidelines are helpful, they are by no means required. Any powerful reason for the children being in a group together may alleviate the need to have the children matched on these other dimensions. For example, I chose to include Danny, the child in this case study, in a group that had members of mixed intellectual functioning and socioeconomic status. Their abuse experiences gave them a common ground that precluded the problems these differences might have caused otherwise.

Role of the Play Therapist

The play therapist serves two primary functions in structured group play therapy. The therapist creates and maintains the structure. This includes

1. All aspects of the creation of the group such as selection of the members, length of the sessions, and duration of the treatment
2. The selection of a format and activities suited to the particular pathologies and developmental levels of the group members
3. The development and maintenance of group goals and a treatment plan across group sessions

4. The maintenance of the structure within each group session
5. Assuring compliance with the basic rules of not hurting self, others, or property so that the basic safety of the group members is protected

The play therapist's other function is as the monitor and interpreter of the group's process. The therapist must put words to the children's individual and group experiences so as to facilitate their cognitive understanding of the process. This insight will, in turn, speed the rate of change for the members and increase the likelihood of generalization of those gains.

Presenting Problem and Background Data

Danny Davis was a ten-year-old European-American male. He was the only child born to a well-educated, upper middle class couple. His parents were both thirty-two years old at the time he was born, having waited to complete their education and become financially stable prior to starting a family.

Danny's early history was unremarkable. He experienced no major childhood illnesses. The family moved only twice. They purchased their first home when Danny was about a year old and moved to their current residence when he was five. Mrs. Davis became aware of the fact that she could not have any more children when Danny was three years old. She reports having become moderately depressed at that time but noted that she came out of it by focusing a great deal of her energy on Danny's upbringing. Mr. Davis worked long hours as an executive in a financial planning firm. Mrs. Davis was a full-time homemaker who did volunteer work for several local groups. Both parents reported that their marriage had been happy until Danny was about eight or nine years old.

About one year prior to Danny's referral, Mr. and Mrs. Davis decided to divorce subsequent to a year-long history of escalating marital problems. Unfortunately, the state in which the family lived did not have community property laws. In some such states, a spouse who first vacates a jointly held property risks losing any right to that property. This tends to force divorcing couples to live together until the financial settlement of their divorce becomes final. Additionally, the state in question required that one partner show cause as to why the divorce should be granted if it is contested by either party. This significantly increased the blame-laying between Mr. and Mrs. Davis.

The Davis family owned a very expensive home in a well-to-do suburb. As neither Mr. nor Mrs. Davis wanted to risk losing their right to moneys acquired from the sale of their home, they chose to live there together while pursuing their divorce. They moved into separate bedrooms with an adjoining bathroom.

The intensity of Mr. and Mrs. Davis' animosity for one another only increased as they moved toward divorce. They became preoccupied with the division of assets and the need to place blame for the divorce, each upon the other. Each of them also became preoccupied with gaining sole custody of Danny in order to punish the other parent and get his or her own narcissistic needs met. Since both were aware that there was little reason for the courts not to grant joint custody, each chose to increase the likelihood of getting sole custody by doing two things. Each parent reported the other for spousal abuse. Indeed, the level of domestic violence increased steadily over the course of the year preceding Danny's referral. Each parent also worked to win Danny over to his or her "side," while turning him against the other parent—he was the rope in their tug-of-war.

Danny was referred by Child Protective Services. This was somewhat unusual as Danny had not been either physically or sexually abused. Instead, the referral was based on a determination that he was being emotionally abused through exposure to the violence between his parents. At this point, the couple had engaged in actual physical violence. Although the mother claimed to be the primary victim, it was later discovered that she was often the aggressor. The mother had begun requiring Danny to sleep on the floor at the foot of her bed in order to protect her from her husband.

The parents also tended to use Danny as a messenger between them so that they could avoid contact with each other. Initially, this was simply a strain for Danny who was literally "in the middle." Later, however, both of the parents tended to become abusive toward Danny when they did not like the content of the messages he delivered. Danny soon learned to change the content of the message so as to mollify both parents and earn their approval and gratitude. In other words he convinced both of his parents that he was really on their side.

The primary referral problem was Danny's generally "out-of-control" behavior. He was not directly aggressive in the manner of many out-of-control children. Instead he was manipulative, controlling, defiant, and verbally aggressive. He had previously been an excellent student and was now getting mostly C's in school. His mother also reported that he had no peer friendships.

Pretreatment Assessment

The first portion of the intake was separate interviews conducted with the parents during which they relayed the above history and description of the presenting problem. It should be noted that Mr. Davis felt that Danny's difficulties were relatively minor and a result of Mrs. Davis dragging Danny into the marital conflict.

Mrs. Davis, on the other hand, saw Danny as a deeply troubled young man with significant internal conflicts arising out of his lack of a significant relationship with his father.

During the intake interview, I also assisted the parents in completing the Developmental Therapy Objective Rating Form—Revised (DTORF) (Developmental Therapy Institute, 1992). The DTORF is a scale made up of a hierarchically arranged list of behaviors in four domains: behavior, communication, socialization, and academics. It is particularly useful for determining the developmental goals toward which a child should be working in group. The results of this administration of the DTORF are discussed in the Developmental section of the case formulation that follows.

The intake interview with Danny prior to his acceptance into treatment was a replication of his usual interactions with adults. His mother was so afraid of his reaction to being brought to therapy that she did not tell him where she was bringing him until they were in the waiting room. He responded by leaving and refusing to reenter the clinic. When I informed the mother that I would not take responsibility for Danny until he was, at least, in the waiting room, she went out and pleaded with him until he returned.

Once in the waiting room, Danny came readily to my office. As he entered the office he informed me, while looking at his watch, that I had better talk fast. He said that he had only agreed to come back in the building when his mother had stipulated that he would not be required to stay for more than five minutes. He also informed me that I could say whatever I wanted, but he had no intention of talking. At this point I let him know that whatever agreements he had made with his mother were null and void in terms of his interactions with me. He was under his mother's control outside the clinic, but under my control once in my office. I would decide what we talked about and for how long.

At this point Danny picked up a chair and moved to throw it through the huge window in my office. With no hesitation I took hold of the leg of the chair and forced it back to the floor. I moved in very close to Danny and, while making direct eye contact, said, "Sit down. Don't talk. And don't move until I tell you it is okay." Danny sat down saying, "Oh, . . . okay." After a brief review of the purpose of the visit and some reflection of his feelings of anger at having been deceived, Danny settled into a very productive intake interview.

Danny was incredibly insightful with respect to his current role in his parents' marital conflict. While I tried to point out the strain the role created, he pointed out the benefits. He said that if he could read his parents correctly and tell them exactly what they wanted to hear from, or about, the other parent then he got rewarded. He said he knew he could make them feel good or guilty as needed. He further noted that in a good week he could woo or cajole thirty to fifty dollars' worth of gifts, cash, or local trips out of each parent. His reality included the fact that his parents' marital conflict was a big money-maker for him.

With respect to his presenting problem, Danny generally responded with denial or blaming. He said he was not really a problem at school, but readily observed that most of his teachers were really stupid. If there was conflict between him and them, he noted, it was generally because he was right and they were wrong about something. Then, because adults hate it when a child is right, they would get him in trouble. He claimed to have many friends, but had difficulty naming any.

Theoretical Conceptualization

The style on which the case formulation that follows is based is fully described in *The Play Therapy Primer* (O'Connor, 1991). The formulation and treatment planning process is divided into four steps. First, the play therapist delineates the child's present pattern of functioning. From this description the play therapist derives developmentally appropriate treatment goals. Second, he or she develops hypotheses as to the factors that contributed to the child's present functional strengths and weaknesses. From these hypotheses the play therapist derives reparative goals. Third, the play therapist develops hypotheses as to the factors maintaining the child's present functioning. He or she develops treatment goals from these hypotheses to facilitate the generalization of the progress the child makes in treatment. Last, the play therapist synthesizes these goals and develops a treatment plan. Because of the focus of this chapter, I will discuss the individual therapy and broader systems goals developed during this process only very briefly.

Danny's Present Pattern of Functioning

Developmental Level

In observing Danny and conducting the intake assessment, it became apparent that, in spite of his intellectual capacity, he was functioning in many ways like a two- to three-year-old. His primary emotional bond was still with his mother. He was obsessed with exerting and maintaining his power in relationships and the world at large. When he could not exert control verbally he would become physically aggressive and demanding. Further, he showed little or no interest in peer relationships. While his social and emotional functioning appeared quite low, it was clear that in other areas he was functioning at or above a level that would be considered developmentally appropriate.

Using the DTORF, the Davises rated Danny as functioning in stage four (ages nine to twelve) in the Behavioral domain, suggesting that his behavior and impulse control were within normal limits. Danny was at the end of stage three (ages six to nine) in the Communication domain, due primarily to limitations in his ability to recognize others' feelings and function as part of a group. He was in stage two (ages two to six) in the Socialization domain, primarily because of his extreme difficulty initiating and maintaining interactions with peers. The Academic domain was not rated. At ten years of age Danny should have been functioning at stage four in all domains.

Goals: Danny's developmental level needed to be equalized across areas of functioning; therefore, addressing his deficits in social/emotional functioning was a priority. Danny would be able to (a) respond appropriately to choices for leadership in the group (B–20); (b) indicate beginning awareness of his own behavioral progress (B–21); (c) use words to show pride in group achievements (C–21); (d) channel feelings or experiences through creative, nonverbal media such as art, music, dance, or drama (C–22); (e) participate in interactive play with another child (S–17); and (f) participate in cooperative activities or projects with another child during organized activities (S–18). [These goals are from the DTORF. The code letters stand for the domain (B for Behavioral; C for Communication; and S for Socialization) and the numbers correspond to the DTORF items.]

Cognitions

Danny had been assessed through his school for potential placement in a program for intellectually gifted children. On the Wechsler Intelligence Scale for Children-III, he achieved a Verbal IQ of 125, a Performance IQ of 115, and a Full Scale IQ of 123. These scores suggest that Danny was able to function well above average in all intellectual areas. It was apparent in conversations with Danny and from reports made by his teachers that he impressed most adults as being very bright. This impression was created largely by his verbal fluency and language complexity.

Danny maintained several dysfunctional beliefs that derived directly from the role he was playing in his family. First, he believed that he was directly responsible for his parents' well-being. It was his duty to make sure they were happy. Second, he believed that his parents would only respond to his needs if he first met their needs, especially their need for emotional support. Third, he believed he had the power to control the outcome of their marital conflict. Fourth, he believed that any interpersonal interaction that he could not control would turn out badly, resulting in his not getting his needs met. Last, he appeared to believe that peers were not a reasonable source of emotional or material supplies.

Goals: Danny would be able to (a) use his verbal skills in a nonthreatening way in interactions with peers, (b) state the limitations of his power with respect to his parents' marriage, (c) ask directly for emotional and material supplies from either or both of his parents, (d) show pleasure in an interpersonal situation that he was not controlling, and (e) approach his peers for emotional supplies and support.

Emotions

Danny's emotional repertoire was relatively appropriate. He experienced and was able to manifest a broad range of emotions, although he often had difficulty expressing these feelings verbally. He tended to be anxious most of the time secondary to his belief that if he were not controlling every situation it would become problematic. He also tended to become intensely angry when he was not allowed to control a situation, fearing that he would not get his needs met.

Goals: Danny would (a) be able to verbally describe his current emotions, (b) report less anxiety in situations he is not controlling, and (c) demonstrate fewer rage episodes.

Response Repertoire

In this area I considered whether Danny tended to adopt one of two overall styles: autoplastic or alloplastic. An autoplastic style is one in which individuals attempt to correct problems they encounter by changing their own behavior. An alloplastic style is one in which individuals attempt to correct problems by expecting/demanding that others or the environment make the necessary changes. Consistent with his belief that he could and should control most of his interpersonal interactions, Danny tended toward a predominantly autoplastic response style. For example, when faced with the dilemma of his enmeshment in his parents' divorce, he figured out a way to play it to his advantage rather than expecting them to alter their behavior. Only when severely stressed by a situational loss of control would Danny resort to alloplastic responses and expect others to change. This was evidenced by his violent acting upon being tricked into coming to my office.

Goals: Danny would (a) more realistically perceive the level of control he could or should have in various interpersonal situations, (b) be able to ask others (parents and peers) directly to meet his needs, and (c) manifest fewer rage episodes in situations he cannot control.

Origins of Danny's Present Pattern of Functioning

In this stage of the treatment planning, my goal is to develop hypotheses about the factors that contributed to the child's present pattern of functioning and appropriate reparative goals.

Child-Specific Factors

Clearly, Danny's intellectual and verbal skills made it possible for him to adopt a primarily internalized, autoplastic mode of responding to his environment. He was capable of interacting with adults on their level and of controlling them in many situations. The subsequent reinforcement he received made this pattern of behavior both predominant and stable. The successful use of this pattern of response, in turn, reinforced Danny's dysfunctional beliefs about his role in the family and his control skills/needs.

With respect to Danny's early history, it seemed likely that his mother's depression when he was three years old solidified certain aspects of the family's interactional style. It seemed likely that Danny reacted to his mother's depression and withdrawal as a partial abandonment. This would motivate him to work to reestablish contact with her and would interfere with his pursuing the normal developmental task of this age, namely, the generalization of his primary attachment to his mother to include his father. The father's general unavailability during this period would have exacerbated this problem. Because Danny never generalized attachment behavior beyond his relationship to his mother to include even his father, there would be little chance of his then generalizing that attachment to peers in subsequent developmental phases.

Goals: Danny would (a) use his intellectual skills to become more proficient at interpersonal problem solving and (b) be able to verbally describe the ways in which his attachment to his mother interfered with his attachment to his father and with his peer interactions.

Ecological Factors

Family. As I have noted, Danny's role as the only child in his family significantly contributed to the pattern of strengths and weaknesses he was displaying at the time of intake. He had been expected to meet his parents' narcissistic needs for some time and had become quite skilled at doing so. As the stress of the divorce increased his parents' need for emotional support, Danny attempted to provide for each of them accordingly. Clearly, his resources had become stressed by these demands to the point that he had begun to act out aggressively.

Goals: Danny would (a) be able to verbally recognize the inappropriateness of his current role in his family and redefine himself as a child, (b) ask his parents directly for emotional support, and (c) demonstrate fewer rage episodes.

Peers. Since Danny had virtually no peer relationships prior to entry into therapy, these did not significantly contribute to his present functioning.

Goal: Danny would demonstrate the beginnings of one or more stable peer friendships.

Broader Systems. The primary system that seemed to have had an impact on Danny's functioning besides his family was his school. Certainly he had received a great deal of positive reinforcement for his academic success until the year prior to his referral. Teachers may also have contributed to Danny's isolation from peers by using his academic achievements to set him apart. This happens when teachers say things like, "Now children, I am very disappointed with the way you did on this last spelling test. I know you can all do better. Danny seems to be the only one who studied because he got a 100 on the test." While such comments are not made with malicious intent, they isolate the child and place him or her in the role of scapegoat.

Goal: Danny's teachers would focus on reinforcing his interactions with peers over academics, at least temporarily.

Factors Maintaining Danny's Pattern of Functioning

Child-Specific Factors

Not only did Danny's intellectual skills contribute to his present pattern of functioning, they allowed for his maintenance of such an autoplastic approach. He engaged adults in long verbal debates about his behavior, thereby avoiding compliance. He was able to manipulate his parents into feeling guilty so as to gain specific rewards. And he was able to control his peers by speaking to them as an adult would.

The dysfunctional beliefs that Danny had developed about his familial interactions over time now served to maintain his pattern of responding. For example, since he believed his parents would only meet his needs if he first met theirs, he was loath to stop meeting their needs for fear that to do so would result in the loss of their love and support. He may have even believed that either or both of them would choose to "divorce" him.

With respect to Danny's early history, it seemed that his mother's use of her relationship to him as a way of pulling herself out of her depression continued to set the standard for their interactions. At the time of his referral, Danny was not only her child, he was her protector and confidant as well.

Goals: Danny would be able to (a) verbalize the inappropriateness of his mother's dependence on him, (b) recognize his own emotional needs as separate from those of his mother, (c) verbalize some of his dysfunctional beliefs and recognize the degree to which they interfered with his getting his needs met, and (d) use his intellectual skills to engage in interpersonal problem solving relative to his peer interactions.

Ecological Factors

Family. The parents' inability to maintain appropriate role boundaries while under the stress of their divorce allowed them to draw Danny into their increasing marital conflicts. Each parent was attempting to pull Danny into the role of spousal confidant and protector. Each parent wanted him to take sides against the other. Each parent also wanted Danny to meet his or her needs for emotional support. All of these combined to force Danny into continuing his pattern of functioning. He perceived himself to be in serious jeopardy of losing what little nurturance he did receive from his parents if he did not comply with their demands.

Goals: Danny would be able to (a) verbalize the inappropriateness of the current demands being placed upon him by his parents, (b) ask his parents directly for emotional support, and (c) reduce his dependence on parental support by identifying other adults and/or peers in the environment who might provide him with emotional supplies.

Peers. By the time children enter the third or fourth grade, they tend to have a substantial network of stable friendships if they have continued to live in the same area since beginning school. These networks are frequently rather rigid and new children may have difficulty entering the system. Danny had managed to complete fourth grade without being included in these peer networks. He had the added disadvantage of not being a new child, but rather one already identified by his peers as a loner or outsider. Because of these two factors, it was likely that Danny would have significant difficulty making initial friendships with his school peers.

Goal: Danny would use the members of the group as a peer support network. This would involve his first developing and honing the skills necessary to gain their support and then using the group as a base from which to generalize to relationships with peers in his neighborhood and at school.

Broader Systems. School continued to support Danny's dysfunctional patterns of responding by focusing on his steadily declining academic performance and ignoring his peer relationships. His teachers ignored the possibility that school failure might be reinforced by Danny's peers because it reduced the pressure on them to perform.

Child Protective Services made a significant impact on Danny's pattern of functioning simply by referring him to treatment in a child abuse clinic. This referral facilitated Danny's seeing himself, not as the person in control of his family situation with all of the consequent rewards, but as the victim of his parents' conflict. This was the first input Danny received that suggested his parents' expectations were inappropriate. Additionally, he understood that the role of that system was to protect him from his parents rather than promoting his role in protecting his parents from one another.

Family Court appointed an advocate to protect Danny's rights in the divorce process. At one point early in his treatment, Danny requested an Order of Protection against both of his parents. Typically, these orders stipulate that the named parties may not come within a certain physical distance of the petitioner so as to inhibit violence. A violation of such an order can result in the offender serving jail time. At the time of his request, Danny's parents had orders against each other specifying that they must remain at least 100 yards away from each other. If either one violated the boundary, the other party could call the police. Danny wanted a similar order aimed at keeping his parents away from him. This represented overwhelming progress as it reflected Danny's view that he no longer wanted to be a part of such an enmeshed relationship. It was also one of the first times he sought support from another adult.

If the order had been granted, Danny would have felt that someone wished to protect him. On the other hand, such an order would also reinforce Danny's sense that he should be responsible for managing his parents' behavior and his view that they were incapable of responding to his needs directly. In consultation with me, the advocate determined that such an order would not be issued. Instead, the original orders were rescinded. The message to each of the family members was that the court expected them to behave appropriately without the threat of incarceration. The advocate also made it clear to Danny, in front of his parents, that she expected them to protect him with or without a court order simply because it was in his best interest. The parents were strongly chastised for creating a situation where their child felt the need to seek outside protection and informed that failure to alter their behavior could result in both of them losing custody. The advocate did not convey the possibility of both his parents losing custody to Danny as it would have significantly heightened his fear of losing his parents altogether. They responded quite appropriately to this and greatly reduced the fighting they did in front of Danny.

Goals: (a) Danny's teachers would reinforce all positive approaches Danny makes toward peers while minimizing their criticism of his academic performance, (b) Danny would continue to use his court appointed advocate as a source of support, and (c) Danny's advocate would maintain pressure on the parents to meet Danny's needs if either of them was to have any custodial responsibility.

Goal Synthesis

By reviewing the many goals developed in the course of writing the case formulation, the play therapist develops an overall set of goals and then sorts these goals based on their priority. He or she will use two criteria to determine priority. Any goals addressing behaviors that are a danger to self or others become a very high priority. The other high-priority goals are those that reflect the child's developmentally lowest areas of functioning. Second, the play therapist must determine which goals can be addressed through psychotherapy and which must be addressed through some other intervention. Third, the play therapist determines the type of intervention or treatment modality that will best address each of the psychotherapy goals. Last, the play therapist determines the specific techniques or activities to be used with the overall intervention model to address client specific goals or content.

In Danny's case, his aggressive behavior was relatively mild and there was very little threat to the well-being of himself or others. Therefore I did not consider any of the goals to be of high priority based on danger. Using the developmental criteria, Danny's very significant delays in social and emotional functioning became the top priority. Since his current functioning in this area was at the preoperational level, I determined that these goals would not be well suited to group therapy. Therefore, I began Danny's treatment with an initial course of individual sessions. Specifically, I wanted the individual treatment to address the issues of Danny's enmeshed relationship with his mother, helping him to separate from her while developing a more positive and stable relationship with his father. Individual treatment was also the context in which I could address the origins and impact of Danny's dysfunctional beliefs about his family and social interactions. Two other therapists in the same clinic also provided individual treatment for each of Danny's parents, with the overall plan of completing some family work prior to termination. The goal of the family treatment was the development of more appropriate role definitions and boundaries within each of the new family units (Danny/Mr. Davis and Danny/Mrs. Davis).

I determined that those goals related to Danny's deficits in peer social skills were second in terms of priority. Once Danny had progressed in individual therapy to the point that his social and emotional functioning was more comparable to that of a four- to five-year-old, I decided to begin addressing these goals in group therapy. I used Danny's attainment of three developmental criteria in making this decision. First, Danny demonstrated decreased dependency upon his mother (age two or older). Second, Danny demonstrated increased use of his father and other significant adults in his life as sources of emotional and material support (age three or older). Last, Danny had become less aggressive and showed an emerging interest in peer interactions (age four or older).

During the initial phase of group therapy, Danny participated in both individual and group therapy simultaneously. The individual therapy sessions were rapidly faded to termination by increasing the time interval between sessions. This transitional plan weaned Danny from his one-to-one dependent relationship on me and facilitated his coming to use the group as a substitute for the individual sessions. Although my having provided both the individual and group therapy in this case was not optimal, it was necessitated by the staffing of the clinic. The problem of jealousy between group members was not an issue in this case because all of the children in this particular group had been in individual treatment with me at some time.

I determined a third set of treatment goals to be of relatively high priority, but not suited to psychotherapeutic intervention. These goals consisted of items that could be best addressed through education/consultation with representatives of the other systems that were affecting Danny's functioning. I established two ongoing consultative relationships. One relationship was with Danny's teachers. I apprised them of the role that the school could play in altering Danny's dysfunctional patterns and presented them with some simple strategies for initiating change. These consultations took place by telephone at irregular intervals over the course of Danny's treatment. I also established a consultative relationship with Danny's court appointed advocate. She was instrumental in setting limits on the family's pattern of interactions that supported the therapeutic goals of establishing appropriate role definitions and boundaries. These consultations continued until the court finalized the Davis' divorce settlement. It is this type of consultation that sets ecosystemic play therapy apart from some of the other, more traditional forms of both individual and group play therapy.

The Process of Play Therapy

Setting Up

Preparation for the group to which Danny was referred was quite limited. I conducted the sessions in a relatively large (eighteen by eighteen feet) room. It was divided roughly into halves, one carpeted, the other with a linoleum floor. The carpeted side of the room was further divided into two areas. One area was defined by a couch, two armchairs, and a coffee table. It very much resembled a traditional living room. The other half contained a table and enough chairs for each of the group members and the group leader.

The purpose of the arrangement was to provide the members with visual and spatial cues for the types of behavior expected in the group. The living room area was reserved for discussions and quiet activities. This was also where snacks were served. When children were in this area, I expected them to make verbal contributions to the group process and to comply with basic "manners." The group used the table exclusively for table games and art projects. In this area, I emphasized sharing, cooperation, and a "product orientation" among the children. The group used the large empty area of the room for gross motor activities and games. When the group was in this area, I emphasized cooperation. The group also went outside frequently to play at a local park, where I expected behavior similar to that required in the open area of the room.

I brought very few materials into the playroom. My goal was to focus the children on their interactions with one another rather than on their interactions with the toys or materials. I provided food, for two reasons. One reason was simply pragmatic: the group met immediately after school and the members tended to be so hungry that they could not focus on anything else until after they ate. The other reason was more symbolic: the food was a way of sharing nurturance among children who had all been the victims of abuse. Snack time was also a good way for me to teach sharing and simple table manners.

At no time were toys or materials freely available to the group. I selected the materials to be used prior to each group session and placed only these on the table. By limiting access to materials, I maintained the structure of the group and maximized members' developmental progression by presenting materials that challenged, but did not frustrate, the children. Initially, I used storytelling cards extensively to provide the stimulus for group discussions. These included pictures that portrayed themes, events, and conflicts relevant to one or more members of the group. I used art materials quite often throughout the course of the group. I provided crayons, markers, small and large pieces of paper, and clay at different times. I did not introduce board games until the majority of the group members had reached a developmental level where they could tolerate such things as taking turns, following rules, and competition (age eight and above).

The group consisted of six boys, ages nine to twelve. All of the boys in the group had been abused in various ways. The severity of the abuse ranged from the child who had witnessed his parent murder his sibling, as the most severe, to Danny's, which was the least severe. In spite of their common histories, the boys were not aware that this was one of the criteria for placement in the group. The members were told that they were in the group because they had each expressed sadness at not having friends and a desire to develop friendships.

Prior to a boy entering the group, the parents were required to agree that the child would attend a minimum of nine consecutive sessions. The treatment contract specified that I would review the boy's progress with both the parents and the child after the eighth session. If we decided to terminate at that point, we used the ninth session to accomplish this. If we agreed upon continuation, then I asked the parents to sign another nine-session contract. For returning children, I used the ninth session of the original contract to help them say good-bye to departing members and to welcome new children who were added to the group only at this time.

The format of each group session was also predetermined. The first segment of the group consisted of having the group members complete a simple, directed relaxation exercise. Initially, this was used to focus the group and habituate them to following directions. Because none of the group members had much difficulty settling into the group's routine and none seemed particularly distractible, the relaxation was given up in favor of extended discussion periods.

During the second fifteen-minute segment of each group, the children sat on the sofa and chairs and had their snack. In this rather relaxed atmosphere, we engaged in "talk time." These were focused discussions about topics of concern to the group members. Initially, I prompted these discussions through the use of selected storytelling cards. As the group became more cohesive, they generated their own discussion topics. I guided them to apply problem solving within the context of these discussions whenever possible.

Following "talk time" came "activity time." For the next twenty to thirty minutes, the boys either sat at the table and completed an art activity or played a table game or moved to the empty side of the room to play a gross motor game. I selected and directed the activities engaged in during this time. I retained primary control of both "talk time" and "activity time" and was responsible for maintaining our established routine during both.

When time permitted, the last fifteen to twenty minutes of the group was free-play time. During this portion of the group session, the boys could select their own activity. They could play together or separately, continue what was started during "activity time," or change to something else.

Beginning

During the beginning phase of treatment, a group member usually progresses through several subphases in the process of adapting and responding to treatment. The first of these subphases is exploration, during which the children are focused on absorbing information about the new situation. This phase is usually quite brief in children who are not seriously disturbed or the victims of severe neglect. During the tentative acceptance phase, children appear to be involved in the treatment, but are subtly noncompliant. They will be most involved when the group is meeting their needs and quite resistant when the group is not. Negative reaction is the final subphase of the beginning phase of treatment. At this point children will act out in response to the situational demands for behaviors and responses that are outside their usual repertoire. Further, they will now feel safe enough within the group to manifest their noncompliance more overtly. Not only do all members of the group go through these phases, but the group as a whole moves through them as well. The play therapist must be able to plan activities that address both the treatment stage of the majority of the group members and that of the overall group.

The play therapist can use interpretation to facilitate moving the group members through these stages fairly simultaneously. In order to avoid scapegoating any member who is lagging behind, it is often helpful to make interpretations that compare the progress of each member to that of the group as a whole rather than comparing members to each other. Although it is a difficult decision to make and implement, it is important that the play therapist not allow the progress of the group to be lost due to a single member who is unable and/or unwilling to progress. Sometimes a child will use refusal to progress as a way of controlling the group and will be reinforced by the power he or she wields. In such cases, it is probably better to move the child to another group that is just beginning and to allow the original group to move on.

Exploration. Behaviorally, Danny did very little during the exploratory phase. He did not talk to the other children. He tended to be very reserved motorically and he did not participate in group activities. At best, he engaged in parallel play while visually scanning the environment and obviously attending to all conversations. Danny engaged in this type of exploratory behavior for the first one and one half group sessions

Here is an example of the types of experiential activities used to address Danny's need to explore his new environment. During Danny's initial session, the group played a simple game designed to facilitate interpersonal focus. One child would stand in the middle of the group allowing all of the other children to visually examine him and try to memorize his exact appearance. The target child then left the room and changed something about his appearance, such as moving his shoes to the wrong feet. When he reentered the room, the group was timed to see how long it would take them to discover the change. Although Danny refused to be one of the target children and made every effort to look like he was not interested, he was among the first to begin guessing what was different when the target child reentered the room.

I used interpretation to put words to Danny's behavior and feelings, as well as to make these a part of the group process. I offered reflections that labeled Danny's anxiety and discomfort with not being in control of this new situation. I interpreted his refusing to play as an attempt (autoplastic) to retain what control he could. I also reflected his ambivalence about participation and noted his interest in the activities.

Tentative Acceptance. Probably because of his previous therapy experience, Danny moved into the tentative acceptance subphase of treatment during the second session. At this point Danny began to talk more, but directed everything he said toward me. He never acknowledged the content of another child's verbalizations directly. Instead, he tended to make very egocentric follow-up statements such as, "Oh yeah, that happened to me once. I . . ." Danny began to complete activities in group that required only parallel play with no more than a minimum of sharing. If possible, he would develop variants on other activities that would allow him to maintain this stance.

While Danny was in the tentative acceptance phase, one of the group activities was a project called "pair pictures." Each of the boys picked a partner and I gave each dyad a single large piece of paper and a single box of markers. I instructed them to draw anything they wanted. I encouraged them to work together, but allowed them to work individually on separate areas of the paper so long as they did not tear it in half. Danny immediately drew a line down the middle of the paper without even consulting his partner. He then proceeded to complete a very small drawing on his half. At this point, most of the other dyads had begun to work cooperatively even if they had initially divided their paper. Apparently, this level of parallel activity was too much for Danny because he found a way to be noncompliant. He folded over one corner of his side of the paper and drew a much more elaborate picture there so it would be completely separate from that of his partner.

While Danny was in this phase, I selected activities that would moderately challenge his usual pattern of behavior. Activities like the "pair pictures" described above were common. The focus of the group was on low-level cooperation. This meant that Danny would not be getting reinforced for the types of parallel play he usually engaged in.

During this phase I used interpretation to reflect Danny's growing frustration with his inability to either get control of the group or to be rewarded for independent activity. When he drew on the back of the paper during the "pair pictures" activity, I labeled his desire to break the rules of the task. Simultaneously, I praised the other children for their compliance. I never directly criticized Danny for his behavior nor did I set any limits. Rather, I consistently reinforced the other children for approximating interactive play. My interpretations always made a connection between Danny's behavior and his belief that if he were not in control he would lose out on reinforcers. I made explicit the fact that, in the group, control would cause him to lose rather than gain reinforcements.

Negative Reaction. Danny moved into the negative reaction phase during the end of his first nine-session contract. He began by becoming more verbally aggressive. His comments were now both egocentric and intrusive. He would talk over other children or label their comments stupid and substitute his own. He refused to participate in any activity other than snack time, verbally labeling everything as stupid. He became very vocal about his past academic achievements and used these as an attack on the rest of the group members, who were experiencing academic difficulties.

Danny also moved to take over my role in the group. This was clearly a manifestation of his move into the parental and spousal roles in the home. He thought he could take control by becoming the adult. He would monitor all of the other members' behavior and report any rule violations to me along with suggestions for consequences. When I would not follow his directions, he would storm out of the room, only to return a few minutes later with a new suggestion. The most benign manifestation of his negative reaction was his tendency to help other members of the group. He would give advice on winning strategies during a game or suggestions for improving another child's art activity. These behaviors were problematic on two levels. Danny tended to use adult language when making suggestions and, therefore, alienated the other children because they believed he was being condescending. Danny also reacted with hostility if they did not take his directions, so that the other children knew he was more interested in control than in being helpful. Danny would also use his role of advice-giver to avoid actually playing a game or completing his own portion of a project.

Activities designed to move Danny through the negative reaction phase were, alternately, ones in which I let him have control and ones in which he had to take direction from others. A simple game of Simon Says proved to be an ideal way of making Danny's behavior evident. He was very enthusiastic when he was picked to be Simon. He gave directions with relish and delighted in getting the other boys to make mistakes. When he had to follow the direction of another Simon, however, he would pout, become argumentative, and then leave the game if he made a mistake.

At this point I regularly labeled Danny's battle to save himself from the anxiety of relinquishing situational control versus the frustration of not gaining my approval for exerting too much control. I also noted the motives for each of his behaviors, and the similarity of his behavior in group to that which he displayed at home and school. I identified the difficulty of the battle and made statements reflecting my belief that he would win in the end. It was at this stage that the other boys really began to talk to Danny—and most of what they had to say was quite negative. They did not like his attempts to control them and he heard "You're not the boss of me" a lot. In spite of this, the group was beginning to coalesce and leave Danny out.

As is often the case, Danny completed the negative reaction phase with a "bang." One day he became furious at being left out of a game when he would not follow the rules. He crashed around the room, and then left. I went to retrieve him and he yelled at me, "You have to make them let me play." I refused and told him he must ask the boys directly to reconsider and include him. When I suggested that he apologize for breaking the rules of the game in the first place, he became further enraged. He threatened never to come back to group. He threatened to tell his parents and then to tell his social worker how mean I was. Then he threatened to hurt me. At this point I grabbed his hands, held him securely and suggested that this was probably the final battle of his war against his old way of handling things and that I knew he would win. He fought for a few seconds then stopped and sat down, resigned.

We then engaged in some problem solving. Danny first identified the problem as the other children being mean. With some help, he redefined it as his feeling hurt and angry at being excluded. He noted that he was really not aware of the behaviors he engaged in that angered other children until after an interaction had already turned sour. Among the many plans we developed was one in which I would cue him to the fact that he was beginning to alienate the other boys by simply saying his name. We also rehearsed what he would say when he reentered the room. As we finished he said he was still not ready to go back to the group. I became aware that Danny was probably gaining a considerable sense of power and reward by keeping me away from the group. I left him saying I knew he would be okay and that he could rejoin the group as soon as he was ready.

While he was out of the room, I coached the boys as to how they might respond if Danny asked for another chance. I had them engage in problem solving with respect to the impact of Danny's behavior on them. Their plan was to provide him with more verbal feedback faster, that is, before they became really angry at him.

A few minutes later he came into the room. At first he said nothing and sat on the sidelines. The other boys kept looking to me for cues as to how they should respond, and I suggested they continue with what they were doing. Eventually, Danny came over and tried to join in, but the boys would not let him so he went back to the couch and sat down. I went to him and prodded him in the direction of the group. He then went over, quickly apologized and asked to play. As cued, the group allowed him back in. Danny had been able to approach his peers directly to get his needs met and had encountered success. His negative reaction phase was at an end and he was ready to begin the real work of his group therapy experience.

The group's negative reaction phase is evident in the scenario described above. During this subphase they were not just passively ignoring Danny. They were actively excluding him from things, stating that they did not like him or his behavior. Gentle interpretive comments from me did not undermine their resolve to exclude Danny. They made their response to Danny even more aggressive by choosing to accept another new boy at this time. Only when Danny was able to demonstrate a clear change in his behavior did the group move to change their response to him. Even then, they needed considerable support from me to do so.

Growing, Trusting, and Working Through

Once Danny had experienced one positive, needs-meeting interchange with his peers in a way that violated a behavior pattern of which he was now aware, his treatment progressed rather rapidly. At this stage in the progress of the group as a whole, each of the boys worked out a personal goal toward which he would work in sessions. For some of the boys, the goal was to refrain from hitting others. For some, it was to be less verbally aggressive, and for still others, it was to approach others in the group cooperatively. We did this goal-setting in the discussion segment of the group so that all of the boys were aware of each other's goals. When it came time for Danny to develop his goal, I had trouble putting the abstract concept of his trying to be less pseudomature into words. Danny finally said, "I know. I should try to stop being the play therapist and remember that I am one of the kids." While this was not exactly the operationally defined type of goal the other boys had set, it reflected Danny's progress in developing an awareness of his problem and an ability to direct his cognitive skills toward its resolution. Danny requested that I continue to remind him when he slipped into an adult role simply by saying his name as I had done previously.

During the growing and trusting phase, the focus of Danny's treatment was his development of mutually beneficial peer friendships. Initially, this required that I constantly refocus him on his peers and away from me as his primary source of emotional support. I continued to verbally cue him every time he attempted to join me in the play therapist role. I also consistently interpreted the similarity between his style of interacting with me in the group and his style of interacting with his parents and other adults in authority positions. The element of this behavior that he seemed most reluctant to give up was the setting of limits on the other children's behavior. He acted as if his identification of the other children's bad behavior would prevent the adult from giving that child nurturance. This, in turn, would make that adult more available to Danny. Further, if he was to join the adult in setting limits the adult would be less tired and even better able to provide for Danny. I interpreted this dynamic to Danny and he accepted it. However, as all therapists acknowledge, insight does not always bring about behavior change. The reinforcement Danny received for this behavior in terms of anxiety reduction was so great that it withstood any amount of redirection from me.

The intervention that produced the eventual change in Danny's pseudomature, adult-oriented pattern was the selection of activities. Consistent with his developmental age, Danny learned much better from experience than he did from language. This is not to discount the importance of the interpretations and the verbal work that I did. It was this language base that allowed me to process changes in Danny's behavior with him, to compare and contrast the costs and benefits of change, producing rapid generalization.

The types of activities that altered Danny's behavior were ones that involved group cooperation, rather than competition. Games like "Snakes in the Grass" (Fleugelman, 1976; O'Connor, 1991), where the group must work together to change each of the humans to snakes, were ideal. Other noncompetitive group games can be found in *The New Games Book* (Fleugelman, 1976), *More New Games* (Fleugelman, 1981), and *The Play Therapy Primer* (O'Connor, 1991). Also productive were group excursions to local parks where the children could explore and, consequently, be reinforced by their environment. In this context, one boy could climb a tree and be reinforced for his skill. He could then help another boy up into the tree and be reinforced for his assisting a peer. The recipient of the help was reinforced for reaching the same climbing objective and by having received support from a peer. It should be noted that, while I continued to model the provision of social reinforcement, the group members largely took over reinforcing one another.

I further strengthened the group members' tendency to reinforce one another by periodically abandoning the adult/therapist role. This would not have been possible if the group as a whole had not made the transition into the growing and trusting phase of the treatment process because they still would have required my focusing on maintaining the structure and limits to maintain their behavior. At this point, I tended to join in as an active participant in most of the group activities. I played side by side with the children. I continued to interpret the group process heavily, but disguised these as comments about my personal feelings or reactions to events as they unfolded. Rather than making an interpretation like, "Everyone wants to be 'It' in this game so badly that they are willing to prevent the group from playing rather than let anyone else be 'It.'" I would say, "I'm getting frustrated with everyone fighting to be 'It.' I'll let someone else be It first if we can just go ahead and play." This shift in presentation accomplished two things. On the one hand, I was modeling the use of group process information in interpersonal problem solving. On the other, I was fading the "therapeutic" tone of the group, making it appear more like a typical get-together of peers in order to foster generalization of the children's learning to their everyday world.

I began to fade the structure of the sessions as much as possible, again attempting to simulate a typical interaction of ten-year-old boys rather than a structured play therapy group. We had long since stopped doing the relaxation training at the beginning of each meeting. The snack and discussion time merged and tended to be much more variable in duration. I no longer initiated discussion topics. Some days, the boys would be finished in five minutes; other days, they would identify a high-interest or emotionally loaded topic and spend most of the hour talking. At this stage, we had also played a wide variety of games and completed many different activities, so that I began to let the boys plan the activity portion of the next group session during the discussion time. Gradually, they introduced their own ideas for games and activities and we incorporated these in our repertoire. Again, this gradual fading of the structure and facilitation of the boys' self-management of the group promoted generalization of their behavior to other settings.

This group made particularly good progress through the growing and trusting phase largely because of the continuity and stability of the group. After the addition of Danny and one other boy, only one child left and one child entered the group over the next five months. The one boy who joined the group was rather quiet and observed the group for a long time before joining in. When he finally became more active, it was apparent that he had been spending his exploration phase learning a great deal about the group's rules and process because he was immediately accepted and integrated into their interactions.

Termination

Danny remained in the group for approximately six months or three nine-session contracts. Danny and his parents made the decision to terminate his group therapy with my full support. At the time of termination, a new DTORF indicated that Danny was functioning at age level in all domains. He was no longer demonstrating any rage episodes and his grades had returned to mostly A's and B's. While problems related to his parents' divorce remained partially unresolved, Danny had made significant gains.

We accomplished termination in the ninth session of his third treatment contract. Consistent with Danny's treatment goals, he was heavily involved in determining the type of termination ritual that would best meet his needs. He chose to have a party similar to that he had seen other children have, which included cake and drinks for snack time. He also chose to ask the other boys for their names, addresses, and phone numbers so that he could call them at some point in the future and get together to play. These types of meetings had already occurred between several of the boys and this was Danny's strategy for retaining some control over the rate at which he separated from the boys in the group.

Results and Follow-Up

Overall, the outcome of Danny's course of psychotherapy was very positive. He met the primary criteria for termination. He had achieved a level of age-appropriate developmental functioning. He had also met his own goal of developing some consistent peer friendships and feeling less anxious and more happy. Mrs. Davis reported that Danny had begun to develop friendships with some of the children in their neighborhood and even showed early signs of having acquired a best friend.

The least successful part of Danny's treatment was the family component. Both of his parents proved to be very resistant to changing their narcissistic styles. They tended to need an incredible amount of emotional support from others and saw Danny as a viable resource for meeting those needs. Neither parent developed any peer friendships of their own as the divorce progressed and so they remained isolated from other, more appropriate resources. At this level, treatment came to be geared more toward helping Danny resist their demands without acting out, rather than significantly altering their behavior. Danny became very good at recognizing when his parents' expectations were inappropriate and either drawing a reasonable boundary to keep them away or insisting that they seek support elsewhere. While this was certainly an improvement, it maintained Danny in a pseudomature role vis-à-vis his parents. He was the one monitoring boundaries and setting limits, rather than being able to trust those of his parents. However, this application of his pseudomaturity did substantially free both his intellect and his emotions, allowing him to pursue getting his needs met through other relationships and to be a child. Further, this stance allowed him to continue to get those supplies that his parents were able to provide in a way that was much healthier in the long run.

Discussion

Ecosystemic play therapy is a model in which the play therapist considers the impact and interaction of the various systems in which child clients are embedded from the point of intake through the assessment, treatment planning, and treatment implementation to the time of termination. The play therapist develops broad goals that address the systemic aspects of the problem with which the child is presenting and addresses these either in the play therapy itself or through referral, consultation, and/or liaison work. Structured group play therapy is one intervention technique through which the play therapist can address children's problems with peer socialization.

It is important in conceptualizing a structured group play therapy intervention that the play therapist not view it as a treatment that can be effectively implemented in isolation. The play therapist must consider the developmental level of the child and his or her life situation if the treatment is to proceed optimally. This model was particularly well suited to the case presented as it was the combination of individual, family, and group therapy along with consultation to the school and family court that served to alter the referred client's pattern of functioning. In each of these interventions the underlying goal was the reestablishment of developmentally appropriate behavior in the child as well as an increase in his ability to get his needs met in a way that did not violate the basic needs and rights of others.

In reexamining this case, it is my sense that the outcome could have been significantly enhanced by including the parents in the treatment process to a greater degree. At the time, family therapy was not implemented for two reasons. One was the ongoing combat between the parents and my concern that, should this erupt in session, it would overwhelm Danny's gradually improving defenses. So long as his parents did not directly interact, they did not have the opportunity to be physically violent. My other reason for not conducting family sessions was my concern about fueling Danny's fantasies that he could force his parents to reunite. If this had occurred, then family sessions would have reinforced his acting-out behavior. In spite of the divorce, Danny and his parents were probably well suited to family therapy. The goals of such an intervention would have been to establish clearer and more appropriate parent-child role boundaries. This would have freed Danny to be a child in his interactions with each parent.

In spite of the minimal involvement of Danny's parents, I believe the outcome was nearly optimal given the pragmatics of this case. Danny learned many new strategies for getting his needs met. Some of these allowed him to maintain better boundaries between himself and each of his parents and to extricate himself from their marital conflict. Other strategies allowed him to function as a child in his interactions with his peers. The latter provided him with a whole range of reinforcers and supplies that were previously unavailable. Although Danny was required, due to his parents' unresolved narcissistic needs, to maintain an overly mature stance relative to his interactions with them, I believe his prognosis is excellent.

References

Camp, B., Blom, G., Herbert, F., and Van Doomick, W. (1977). "Think aloud": A program for developing self-control in young aggressive boys. *Journal of Abnormal Child Psychology, 5:* 157–169.

Developmental Therapy Institute. (1992). *Developmental therapy objective rating form—Revised.* Athens, GA: Developmental Therapy Institute.

Dinkmeyer, D. (1973). *Developing understanding of self and others* (DUSO). Circle Pines, MN: American Guidance Services.

Fleugelman, A., ed. (1976). *The new games book.* New York: Doubleday.

Fleugelman, A., ed. (1981). *More new games and playful ideas.* New York: Doubleday.

Goldfried, M., and Davison, G. (1976). *Clinical behavior therapy.* New York: Holt, Rinehart & Winston.

Jacobson, E. (1938). *Progressive relaxation: A physiological and clinical investigation of muscular states and their significance in psychology and medical practice. 2nd ed.* Chicago: University of Chicago Press.

Meichenbaum, D. (1977). *Cognitive-behavior modification: An integrative approach.* New York: Plenum.

Meichenbaum, D., and Goodman, J. (1971). Training impulsive children to talk to themselves: A means of developing self-control. *Journal of Abnormal Psychology, 77:* 115–126.

O'Connor, K. (1991). *The play therapy primer.* New York: John Wiley & Sons.

O'Connor, K., and Lee, A. (1991). Advances in psychoanalytic psychotherapy with children. In M. Hersen, A. Kazdin, and A. Beflack (eds.), *The clinical psychology handbook, 2nd ed.* Elmsford, NY: Pergamon Press, pp. 580–595.

CHAPTER EIGHT

CIRCLE TIME IN DEVELOPMENTAL PLAY THERAPY

Viola Brody

Group play therapy is an integral part of the Developmental Play Therapy (DPT) model: a three-pronged, three-hour weekly program that provides training for five or six adults along with individual and group therapy for five or six children, each of whom is paired with one of the adults. That adult is called the child's *Partner*. The program starts with one hour of training with the adults (or therapists) followed by one hour with the children—a half-hour of individual therapy followed by a half-hour of group play therapy called *Circle Time*—and ends with a one-hour training session. Thus, DPT has three parts in one weekly session: training, individual child therapy, and group play therapy. The therapist in charge of the program is called the *Leader*.

Background

In *The Dialogue of Touch: Developmental Play Therapy* (Brody, 1997), I presented only two parts of this program—the therapy of one child and the training of the adult Partners. The group play therapy process that took place in the Circle Time was not fully presented. Using the same five children and the same Leader described in the book, this chapter will present the group play therapy part (Circle Time) and in so doing, complete the picture of the DPT model of child therapy.

The Setting

Picture a room where five adult-child pairs are seated on the floor facing each other in specific spaces identified by a rug or blanket. The individual session ends when the Group Leader announces "Circle Time." Each adult brings her child to the Circle, sits down, and holds her child ready for the Leader to start. *Note to the reader: in referring to the children and therapists, I use the feminine pronoun.*

The fact that the five adults and the five children together with the Leader carry out the individual work in the same room and then come together for Circle Time in the same room gives the DPT approach a familylike experience for everyone. From the beginning all the participants, both adults and children, are together in the same room. The DPT is modeled after real life: a child is born into a family but first becomes attached to the mother in the presence of the family. Then she relates to the others but always in the presence of and with the support of the mother. The Circle Time is like the second stage where the children play together with each other, say in the park under another's leadership, while parents observe and support. The fact that every child in the DPT group play therapy has her own "mother" present in the Circle Time for support—even physical support—differentiates the DPT group play therapy approach from most other models right at the beginning.

Belief System

To understand any therapeutic model, one must understand the belief system of the therapist doing the therapy. Being aware of your belief system changes the quality of your work because then you work with a specific intent. It took me over forty years to realize that the condition I provided for children's growth was touch. Thus what I do now as a DPT group play therapist is guided by my belief that the child's experience of her body through caring touch is the basic experience she needs for everything she does. As Montagu (1986) says, the skin never forgets.

The child learns who she is first through touch from a caring adult, hopefully the mother. In DPT touch is the condition that enables the child to relate to the Partner in the individual session that precedes the Circle Time. The child's inner self gained through her attachment relationship with her Partner enables the child to take the next step—relating to peers in the group setting (Circle Time).

In other words, in the DPT model of group play therapy, the children do not play with dolls, toys, or games. Instead, they play with each other. At no time is a child by herself in the Circle Time. All the children are involved in the group process either with each other or with the group Leader, who is either providing the structure or responding to the children as they create their own activities.

DPT group play therapy is a presymbolic form of group play therapy—a second way in which it differs from most other models. That is, it is a highly interactive, body-contact, body-focused approach that provides children with the basic experiences needed to learn to engage in symbolic play. For example, doll play is not meaningful unless the child has an attachment relationship that can be represented in the doll play. A child cannot give form or symbols to something she has never experienced. Thus, the DPT group play therapy model is the first or *basic group play therapy* because it provides the foundation for all other group therapies.

In the beginning stage, the role of the Leader involves providing the structure and the focus the children need to create a group. The Leader does take charge. The goal, however, is to create conditions that enable the children to provide their own structure so that what happens in the group comes from the children instead of being the result of preplanned activities dictated by the Leader. In other words, the Leader looks for opportunities to respond to cues from the children and to acknowledge what is happening in the group.

Thus the goal of the DPT group play therapy is to provide the child with what she needs to experience herself as a member of this group. To be a group member, the child has to be *present*. The Leader provides the condition the child needs to be present, and this is touch. For example, as the Leader, she says hello to a child by touching the child's hand and calling her by name. To be a group member, the child has to be a *participant*. The group Leader provides the condition the child needs to be a participant: she asks the child to choose a member of the group, touch that child, and say her name. Acknowledging each other through touch makes children move toward each other and look at each other—one as the giver and the toucher, the other as the receiver and the one touched. This, in turn, leads to children's sharing experiences verbally. By the end of the program most of the children will demonstrate their ability to use the group as a vehicle to express where they are through some symbolic form.

The goal of the DPT group play therapy, then, is for the children to become a group by providing their own focus, which guides and gives meaning to their interactions with each other as they use the group as an avenue to give form to their experiences through inviting others to participate in the acting out of their fantasies. The Leader supports, reflects, and provides boundaries as needed.

The Structure of Circle Time

Circle Time has three clearly defined parts: the beginning or Hello part, a middle or creative play part, and a parting or Good-bye part. Each part has a specific purpose or focus. The Leader takes charge of the Hello and Good-bye parts, which are more or less set. The purpose of the Hello part is to provide the children with what they need to be present. The Leader does this by singing the Hello song in which the children are seen, named, and touched and they take turns doing the same to others. At the end of the session, the Leader provides the children with what they need to feel secure leaving the group—activities that provide memories they can take home with them—eating a snack, being cradled while the Leader sings a lullaby, saying what they like best, and singing a good-bye song. The middle part is reserved for creative play initiated by the children. The unfolding of new behavior takes place here.

Cradling is the touchstone of DPT and reflected in the logo. In DPT group play therapy, the cradling is a group experience. Children who can learn to relax and allow themselves to be held by their Partner in this group cradling experience do change. When they are relaxed, they are present and participating.

Understanding an approach begins with experiencing it. To help you experience what it would feel like to be a child in a DPT Circle Time and what it would feel like to be the Leader of a DPT Circle Time, here are transcripts of an early session and the terminating sessions of the group described in my book (Brody, 1997).

Case Example

This play group consisted of five children from a regular day care center, five adults in training, and a group Leader, Mary, an experienced certified DPT trainer. To experience firsthand what it's like to be a participant in a DPT group therapy program, I became one of the five adults in training.

The Participants

This play group consisted of three girls, all age four (Mira, Mona, and Jeanne) and two boys (James, age four, and Amos, age five.) These children were not referred. They were in the group because children were needed for training purposes; the day care center approved and the parents signed a release. Except for Mira's mother, no parent expressed any need for help with her child. Mira's mother clearly wanted her child to be in this one-hour weekly program because she did not know how to handle the fighting between Mira and her older sister, age six. We had no diagnostic data—only information from observing the children in the classroom. Clearly they were all attachment-problem children. Mira revealed her attachment problem in her constant need to control and need for attention. These five children attended both parts of DPT—the individual therapy and the group play therapy. This paper focuses on the group process as it unfolds in the Circle Time.

Like the children, the Partners or therapists included three females and two males. Two of the women were experienced DPT therapists (Brenda and Vi); Selma was a beginner. Of the two men, Shawn was an experienced DPT therapist and Mort was a beginner.

The Beginning Process

In the first Circle Time, the adults need to meet the children and choose the child they want for their Partner, and the Leader needs to introduce the children to the play program. That is the purpose of this first Circle Time. The adults sit on the floor in a circle with a child sitting between two adults. The Leader begins by introducing everyone with a Hello song in which everyone learns all the names. She tells the children about a playtime they will have every Monday and that one of these big people will be their Partner. Then the Leader starts a game called Pass-the-Child. Each adult picks up the child next to her and holds her on her lap and plays with her for five minutes (games like counting fingers). At the end of that time the adult passes that child to the next adult and takes a new one on her lap until all the children have had a turn. A good-bye song is sung to the children and they leave.

The Leader then asks the adults to choose the child they want and to say why they want a particular child. If more than one adult wants the same child, the two have to work it out. In this case, however, there were no conflicts. Each adult got the child she wanted. For whatever it means, the two men chose the two boys and the three women chose the three girls.

The transcript that follows is from Session 3. As you read this transcript (Brody, 1997, pp. 225–230), ask yourself what did the play group Leader do to enable these very disturbed children to start experiencing themselves as a group. What did she provide? To set the scene, picture the adults each holding their child and sitting on the floor in a circle; the Leader sits between the two male Partners.

Leader:	*[looking around]* Everybody is here. Follow my hand. Listen to the music. *[moving her hands to the music and observing the children]*
Children:	*[imitate Leader and move their hands to the music]*
Leader:	That's right, Jeanne. *[touches the palms of a child across from her]* Anyone across the circle you'd like to touch their hands?
Amos:	*[touches Leader's hand]*
Leader:	That's right, Amos.

Mira: *[yells]* Mona!

Leader: Here's Mira and Mona. Here's Mona saying Hello to Amos. That's very nice. There you are.

Jeanne: *[reaches toward Amos]*

Leader: Here, Amos. Jeanne wants to touch you.

Jeanne: *[crawls on all fours to reach Amos and touches his hand]*

Mira: *[in loud voice]* I want to touch James. *[moves toward James]*

Leader: Very gently. Well, let's ask James if it's OK. *[to James]* James, Mira wants to touch hands with you. Is that OK with you? Can she come over and touch your hand *[touching him]* like this? *[to Mira]* I think he said yes.

Mira: *[crawls over on all fours to reach James and touches his hand]*

Leader: Very gently . . . very gently, Mira.

Mira: *[returns to Vi's lap and screams]*

Mona: *[screams]*

Leader: *[in louder voice]* Everybody follow me. *[moves her hand to the music in large movements]* Move your hands up. Both hands straight up.

Children: *[follow her and screaming stops]*

Leader: Here they come down. *[moving her hands toward the floor]* You've got to watch closely. Here they go. *[in sing-song tone]* That's the way, Amos. *[smiling at him]* That's the way, Jeanne. *[smiling at her]* Let's see how high we can stretch. *[moving her hands up]* Oh, Amos is really high. *[laughing at him]* Now let's see how far we can go forward and then up again *[moving hands up]* and then fall down again. *[moving hands to floor]*

Children: *[follow]*

Leader: And now, while the music is very quiet, we're going to take turns. Mona, who would you like to touch? . . . very gently . . . reach across.

Mona: *[crawls over and touches Mira]*

Leader: Mira, OK?

Mira: *[looking at James]* Hi, James.

Mona: *[continues touching others, guided by her adult partner]*

Leader: *[names them as she touches them]*

Mira: *[making noises]*

Leader: *[continues naming]* And Mary, and Vi, and here's somebody else ready *[looking at Amos]*

Mira: Me.

Mona: *[touches Amos]*

Leader: That was very nice, Mona. And you said Hello to everybody. OK, Jeanne, it's your turn. Listen to the music and see who you'd like to touch.

Jeanne: *[touches all of them in turn]*

Mira: *[pulls her hand back when touched by Jeanne]* Eh!

Leader: That was very nice, Jeanne. And now it's James's turn. Who would you like to touch with your hands, James? Listen to the music.

Amos: *[holds out his hand]*

Leader: Oh, Amos, would you like him to touch you?

James: *[reaches over and touches Amos in the stomach]*

Leader: *[laughs]* Oh, right in the tummy, OK. Well, that was very nice, James. And now we'll move right around here and it's Amos's turn. Hi, Amos.

Amos: *[names the children he touches in a quiet, gentle way]*

Mira: *[making noises and hitting Vi's knee]*

Leader: And now there's one person left. And you know who that is.

Mira: *[points to Vi]*

Leader: *[laughs, and so do the children]* I think it's Mira. Anybody you'd like to touch? Very gently. *[names them as Mira touches them]* Very nice.

Mira: *[ends her touching with a little yell]*

Leader: *[in a louder voice]* And everybody had a turn. Sometimes, it's hard to wait your turn, isn't it? But everybody got a turn, huh! I'll tell you what we're going to do now.

James: *[softly]* I want a turn.

Leader: You'd like another turn.

Mira: *[in a loud voice]* I want a turn.

Leader: Hold on here a minute. We'll see how turns go. Your turn, James.

James: *[touches others]*

Mira: *[loudly]* My turn.

Leader: Just a minute. Let's see if there's anybody else he wants to touch.

Mira: *[softer voice]* My turn.

Leader: We're going to go in a different order than we did before. And so it's Mira's turn. So who would you like to touch?

Mira: *[touches each child]*

Mona: *[loud voice]* My turn.

Leader: And now it's Amos's turn. Who would you like to touch?

Mira: I touched myself. *[touching her knee]*

Vi: She said she touched herself.

Leader: Oh, OK. And now it's Jeanne's turn.

Jeanne: *[reaches over and touches each child]*

James: *[while touching going on]* I'm hungry.

Leader: OK, everybody. It's cradle time. Everybody in our Circle, we're going to have a cradle time. So big people, get in a comfortable place. *[shuts off the music]* Here we go.

Vi: *[turns Mira around in the cradling position]*

Mira:	*[screams, stiffens her body, then relaxes]*
Leader:	*[sings Brahms "Lullaby"]*
Mira:	*[lets herself be held. She turns her face toward Vi, reaches up, and touches Vi's hair. She closes her eyes and lies totally still during the singing.]*
James:	*[sits up in Shawn's lap during the singing]*
Jeanne:	*[in cradling position she is very tense and moves her body a lot]*
Mona:	*[stiffens her body, fights the cradling by moving her body in strange positions with her legs up in the air]*
Amos:	*[sits up, leaning against Mort]*
Leader:	*[continues singing, then chants]* Just lean back right on your partner and see how warm it feels to rock. James and Shawn are rocking close, and Mona and Brenda are rocking, too. Jeanne and Selma are rocking, and Mira and Vi are rocking, too. Amos and Mort are rocking, la la la . . . *[to end the singing]* Now everybody stay real still with your partner and the two of you remember what the trick is you're going to do. You want to be the first, Amos?
Amos:	*[nods yes]*
Leader:	Let's make a little bit of room in the center of the circle. Now wait a minute, you guys, because we've got a lot of people in this group, and the first one to do a trick is gonna be right here. *[pointing to Amos and Mort]* Does anybody know who they are?
Jeanne:	Amos and Mort.
Leader:	Right. Which one is Amos? And this one? OK, everybody pay attention because in the center ring of our circus, we have Amos and Mort.
Amos:	*[with help from Mort, does a headstand]*
Leader:	Stand up and take a bow, Mort and Amos.
Amos and Mort:	*[stand up and bow]*
Others:	*[applaud]*
Leader:	*[introduces Mira and Vi in the same way]*
Vi:	*[removes Mira from her lap and lays her down in the center; she has one knee bent]* This knee won't work. How many kisses does it need to make it move?
Mira:	*[holds up her two hands]*
Vi:	*[kisses her knee ten times and then the knee does move]*
Mira:	*[stops Vi from picking her up]* The other knee.
Leader:	This is a two-knee trick.
Vi:	*[repeats the trick, asking the others to help her count]*
Leader:	It does work. That's a very nice trick. Now will you stand up and take a bow? You could do a curtsy. *[stands up and shows her]*

Mira:	I don't want anyone to see my underwear.
Leader:	Oh, no. They won't see your underwear. Just hold your skirt.
Mira:	*[giggles, gets silly, loses her balance, and then loses her composure]*
Vi:	*[reaches out and pulls her back into her lap]*
Other children:	*[do their tricks, except Mona, who can't]*
Leader:	*[passes out rice cake snacks and asks each child to share with her partner]*
Mira:	No.
Others:	*[share snacks]*
Leader:	*[sets up a game with the snacks]* Let's see if we can make them crunch together. *[holding up her cracker]* Everybody get it ready right in front of your mouth. Ready; one, two, three. *[bites into cracker]*
Children:	*[follow; each child has a turn to be the leader and count]*
Leader:	*[offers Vi a bit of her cracker]* That's all for turns today.
Mira:	*[screams]*
Leader:	Wait a minute. I would like for you all not to yell in here because it hurts my ears.
Mira:	*[screams]*
Leader:	Did anyone have a good time in here today? Did you, Jeanne?
Jeanne:	*[nods yes]*
Leader:	Would you turn around and tell Selma?
Jeanne:	*[to Selma]* I had a good time today.
Leader:	Did anyone else have a good time today?
Children:	*[all put their hands up, including Mira]*
Jeanne:	I had a good time with Selma.
Leader:	I'm glad to hear that. OK, it's time to put your socks and shoes on. If you want to give your partner a hug, you can. Anyone who wants to give their partner a hug?
Mira:	I don't want to give her a hug. I don't need one.
Other children:	*[hug their partners]*
Leader:	*[sings the Good-bye Song; says time to put on shoes and socks]*
Mira:	*[at end of song, goes around and hugs each child]*

Comments

This transcript showed what this beginning DPT Group Play Therapy looked like and felt like—what each child did and what the Leader did to provide the much-needed structure. As you read it, you experienced how hard this session was for both the children and the Leader. At the same time you probably admired the Leader's ability to keep these very immature children focused on a group task. Let's look at the process.

What the Leader Did. First, she started with a whole-group activity led by her—all moving their hands to soft music. When the group were in unison and while she was leading them with her hands, she reached over and touched one child. Asking that child to touch another child started a chain reaction of one child touching another child, one at a time. Thus, the Leader moved from a whole-group activity to an individual activity.

When the children could not handle the individual focus, a reaction they expressed in screams and yelling, the Leader returned to a whole-group activity, again moving their hands to music. The Leader's hypnotic voice relaxed the children so that she could return to calling on individual children to repeat the touching-hello exercise. This time the children could stay focused a longer period before they became tense and noisy.

The next whole-group activity was the cradling, initiated early (usually it comes at the end) because the children were all wanting attention at the same time. The Leader asked the Partners to cradle their child while she sang a lullaby.

The two male Partners did not place their children in a cradling position and these boys (Amos and James) remained sitting up with eyes open. The women did change the position of the three girls. Jeanne and especially Mona were very tense. They kept moving their legs the whole time. Mira, in contrast, not only accepted the cradling but liked it, which she showed by her total relaxation and her reaching up and touching the Partner's hair—the only time during this half hour that she was quiet and relaxed.

Again, the Leader followed a whole-group activity with an individual activity called *Trick Time.* Each partner and her child took turns coming to the center to do their trick. It was very obvious, however, that none of these children had any trick in mind nor were they able to create one. Therefore, the Partner and the child did something that the Leader called their trick. When Mira and Vi did her knee trick, Mira asked if she could complete her trick by doing "the other knee," which the Leader allowed. After each performance, the Leader applauded and asked the others to applaud while the pair who performed were asked to stand and bow.

As before, whole-group activity followed individual activity. The Leader prepared the group for the Good-bye part of the session by making snack time a whole-group activity. She asked the children to hold up their cracker and count with her, "one, two, three," and then take one bite all at the same time. Each child had the experience of being the Leader in this game.

When Mira responded to the Leader's demand to stop screaming by screaming again, the Leader stopped giving her attention and turned to Jeanne, asking her if she had a good time and she said yes. After the Good-bye song the Leader closed the session by inviting the children to give their Partners a hug. In other words, she offered the children the opportunity to be the one initiating the touching—being the toucher. Mira's response to that offer showed her confusion over who the "I" is and her constant need to be in charge—doing it her way.

The Structure the Leader Provided. To be called a group, people need to have a focus and a structure. The Leader provided both in the simple act of saying Hello to a child through touch. The focus and the structure are in the act itself. In other words, instead of telling the children why they are here and what they'll be doing, she enabled them to experience both immediately in the here-and-now without words. The touching provided the child with the condition she needed to be present and to be a participant—that is, to be a group member.

The Leader provided activities that helped a child contact another child through touch, through performing, through observing and being observed, through acknowledging others and being acknowledged, and through being a member of a group all doing the same thing at the same time.

The Leader set limits in two ways. First, instead of trying to get a child to change her disruptive behavior, the Leader changed *her* approach. That is, she looked at a child's disruptive behavior as a signal to her that she was not connecting with the child and she needed to do something different. Instead of trying to make the child change her behavior, the Leader changed her own behavior. The Leader did this often. For example, when the children could not stay focused on the individual child work, she returned to some quiet whole-group activity, such as moving hands to soft music. Similarly, the Leader shifted her attention from Mira to the whole group when she recognized Mira's inability to make use of the Leader's demand to stop screaming. Second, the Leader set limits by requiring the children to wait their turn when they all wanted a turn at the same time. The children were able to do that.

The Leader supported the children's request to do something that was new for them—for example, when Mira wanted to add something to the trick she and her Partner did and when James wanted to repeat the touch game. Thus the Leader differentiated between demands for attention and requests to try something new. The request to do something new is an expression from the child's inside as opposed to trying to control the outside world. The Leader responded to the new behavior by applauding and having the children applaud each other.

Summary of the Leader's Work. This transcript demonstrates how to start a beginning DPT group play therapy session. The Leader provided the condition the children needed to be present and to be participants in this group. That condition was touch. The touching activity equalized this very uneven group because every child could do it—touch another and accept someone else's touch. They could all start out at the same place by feeling their own physical presence. ("I touched myself," said Mira as she touched her own knee.)

The inner self born through the awareness of the physical body enables the child to feel and to ask for what she needs. That's the basic equipment the child needs to be present and to be a participant. The basic and first communication illustrated in this session is direct, physical, and visual—nonverbal.

Reading this transcript evokes a feeling of the organic quality of this Leader's work. Under her guidance the group behavior had a rhythm and flow like the ocean, which is sometimes quiet (like the cradling) and sometimes breaks up into individual waves of different sizes (like individual children touching, screaming, yelling, talking, performing). The ability of these very immature children to experience so many different group activities in this half-hour is largely due to the ability of the Leader, who ran a tight ship while at the same time providing space for each child's individual needs.

The Children. This group of five children included one very active, controlling child and four very quiet children. Having a diagnostic label for these children would not have told the Leader what to do. Yet under her leadership and understanding, these children began to define themselves through their behavior.

Mira. Mira's behavior defines her as an ADHD child. She exhibited twelve of the fourteen behaviors of ADHD children listed in the DSM-III-R. She was constantly moving her body and her mouth (screaming, yelling, talking). When she was given the attention she seemed to be demanding, she didn't know what to do with it. She screamed when she did something well and got very silly. She was extremely nervous doing her trick performance. Yet she quietly (new for her) asked to complete her trick. She would touch others but didn't want to be touched by them. However, she did respond to being cradled by her Partner—the only time she was relaxed and quiet. *Issue:* Mira's behavior represents her attempt to control the outer world because she has no inner self. She was totally lost and very scared. *Need:* Mira needs an inner self but she can't get that by herself. Responding to her demands for attention didn't do it but the cradling did. When she could let herself relax in the arms of her Partner, she found her inner self, which was born when she relaxed and reached up and touched her Partner's hair.

Mona. Mona's behavior showed some autistic quality. She was uncomfortable just sitting in her Partner's lap. The only thing she said during the session was "My turn"—a repeat of Mira's words and Mira's screaming and yelling. She did, however, take her turn in the touch-hello exercise, but she needed some help from her Partner to do it. She could not participate in the Trick Time. She fought the cradling by moving her legs as if trying to get up. *Issue:* Mona copied Mira because she has no inner self. Unlike Mira's, however, Mona's behavior showed no awareness that she needed anything. She was very tense in the cradling, but she showed no awareness that she felt it. *Need:* Mona has no inner self. Mona needs to learn to feel her physical body and to be comfortable being held by her Partner.

Jeanne. Jeanne was also a very quiet child, but she participated in all the group activity. She did say one sentence in response to the Leader's question at the end: "I had a good time today." Like Mona, Jeanne was very uncomfortable in the cradling position. Like Mona, she gave no evidence that she felt her uncomfortableness. *Issue:* Jeanne lacks an inner self. *Need:* Jeanne needs an inner self, which the cradling provides and which she resisted.

James. James had a sweet, babylike quality expressed in his voice when he said, "I want a turn. I'm hungry." He was very present, playful, and creative in the touching games, especially with Amos. James asked for what he wanted. *Issue:* James does have an inner self, but it is the inner self of a much younger child. *Need:* James is in the baby stage. He needs to be allowed to be there and pick up what he needs to be able to move on. James, however, did not get the cradling experience because his Partner did not place him in the cradling position, and James would have loved it.

Amos. Amos, one year older than the others, was a very quiet, gentle boy. He was very present. When the Leader invited a child to start the touching-hello game, Amos was the first one to accept her invitation when he reached out and touched the Leader. Like the others, he communicated nonverbally, for example, when he held out his hands to invite James to touch him. The only time he talked was when he named those he touched in the touching exercise. *Issue:* Amos has an inner self, but it's an inner self that doesn't allow him to assert himself very much. He has to be invited before he does something. *Need:* Amos needs a relationship with someone who will take an interest in him. When he is touched, seen, and stimulated he can do things. He needs a friend. Like James, Amos did not get the cradling experience because his Partner did not cradle him.

Summary for the Children. The children's behavior in Session 3 defined where the children are and what they need. Four (Mira, Mona, Jeanne, James) show that they need to be provided with the condition that enables them to experience themselves at level 1—what I call the baby stage—that is, the stage where they can totally relax and let the adult take care of them. That condition was the touching and the cradling. James was already functioning at this stage when he kept asking to be fed. Mira didn't know what she needed, but when she got it—the cradling—

she recognized it at once. Mona and Jeanne were the most disturbed because they did not recognize what they needed when it was provided. Amos asked for the touching when he invited others to touch him.

In this session, the children followed the Leader. They were very involved in the activities the Leader provided. No one ran out of the Circle (as sometimes happens).

The Termination Process

The child's response to the termination phase reflects how well the child is ready for termination and how well the final session prepares the child for the ending. Thus a great deal of attention is given to the termination process which usually consists of three experiences for children in a DPT group play program: first the child reacts to the first reminder of the ending when the program is very meaningful to her—sadness, anger; second, the child expresses positive feelings—an awareness of her attachment; third, a sense of joy, self-empowerment, and a memory the child herself has created in the last session to take home with her. In the DPT approach, the termination date is set at the beginning. Three sessions from the end, the children are reminded, "We play today and two more times and then we have to say good-bye."

In Session 3, you saw the beginning stage of DPT group play therapy. In Session 14, you will see the beginning stage of terminating a DPT group—the session in which the children have been told of the ending. When the children come to Circle Time, they will have already talked about the ending with their Partners.

Session 14. As soon as the group assembled for Circle Time, Mira broke out with huge sobs that lasted for about half of the Circle Time. As she sobbed she leaned against her Partner, and the children quietly observed. The Leader started singing, "It's all right to cry. Crying takes the sad out of you. It might make you feel better." The children were very quiet—a whole-group activity—just listening. Then the Leader asked Mira if she were sad. She was still crying but a little less and did not respond. The Leader then took the focus off of Mira and turned to Amos, asking him if he thought Mira was sad. He said yes. Mona blurted out, "No, she's not." Amos added that she was sad because they were stopping after two more times. The Leader made an interpretation when she asked Amos if he thought Mira liked her Partner (Vi), and he said yes. Then, as she has done often, the Leader changed from an individual activity to a whole-group activity when she quietly reviewed the history of this group, asking the children to name each adult and child as she pointed to them. Mira said nothing for the whole Circle Time— unusual for her.

What the Leader Provided. Many therapists feel at a total loss as to how to respond to a crying child—a child crying from the heart as Mira did. In this session the Leader's role differed from her role in Session 3 because the children, led by Mira, provided the focus and the structure. Through her sobbing, Mira enabled all the children to experience their own reaction to the termination. She gave them the opportunity to experience it too. They felt it in their quietness.

The Leader's role here was to provide the space and be a container for all these feelings. Because she was holding this space for the children, they didn't have to do anything and all of them stayed quiet and focused. These children were thus all group members sharing a group experience expressed by one of the members who provided the focus, not the Leader—a very different group from the one in Session 3. Here, the Leader followed the children.

The Meaning of the Crying. Crying from the heart as Mira did gets the child in touch with the caring, loving part of herself (Levin, 1988). It represents the birth of her true inner self—the self that cares about her. Being held while crying in the presence of a group of friends is one of the most healing, powerful, loving experiences any child can have, or any adult.

Session 16, the Last Session. As you read the excerpts from this session (Brody, 1997, pp. 235–240), put yourself in the place of the children having to say good-bye to this group and in the place of the Leader who has to provide them with what they need to say good-bye. Compare the changes you experienced in reading sessions 3, 14, and 16.

Selma: *[walks in with Jeanne]*

Vi: *[walks in carrying Mira]*

Mira: *[to Vi]* Pretend I'm your tiny little baby.

Leader: Vi has a little tiny baby. Don't wake the baby. *[looking at Jeanne]* Oh, my goodness. Looks like Jeanne is asleep, too. There are two sleeping girls with their Partners, and we've got one boy watching the girls sleeping. And here comes another Partner with a little one. *[Amos was absent.]*

Brenda: *[enters carrying Mona]*

Mira: *[sits up and starts rubbing her eyes, which are closed]*

Leader: Mira is starting to wake up a little bit. Everybody just be quiet with your Partner just a minute. Lean back on your Partner.

Mira: *[rubbing eyes and yawning, eyes still closed, moves into center]*

Leader: I think Mira is starting to wake up.

Mira: *[with eyes still closed, lifts her face up toward the Leader]*

Leader: And there's her little face. *[reaches out and touches her face]* OK, everybody, big folks, let's rock.

Mira: *[leans her face out toward James]*

James: *[reaches out and touches her face]*

Leader: How about Shawn?

Shawn: *[reaches over and gently touches her face]*

Mort: I'd like to touch her face.

Leader: Right over here, Mira.

Mira: *[leans her face toward Mort, with her eyes still closed]*

Mort: *[touches her upturned face]*

Brenda: I want to say "Hello" to her face. *[touching her face]*

Mira: *[sitting in center of circle; eyes closed, pretends to yawn, then moves over toward the Leader with her face upturned]*

Leader: You want some more. Big yawn here. *[Cups Mira's face in her hands]*

Group: *[laughs a little]*

Leader: Would anyone else like to have their face Helloed to?

Jeanne: *[touches Mira's face]*

Leader: And Mira's trying to say Hello to Jeanne and they've both got their eyes closed, and now she's patting her. And now let's see—I want to say "Hello" to Jeanne's foot, too. *[touches her foot]* And Mira's saying "Hello" to Mona, and Mona's saying "Hello" to Jeanne's foot over here. And Jeanne is looking to see who's saying "Hello" to her.

Comments. *The children provided the focus.* Led by Mira, the children provided the focus and the structure through this family play they had created: one girl (Jeanne) is asleep in her Partner's lap, Mira and Mona had asked their Partners to "carry them like a baby," and Mira said, "Pretend I'm *your* tiny baby." The play started when Mira came on stage (the center of the circle) and portrayed herself as the new baby in this family who are here to welcome her. The children got this image of her as the new baby and played the part of her family—all without words either from Mira (new babies don't talk) or the children. It was a play without words. In this role, Mira did invite the contact—but what was new, she loved receiving it and she couldn't get enough of it. Playing a role was also new for her (in Session 3, she did not have the basic experience of *being* a baby to role-play anything). Here she was aware that she was role-playing, and she loved doing it. In her play she was simply presenting herself as she is, what she needs—to be touched, seen, and loved. In other words she's ready to be a receiver and let people in instead of trying to control them as she did in Session 3.

The children and their Partners responded to Mira's invitation to see her and touch her by reaching over and gently touching her face. Everyone was very focused and present (even Mona). There was a loving quiet energy in the room— no yelling, screaming, or talking out of turn. After Mira completed her act twice, the focus of the group just naturally changed from one person receiving all the attention to everyone being touched and noticed. It became a family party. They had fun with each other. The children did this naturally without any direction from the Leader. Mira became a giver too. She even went over and touched Mona. This interaction between the members had such a nice flow and enjoyment and freedom—again nonverbal. In Session 3, the Leader provided this touching experience by doing it with them. Now the children can do it by themselves because they have an inner self.

The Leader followed the children. The Leader simply put into words what she saw the children doing ("I think Mira is starting to wake up") or guided them ("Right over here, Mira"). She also joined the family party ("I want to say 'Hello' to Jeanne's foot, too").

Summary. Instead of talking about this being their last time together these children prepared themselves for the termination and gave it meaning through the play created by Mira. In other words, they can represent experiences symbolically because they've had the experiences. For example, when a new baby comes into the family, the child already there has to move out of the nest and become a caretaker. That is exactly what Mira did in her play—first she was the new baby and then she became a family member. Through the play, she relived the experience of being touched, seen, and loved. Now she will remember it because she's the one that created it.

The Good-bye Part of Session 16. The Leader took charge of the good-bye ritual. This time it included more activities needed to say the final good-bye so that the children can leave feeling whole, happy, and competent—and have something to take home with them. The Leader took Polaroid pictures of each child-Partner pair, one for the child and one for the Partner. She invited the children to walk around and share their pictures with each other. Excerpts from the transcript:

Leader: *[to Mona]* Who would you like to show your picture of you and Brenda?
Mona: *[hides her picture]*
Mira: *[in her old baby-talk voice]* I'm not going to let anybody see mine.
Leader: Mira, may I see yours?
Mira: *[holds it up for the Leader to see]* Don't show it to Mona.
Leader: Thank you.
Mona: *[yelling at Mira, who was stealing a glance at hers]* Quit peeking, cheater.
Leader: Mona doesn't want to show hers right now. For one last time we're going to say Good-bye to our Partners.

James: *[interrupting]* We going to have snacks?

Leader: We are going to have snacks. One of the things I remember, James is your saying, "I want snacks." While you're eating your crackers, would anybody like to say the thing you liked the best out of the whole time?

Mira: *[raises her hand immediately]* Me! I liked it the best when we did our trick, Vi couldn't get me up! *[laughs]*

Group: *[laughs]*

Leader: You liked that. Who else?

James: I like my friends.

Leader: Are these all your friends? Can you say everybody's name?

James: Yes.

Later:

Leader: Instead of the cradling, we're going to do this—hold hands.

James: I want to cradle in the blanket!

Leader: That's OK. First, we're going to do this.

The leader told the story of how this group came together and asked the children to repeat each statement after her. She touched each child's nose and asked that child to name her Partner.

Leader: Before we go, James wanted to do something all you guys like to do. So we're going to swing James in the blanket. Anyone who wants a turn can have one.

Mira: I want a turn.

Leader: *[to children]* Put your pictures down and help swing James.

All the children had a turn. Each Partner picked up her child, put her in the blanket. The Partner and the Leader took the ends and swung the blanket while the others stood on the sides and helped in the swinging as they sang the good-bye song to the tune of "Goodnight Ladies": "Good-bye James. We're glad you came to play." Then Shawn lifted James up out of the blanket. After his turn, James said, "I want to help," and he joined the other children swinging the next child. That is the way Session 16 ended.

Comments. In the good-bye part of this session, the Leader took charge in two ways; by providing the structure, that is, activities she felt the children needed to feel good about the ending, and by honoring the request of the children. She provided space for the children to walk around and share their snapshots with each other. That invitation increased the physical space of the group and gave responsibility to the children. The Leader served as a go-between for Mira and Mona in their not wanting to share their pictures with each other by asking Mira to share her picture with her (which Mira did) and by saying to Mira, "Mona doesn't want to show hers right now." Thus both children felt seen and supported by the Leader.

As a substitute for the cradling at the end, the Leader wanted to end the session by having the group stand and all hold hands to say good-bye, but she was interrupted by James, "I want to cradle in the blanket." The Leader said yes to James but he would have to wait until later. In other words, the Leader did her version of the last good-bye and then the children did theirs. *The Leader:* Since the children now would be going back out into the world, she wanted the children to experience a more grown-up way of parting (they still would be touching via hands). *The children:* They wanted one last cradle time at the end because that would be an image that they could take home to remember whenever they needed to feel loved. In other words, they could just sit still and feel loved simply by remembering the cradling. The children had the last word.

As it turned out, the cradling-in-the-blanket was a perfect substitute for being cradled by a Partner, who still had some individual contact with the child when she put the child in and lifted the child out of the blanket. The child is being rocked by the whole group standing on each side looking at her and singing the good-bye song. A perfect ending! A total group experience that combined individual child-pair activity within a whole-group activity.

In Session 16, the children provided the focus and the structure—Mira for the beginning (the play) and James for the end (cradling in the blanket). A very different session from the first one, where the Leader had to do everything! In Session 16, the Leader met her goal. She provided the conditions that enabled the children to do what they needed to do. Every child, at her own level, was present, was a participant, and used the group to get her needs met.

The Children. The children could ask for what they needed because they had an inner self that made them aware of what that was—the need to be touched, seen, and loved.

Mira. In this session, Mira expressed her needs quietly without words (new for her) in the form of a drama in which she invited the others in the group to participate because she needed them to complete her picture of the arrival of a new baby in the family. They got the message and became part of her play—a symbolic creation. When the Leader asked the children at the end to say what they liked best, Mira immediately knew her answer. While laughing she said, "What I liked best was when we did our tricks, Vi couldn't get me up." That is, she had created a trick that her Partner could not do. This is an example of a child using the Circle Time to share something she did in her individual session with her Partner. Thus she ended the program having had fun (that she had created), with a feeling of joy and self-empowerment. This is the same child who screamed in Session 3, who sobbed in Session 14. She has become a child who can let herself feel whatever she feels because it come from the inside.

Mona. Mona showed her awareness of her need to be held when she asked her Partner to carry her to the Circle Time. This was a child who could not tolerate the cradling at all in Session 3. She was very present and relaxed during Mira's play. When she didn't want Mira to look at her picture, she said so. Nevertheless, she could not answer the question about what she'd liked best.

Jeanne. Jeanne also realized that she had a need to be held when she pretended to be asleep in her Partner's arms. Jeanne and Mira had fun sharing their pictures with each other. Like Mona, Jeanne could not answer the Leader's question.

James. James became more and more assertive in making his needs known—the need for food (he always asked for snacks as if they might be forgotten) and cradling. James and Mira followed the same course: both relived their baby place, after which both took a more grown-up place. After being cradled James asked to help cradle the others; after being touched, Mira became a toucher. James could answer the question as to what he liked best from the program—"I have friends and I know their names."

Theoretical Conceptualization

Developing the theory presented in this chapter, the organization of the DPT group play therapy is based on two premises.
   • *To be a participant in a DPT group play therapy requires that the child have at least the beginnings of an inner self.* This sense of who she is comes about through an attachment relationship with the mother or surrogate mother, who provides the child with the condition she needs to be able to relate and to communicate. That condition is caring touch, which is the first communication.
   To provide the child with this attachment relationship, the DPT group play therapy session is preceded by an individual session with her Partner. This provides continuity between the individual therapy and the group therapy. The child can share and practice what she has learned in the individual therapy in the larger world of the Circle Time. Thus the child brings to the Circle Time some

sense of who she is because the Partner chose her and the child has some sense of who her Partner is because her Partner has already communicated with her through touch.

• *The adult (Partner) needs to experience caring touch in order to be able to provide caring touch for the child.* To provide them with this experience, the Partners have two one-hour meetings with the Leader—one before and one after the children's sessions. This means that the Leader, in taking charge of the Circle Time, is not only aware of where the children are developmentally but also of where the Partners are developmentally. This information is needed to understand that the Circle Time presented in this chapter is only one part of a very intense, integrated structured play therapy program that includes individual and group therapy for the children and training for the adults (Brody, 1997).

Process of Group Play Therapy

The DPT process has already been illustrated in the transcripts. Nonetheless, it is worth looking at the stages in some detail.

Stage 1. In the beginning, the Leader took charge—not by telling the child what to do but rather by making physical contact with the child—touching the child to enable the child to experience her physical body, her aliveness, and the presence of the Leader. Then the Leader took her cues from the child's response to that touch. You saw the Leader do that in Session 3 all the time. The Leader provided two conditions that the children needed to develop an inner self—the touching to say hello and the cradling. The cradling and the touching are not forced on the child but are offered over and over, trying to find a way that the child can accept. Some children really enjoy the touching when it is combined with some movement or some game when they could not tolerate the cradling at first. In the first stage, the children follow the Leader (a game you saw the Leader play in Session 3) because the children don't know what to do. In Stage 1, the children learn to relax, to enjoy the cradling, to receive, to be touched.

Stage 2. When the children get an inner self, they show a marked change. They plan the hour because they know what they want or they have some idea. The Leader stands back and lets the child take responsibility for her action. The Leader follows the child. This is a very creative and exciting period for both the child and the Leader. The child builds her own self-esteem through the activities she creates. The Leader, in turn, has more freedom to be creative and supportive in her responses to the child (for example, the Leader's response to Mira and Mona regarding their pictures). In Stage 2, the children learn to give, to touch, to relate, to ask for what they need, to define themselves through play.

Stage 3. The termination is the time the child becomes aware that she feels, and she gives form to those feelings. It is the time the child gives form to the new self she has become so that she can take that new self with her with awareness. You saw the children do that in Session 16. In Stage 3, the child knows who she is. If the DPT is done well, both the children and the Leader end this program with a sense of pleasure and accomplishment.

Applications

The Developmental Play Therapy approach (which includes the Circle Time group time) has been found to be very effective in the following groups or agencies:

• *The public schools.* School counselors run DPT groups within the school day using teachers, psychology students, parents, and senior citizens as adult Partners. Speech and hearing departments, pre-K schoolteachers, and pre-K therapeutic day care centers are using DPT. The effectiveness of the DPT approach with elementary grade school children was demonstrated in a study under a grant from the U.S. Office of Education in 1974. In 1995, I was asked to train pre-K teachers in the Orlando public schools because the teachers were reporting that they had not seen young children like this before.

• *Parent groups.* I ran one parent group in the Manatee County Schools in Florida. The parents were the Partners for the children. They met one evening a week. It included some fathers—a group of ten parent-child pairs. Both the children and the parents loved it. When the parents chose the child they wanted to play with, some parents chose their own child and some chose other parents' children. Those who chose a child other than their own had the best time. This was true for the child also.

• *Day-care treatment centers.* See the study described in my book (Brody, 1997).

• *Headstart.* I trained Headstart staffs in Chicago, Pinellas, and Manatee Counties in Florida.

Many groups of children benefit from the DPT program:

1. All attachment-problem children of all ages—basic for them.
2. Young children born of alcoholic and cocaine-addicted mothers.
3. Sexually and physically abused children. (These children long for caring touch by someone who knows how.)
4. Hyperactive young ADHD children. These children—like Mira—are hyperactive because they are not in their bodies. They are not grounded. *They don't need Ritalin. They need the kind of touching illustrated in this report.* You saw its effect on Mira (Brody, 1997).

Conclusion

Through the transcripts and comments, I hope you were able to experience this DPT Play Group Therapy—how the Leader took charge in a way that enabled the children to relate to each other and to the Leader, first through touch and second through symbolic play. The complete story of the change in Mira, an ADHD child, is told in Chapter 5 of my book (Brody, 1997).

References

Brody, V. A. (1997). *The dialogue of touch: Developmental play therapy.* Northvale, NJ: Aronson.

Levin, D. M. (1988). *The opening of vision.* New York: Routledge.

Montagu, A. (1986). *Touching: The human significance of the skin* (3rd ed.). New York: Harper-Collins.

CHAPTER NINE

GROUP PLAY THERAPY FROM A GESTALT THERAPY PERSPECTIVE

Violet Oaklander

Gestalt therapy, originally developed by Frederick and Laura Perls, has at its base principles from psychoanalytic theory, gestalt psychology, humanistic theories, as well as aspects of phenomenology, existentialism, and Reichian body therapy. From these roots a large body of theoretical concepts and principles has developed underlying the practice of Gestalt therapy.

Theoretical Background

Basically, Gestalt therapy is a phenomenological, process-oriented therapy concerned with healthy functioning of the organism: senses, body, emotions, and intellect (Latner, 1986; Perls, 1969; Perls, Hefferline, & Goodman, 1994). This chapter will discuss some theoretical concepts that are particularly pertinent to group work with children.

The I/Thou Relationship

The I/Thou relationship, derived from the philosophical writing of Martin Buber (1958), is the essential basis for therapeutic interaction between the therapist and the child. Some of the pertinent fundamental principles of this kind of relationship are highly significant in work with children. The therapist is cognizant of the fact that she, despite differences in age, experience, education, is not superior to the client; both are equally entitled. The therapist has a responsibility to bring herself fully to the encounter, genuinely and congruently.

The therapist meets the child with acceptance and honor, regardless of how the child presents himself while she, at the same time, is cognizant of the wider potential of the child. The therapist, further, honors her own limits, boundaries, and feelings and engages with the child authentically without manipulation or role-playing. Though the therapist may have goals and plans, there are no ex-pectations—each session is an existential experience. The therapist creates an en-vironment of safety and never pushes the child beyond his capabilities or consent. The relationship itself is therapeutic; often it provides an experience for the child that is new and unique.

Contact

Contact involves the ability to bring oneself fully into an encounter whether it be with the therapist, teachers, other children, books. Healthy contact involves the use of the senses (looking, listening, touching, tasting, smelling), awareness of and appropriate use of aspects of the body, the ability to express emotions healthfully, and the use of the intellect in its various forms, as learning, expressing ideas, thoughts, curiosities, wants, needs, resentments, and so forth.

When any of these modalities are inhibited, restricted, cut off, or blocked in some way, good contact suffers. Fragmentation, rather than integration, occurs. Healthy contact involves a feeling of security with oneself, a fearlessness of stand-ing alone. "What distinguishes contact from togetherness or joining is that con-tact occurs at a boundary where a sense of separateness is maintained so that union does not threaten to overwhelm the person" (Polster & Polster, 1973).

Contact-Boundary Disturbances

We make contact with others from a place beyond ourselves, from the edge of our-selves—the boundary of the self. "The contact boundary is the point at which one experiences the 'me' in relation to that which is not 'me' and through this con-tact, both are more clearly experienced" (Polster & Polster, 1973). If the self is weak and undefined, the boundary is fuzzy and contact suffers. As the child strug-gles to grow up, survive, and cope with life, he may manifest a variety of inap-propriate behaviors and symptoms that serve to avoid contact and protect the self. He does not have the inner support, cognitive ability, or emotional maturity to di-rectly express deep feelings, particularly anger. Some contact-boundary distur-bances commonly seen with children involve *projection*—projecting feelings or blame onto others; *deflection*—turning away from that which is uncomfortable, yet needing to hit and kick to release the energy of anger or other deep feelings; *retroflection*—pulling the energy inward, causing a variety of physical ailments; and *confluence*—desperately needing approval to feel some segment of self and blending into the feelings and beliefs of others. The phenomenon of introjection is of great significance in the development and behavior of children. Since the young child is cognitively unable to discriminate both overt and covert messages about himself, he believes everything he hears or imagines he hears and defines himself in this way. He develops a belief system about who he is and how he is supposed to be in the world in order to ensure approval and love and avoid rejection and abandonment. These introjects lurk inside the individual even into adulthood. How the child copes with these faulty messages often determines his process well into adulthood.

These symptoms and behaviors, the very ones that bring children into therapy, are actually the organism's way of attempting to achieve homeostasis and balance, albeit unsuccessfully. The quest for equilibrium is unrelenting, but the child has little awareness of cause and effect in his attempts to cope, get his needs met, and protect himself. The child has a powerful thrust for life and growth and will do anything he can to grow up. Paradoxically, in the service of this quest, he will restrict, inhibit, and block aspects of the self. He will desensitize himself, restrict his body, block his emotions, and inhibit his intellect. The consequence of this process is an increased diminishing of the self and impairment of his contact abilities.

Resistance

Inappropriate behaviors are often viewed as resistance. Most children will be resistant—self-protecting—to a degree. Resistance is actually a healthy response and those who appear to have none are children who have such a fragile self that they are unable to pause and consider. Good contact involves some level of resistance—it is difficult to have good contact with someone who does not have a clear boundary. Just as having no resistance affects contact skills, having a high degree of resistance makes achieving satisfying contact impossible. The resistance must be flexible. The therapist expects some resistance and recognizes it as the child's ally. She is respectful of the resistance. As the child begins to feel safe in the sessions, he will soften and move through it for a time. However, when he has experienced or divulged as much as he can handle, as much as he has inside support for, the resistance will come up again. In this way, resistance surfaces over and over again and must be honored each time. Often it is the child's signal that he has reached his limit of capability at this time.

Resistance can be viewed as a manifestation of energy, as well as an indication of the contact level of the child. When the energy fades and the contact shifts, it is a manifestation of resistance. Some children indicate the resistance in passive ways, that is, they will ignore, act distracted or appear not to listen. The child who can say, "I don't want to go any further with this" needs reinforcement for such a direct, contactful statement.

Awareness and Experience

Guiding the client toward awareness of one's process—what I do and how I do it—is an important aspect of Gestalt therapy. A client who achieves awareness of those specific behaviors that have led to difficulties can then choose to experiment with new, more satisfying ways of being. Awareness comes with allowing the self to engage in these behaviors with full knowledge and acceptance—thus leading, paradoxically, to new choices and change. Children have little cognitive understanding and emotional maturity to follow this approach. Experience plays a key role in therapeutic work with children. Presented with varied experiences and experiments, the child may become more aware of himself: who he is, what he feels, what he likes and doesn't like, what he needs, what he wants, what he does, and how he does it—he finds that he has choices he can make—choices for expression, getting needs met, and exploring new behaviors (Oaklander, 1988). The self becomes stronger as he defines himself. This kind of awareness is not necessarily articulated; it becomes a visceral experience. Experience can be powerful—once a child experiences himself in a new way, integration of this aspect of the self takes place.

The healthy, uninterrupted development of a child's organism—senses, body, emotions, and intellect—is the underlying basis for the child's sense of self, and a strong sense of self leads to good contact with the environment and the people in it. As each need surfaces and is met without hindrance, not only homeostasis and balance but new levels of growth and development are achieved (Oaklander, 1988).

Purpose

A therapy group has the advantage of being a small, insulated world in which present behavior can be experienced and new behaviors tried out. The child's way of being in the group, and how that behavior affects others positively or negatively, becomes clearly evident. The group becomes a safe laboratory for experimenting with new behaviors through the support and guidance of the therapist.

Example 1

Jimmy, age nine, was extremely disruptive in group meetings. Often group time was spent focusing on his unacceptable behavior, with the group members offering varied suggestions to no avail. The therapist began to look at what actually took place: Jimmy received all the attention he could muster—actually, it seemed, getting exactly what he wanted and needed (attention) regardless of the affect on the group.

At the next meeting the therapist presented a scenario to be acted out by Jimmy and the group. She asked Jimmy to imagine that he was a new baby, perhaps the baby Jesus (it was close to Christmas), and the rest of the group would be all the people who brought gifts to the baby. So with much giggling Jimmy lay on a mat spread out for him. The therapist modeled bringing him an imaginary gift talking with great emotion about what a beautiful baby this was and how fortunate we were that he was born. The other children followed suit, and many gifts were presented to the baby with much ooing and ahhing over this baby. Jimmy lay quiet with a big smile on his face during this time. Finally the group was called together, and the therapist asked Jimmy to report how he liked our gifts and attention. He said he loved it, and the truth of this was evident from his smiling face and calm demeanor. He commented that he felt as if he were receiving actual gifts. The therapist wondered out loud if Jimmy felt he received much attention in his life. Jimmy spoke with deep feeling about this lack, eliciting thoughtful comments from the other children about their own experiences with attention. (In this type of discussion the children are encouraged to report their own experience and discouraged from any advice giving.)

Following this session, the therapist made sure that she smiled and spoke to Jimmy as soon as he came into the room, as did the other children. Jimmy no longer created a disturbance at the group meetings. This kind of acting-out scenario allowed Jimmy to experience exaggerated positive attention. Though this was a play situation, the experience was quite real to him. Feeling safe and loved, Jimmy could talk about the polarity represented in his real life. Expressing his feelings and learning how to ask for what he needed in a direct manner were subsequent themes in the sessions. Though Jimmy's situation was somewhat extreme, all the children could identify and benefit from the activity. An important aspect in the sessions is the modeling of the therapist. When the therapist treats a child with honor and respect, that child responds in kind and the others in the group begin to follow suit.

The group is an ideal setting for children to enhance their contact skills. Contact skills, or contact functions, include the use of all the senses—how we look, listen, touch, smell, and taste; the body—how we move in the environment, the awareness and expression of emotions in appropriate ways; and the use of the intellect—through language to express thoughts, ideas, opinions, and curiosities. Poor contact skills are an indication of a poor sense of self leading to poor social skills. It is natural—as well as being an important developmental task—for children to seek out other children. The group provides an arena for those who have social difficulties to discover and work through whatever is blocking the natural process of connecting and relating well with others. One's process in a group may be much different in a one-to-one therapy setting. When the behavior becomes foreground, we can examine it from all sides, play with it, change it.

Example 2

The therapist brought in a variety of small games—jacks, pick-up sticks, dominoes, Blockhead, Connect 4—to a therapy group of eight children, ages eleven and twelve. The children were paired off and each pair was instructed to choose a game. (This task in itself was interesting to observe.) A kitchen timer was set for ten minutes. At the end of the time the group was asked to switch partners as well as games. All the games and partners were rotated. At the end of this time, the group talked about the experience.

Some comments:

"This is the first time I ever played jacks with a boy. I had to teach him how to do it. It was great!"

"And I was the first boy who probably ever played jacks."

"I lost and felt bad and was glad when the timer rang."

"Chris cheated, but stopped when I told him I didn't like it."

"He didn't cheat at all with me. He was really cooperative."

The general tone of the children was gentle and tolerant. An air of contentment and calmness permeated the room during and after the game period. There was a lot of noise, the kind of noise one hears when people talk with each other (Oaklander, 1988).

Example 3

Projections often interfere with the child's ability to relate to other children.

Phillip: I don't like the way Allen's looking at me!
Therapist: What do you imagine he is saying to you with that look?

Phillip: He's saying, "You're stupid!"

Therapist: Pretend this monkey puppet is you and you are Allen and say those words to yourself. *[therapist holds puppet in her hand.]*

Phillip: *[to puppet]* You're stupid!

Therapist: Phillip, do you have a voice inside of you that says this to yourself sometimes?

Phillip: Yeah!

Children need to learn that seeing a facial grimace is not the same as knowing the thoughts behind it. The other child might have a stomachache. Of course, projections are most active with children who have a low self-image and fuzzy boundary.

Many activities to strengthen the self are effective in group settings, and actually are more fun and interesting to do with other children. Games involving the use of the eyes, such as I Spy (a UNICEF game) or working through the *Where's Waldo* books; games involving listening, such as Sound Safari; and games involving smelling, tasting, and touching are productive and pleasurable.

Example 4

Each member of a group was given an orange. They all examined their own oranges thoroughly, then put them back in the pile—and could find their own oranges again easily. The children, along with the therapist, began to peel the oranges and carefully examine the skin, smelling it and tasting it. Next the white part was peeled, smelled, and tasted. After noticing and feeling the glistening layer, the oranges were broken into segments and tasted. Each child then traded segments with other children. They noticed that some were sweeter, some tarter, some juicier, and so forth. And all were delicious (Brown, 1990). This exercise has been used with many different groups of all ages. Comment of a twelve-year-old girl to the therapist: "I can never eat any fruit anymore without thinking of that orange exercise we did!" This kind of exercise allows children to freely use all of their senses, a necessary prerequisite to owning the self.

Example 5

Often, sensory-type experiences encourage good social conversation in groups. Clay and finger painting are particularly good for this purpose.

A group of children in a special class for severely emotionally disturbed children were given old cafeteria trays on which were dabs of finger paint. Twelve boys, ages eleven to thirteen, made up this group. Their reaction to seeing the finger paint was, predictably enough, "What is this baby stuff?!" Rather than sitting at desks, the therapist felt the boys needed to face each other to promote communication and perhaps find some way to relate other than hitting, punching, kicking, and name calling. Tables were set up so that there were six boys on each side facing each other. The boys were asked to finger paint in the trays and when ready, the therapist would make a print of each painting by spreading paper over the painting, pressing down, and lifting it off. Each boy finished the first painting quickly and was delighted with the results.

Many of these children had difficulty with both small and large muscle coordination and usually shied away from drawing and brush painting. Finger painting is soothing and flowing, trial designs and figures can be made and quickly smoothed over, and success is guaranteed. During the activity the boys began to converse with each other, first about their designs and then about other things. One boy made something that looked like a bird, and the conversation began to focus on flying and airplanes. Many topics were discussed calmly and amicably. Yes, there was noise—but it was the noise of laughter, happiness, and good talking. Not once did anyone hit, kick, or say anything abusive. Contentment permeated the whole group (including the therapist). These children often requested this finger painting experience again, and sometimes the therapist was able to elicit stories about their designs, promoting self-awareness and taking the experience into wider and deeper realms. Most of these boys had not had the experience of making a friend, or, for that matter, of being treated or treating others respectfully, so the experience was particularly useful to them and they recognized it as such. The atmosphere during the finger paint sessions generalized to the rest of the class time, and although there was occasional acting-out behavior, the general milieu was one of respect and friendship.

Certain variables are present in this kind of experience. The therapist has set up clear limits and boundaries, though she is at all times respectful of each child. The children are dealing with a medium that they soon discover can only lead to success. (The block prints were astounding.) They can experiment and explore color and design. (They quickly discover that red, yellow, and blue make a murky brown.) There is a soothing quality to the kinesthetic and tactile motions. The self is strengthened and good contact takes place. They find that they *like* this kind of contact.

Example 6

A common theme among children in therapy, and probably outside of therapy, is the feeling of being different. The child struggles to establish the self and moves back and forth from confluence to isolation. Confluence involves getting a sense of self from someone else—he must be like everyone else since he does not have a sense of who he is. Since healthy contact involves having a good sense of self, feeling enough support to be able to meet someone without losing the self, the disturbed child must often retreat to a very lonely place to perhaps find something of a self. The group is an ideal setting for helping children maintain their own integrity while relating to others. The group is a safe microcosm of the outside world, and with the guidance of the therapist, and clear boundaries, the child can indeed find himself among others.

A group of children, all with fathers in an alcoholic treatment center, were asked to share their dreams. This group ranged in age from eight to sixteen and included several sets of siblings. At the time in question, this unorthodox group had been meeting for most of a year, and the members were quite comfortable with each other in spite of the age differences. They had discovered that they shared many common experiences. One girl, age twelve, described a dream in which she is in a car driven by her father going down a steep hill. At the bottom of the hill there is a lake. The car is going very fast and she is screaming at her father to slow down. She fears the car will go right into the lake. Her father ignores her, and just as the car is about to take its plunge, she wakes up. The other children listened intently to this dream. As soon as she stopped speaking, an eight-year-old boy said, "I have a road in my life just like that."

Example 7

Discovering that other children have similar thoughts, concerns, worries, fears, ideas, wonders, as well as experiences, is a revelation to most children. The more they feel this linkage, the more support they appear to feel. This outside support strengthens their inner support and a stronger self develops. Paradoxically, they are then more willing and able to present those parts of themselves that are different to the group.

Several young adolescent boys were given clay and asked to make something with their eyes closed. The group had been meeting weekly for about two months and Joe had not participated in any of the activities. He was not disruptive and just sat quietly, appearing to listen and watch. The therapist directed the children to complete their pieces with their eyes open and each was asked to become the piece and describe themselves.

> *Joe:* I didn't make anything.
> *Therapist:* Joe, you have something there so just describe it.
> *Joe:* *[staring at his clay]* It's just a lump of nothing. *[looking up at the therapist]* And that's what I am! A lump of nothing!
> *Therapist:* How do you feel right now in this group with all of us?

Joe: I feel like a lump of nothing.

Therapist: I think you're saying that you feel like you're not worth much.

Joe: That's right. I'm not.

Therapist: Joe, I feel very appreciative of you for sharing how you feel with us. It shows that maybe you trust us a little. Thank you.

Joe: [*slight smile*] That's OK.

What is evident here is Joe's low self-esteem, which he openly shared with the group. In doing so, in telling about his existence in life as he perceives it, he made a giant step toward renewed self-hood. Although the therapist was tempted to tell Joe all about his good points, that would have invalidated his feeling at this moment. The therapist must respectfully accept Joe's self-perception so that he can begin to accept himself. Later she overheard one of the boys telling Joe how he used to feel the same way a lot, and sometimes still does, but not so much anymore.

Group Process

A group, though made up of individual children, has a distinctive life of its own. Every group seems to follow more or less the same pattern. The children in the groups described in this chapter generally have had some experience with the therapist, and a relationship with her has been established. However, the children do not know each other and come into the group usually feeling very much alone. In the beginning the child is self-conscious and may tend to manifest a variety of negative behaviors to cover up his anxieties. The therapist makes use of this time to help the children feel safe and respected and to get to know each other through noninvasive, nonthreatening activities. Limits and boundaries are made clear as needed.

After about four to six weeks with a group that meets weekly, the group begins to gel; children feel comfortable in the setting, and anxieties about sharing themselves below that superficial veneer drop away. There is generally a feeling of companionship with each other and a knowledge that the others will provide support and understanding when needed. Roles emerge: one child becomes the leader, another appears to act out for everyone, one is labeled as the smart one, another the clown, and so on. The therapist, as these roles become evident, can bring them into the awareness of the group through various techniques. And sometimes the children themselves invent ideas for experimenting with roles.

Example 8

A group of eight boys and girls, ages eleven and twelve, had been meeting together weekly for several months. They knew each other quite well. Susan clearly emerged as the leader. The therapist had presented an exercise to promote direct communication called "I like, I don't like." Each child had a turn to make statements to everyone else. One member said to Susan, "I don't like it that you always decide what we should do." At the end of the exercise the discussion was open for reaction. Susan said, "I know what we should do. Let's have each person be the therapist for one meeting and decide everything." The children liked Susan's idea—actually she had many good ones. So each week for a while a child decided whether we should draw pictures relating to a theme of some sort, use puppets or clay, have a discussion about something, or engage in another activity. The child who was "therapist" not only decided what the group would do but modeled the therapist amazingly accurately. All had a turn to be leader, often finding a side of themselves that had never before been presented openly.

Group Structure

The author has experimented with a variety of group sizes, from pairs to groups of twelve. Generally six or eight children who are over eight years old is a good size, and three to six children who are under eight. It is important to have a cotherapist present in the group if at all possible, since there may be times when a child must have individual attention. The group, however, is an ideal setting for children who need connection with other children.

Some groups can be time-limited rather than ongoing. This therapist is of the belief that ongoing groups for children with similar experience, as for those who have suffered child abuse or are victims of divorce, tend to label these children and isolate them from other children. It is nonetheless sometimes worth establishing such a group; the children described in example 6, who had fathers in alcoholic treatment, were quite successful as a group even though the grouping did tend to set these children apart.

The groups, which meet for one and a half to two hours depending on the ages of the children, are fairly structured. Each group begins with "rounds"—a time when each child reports anything they choose to share about their week. This in itself becomes a lesson in listening. In the beginning children are reluctant to say much, but as the weeks go by it becomes necessary to set a time limit for each child. There can be no discussion or questions (except for occasional clarification)—the child has the floor. The therapists participate as well. Passing around a "talking stick" is helpful. Some children cannot help making remarks, poking others, wiggling, and so forth. As long as these noises are in the background and the child speaking is not disturbed, they are ignored by the therapist. It appears that children can tolerate much more commotion than adults can. However, if the hubbub becomes disruptive and disturbing, the therapist calls a halt and the matter is discussed with the group. In effect, this becomes the group's business for a portion of the session. Toward the end of the meeting the children clean up and take their seats once more. This is a time for closure; everyone is given the opportunity to say anything they would like to say to the therapist or anyone else in the room, to critique the activity, to mention something they particularly liked during the time, or something that annoyed them. The therapist must pace the group session to allow time for cleanup and closure.

Example 9

At the closing time eleven-year-old Carrie, with much hesitation and caution, told Tommy, "I didn't like it that you always tried to sit next to me today, and when you did, it was too close and I didn't like it." The therapist reinforced Carrie's effort to tell Tommy about her discomfort. She said, "Tommy, I'm glad you are listening to Carrie; what she is saying is very important to her." At the next meeting's closure Carrie said, "Tommy, I really appreciate that you didn't try to sit next to me all the time, and when you did, you weren't too close." Tommy smiled as if he had received a great gift.

Group Content

The content of the group varies, of course, according to the age range and the specific needs of each child. Unless the purpose is to observe free play, the group is structured. It begins with rounds and ends with closure. In between the therapist plans the experience for the meeting. Although the therapist has goals and plans, they can be discarded at any time. Sometimes something emerges from the rounds that needs attention; sometimes the children make an alternative decision. Often the session evolves from a prior session.

The activities are varied and generally enjoyable. Basically they facilitate expression of feelings, definition and strengthening of self, and experiences with healthier aspects of the self. Many projective techniques are used, such as drawings, clay, collage, sandtray scenes, puppetry, music, body movement, creative dramatics, metaphorical stories, fantasy, and imagery. Often themes of relevance to the children are presented, such as loneliness, teasing, rejection, embarrassment, loss, divorce, and so forth. These themes often emerge during group sessions, are suggested by the children, or are presented by the therapist. Many games are used as well as projective tests as therapeutic vehicles. At one session the children may draw their safe place and share their efforts with each other. The therapist may at times focus on one particular child's drawing. The children rarely make fun of anyone's drawing—the therapist's attitude of respect for each effort sets the tone.

An important theme in almost every group is anger. Children may be asked to draw something that makes them angry, or make a figure out of clay representing someone they are mad at, or play a variety of percussion instruments representing their feelings, or put on a puppet show for the others depicting an angry scene, and much more. Gaining skills for expressing angry feelings safely and appropriately is an important aspect of these activities.

Example 10

The video camera is a wonderful tool to use with many children.

Sam, age fourteen, has a friend his parents do not approve of. Recently Sam invited a boy into his house, ignoring his parents' rule of not having friends in the house when they weren't at home. As Sam stood by helplessly, the boy went into the parents' bedroom and threw things around as he examined everything. Sam had been working hard to feel a stronger sense of self and stand up for himself; however, he totally capitulated with this boy. Since he was in great trouble with his parents over this incident, the therapist made it the central theme of the group session. She suggested that the group act out the event in front of the video camera.

Sam selected someone to play the part of the unruly boy, and with the camera rolling they proceeded to act out the event. The therapist encouraged exaggeration in order to make the situation more obvious. With great energy, the "bad" boy knocked on the door, entered the house, and proceeded to trash the place, describing loudly what he was doing. Sam meekly stood by trying to protest. When this scene ended, I suggested they try another one in which Sam would act in an opposite way. In this scene Sam loudly admonished the other boy, forcing him to leave the house. At the suggestion of one of the group members, a third scene showed Sam's mother (the therapist was recruited for this role since all the members of the group were boys) returning home and showing that she is thrilled and proud that Sam has obeyed the rules. The group immediately viewed the whole enactment on the monitor to much laughter. Sam announced he knew that he could be assertive with that boy if it happened again, and, in fact, wondered why he had even befriended him at all.

Conclusion

Working with groups is a gratifying, effective way to work with children. The group lends itself to the development of social skills, a feeling of belonging and acceptance, a place to express heretofore unexpressed feelings, and a place to experiment with new behaviors. A successful group is one in which each child feels safe to be vulnerable. Group sessions need to be enjoyable for the children, regardless of the subject matter. In fact the enjoyment and nurturing that children feel in a group actually encourage delving into painful places. As each child feels free to reveal his emotions, thoughts, opinions, and ideas, he knows that he will find support from and connection with the therapist and the other children. In this way each child makes discoveries about himself that lead to increased self-support and healthy contact in and out of the group.

References

Brown, G. (1990). *Human teaching for human learning.* New York: Gestalt Journal Press.

Buber, M. (1958). *I and thou.* New York: Scribner.

Latner, J. (1986). *The Gestalt therapy book.* New York: Gestalt Journal Press.

Oaklander, V. (1988). *Windows to our children.* New York: Gestalt Journal Press.

Perls, F. (1969). *Ego, hunger and aggression.* New York: Vintage Books.

Perls, F., Hefferline, R., & Goodman, P. (1994). *Gestalt therapy.* New York: Gestalt Journal Press.

Polster, E., & Polster, M. (1973). *Gestalt therapy integrated.* New York: Brunner/Mazel.

PART THREE

GROUP PLAY THERAPY
ISSUES AND TECHNIQUES

CHAPTER TEN

ART IN GROUP PLAY THERAPY

Linda Chapman and Valerie Appleton

Art media such as paper, crayons, markers, paint, and modeling clay are considered standard playroom supplies, and are normally employed by clinicians in individual play therapy sessions. The introduction of art media in an active group play therapy session is often a challenge for clinicians, but group art experiences can be enjoyable and valuable with careful consideration and planning.

The uses of art with groups have been documented by numerous authors (Horowitz, 1970; Landgarten, 1981; Liebmann, 1986; Oster & Gould, 1987; Rhyne, 1971; Riley, 1996; Vogt & Vogt, 1983; Wadeson, 1980). Specifically, there are references to art in groups with children (Bender, 1952; Crawford, 1962; Kramer, 1958, 1971, 1972; Rubin, 1978), specific references for art in groups with adolescents (Raymer & McIntyre, 1987; Schneider, Ostroff, & Legow, 1990), in school settings (Davis, 1969; Lowenfeld, 1971), in hospital settings (Allen, 1983; Appleton, 1993; Chapman, 1993; Prager, 1995), with sexually abused clients (Anderson, 1995; Haygood, 1991), and with families (Harvey, 1990).

Other authors have written about the use of the arts in group play therapy (Fryrear & Stephens, 1988; Klorer, 1995; Leavitt, Morrison, Gardner, & Gallagher, 1996; Lowenfeld, 1971; Nickerson, 1973, 1983; O'Doherty, 1989; Schiffer, 1969). Furthermore, the ways art can help bridge across cultures is an exciting new direction in the applied uses of art for groups (Appleton, in press; Hiscox, 1993).

This chapter is designed to provide the play therapist with knowledge and skills to use art media in a group play therapy setting. Art in group play therapy will be viewed through two lenses in this chapter; as an approach to work with hospitalized children, and as a method of communication across cultural differences between group members and between clients and play therapists. Particular emphasis will be placed on the unique issues that must be considered in planning, facilitating, and ending group art experiences. The goal is for this practical information to be used by play therapists to provide safe, enjoyable, and enlivening experiences for their clients. It is further hoped that play therapists will explore art materials to learn about their own art expression and its relationship to the artwork of their child clients.

Definition of Terms

It is helpful to begin a discussion of this type by establishing a common vocabulary. This chapter uses terms as follows:

Art media: Any art materials used for the art therapy process, including graphic media (pastels, felt pens, crayons, pencils), painting media (watercolor, oils, acrylics, tempera), and sculptural media (clay, collage and glue, wood, metal, found natural objects such as leaves).

Art media continuum: Art materials form a continuum ranging from those that are easy to control (pencils, crayons, felt pens) to those that are less easily controlled (watercolor, finger paint, wet clay).

Impromptu art making: Art activities or themes that are suggested by the therapist, such as "draw a house" or "draw a picture of your family doing something."

Product: The finished artwork.

Spontaneous art making: Art activities in which themes are not suggested by the therapist. The client works spontaneously to create the art product.

Structured group experience: A group experience that involves a specific directive and limited materials, with clear limits and boundaries related to the art experience.

Unstructured group experience: A group experience that allows media and activity choices and has loose limits and boundaries associated with the art experience and processing of the image.

Initial Considerations

As in any group, one must consider the members and goals for an art therapy group, as well as the selection and uses of interventions and materials. The members of a children's group should have similar developmental levels, presenting issues, and abilities to function in a group setting. Other considerations in forming a therapeutic group might include each child's level of sophistication, balance of males and females, racial diversity, and the physical, emotional, and social issues to be addressed.

To develop an effective group art session, the art materials and interventions require special consideration. Attention must be given to any physical limitations that may prohibit participation in art activities, such as allergies, physical disabilities, or phobias. The assessment of the level of ego function and responses to various art media can be accomplished during one or two individual sessions involving experimentation with various art media. Since the knowledge of a given medium, its properties and impact, is so critical, the play therapist must consider his or her own skills and abilities. Children often require technical assistance when creating art. The therapist's lack of ability to provide help with the mechanics of art making can hinder the child's experience, self-esteem, and trust of the therapist. Further, to ensure therapeutic progress, a reasonable staff-to-child ratio is also essential when working with art media. This is particularly true when working with highly impulsive or behavior-disordered children who might have special difficulty using unstructured and hard-to-control art materials. A further discussion of the specific properties of art materials and their impact on children is presented in the subsequent sections on media and case studies.

Along with a consideration of the art media, the physical space must be considered. To make art, children must have a safe and comfortable working situation. In the room where art materials are stored, some children can safely and comfortably explore media options and make choices while other children may be overwhelmed and overstimulated by access to closets and drawers. Distractibility factors such as windows and hallways or potential hazards such as kilns or saws can be highly stressful to some children. Self-hurtful children must be monitored at all times, and all art media must be assessed for the potential for causing harm. Kite strings and tails, hard ceramic sculpture, clay and woodworking tools, and ingestible items may not be appropriate for some populations. The play therapist must evaluate the needs of each child when selecting and using art media for the group.

Goals are critical to consider when using art to assist the progress and development of therapeutic groups. The goals may vary widely according to the needs of different populations. For example, in crisis intervention or disaster work art projects may be done with very little group cohesiveness. In such groups, art may provide early opportunities to calm and stabilize overwrought children through facilitating expression of feelings and fantasies associated with the experience. Further, the artwork and art-making processes provide a preliminary assessment of the children's levels of coping and needs for future counseling. On the other hand, when used as a part of long-term therapy with consistent group members and similar histories, the goals for the art processes may be to build a sense of cohesion and trust. A long-term goal for an art group with children who are victims of abuse or multiple transitions and losses would be to develop trust through projects designed to facilitate working together and relying on others. Over time, a loss group might work to build trust by creating a joint mural that is displayed for family and friends. Overall, art making offers a unique opportunity to groups that can foster the broader group goals of socialization through activity that is enjoyable and relaxing.

Structured or Unstructured Groups

In planning to include an art experience in group play, one must first decide whether the art making will be a structured or unstructured experience (Rubin, 1978; Liebmann, 1986). A structured group experience involves a specific directive for the entire group, limited access to materials, and clear limits and boundaries related to the art experience. Structured groups often have consistent time, meeting space, and group members. An unstructured group experience provides the children the opportunity to select their own directive for the experience; it allows media choices and has loose limits and boundaries associated with the art experience and processing of the image. Unstructured group experiences may have fluctuations in time, meeting space, and group members.

Art Media

An understanding of the properties of art media is essential if they are to be used therapeutically. The play therapist must experiment with media to learn about the properties of different media, to learn to mix colors, and to understand the process of sculpting with various materials. Similarly, the therapist will discover the various applications and maintenance of art materials. Most important, the play therapist will observe the various physical and emotional impacts of the art materials explored. When these properties are understood, art media can have tremendous therapeutic power. When misunderstood or used indifferently, art media have the potential for creating more suffering. The impact of misunderstood media can be countertherapeutic and may result in sequelae such as increased disorganization and fragmentation.

Various media have different psychological effects on the art maker. To map these effects, art media may be seen on a continuum from those that are resistant and more easily controlled, such as pencils, to those that are more fluid and less easy to control, such as watercolors. Along this continuum, the physical properties of art media can be observed to arouse varying degrees of freedom, emotion, and ego defense in the person using them. For example, structured media such as pencils and erasers, colored pencils, wood and glue, and collage are restrictive and provide physical limits or boundaries of the image being created. These materials are easily controllable and require less tolerance for frustration. They are viewed as offering ego support, tending to reduce impulsive behaviors, and inviting control through sublimation.

In contrast, the use of unstructured media is very fluid and regressive, and there is an inability to define or control the edges or boundaries of the image. Unstructured media may include watercolors, finger paints, or clay with water. These media may be satisfying to use but will facilitate access to deeper unconscious content and must be selected and used carefully with children with poor sense of ego boundaries or impulse control. Along these lines, media that provoke aggressive responses—wood and nails, splatter painting, torn paper collage—can elicit angry feelings. Used with careful intention these provocative art media can provide a vehicle to sublimate aggression while providing a creative and productive alternative to poorly directed anger or rage.

Markers, pastels, and paint with brushes are familiar to most children and are typically used to facilitate expression. These expressive media allow most children a moderate and comfortable level for the nonverbal expression of thoughts and feelings.

It is advisable that the play therapist begin with fairly structured media, following them with expressive media, and lastly with unstructured media to ascertain how the children respond. By observing the affective and emotional responses to the media—and to any decrease in limits and structure—the therapist can assess the children's internal control levels.

Getting Started

After these initial considerations, it must be determined whether the art activity will be a part of a play therapy session or designed to occupy the entire session. For very young children with limited attention spans, art activities can provide a break from the usual play therapy or can be a calming activity. For example, when a very active group of three- and four-year-olds were halfway through a group play therapy session, the energy level and chaos were escalating. The boys were invited to sit at a small table, given markers and paper, and instructed to follow impromptu suggestions for a drawing sequence.

The art process began by having the children draw small circles, then big circles. This was quickly followed by asking them to draw circular motions very fast, then slow, to draw tall lines, then short, and so on for about four minutes. The boys became calm and focused. When invited to, each boy took a turn leading the group in drawing lines, squiggles, fast, slow, and so on. As they lost interest in the art experience, the children were invited to stay at the table and draw, or return to their group play therapy activities.

This activity was designed to divert the children from escalating gross motor activity and chaotic play to more focused and controlled processes. It provided a developmentally appropriate and enlivening activity for containing their impulsive behaviors. The experience also provided an opportunity to delay gratification by waiting for turns and to develop self-esteem as each child could participate in this no-fail activity and assume a position of leadership within the group. This activity allows for the assessment of motor skills and control and of the child's ability to respond to limits and structure, and also for a decrease in limits and structure.

Children presented with art media are often unsure of what is expected and may experience performance anxiety—art media can be intimidating. To reduce this stress, it is advisable to discuss the parameters of the group art experience, including the fact that all art productions will be different and exhibit different levels of skill and ability with media. Ground rules can be developed with the children and modeled by the therapist. Examples might include statements such as "no mean things are said about other people's art" and "everyone in our group looks to find what is special about the other person's art." The development of ground rules can include an open discussion about the parameters for self-disclosure and the members' fears and anxieties about art and about group therapy. These discussions are recommended as children may have comments or questions pertaining to these issues, and clarifying what can be expected to happen in the group reduces anxiety for the members.

Discussing leadership (including the roles of students, volunteers, or other staff), expectations of the participants, limits, and confidentiality provide the necessary physical and psychological safety that allows the child to relax and experience greater freedom of expression. A few clear, simple rules are best and must be fully explained to the children. For example, when discussing the destruction of art materials, one can define the difference between accidentally breaking materials and tools and deliberately destroying them, and between needing lots of paper and deliberately wasting materials. These clarifications help a child feel safe and comfortable in exploring art media.

Having considered these important start-up tasks, one can begin the art activity. The art activity can be seen as consisting of four components: motivation, the art activity itself, discussion of the process and product, and closure. The following case examples will demonstrate these four components of group art experiences.

Case 1: Structured Pediatric Art Therapy Group

A group play therapy session was offered to five children who were hospitalized for asthma. They were all boys, aged eight and nine years old; each had been hospitalized for asthma-related illnesses, and most were newly diagnosed with asthma. The boys were not oxygen dependent at the time of the session, but each was required to wear an oxygen mask several times throughout the day for asthma treatment. Each had IV lines and was required to have oxygen checks several times per day. The boys had been seen two previous days for two hours of group play therapy. Play consisted of interactive and imaginative play with toys, medical supplies, and art materials. During this particular session, the boys were directed to the art table and invited to participate in an art activity.

The motivation for the group began with a discussion about asthma, what it is, is not, how we can help ourselves, how we cannot, and the problems of having a chronic illness and ways of dealing with the illness to make it easier to live with. The typical negative responses focused on the fact that people who did not have asthma could not understand what it was really like. The coping strategies included breathing exercises and avoiding dust and pets as ways to help make breathing easier. The discussion soon focused on the need to come to the hospital when breathing is difficult. The children felt the advantages of the illness were staying home from school and getting special attention. The disadvantages were being different than other kids and being sick.

Following this discussion, each child was given paper, magazines, markers, and glue for the art activity. The directive was to make a collage of "Who I was before I had asthma" on one half of the paper and "Who I am after I had asthma" on the other. The boys wrote the descriptions across the paper and eagerly began looking through the magazines to find photos to glue in each area that represented themselves. They quietly and thoughtfully created collages for about twenty-five minutes.

To provide an opportunity for discussion of the product and process, the boys were then given the option of showing their collage to the others and talking about the collage. Each boy did so, and typical responses centered around their sense of self, body image, coping with a chronic illness, and the limitations the illness imposes on activity. One child looked at his collage and stated, "The only way I am really different is with taking medicine and having to rest more often. I am really not very different." Other boys agreed, and they discussed their common understanding of asthma.

Closure for the session consisted of asking each child to comment on one thing he learned about himself and asthma. Each boy had a unique response, yet the universal theme among their responses related a greater feeling of self-acceptance. Other comments related to coping with their situation, such as methods of helping oneself during an asthma attack, dependence on medication, and living with a chronic illness.

This activity was designed to address the issues the boys brought up: sense of self, body image, and medications and procedures associated with a chronic illness. The boys also had an opportunity to understand their common situation, develop ways of coping, and display empathy and understanding for themselves and their peers. The art making was fun for the boys. It provided a safe way to reframe the stigma of illness through participation in a typical childhood experience of exploration with glue, magazines, and imagination.

Case 2: Multicultural Images in an Unstructured Art Group

Truancy among the Native American children at a school was very high, with about 40 percent of students from the adjacent reservation missing half the week or more. In an effort to increase attendance, the school district approved an experimental art group to be offered to one class of children from the reservation (members of the Nez Percé, Salish, and Crow tribes). The parents of the children were contacted about their receptivity to the idea. Following traditional customs, the parents sought the tribal community leaders and elders for approval. The community agreed on the condition that the goal of the group was to explore and reinforce heritage and native culture. They expressed concern that their traditions were not respected by the school. The group was held at a separate time from regular classroom activities, over seven weeks, for fifty minutes a session. The group was composed of five girls and five boys from the fifth-grade classrooms.

The group began with a discussion of the purposes and goals of the group facilitated by the therapist. Early on the students requested a "talking circle" be used to develop motivation for the group goals and determine the activities. In a talking circle, each person speaks in turn while holding a "talking stick." The children stated that they wanted to make art and to be, as they said, "more Indian." It was determined that the way to be more Indian was to develop the art group plans together. In this way each person's contributions could be considered, and harmony for the whole group achieved. Thus the art group developed according to an unstructured format.

Since the therapist was not Native American, the unstructured nature of the group was consistent with cultural sensitivity and allowed the students to teach the therapist. The role of the therapist in an unstructured art group format is to support the inclusion of all members and allow the group members to develop the art process and choices of media. The therapist further should provide a variety of materials that are available for whatever processes evolves and allow flexible limits. It was agreed that art processes would be shared spontaneously and in the closure through the talking circle.

Following the planning stage, the children selected different art media to represent their goal for the art activity to represent their experiences with, as they described it, "being Indian." A variety of media were selected by the therapist within the range described in this chapter as easily controllable, comfortable, and familiar. These included pastels, felt pens, and crayons. The children drew personal symbols of their names, including animals (eagles, bears, trees) and popular images of Native American culture, such as tepees and warriors on horseback. The children worked busily and admired one another's ideas and artwork.

The discussion of the product and process included each person who wanted to share their artwork. The common theme that emerged among their drawings was that of ambivalence about being Native American. The artwork reflected the students' sadness about rejection of their tribal ways by Caucasian children and by the school. This inspired a discussion of the fact that the group members did not trust their teachers. They also expressed anger that the school system refuses to acknowledge the Indian sense of time—*Indian time* being cyclic and not linear as it is when the school bell rings. The therapist worked to help all members who wished to contribute. Further she modeled and directed the children toward avoiding judgment statements when the group was looking at one another's artwork. In this way the therapist created a safe environment for sharing art products.

The closure conformed to the children's original plan of a talking circle. Since some of the children were not aware of the customs of the talking circle, the therapist worked to help the children explain to one another the two-part procedure: speaking from the heart, and speaking only when you receive the stick except to ask a question for clarification. It was stated that the talking circle is one of honoring and respecting one another. This model was useful since it is also the appropriate attitude for viewing artwork in a group. The talking stick was passed, and each child spoke about their artwork and about the experience of being in the group that day. The children were relieved that they were able to express their concerns and anger about the school system without reprisal from the therapist. They decided their artwork would be saved by the therapist in a folder for a final group art show.

Interestingly, the nonstructured group appears to have been an effective approach with these children. The groups were successful because they allowed the children to control the structure. For a population whose history is replete with experiences of exploitation and cultural genocide at the hands of the white culture, this approach was advised. Truancy declined within the first two weeks of the art group. Teachers reported that the students always attended on group day. Perhaps more important, by the end of the final art group the tribal leaders approached the therapist to request an extension of the art groups and the inclusion of more of their children.

The art processes in this unstructured group created a sense of control that made the school experience less frightening and rigid. The effectiveness of the unstructured approach lay in encouraging the experts, the children themselves, to guide the group. The art processes offered freedom and furthered cohesion, closeness, and a sense of purpose and identity among the group members. It is only with this assurance of safety that Native American students can achieve the healing, growth, and courage necessary to enter into cross-cultural dialogues.

Summary and Recommendations

As we have explored in these two cases, both structured and unstructured art groups can provide safe ways to facilitate self-expression and personal disclosure. Art expressions have tremendous capacity for the revelation of unconscious material in a very quick and surprisingly accurate form. In this way they may be viewed by the novice as magical techniques. However, several critical aspects of art processes and the use of art as a therapeutic technique must be considered by the play therapist. To use art effectively and reduce the potential for misuse, it is essential to approach the subject cautiously, paying particular attention to the power of symbolic imagery; the potential for disclosure of troubling or disturbing imagery, which may indicate the need for further assessment; the impact of client imagery on the therapist; the need to discuss and care for art products with respect; and the status of art media as a therapeutic other with which the clients develop an ongoing relationship.

As in other forms of group play therapy intervention, the therapist's personal issues are considered in building the alliance with the child client. However, the addition of artwork and evocative or disturbing images can influence the clinician on an unconscious level that remains symbolic. It is important for the play therapist to be in supervision when using art processes. Supervision should include a review of the reactions and responses to the artwork of the clients, the way art materials are used, and reaction to the product. Although the therapist tries to avoid judgment about therapy products, it is difficult to avoid reactions of tremendous pride or delight when a child has created a particularly beautiful piece of artwork. Art is seductive especially to the therapist feeling fatigued with the more mundane tasks of practice.

Since groups generate more images and more content, this supervision becomes critical. When the imagery includes evocative issues of victimization, abuse, and trauma, the cumulative impact on the therapist can be severe. This impact may manifest in the play therapist as vicarious trauma or secondary posttraumatic stress disorder. The play therapist may notice sensitivities to images from popular culture. Further, once seen, trauma images do not disappear; they become integrated into our perspectives and personal lives outside the office, hospital, or school. As current studies in medicine have shown, the impact of imagery is physical and alters brain chemistry. Thus, debriefing imagery is as important as other aspects of the case management. In these cases, consultation or supervision with an art therapist trained in traumatology may be indicated.

We have discussed the importance of selecting art materials that are suited to the developmental and psychological strength of the child client. Similarly, art processes may go out of control, and the therapist will want to create ways to help the client contain both the physical and imagistic aspects of the process. Providing time to talk about the process is as important as talking about the product. However, art products should not be treated casually. The powerful message given by a therapist who folds, creases, or discards a child's masterpiece is blatant and countertherapeutic. Art products must be honored as the metaphorical extension of the child and his or her universe. They must be carefully handled, spoken about, and preserved. Prying questions are as violating to the art maker as crumpling up the finished art product. Children are comfortable with their images remaining on symbolic levels and usually do not share the adult need for explanation.

Finally, art media provide a vehicle for exploration, relationship, and opportunities for growth and mastery. As such, they are a form of therapeutic other with which the child develops a relationship. The media will challenge, frustrate, delight, and grieve the child. Usually, we will find art groups deeply involved in the tasks of art processes. Interruption of this relationship with the media should be weighed against therapeutic goals. For this reason, the play therapist may want to remain silent while art is being made. For children with high levels of ego strength and internal locus of control, such a stance can facilitate expression. For children who display low impulse control, anxiety in performance, and a poor sense of self, a more involved stance is required to ensure safety and success. The relationships that children form with the media provide the therapist with useful assessment information. It is these metaphoric interactions with media and the symbols evoked that offer the play therapist guidelines for understanding and helping the group.

Art is a powerful therapeutic tool, but it is no accident that it is so. The therapeutic potential of art lies in two areas: the opportunity art offers for integration and the creation of meaning, and the vehicle art provides for mastery through creation and exploration of images. Although art may be experienced as intrinsically therapeutic, it becomes a method of change and healing when used responsibly and with skill.

References

Allen, P. (1983). Group art therapy in short term hospital settings. *American Journal of Art Therapy, 22* (3), 93–95.

Anderson, F. (1995). Catharsis and empowerment through group clay work with incest survivors. *The Arts in Psychotherapy, 22* (5), 413–427.

Appleton, V. E. (1993). An art therapy protocol for the medical trauma setting. *Art Therapy: Journal of American Art Therapy Association, 10*(2), 71–77.

Appleton, V. E. (in press). Using art in group counseling with Native American youth. *Specialists for Group Work.*

Bender, L. (Ed.). (1952). *Child psychiatric techniques.* Springfield, IL: Thomas.

Chapman, L. (1993). Establishing a pediatric art and play therapy program in a community hospital. In E. Virshup (Ed.), *California art therapy trends* (pp. 219–230). Chicago: Magnolia Street.

Crawford, J. (1962). Art for the mentally retarded. *Bulletin of Art Therapy, 2*(2), 67–72.

Davis, R. (1969). Teaching art in a therapeutic milieu. *American Journal of Art Therapy, 9*(1), 17–23.

Fryrear, J., & Stephens, B. (1988). Group psychotherapy using masks and video to facilitate interpersonal communication. *The Arts in Psychotherapy, 15*(3), 227–234.

Harvey, S. (1990). Dynamic play therapy: An integrative expressive arts approach to the family therapy of young children. *The Arts in Psychotherapy, 17*(3), 239–246.

Haygood, M. (1991). Group art therapy with mothers of sexually abused children. *Arts in Psychotherapy, 18,* 17–27.

Hiscox, A. (1993). Clinical art therapy with adolescents of color: Current trends in health care. In E. Virshup (Ed.), *California art therapy trends* (pp. 17–25). Chicago: Magnolia Street.

Horowitz, M. (1970). *Image formation and cognition.* Englewood Cliffs, NJ: Appleton-Century-Crofts.

Klorer, G. (1995). The use of anatomical dolls in play and art therapy with sexually abused children. *Arts in Psychotherapy, 22*(5), 467–473.

Kramer, E. (1958). *Art therapy in a children's community.* Springfield IL: Thomas.

Kramer, E. (1971). *Art therapy with children.* New York: Schocken Books.

Kramer, E. (1972). The practice of art therapy with children. *American Journal of Art Therapy, 11*(3), 89–110.

Landgarten, H. B. (1981). *Clinical art therapy.* New York: Brunner/Mazel.

Leavitt, K., Morrison, J., Gardner, S., & Gallagher, M. (1996). Group play therapy for cumulatively traumatized child survivors of familial AIDS. *International Journal of Play Therapy, 5*(1), 1–17.

Liebmann, M. (1986). *Art therapy for groups: A handbook of themes, games, and exercises.* Cambridge, MA: Brookline Books.

Lowenfeld, V. (1971). *Play in childhood* (2nd ed.). New York: Wiley.

Nickerson, B. (1973). The use of art as a play therapeutic medium in the classroom. *Art Psychotherapy, 1* (3–4), 293–297.

O'Doherty, S. (1989). Play and drama therapy with the Down's Syndrome child. *The Arts in Psychotherapy, 16*(3), 171–178.

Oster, G., & Gould, P. (1987). *Using drawings in assessment and therapy.* New York: Brunner/Mazel.

Prager, A. (1995). Pediatric art therapy: Strategies and applications. *Art Therapy: Journal of the American Art Therapy Association, 12*(1), 32–38.

Raymer M., & McIntyre, B. (1987). An art support group for bereaved children and adolescents. *Art Therapy: Journal of the American Art Therapy Association, 4*(1), 27–35.

Rhyne, J. (1971). The gestalt art experience. In J. Fagan & I. Shepard, (Eds.), *Gestalt therapy now* (pp. 274–284). New York: HarperCollins.

Riley, S. (1996). An art psychotherapy stress reduction group: For therapists dealing with severely abused client populations. *Arts in Psychotherapy, 23*(5), 407–415.

Rubin, J. (1978). *Child art therapy.* New York: Van Nostrand Reinhold.

Schiffer, M. (1969). *The therapeutic play group.* New York: Grune & Stratton.

Schneider, S., Ostroff, S., & Legow, N. (1990). Enhancement of body-image: A structured art therapy group with adolescents. *Art Therapy: Journal of the American Art Therapy Association, 7*(3), 134–138.

Vogt, J., & Vogt, G. (1983). Group art therapy: An eclectic approach. *American Journal of Art Therapy, 22*(4), 129–135.

Wadeson, H. (1980). *Art psychotherapy.* New York: Wiley.

CHAPTER ELEVEN

THE USE OF STRUCTURED EXPRESSIVE ART ACTIVITIES IN GROUP ACTIVITY THERAPY WITH PREADOLESCENTS

Sue Carlton Bratton and Kelly Webb Ferebee

There Was a Child Went Forth

There was a child went forth every day,

And the first object he look'd upon, that object he became,

And that object became part of him for the day or a certain part of the day,

Or for many years or stretching cycles of years.

—Walt Whitman

McNiff (1992) suggested that Whitman's poem is a reflection on how experiences form a person. *Experience* can be defined as "the act of living through an event or events; personal involvement in or observation of events as they occur." Play and other expressive art forms are by their nature experiential. They are uniquely ours as we creatively build, draw, paint, or dramatize our lives.

For decades, play therapists have understood the value of play and creative expression in treating children with emotional or behavioral problems. Although play therapy is widely accepted as the developmentally appropriate mode of treatment for children, preadolescents may view conventional play therapy as juvenile (Ginott, 1961). Slavson (1944) first suggested the need for a specialized treatment modality for troubled preadolescents, one that provided a setting and activities consistent with the developmental needs of this age group. The authors propose the use of expressive arts and other age-appropriate play activities in a group context as an effective means for preadolescents to work through thoughts and feelings that they are unable to express verbally. Appropriately structured creative art activities provide preteens with opportunities to change perceptions about self, others, and the world as they try out new roles and solutions in the safety of the group. Furthermore, the use of expressive arts facilitates a process of creative self-development that can continue long after termination of therapy—providing the preadolescent with the inner resources to cope with future difficulties.

This chapter explores the developmental and therapeutic rationale for the integration of expressive arts in an activity group format for preadolescents. Also included in this chapter are a description of the activity room and materials, the structure for a sixty- to ninety-minute group, and detailed descriptions of developmentally appropriate expressive art activities that foster creativity and interaction in a group format.

Developmental Needs of Preadolescents

According to Piaget's theory of cognitive development, children in the preadolescent stage of maturation are not likely to have developed formal operational thought processes that allow for abstract thought and expression (cited in Kottman, Strother, & Deniger, 1987). Therefore, preadolescents often have difficulty verbally communicating their concerns and feelings. Landreth (1991) stated that children of all ages naturally and comfortably use play and activity to express themselves and interact with others, adding, "to restrict therapy to verbal expression is to deny the existence of the most graphic form of expression, activity" (p. 14). Activity is also important in the preadolescent's physical development, providing opportunities for movement and discharging excess energy (Frank & Zilbach, 1968).

In addition, preadolescents are entering a phase of development when socialization becomes very important—where they become sensitive to influences beyond the immediate family. Developing positive peer relations is an important developmental task that has significant impact on later developmental stages. Indeed, Ginott (1961) stated that the opportunity to discover and experiment with new and more satisfying modes of relating to peers was the major advantage of group over individual activity and play therapy.

Preadolescents are also beginning to form their sense of identity as they broaden their social parameters and explore who they are within the context of their peer group. The necessary work on identity during this phase of development can be supported and enabled by a group therapy format as group members respond to the individual's trying on different roles in an atmosphere of acceptance, nonretaliation, and nourishment (Frank & Zilbach, 1968). Because peer acceptance is so important to the preadolescent, the group setting provides impetus for members to modify their behavior and develop coping skills that are more socially acceptable and cooperative. As group members begin to evaluate their behavior in light of their peers' reactions and make decisions to choose alternative ways of interacting, self-regulation and self-responsibility for behavior begin to develop. Thus a therapeutic approach that provides the preadolescent with opportunities for creative expression through activity and play in a group format would seem to be most consistent with the developmental needs of this age group.

The Activity Group

Slavson (1944) introduced the therapeutic use of activities, toys, and games with preadolescents in 1934, with his concept of activity group therapy. In Slavson's model, therapy occurs in a group setting where much of the interaction involves play, food, and materials. Slavson proposed that preadolescents would reveal their characteristic behavior patterns through self-directed activities. He avoided interpretation of their behavior, relying on group dynamics to bring about behavioral change. Schiffer (1952) worked closely with Slavson, becoming the director of the Activity Group Therapy Center in New York City and implementing Slavson's model in the public schools.

Ginott (1961) recommended activity therapy as a compromise between play therapy and traditional talk therapy for children between ten and thirteen years old. He further stated that in his experience, most preteen children are referred for therapy for difficulties related to either acting out or social inhibition, both of which are more appropriately addressed within a group format. MacLennan (1977) described activity group therapy as well suited to the needs of preadolescent children: increasing self-esteem, dealing with problems of authority and sibling rivalry, accepting success and defeat, coping with competing individual demands inevitable in group settings, formulating self-identity, developing a sense of competency, overcoming social fear, satisfying the need for a sense of belonging, and developing satisfying peer relationships (p. 86).

There has been a scarcity of research and writing on activity group therapy over the last two decades; the most recent writings include Celano (1990), Kottman et al. (1987), Lev (1983), Nickerson and O'Laughlin (1983), Roos and Jones (1982), and Schaefer and Reid (1986). Celano focused on the use of games and activities in group psychotherapy with sexually abused children and stated that there is a trend for the development of and specialization in the use of games and activities in therapy. Kottman et al. discussed benefits of activity therapy and how to set up the activity room and materials, citing an individual activity therapy case study. Lev described a short-term activity discussion group for severely disturbed children in an inpatient psychiatric unit, where a greater emphasis was placed on verbalization. Roos and Jones discussed the use of an activity group for girls experiencing family losses and recommended the structuring of group activities in the initial stages of activity therapy. Nickerson and O'Laughlin recommended the development of structured games for specific therapeutic purposes in treating preadolescents, as did Schaefer and Reid. Based on this brief review of the literature, there is clearly a need for further research and writing on the continuing evolution of group activity therapy.

Selection of Group Members

Ginott (1975) emphasized the benefits of group activity therapy over individual therapy for most preadolescent children, stressing the importance of careful screening of group members. His main criteria for group membership were that prospective members demonstrate appropriate ego strength and social hunger, which he defined as a desire to be accepted by the group. Ginott further emphasized that the potential for help *or for harm* is greater in the group; hence, selecting the appropriate combination of group members is critical. A well-balanced group would consist of preadolescents whose personality characteristics, presenting problems, and coping styles complement each other, so that group members may have a therapeutic effect on each other (Ginott, 1975; Slavson, 1944). Group members should be of the same sex and generally not more than one year apart in age. Preadolescents who are overly insecure and seem to have great difficulty forming attachments would benefit from individual treatment to strengthen their self-concept and develop their capacity for, and interest in, establishing relationships before entering into group treatment. Preadolescents with a history of acting out sexually would also be contraindicated for group membership. Due to the significance of proper screening of group members, the authors recommend an initial parent interview and at least one individual session with each prospective member prior to forming the group.

The Activity Room

The environment should be inviting and stimulate both self-expression and interaction with others. Since preadolescent children are highly active, they require adequate space to explore, create, and expend excess energy. Schiffer (1969) suggested an optimal size room of about three hundred square feet for five or six preadolescents; Ginott (1975) recommended four hundred square feet for a group of five to eight children. However, the authors have found that most play therapists do not have that much clinic space to dedicate to a fully equipped activity room. Our experience is that a carefully planned two hundred square feet can accommodate up to four preadolescents, including the necessary equipment and materials, and with minor rearrangement, can also serve as a group room for working with parents and other adults. The well-designed activity room should include carefully selected age-appropriate equipment and materials, a sink and counter area, adequate open floor space, and allow for flexibility in room arrangement. The room should also provide opportunities for group members to work individually or in pairs, as well as provide a place for hiding or being alone.

Adequate space for moving about is a top priority—inadequate open space creates a greater need to set limits and can lead to hostility among group members. Preadolescents need plenty of space to move freely without the frustration of bumping into each other. We also recommend providing adequate floor space for the group to sit in a circle, eliminating the need for a large table. A large round vinyl tablecloth placed on the floor can serve as a work space for arts and crafts and serve as a place to gather around for snack time and other structured group activities.

Equipment should be carefully selected to provide preadolescents with opportunities to express themselves in a variety of creative activities, while keeping space needs in mind. Major equipment requirements include a sandplay unit, a puppet theater, a woodworking table and pegboard for tools, shelved storage units, a multigame activity table (air hockey, pool, and so on), a double easel, two beanbag chairs, a mirror and wall hooks for displaying a variety of dress-up and fantasy items, a small table for one to two group members to work, and a folding chair for each group member. Installing locking wheels on the large items (sandplay unit, theater, storage units, activity table, and so on) allows for flexibility in room arrangement and also allows equipment not being used to be moved out of the room to make more floor space.

The authors have found that preadolescents enjoy rearranging the room to meet their needs and seem to develop a sense of ownership in creating their own space. Other floor-space–saving ideas include mounting a double easel on the wall; building a puppet theater that doubles as a room divider, hiding place, storefront, writing board, and so on by mounting it on wheels and making the front out of a sheet of whiteboard; having a lid made for a multigame activity table so it doubles as a work table for crafts, drawing, and so on; and mounting shelving on the wall above permanent items such as the easel, sink and counter area, or woodworking table.

When possible, equipment should be designed to accommodate the entire group of preadolescents so as to facilitate group dynamics. For example, a puppet theater approximately five feet wide by five feet high (or a five-foot table turned on its side) is required for four adolescents. It's also useful to have a sandplay unit that holds two sandtrays on top, two more underneath, and includes space for storing baskets of miniatures, which allows group members to work all together, individually, or in pairs. A sturdy woodworking table approximately three feet by four feet, with two large vises and a large selection of carpentry tools and supplies—from the hardware store, not toys—also encourages group projects. (*Note:* The authors have found the need to custom-build most of this equipment, as similar items available commercially are not large enough for group use and are also designed for younger children. The commercial items tend to be too low for most preadolescents and too fragile to withstand their activities.)

Toys, games, and other materials for the activity room should be selected purposefully and provide a wide variety of choices for group members. The authors recommend materials that stimulate interaction, promote creative expression, encourage exploration and release of feelings, facilitate the acting out of real-life concerns, and encourage the development of effective problem-solving and coping strategies. We suggest the following categories of materials for the activity room:

• *Expressive arts and crafts media:* Clay, tempera paints, fingerpaints, water colors, Play-Doh, charcoals, pastels, chalk, crayons, markers, assorted magazines, glue sticks, adhesive tape, hot glue gun, air brush, pipe cleaners, tissue paper, colored paper, assorted paper for drawing and painting, rolls of butcher paper and newsprint, feathers, shells, rocks, assorted beans, beads, buttons, glitter, sequins, yarn, felt, fake fur, assorted fabrics, leather craft items, Popsicle sticks, assorted plastic foam items, foil, paper plates, clear plastic wrap, and so on and on. We organize these items in clear storage bins and store them on open shelves.

• *Toys useful for symbolic acting out:* All sorts of items that can be associated with important people and real-life events come in handy here. It's useful to have an assortment of puppets (people, animal, and fantasy); face masks; dress-up clothing and fantasy costumes; an assortment of toy guns, knives, swords, and handcuffs; a large inflatable plastic figure or punching bag; some Barbie and Ken type dolls; anatomically detailed dolls (boy and girl only); and an assortment of sandtray miniatures, including a bendable doll family.

• *Manipulative skill-building materials and equipment:* Lego and other types of building toys, lumber and carpentry tools and supplies, do-it-yourself building project kits, model airplane and car kits, sewing machine and supplies, weaving loom and supplies, and a toaster oven and basic measuring and cooking utensils (a small refrigerator that will sit on the counter is useful). Older preadolescents enjoy discarded household items (phone, VCR, and so on) that can be taken apart and put back together.

- *Games that encourage large movement:* Basketball (mount hoop on door), bowling set, foam bats, assorted soft balls, Ping-Pong balls with paddles and rackets, ring toss, plastic dart set, and so on. (As mentioned earlier, a small activity table that converts to a variety of games such as pool, air hockey, and Ping-Pong is a popular item if space allows.)
- *Commercial board games:* Checkers, chess, Life, Break-the-Ice, and so on, as well as games designed for therapeutic purposes such as the Talking, Doing and Feeling Game, The Ungame, and Reunion.

Activity Group Format

Although most activity therapy researchers agree that some combination of expressive arts and crafts, building materials, and games used in a small-group format is useful in treating troubled preadolescents (Celano, 1990; Cermak, Stein, & Abelson, 1973; Frank & Zilbach, 1968; Gardner, 1971; Ginott, 1961; Kottman et al., 1987; Nickerson & O'Laughlin, 1983; Schiffer, 1984; Slavson, 1944), they differ regarding the format or structuring of the group. Philosophically, there seem to be two main schools of thought regarding the therapist's role and the use of structure in activity groups. Slavson (1944) and Schiffer (1984) are representative of researchers who propose that preadolescents benefit most from an unstructured, nondirective therapy group where members are free to direct their own activities. Other researchers contend that structured groups, where the therapist plans and directs the activities, are the most therapeutic for preadolescents (Celano, 1990; Crocker & Wroblewski, 1975; Gardner, 1971; Schaefer & Reid, 1986). Gil (1994) stated that therapists often rigidly adhere to either an unstructured or structured approach and suggested that an integration of the two approaches is more appropriate in meeting children's unique needs.

The authors find both approaches useful and necessary in working with groups of preteen children. We suggest the following format for a sixty- to ninety-minute group: a structured, therapist-directed group activity time, followed by a period of unstructured free play where members may work or play alone or together in activities of their choice, and ending with a structured group time for snacks and sharing. A well-designed activity room provides many opportunities for spontaneous creative expression, but preadolescent children are often self-conscious and hesitant to interact with the other group members. Structured activities can reduce anxiety and encourage group members to begin to interact with each other more quickly than they would if left to do so on their own. A therapist-structured activity is an effective means of introducing an expressive art form that group members may be unfamiliar with, providing them with instructions and ideas about how to use the medium. Structured activities can be planned for assessment purposes, to facilitate individual self-expression, and to facilitate group dynamics.

The amount of time allotted to structured versus unstructured activities should be adjusted to meet the particular needs of the group as therapy progresses. As group members begin to feel safe with each other, they generally require less structure and direction and can begin to assume more responsibility for the activities of the group. Leadership skills can be fostered during the structured activity time by assigning a different group member each week to be responsible for selecting and directing the activity for the group, instead of the therapist. Although structured activities offer many benefits for the preadolescent group, self-directed free play in a stimulating environment is equally important. Group members need plenty of opportunities to explore, experiment, create, and make decisions without interference from the therapist. Problems between group members will inevitably arise, providing opportunities for problem solving, resolving conflict, and exploring alternative behaviors.

Following the period of free play, the authors recommend devoting the last ten to twenty minutes to a snack and sharing time. Slavson (1944) and Schiffer (1969) also made food an integral part of their activity play groups and recommended simple snacks requiring little preparation. The authors have found that preteens enjoy cooking their own snacks and recommend providing a small toaster oven for making simple snacks like cheese toast, slice-and-bake cookies, or cinnamon toast. A small refrigerator for storing ingredients and juice is beneficial. Other healthy snacks that do not require cooking should also be kept on hand. Group members can take turns playing host, with everyone assisting with the cleanup. The host is responsible for selecting, preparing, and serving the food. It is important for group members to sit together, preferably in a circle, either at a table or on the floor. The benefits of snack time are numerous—the sharing of food creates a family-type atmosphere and is a concrete act of nurturance. In addition, snack time encourages interaction among group members and provides the opportunity for sharing thoughts and feelings. Snack time also serves as a closing ritual, providing a transition from therapy to the real world.

Therapeutic Use of Expressive and Creative Arts

Rogers (1993) stated that part of the therapeutic process is to awaken creative life-force energy, pointing out that what is creative is frequently therapeutic. Expressive art forms that provide opportunities for creativity include drawing, painting, sculpting, music, movement, writing, phototherapy, collages, sandplay, imagery, fantasy, drama, improvisation, puppetry, and woodworking. Through these various expressive art forms the individual has the opportunity to take elements of his or her own personality and restructure them into new forms. The individual becomes the author of both the process and the product of creativity (Fleshman & Fryrear, 1981). Expressive art activities stimulate all the senses: visual, aural, kinesthetic, and tactile, and often elicit thoughts and feelings the individual may be unaware of or have difficulty expressing. Segal (1984) explained the relationship between sensory experiences and expression of emotions: the brain responds to sensory experiences by tapping into stored memories and feelings—bringing to awareness that which has been previously denied. This process facilitates healing as all aspects of the self are expressed and integrated.

Rubin (1984b) emphasized the therapeutic value of creative arts for clients of all ages, particularly preteen children who naturally use art materials and play to express themselves symbolically. In addressing the healing aspects of the expressive arts for children, Rubin (1984a) stated:

> In art or play the child may do the impossible. He or she may fulfill symbolically both positive wishes and negative impulses, without fear of real consequences. He or she can learn to control the real world by experimenting with active mastery of tools, media, and the ideas and feelings expressed in the process. He or she can gain symbolic access to and relive past traumas, and can rehearse and practice for the future. He or she can learn to be in charge in a symbolic mode, and thus come to feel competent to master reality. The child cannot learn to control and organize himself, if the structure does not ultimately come from within [p. 29].

The integration of expressive arts in an activity group format can provide preadolescent children with opportunities to express themselves in an endless variety of creative activities. Through this process of creative expression, preadolescents are encouraged to reach more deeply into their own resources, which can enable them to handle future challenges more effectively.

Structured Expressive Art Activities

Segal (1984) stated that therapists do not need to be art experts to use expressive arts in therapy, but the authors strongly recommend that therapists experience working with the various expressive art forms before using these media with clients. The therapist's structuring of specific activities is designed to engage group members in the creative process and to encourage interaction. Segal also points out that through the use of symbols and metaphors, creative art activities provide group members a nonthreatening means to express and share themselves with their peers. In addition, these activities can provide preteens with a sense of control over their anxieties, as well as promote emotional catharsis. However, careful consideration and sensitivity should be used when selecting and structuring an activity—the experience may well elicit thoughts and feelings that individual group members are not ready to address. The authors recommend that the therapist structure an activity by selecting the art form to be used and providing materials and basic directions, while permitting group members the freedom to creatively interpret the assignment. Members should be encouraged to share their work with each other and reflect on the process, but they should never be required to participate. The value of the activity lies in the creative process, not in the final product.

There are many excellent books that discuss expressive and creative art activities (see the Resources section at the end of this chapter). We have included several of our favorites, but particularly recommend *Windows to Our Children* by Violet Oaklander (1988). The following structured activities were selected because of our repeated success in using them with groups of preadolescents. In addition, they are simple to use and can be easily adapted to meet the needs of a particular group. The degree of structure and direction from the therapist can be modified in keeping with the therapist's theoretical orientation.

Drawing and Painting Activities

Rubin (1984b) suggested initially exposing clients to the creative process through the basic art media—paper, crayons, and paints. Most people are familiar with these media and tasks may be structured to promote group process or individual self-expression. Relaxation exercises, guided imagery, and music can be used with any drawing or painting activity to enhance the process. When using these exercises in a school setting where you are not allowed to ask students to close their eyes, you can suggest that they may want to rest their eyes while they listen or rest their head on the table. There is a tendency for children—and some therapists—to want to display artwork, but any artwork that identifies group members in any way should never be displayed, other than during the group's own sessions.

Fighting Back. This drawing activity about a small boat in a big storm is designed to reveal group members' perceptions about their place in their world and how each copes with outside forces. The therapist does a short relaxation and breathing exercise, then asks the group to close or rest their eyes and imagine that each of them is a small boat in a big storm. The therapist describes the waves, the wind, and the small boat's struggle. Group members are asked to be the boat, to be aware of how it feels to be the boat, imagining what is happening now and what happens next. Members are then asked to individually draw a picture of themselves as the boat in a storm and share their drawings with the rest of the group. The therapist may find it useful to ask additional questions, such as "I wonder what would have happened if . . ." or "Now, imagine you are the storm, how does it feel to . . ." (Oaklander, 1988, pp. 16–17).

The Spider Web. Group members are shown a picture of a spider web and then asked to imagine, and then individually draw, what it would be like to be a spider trying to build a web on a rainy, stormy day. The therapist may also use the spider web to facilitate group interaction. The therapist begins by showing the picture of the web and saying, "Once upon a time there was a little spider trying to spin a web. A big storm blew in, and it began to rain. Then . . ." Each child is asked to add something to the story (Oaklander, 1988, pp. 18–19). This activity can be expanded by asking the group to illustrate their story by drawing together on a large sheet of butcher paper or newsprint to encourage group interaction.

The Rosebush Fantasy. After a brief relaxation and breathing exercise, group members are asked to close or rest their eyes and imagine that they are rosebushes. The guided imagery includes questions designed to help develop the imagery: What kind of rosebush are you? Are you very small? Are you fat? Are you tall? Are you in full bloom or do you only have buds? What are your roots like? Where are you? What's around you? What's it like to be a rosebush? How do you survive? Who takes care of you? What's the weather like for you right now? (Allan, 1988). Group members are asked to open their eyes when ready and draw their rosebushes. When everyone is finished, the therapist asks members to describe their rosebushes in the present tense. Allan points out that the therapist may find it necessary to ask focused questions, such as those asked in the guided imagery, to generate discussion. Although the authors believe that it is less threatening—and thus safer—to stay with the metaphor of the rosebush when asking questions, we have occasionally found it helpful to extend this activity by asking a group member, "Is there anything about your rosebush that reminds you of your own life?" As in all the activities presented in this chapter, the therapist must be sensitive to group members' readiness, in selecting specific questions during the sharing and processing phase of an activity.

Your World—in Colors, Shapes, and Lines. This activity allows children to create their own world on paper, using only colors, shapes, and lines. The therapist gives a directive to group members to close or rest their eyes and to imagine their world and the colors in it, what it is like for them, how they would show it, how much space each figure would take on a piece of paper and where they would put themselves in the picture. The therapist then has group members describe their drawings to each other, pointing out which shape represents themselves. The experience can be further developed by asking a group member to become that shape and talk to the other shapes in the drawing. This activity provides opportunities for the therapist to gain insight into how group members view themselves in relation to their world (Oaklander, 1988, p. 21).

Cooperative Group Art. This collaborative drawing project is a favorite of the authors and can be used for a variety of purposes: to screen potential group members, to facilitate interaction, to assess group dynamics, and to facilitate group members' insight into their behavior with their peers. The first author adapted the activity from Landgarten's (1987) description of a family art assessment activity. Materials needed include two three-by-six-foot sheets of paper mounted low on the wall and a set of colored markers, with no duplication of colors. The group is told that they will be working together on two drawings during the session. Members are asked to choose one of the colored markers, and told that they must use only that marker for both drawings. For the first drawing, the group is asked to draw a picture together on the first sheet of paper and are told, "There can be no talking, signaling or writing notes to each other while working on your drawing." Group members are told that when they have completed their part of the drawing, to put the lid on their marker to signal others that they are finished. They are told that it is OK to finish at different times. After the group has completed their drawing, the verbal ban is lifted and the group is asked to give a title to their artwork and write it at the top of the paper. For the second drawing, the group is asked to again draw a picture together; however, this time group members are told that they can talk with each other about what they would like to draw as they work together. Group members are reminded to keep their same color marker. Upon completion, the group is asked to again assign a title to their art project.

During both drawings, the therapist should participate only as an observer, giving minimal responses to any questions asked by group members. We find it helpful to consider the following questions (adapted from Landgarten, 1987) as we observe the group, making a few notes as needed:

1. Who initiated the picture and what was the process that led up to this person making the first mark on the page?
2. In what order did the rest of the members participate?
3. Which members' suggestions were used and which were ignored?
4. What was the level of involvement on the part of each person?
5. Which participants remained in their own space and which ones crossed over?
6. Did anyone "wipe out" another member by superimposing their image on top of someone else's?

7. What roles did each group member assume?
8. Did the members take turns, work in teams, or work simultaneously?
9. Where are the geographical locations of each person's contribution and how much space did each person occupy?
10. What was the symbolic content of each person's contribution?
11. Who acted as initiators—who were followers or reactors?
12. Were emotional responses made during the activity?

Because group members are easily identified by the color of the marker each uses, the finished products provide a snapshot of the group's interaction and facilitate reflection on the process. The therapist can use the drawings to comment on the group dynamics in a nonthreatening, noninterpretative manner. For example, the therapist can point to the area where blue has been scribbled on top of red and say, "Mary, I noticed that when Kate marked over your drawing that you moved all the way over by Anne and helped her draw flowers." These kind of comments don't require an answer but generally facilitate responses from one or more of the group members.

This group art activity is especially useful in screening potential group members and assessing whether they are appropriate for a particular group. Using a large sheet of paper mounted on the wall is an important component of this activity—it facilitates movement and allows preadolescents to more readily reveal themselves and their style of interacting with others. This activity also encourages social interaction, cooperation, and negotiation as group members decide how to carry out the tasks. Most important, this activity provides opportunities for group members to become more aware of the impact their behavior has on others.

The Scribble. We find this activity effective in introducing art and drawing to group members, due to its simplicity. There are several adaptations of the activity—the most basic method involves the therapist giving group members each a sheet of paper with the same scribble on it and then asking them to each make a drawing out of it. Drawings are shared when everyone is through. Another method involves both body movement and drawing. Group members are directed to pretend there is a giant piece of paper standing in front of them. Then, they are asked to close their eyes and imagine they are holding a crayon in each hand and to scribble on this imaginary paper, making sure every corner and every area of the paper is touched. Following the imaginary exercise, the group members are asked to draw the real one, sometimes with eyes open, sometimes with eyes closed. The group members then find forms that suggest a picture and complete the picture. When everyone is finished, members take turns describing their drawings to each other. An idea for expanding this exercise is to incorporate drama, music, and dance by asking group members to become their pictures and begin to move about (Oak-lander, 1988, p. 37).

Another group method of using the scribble is an adaptation of the Cooperative Group Art activity described earlier. The group works together on a single large piece of paper, and each member chooses only one color marker. The therapist asks one member to make the first scribble (or the therapist can make it), and then group members take turns adding to the scribble until no one has anything to add. As in Cooperative Group Art, the activity can be done nonverbally or verbally, titled, and processed afterward. Another adaption of this method is to have group members sit in a circle on the floor or at a table, giving each a sheet of paper. Ask them to write their name at the top of their sheet and then to make a scribble somewhere on it. Then instruct them to pass their sheet of paper to the right, each member adding to the drawing as it goes around—again, group members each use a different color marker. Continue until no one has anything to add to any of the drawings. Then ask the group, as a whole, to look at each drawing and decide on a title for each. Or you can ask each group member to title only the drawing with their name on it. Many questions can be generated regarding the ideas each member had in mind as they contributed to the drawings and how their ideas changed as the other group members added to each drawing. Each member's contributions are easily noted by the color marker they used. An added benefit of this activity is that group members each get to keep a drawing that everyone contributed to.

Group Phototherapy and Collage

According to Rogers (1993), collage engages clients in the creative process easily as they look through magazines to pick out images that have personal meaning. Collage is generally more easily done than drawing and allows for a focus on the process rather than the product. Fryrear, Corbit, and Taylor (1992) stated that photographs are a unique way to deal with emotional and therapeutic issues because of their ability to capture a moment entirely and exactly the way it is.

Phototherapy and collage can be combined into a structured group activity that still leaves room for ample creative endeavor. Materials needed include a Polaroid 600 camera, film, marking pens, crayons, oil pastels, package of assorted colors of tissue paper, package of colored construction paper, magazines, scissors, assorted colors of ribbons and yarn, white glue or glue sticks, pieces of white posterboard. Optional materials to consider: stapler and clear tape, colored paper, colored feathers, fabric, and found objects from nature such as leaves, twigs, and feathers (Rogers, 1993; Fryrear et al., 1992). Have group members take two photographs of each other in poses that express who they are. Group members each select one photograph and create a self-portrait. Photographic images may be cut out from the frame prior to gluing them on the posterboard, but the back portion of the photo should be peeled off prior to gluing. Instruct the group to be sure and wash their hands after handling the layers of the photograph to avoid irritation from the chemicals (Fryrear et al.). Group members are encouraged to add to the background of the posterboard using the other art supplies. The second photograph can be used in the creation of a group portrait on a very large piece of posterboard. The group works together, using the available art supplies to personalize their portrait. The final product is titled, and group members are encouraged to share how their portrait represents them as a group. The group portrait activity can be used as an assessment of social skills, as a way to observe communication skills, and as an assessment of individual and group progress (adapted from Fryrear et al.).

Clay

The authors have found that, of all the expressive art media, potter's clay has a tactile and sensual nature that seems to facilitate expression of feelings most quickly. Oaklander (1988) proposed that individuals who have difficulty acknowledging and expressing emotions are out of touch with their senses. The tactile quality of the clay provides a sensory experience that can facilitate awareness and expression of feelings. Oaklander further stated that working with clay facilitates a flow between the clay and the user and, because of this flowing quality, "it promotes the working through of the most primal of internal processes" (p. 67). Clay, as an art form, is unequaled in its flexibility and malleability. The opportunities it provides for a sense of control and mastery without fear of failure make it especially well suited for children and adolescents who need to build a stronger sense of self. The clay can be rolled, pounded, cut, and shaped, and then just as easily "wiped out" for a fresh start at the whim of the creator.

Some preadolescent children (and therapists) are put off by the messiness of the clay. Providing wet paper towels or premoistened towelettes—along with assurances that the clay dries to a fine powder that easily comes off—encourages participation. The authors have also found that if we, as therapists, begin to work with the clay as we introduce an activity, preteens are more likely to begin to experiment with their own clay.

Materials needed include potter's clay, sturdy paper plates, water, paper towels, premoistened towelettes, and assorted clay tools such as a rubber mallet, a wire clay cutter, a cheese cutter, a putty knife, a garlic press, a scraper or hand food chopper, a pencil for poking, a potato masher, and other unusual tools a therapist may wish to incorporate in the exercise (Oaklander, 1988; Rogers, 1993). Rogers also recommended an assortment of compact discs or cassette tapes to allow the therapist to select music appropriate to the kind of activity and the needs of the group. A round vinyl tablecloth placed on the floor can provide a working space for the group if a large round table is not available. We also provide each group member with a plastic cafeteria-style tray—it makes a good work surface and can be taken to the sink for cleanup. Newspapers can also be used as an inexpensive, disposable covering for the work surface.

Introduce clay by giving group members each a block of clay on a sturdy paper plate and encouraging them to spend a few minutes becoming familiar with the clay by closing their eyes and exploring it with their hands. Appropriate music played softly in the background can facilitate relaxation. (Selecting music suitable for this age group can be a challenge!) Instruct group members to squeeze, pinch, poke, pound, and roll the clay, while keeping their eyes open and then closed. Ask members to notice any differences when their eyes are closed versus when they're open. Working with clay, especially with one's eyes closed, has a calming effect— preadolescents often feel less anxious just from the experience of handling the clay. After all group members seem comfortable with this medium, you can introduce a structured clay activity.

The authors have found the following animal sculpting activity well suited for a group of preadolescents. This age group often has difficulty creating free-form clay figures. Animal sculpting allows them to create something familiar, while at the same time providing many choices for symbolic expression. Begin the activity by telling group members, "Think of an animal you identify with or that you are most like or best symbolizes you; then make that animal out of your lump of clay—your animal doesn't have to be real—it can be a creation or a compilation of several animals." After all group members have finished, ask them to tell each other about their animals and why they chose that particular animal. Other questions that we have found helpful: What are the strengths and shortcomings of your animal? How does your animal get along with the other animals? What kinds of things does your animal like to do? What does it wish it could do? What does it wish it didn't have to do? What does your animal need?

We find that the clay animals have personal meaning for group members and recommend keeping them for use in future group sessions. A variety of activities can be developed using the animals; use your creativity and knowledge of the particular needs of the group members as your guide. In our work with preadolescents, the following activity has been a favorite. Begin by telling the group to pretend that each of their animals is homeless. Their task is to create the ideal home place for all their "homeless" animals to live together, out of the materials you give them. (Provide a variety of materials such as twigs, moss, sand, rocks, shells, and so on. Also string, foil, cellophane, paint, paper, craft sticks, tape, glue, and so on and on—the sandtray and miniatures may also be used.) As the home develops, encourage group members to talk about why their animal is homeless and what the perfect home would be like. When they are through, ask members if they were that animal, where would they feel most comfortable in their new home, and then ask them to place their animal in that location. Next, ask them to be their animal and tell what it would be like to live in this ideal place. Other questions we find helpful: Why did you pick that spot for yourself? What do you like best about it? If you could change something, what would it be? Does your place (or home) need anything else? Is there anything you would miss if you lived here? Again, tailor your questions to the needs of the group, being careful not to overwhelm them. This activity can be adapted by having each group member make their own ideal home and then sharing it with the others; or you can modify the directions to ask them to create an ideal "animal school."

Sandplay

Dora Kalff, a Jungian analyst, first introduced the use of a sandtray and assorted miniature toys as a therapeutic medium for working with children (cited in Carey, 1991). Margaret Lowenfeld (1979), also a pioneer in the development of sandplay therapy, described the value of sandplay, emphasizing its tactile nature: "Sand and water lend themselves to the demonstration of a large variety of fantasies, for example, tunnel-making, burying or drowning, land and seascapes. When wet, the sand may be molded, and when dry it is pleasant to feel, and many tactile experiments can be made with the gradual addition of moisture" (pp. 47–48).

The authors have found sandtray play a particularly useful medium in their work with preadolescent groups. The miniatures and sandtray provide more concrete opportunities for symbolic expression than many of the other creative art forms, which tend to be abstract in nature (drawing, painting, clay, and so on), and the small size of the toys allows for storage of a large assortment of symbolic figures for group members to choose from. In addition, preteens seem to find the miniature toys less childish than toys found in a traditional playroom. A further advantage of miniatures is that it requires no skill or artistic ability to use them. Preadolescents can construct their own miniature world in the sand, developing a sense of control and mastery. Through this medium, they can create, destroy, rearrange, and change their world as needed. Kalff has stated that "the symbols speak for inner, energy laden pictures of the innate potentials of the human being" that, when expressed, facilitate emotional growth (cited in Allan, 1988, p. 214).

Traditional sandtray therapists are very specific in their requirements for the both the size of the sandtray and the selection of miniatures. Kalff (1980) recommended a tray of 19.5 by 28.5 by 3 inches, made of wood painted blue on the inside to simulate water, while Lowenfeld (1979) specified a wooden tray, also painted blue on the inside, with a 2-inch rim and measuring approximately 30 by 21 by 3 inches. For the group activity room, the authors use blue plastic storage containers, approximately 18 by 27 by 4 inches, providing one for each group member. These containers are inexpensive and lightweight, and come with lids so they can easily be stacked in a corner or be stored on a cart for portability. We recommend providing two types of sand: a fine-grained white sand and a coarser-grained play sand that is free of any gravel (the play sand works better when using water).

The miniature toys should be organized by category and displayed on open shelves or stored in small baskets. As described in the section on equipment and materials, the authors use a portable cart to store the sandtrays and miniatures. We purchased a metal frame system and assorted sizes of wire baskets, with divided plastic liners, from a container store and mounted the system on a cart. On one end of the cart, hang a container to hold a spray bottle of water and an assortment of tools for moving, shaping, and smoothing the sand (for example, a pastry brush and wooden spatula). The wire baskets are labeled by category and can be pulled out from either side of the cart, so group members can work from both sides. When each group member is creating an individual sandtray, the baskets can be taken out and put on the floor to allow everyone easier access. We recommend the following categories of miniatures:

- *People:* Multicultural families, babies, pregnant woman, bride and groom, ballerina, sports figures, military figures and soldiers (two colors), nun, priest.
- *Fantasy and mythological figures:* Walt Disney characters, action figures (Batman and so on), pirates, devil, witch, sorcerer, wizard, knights, royalty, Santa Claus.
- *Animals:* Assorted domestic, farm, wild, zoo, marine, and prehistoric animals—being sure to include some birds, as well as sharks, alligators, crocodiles, rats, snakes, large spiders, soft wiggly things, dinosaurs, and dragons. (*Note:* Include babies, at least one family set of domestic animals and a few larger animals, such as a bear, gorilla, lion, or dinosaur (preferably hollow).
- *Vehicles:* Assorted land, air, water, space, rescue, and war vehicles—cars, trucks, boats, motorcycle, train, army jeep, tank and cannon, planes, helicopter, ambulance, police car, fire engine, spaceship.
- *Buildings:* Houses, school, church, castle, igloo, tepee, Lego blocks.
- *Vegetation:* Trees, shrubs, plants, silk flowers.
- *Structures:* Bridges, fences, gates, doorways; also stop signs, telephone poles, flags, totem pole.
- *Natural objects:* Shells, driftwood, feathers, bones, and a large assortment of rocks and stones (pyrite is a must).

- *Symbolic objects:* Wishing well, fire, rainbow, treasure chest and jewels, tombstone, and crosses and other religious symbols from a variety of cultures.
- *Odds and ends:* Popsicle sticks, birthday candles, yarn, bits of fabric, foil, tissue paper, beads, buttons, and other miscellaneous craft items.

The therapist can structure the activity so that group members create a sandtray individually, in pairs, or as a group, depending on the therapeutic goal. The authors prefer to introduce sandtray play to the group by asking members to create individual trays and then share them with each other—the purpose is to allow them to become familiar with the sand and symbols and to foster self-expression. Working individually allows preadolescents to focus more on the creative process, freeing them from the added responsibility of having to share, cooperate, and negotiate with their peers. Sharing their individual sandtrays provides a nonthreatening, symbolic means for members to begin to interact and reveal themselves to their peers.

Later on, directing group members to work in pairs or as a group on a sandtray serves to facilitate interaction among members and provide opportunities for social skill development and problem solving. There are various methods of introducing a sandtray activity; "I'd like you to make a 'scene' or 'picture' in the sand using any of the items in the baskets and shelves," and "Look through the figures and choose several that appeal to you [you are attracted to, you like]—using those figures, make a scene or tell a story in the sand" are two that the authors have found especially useful. Therapists may find it helpful to give such directives as: "Imagine you are making a movie about your life, make a scene to show a typical day [or best day, worst day, most embarrassing time, and so on] in the life of—" If your goal is for group members to share about their families, use the same ideas, directing group members to make a scene showing a typical day for their family. The authors have also found that limiting the number of figures that members can select initially (for example, "select five figures that you like") makes it easier for them to get started, which is helpful when there is a limited amount of time for the activity. (*Note:* In either method, members are always allowed to get additional miniatures as needed.)

When the scene is completed, group members can be asked to describe their scenes or tell stories about them. Ask them to think of a moral for their story or to make up a title for their scene or story. Helpful questions: What is happening? What happened before this? What will happen next? If you could be one of the figures, which would you choose and why? The therapist can then talk directly to that figure—for example, address a figure of a lion and ask, "Lion, what do you think about this scene . . . is there anything you would like to change?" The therapist can ask the lion to talk with another figure or to act out what he'd like to be different in the scene, what happens next, and so on. (For example, "Show me what . . ." The therapist can also ask to talk to other figures in the scene: "I'd like to talk with the dragon behind the tree. . . . Dragon, I noticed you seem to be hiding behind the tree, while the other animals are all together over there." One note of caution: avoid overwhelming group members with interpretations and never coerce them to share their tray. When processing individual sandtrays in a group setting, avoid focusing more than a few minutes at a time on any one group member. For example, ask each member to describe their tray, then go around the group again, asking each member another question or two. Use this opportunity to comment on similarities of descriptions, ideas, and feelings expressed by group members.

There are many variations of structuring sandplay activities to fit the needs of group members. When the group, or a group member, continues to play out a similar scene depicting a problem or traumatic event with no resolution, we have found that a variation of the mutual storytelling technique (Gardner, 1971) can be effective. The therapist asks if he or she may use the figures to tell a similar story. Follow the original story line, but select an alternate ending that presents a possible resolution to the problem or traumatic event. Timing is important in using this technique—more than once, the first author has been told that a proposed version of the story wouldn't work! The technique outlined in the Cooperative Group Art activity can also be adapted for use with sandtray play.

Photographs of completed sandtrays are helpful in observing the progress of group members. The authors keep a 35mm camera in the room for taking pictures of the trays for group members' files. Although the prints are more expensive, we also provide a Polaroid camera for group members to use if they would like to keep a picture of their sandtray.

Conclusion

Almost since the beginning of time, expressive arts have been used in connection with physical and mental healing practices (Feder & Feder, 1981; Peters, 1987). The integration of the expressive arts and therapy expands the scope and depth of each. Both play therapists and art therapists have extolled the value of creative expression in therapy for preadolescent children. Landy (1993) stated that:

> If given free rein to paint, to sing, to dance, to play, to experiment with language and to dramatize, children will do so spontaneously. They express themselves aesthetically for a wide variety of reasons: to explore the world and their developing identities, to give shape to their feelings, to amuse themselves and to

engage in social interactions with others, to create order and to create disorder and to play with possibilities. Even when children are not free to tell us that they have been violated in some way, they will most likely express their hurtful and angry feelings in their sounds and movements, in their sketching and scribbling and in their dramatic play [p. 360].

The integration of expressive arts within an activity group format provides a developmentally appropriate treatment modality for preadolescents that offers many potential benefits. Expressive art activities provide preadolescents with an effective means to express thoughts and feelings that they may be unable to communicate verbally. The use of structured activities encourages interaction between group members, thus providing opportunities to experiment with new and more satisfying ways of relating to peers. Finally, the self-creative process awakened during therapy can continue long after group members leave the group setting, providing internal resources for meeting life's challenges.

Resources

There is an assortment of structured expressive art activities that may be used with preadolescents in group activity therapy. The authors recommend the following titles as resources for a variety of expressive art exercises.

Allan, J. (1988). *Inscapes of the child's world: Jungian counseling in schools and clinics.* Dallas, TX: Spring.

Burns, R., & Kaufman, S. H. (1972). *Actions, styles and symbols in kinetic family drawings.* New York: Brunner/Mazel.

Dileo, J. H. (1983). *Interpreting children's drawings.* New York: Brunner/Mazel.

Fluegelman, A. (Ed.). (1976). *The new games book.* New York: Doubleday.

Fryrear, J., Corbit, I., & Taylor, S. (1992). *Instant images: A guide to using photography in therapy.* Dubuque, IA: Kendall/Hunt.

Furth, G. M. (1988). *The secret world of drawings: Healing through art.* Boston: Sigo Press.

Gil, E. (1994). *Play in family therapy.* New York: Guilford Press.

Kaduson, H., & Schaefer, C. (Eds.). (1997). *101 favorite play therapy techniques.* Northvale, NJ: Aronson.

Kramer, E. (1975). *Art as therapy with children.* Chicago: Magnolia Street.

Landgarten, H. B. (1987). *Family art psychotherapy: A clinical guide and casebook.* New York: Brunner/Mazel.

Liebmann, M. (1986). *Art therapy for groups: A handbook of themes, games, and exercises.* Cambridge, MA: Brookline Books.

Linesch, D. G. (1988). *Adolescent art therapy.* New York: Brunner/Mazel.

McNiff, S. (1992). *Art as medicine: Creating a therapy of the imagination.* Boston: Shambhala.

Mitchell, R. R., & Friedman, H. S. (1994). *Sandplay: Past, present and future.* New York: Routledge.

Nachmanonitch, S. (1990). *Freeplay: The power of improvisation in life and the arts.* New York: Putnam.

Nelson, E. (1975). *Movement games for children.* New York: Sterling.

Oaklander, V. (1988). *Windows to our children.* Highland, NY: Center for Gestalt Development.

Oster, G. D., & Gould, P. (1987). *Using drawings in assessment and therapy.* New York: Brunner/Mazel.

Otto, H. A. (1974). *Fantasy encounter games.* New York: HarperCollins.

Rogers, N. (1993). *The creative connection.* Palo Alto, CA: Science & Behavior Books.

Wadeson, H., Durkin, J., & Perach, D. (1989). *Advances in art therapy.* New York: Wiley.

Waller, D. (1993). *Group interactive art therapy.* New York: Routledge.

Wohl, A., & Kaufman, B. (1985). *Silent screams and hidden cries.* New York: Brunner/Mazel.

References

Allan, J. (1988). *Inscapes of the child's world: Jungian counseling in schools and clinics.* Dallas, TX: Spring.

Carey, L. (1991). Family sandplay therapy. *Arts in psychotherapy, 18,* 231–239.

Celano, M. (1990). Activities and games for group psychotherapy with sexually abused children. *International Journal of Group Psychotherapy, 40*(4), 419–429.

Cermak, S., Stein, F., & Abelson, C. (1973). Hyperactive children and an activity group therapy model. *American Journal of Occupational Therapy, 27*(6), 311–315.

Crocker, J., & Wroblewski, M. (1975). Using recreational games in counseling. *Personnel and Guidance Journal, 53,* 153–158.

Feder, B., & Feder, E. (1981). *The expressive arts therapies.* Upper Saddle River, NJ: Prentice Hall.

Fleshman, B., & Fryrear, J. (1981). *The arts in therapy.* Chicago: Nelson-Hall.

Frank, M., & Zilbach, J. (1968). Current trends in group therapy with children. *International Journal of Group Psychotherapy, 18,* 447–460.

Fryrear, J., Corbit, I., & Taylor, S. (1992). *Instant images: A guide to using photography in therapy.* Dubuque, IA: Kendall/Hunt.

Gardner, R. A. (1971). *Therapeutic communication with children: The mutual storytelling technique.* New York: Science House.

Gil, E. (1994). *Play in family therapy.* New York: Guilford Press.

Ginott, H. (1961). *Group psychotherapy with children: The theory and practice of play therapy.* New York: McGraw-Hill.

Ginott, H. (1975). Group play therapy with children. In G. Gazda (Ed.), *Basic approaches to group psychotherapy and group counseling* (2nd ed., pp. 327–341). Springfield, IL: Thomas.

Kalff, D. (1980). *Sandplay.* Santa Monica, CA: Sigo Press.

Kottman, T., Strother, J., & Deniger, M. (1987). Activity therapy: An alternative therapy for adolescents. *Journal of Humanistic Education and Development, 25* (4), 180–86.

Landgarten, H. B. (1987). *Family art psychotherapy: A clinical guide and casebook.* New York: Brunner/Mazel.

Landreth, G. (1991). *Play therapy: The art of the relationship.* Muncie, IN: Accelerated Development.

Landy, R. (1993). The child, the dreamer, the artist and the fool: In search of understanding the meaning of expressive therapy. *Arts in Psychotherapy, 20,* 359–370.

Lev, E. (1983). An activity therapy group with children in an in-patient psychiatric setting. *Psychiatric Quarterly, 55*(1), 55–64.

Lowenfeld, M. (1979). *The world technique* (2nd ed.). London: Allen & Unwin.

MacLennan, B. (1977). Modifications of activity group therapy for children. *International Journal of Group Psychotherapy, 27*(1), 85–96.

McNiff, S. (1992). *Art as medicine: Creating a therapy of the imagination.* Boston: Shambhala.

Nickerson, E., & O'Laughlin, K. (1983). The therapeutic use of games. In C. D. Schaefer & K. J. O'Connor (Eds.), *Handbook of play therapy* (pp. 174–187). New York: Wiley.

Oaklander, V. (1988). *Windows to our children.* Highland, NY: Center for Gestalt Development.

Peters, J. (1987). *Music therapy: An introduction.* Springfield, IL: Thomas.

Rogers, N. (1993). *The creative connection.* Palo Alto, CA: Science & Behavior Books.

Roos, B., & Jones, S. (1982). Working with girls experiencing loss: An application of activity group therapy in a multi-ethnic community. *Social Work with Groups, 5* (3), 430–437.

Rubin, J. (1984a). *Child art therapy.* (2nd ed.). New York: Van Nostrand Reinhold.

Rubin, J. (1984b). *The art of art therapy.* New York: Brunner/Mazel.

Schaefer, C., & Reid, S. (1986). *Game play: Therapeutic use of childhood games.* New York: Wiley.

Schiffer, M. (1952). Permissiveness versus sanction in activity group therapy. *International Journal of Group Psychotherapy, 2,* 225–261.

Schiffer, M. (1969). *The therapeutic play group.* New York: Grune & Stratton.

Schiffer, M. (1984). *Children's group therapy: Methods and case histories.* New York: Free Press.

Segal, R. (1984). Helping children express grief through symbolic communication. *Social Casework, 12,* 590–599.

Slavson, S. (1944). Some elements in activity group therapy. *American Journal of Orthopsychiatry, 14,* 578–588.

CHAPTER TWELVE

GROUP SANDTRAY-WORLDPLAY

New Dimensions in Sandplay Therapy

Gisela Schubach De Domenico

Play with water and miniatures in a tray of sand was first developed by Margaret Lowenfeld in the 1920s in England. She used it with children, developing a rationale along the following lines:

> The child, unable for the most part to talk about its experience, is able to create
> something whole in a limited, safe space. No particular knowledge or skill is re-
> quired. Free, spontaneous and self-generated sandplay readily emerges when
> no restrictions or specific patterns of play behavior are imposed upon the child.
> The play, itself, represents an actual, physical manifestation of the child's multi-
> dimensional experiences of being human. The manner in which these uniquely
> individual experiences become visible in the sandtray outlines the way in which
> the child's psyche is sorting them into cognitive and behavioral schemata that
> support its habitual operative consciousness. The child's concerns about the
> nature of its internal and external reality, notions regarding time, space, move-
> ment, sensations, feelings, and so on, can be simultaneously expressed using
> the sandtray medium. Often emotionally and temporally conflicted experiences
> can be expressed in the sandtray, thus revealing a fuller flavor of the child's
> personality and the situation the child finds itself in [Lowenfeld, 1979].

The medium, furthermore, allows for the stimulation of the sensorimotor, feeling, thinking and intuitive functions of the child's psyche, thereby evoking natural growth and development. Finally, because the medium is to be used without any particular concern for depicting consensual reality and without adult interference, modeling, or interpretation, the World that emerges during the session is there to "confront the maker." The therapist, as witness, does not need to confront the child. The therapist does not need to interpret the World to the child. Thus Lowenfeld was the first to recognize sandplay as the true mirror of the child's psyche: a mirror in which the child can discover itself. It also becomes a mirror in which the therapist can get to know each particular child and how that child experiences itself and the community that she is a member of (Lowenfeld, 1979).

This very special Lowenfeld play therapy technique became known as sandplay, worldplay, the Lowenfeld World Technique, sandtray, sandbox play, and Sandtray-Worldplay. The term preferred reflects the theoretical bias of the therapist who uses it.

Although Margaret Lowenfeld used sandplay in her clinic's group playroom, neither she nor her students used the sandtray for group psychotherapy. Each child was with its own psychotherapist while playing in the presence of other child-therapist dyads who were also playing in the group playroom. The children's play clearly became communal at times. Rather than letting sandplay evolve into a group process, however, it seems that the institute staff continued to promote parallel sandplay focusing on each child's work individually. In such a group sandplay room everyone uses one collection of objects, creating their own sandtray while engaged with their own observer.

John Hood-Williams, also from Lowenfeld's institute, experimented successfully in the 1980s with families playing together in a single sandtray. He had no interest in group sandplay and actually confided in me that the institute staff found Lowenfeld's communal sandplay room a nuisance (personal communication, 1983). The uncontrolled play intrusions by other therapists' child clients in the room were counterproductive to individual sandplay sessions. After Lowenfeld's death almost all sandplay therapy was shifted to private therapy offices. This illustrates an important point: if the therapist wishes to conduct individual sandplay sessions then these need to be conducted in a private space. As soon as therapists create opportunities for parallel sandplay, a communal or group factor will enter the picture. If the therapist has created an environment that facilitates group sandplay processes, it is only logical that the group process be fostered, supported, and made functional, whether there is one group therapist or five therapist-child dyads in the sandplay room. The psyche moves into the expression of group psyche when two or more people create sandplays at the same time, a point I return to later in the chapter.

Dora Kalff, a Jungian analyst, trained with Margaret Lowenfeld during the 1950s. She saw sandplay as a perfect opportunity for using active imagination with archetypal images. She quite naturally began to translate the child's and adult's uniquely individual sandplay into the psychomythological pack and archetypal patterns that had been so meticulously described by her mentor Carl Jung. Because her primary therapeutic focus remained client individuation, she refrained from using the sandtray in a group setting. She would decry the use of communal, familial, and joint sandplay in the playroom (Kalff, 1966, 1980).

The Evolution of Sandtray-Worldplay Group Therapy

Sandtray-Worldplay therapeutic communication techniques originated in 1984 in Oakland, California, after I completed my phenomenological research of normal preschool children's nondirected sandtray play (De Domenico, 1986). I have used both group and individual sandplay extensively. From 1981 through 1984, this included conducting experimental groups with normal preschool children, and I found that preschool children readily played for two to four hours using the sandtray. When each child was provided with a personal play station and used a communal collection of objects, each of the children created their own World, or a series of evolving play worlds. Although the children tended to respect the other Worlds, they frequently visited one another's Worlds, thus creating opportunities for interaction. They would comment on the ingenuity of the other players, admire their creation, and help each other solve problems that arose during the play period, and they were always eager to be initiated into the stories and dramatic actions that animated their peers' Worlds. It was astonishing how consistently the children were actively receptive to the others' play. They rarely disturbed, destroyed, or played uninvited in someone else's World. They maintained a demeanor of curiosity, trust, and helpfulness. Sharing of objects was easily accomplished, as they had plenty to choose from. Absorbed in their own choreography of play in a group, they required very little adult supervision. The children found their own way of interacting with each other: they never ignored the presence of their peers, even when very involved with their own World. A friendly, nondirective adult presence seemed sufficient most of the time.

One particular group's play ended after the children decided that each of their Worlds was a separate planet in the solar system. With the researcher's help, they insisted on connecting the Worlds with a bridge, which soon became a landing station for interplanetary spaceships. They traveled from World to World with their spaceships, practicing the skills of communal living, hospitality, and creating friendship. This memorable session served to illustrate how sandplay readily evokes group process without explicit directions from the therapist.

Encouraged by normal children's love of group sandplay, I developed formats for working with latency, adolescent, and adult groups in clinical settings

(De Domenico, 1987). At first it was arranged so that each participant had access to their own sandtray. The miniature collection was always generous, so that multiple objects of different categories offered plenty of choices to the participants. Sometimes everyone worked at the same time, the group leader being the only witness. At other times participants worked in dyads, with one building or sharing and one witnessing or listening. There was, in each session, a communal sharing time during which each builder shared their World with the group. No matter which group format was used, each participant had an opportunity to individually create while in the presence of others who were also actively creating their World. This was very successful.

Participants learned that appreciation of each person's uniqueness did not eclipse the often joyous discovery of similarities and commonly held beliefs with other group members. This helped improve self-esteem. It also furthered the experience of a more solid core self, which could be quite different from others and still be connected to them. Generally, group sandplay decreased isolation and withdrawal or extreme introversion. At the same time, those who were antisocial or dominating the group with an overbearing, energetic presence tended to become increasingly more self-reflective and curious about others' reality. Each became more respectful of the others. Group members appeared to astonish one another with their abilities to tolerate and even embrace different viewpoints when these were allowed to be played out. This led to participants' increasingly taking risks of sharing very personal material. They learned that "being with their differences" and "playing with their differences" are quite different from "attacking each other with their differences" or "hiding from their differences" or "converting differentness into sameness." They learned that consensus is not sameness. Relationship does not require sameness. It requires trust. Relationship seems to thrive on the celebration of differentness. Acceptance and trust grew with each session. Unconditional regard for self and others slowly followed.

An example of this dynamic occurred during an adolescent boys' group, which consisted of six boys ranging from thirteen to seventeen years of age, with each young man creating his own tray. A seventeen-year-old participant who had been referred to the group because of his rather belligerent, acting-out, destructive behavior used the sandtray to blow up one world after the other. One day, he was blowing up his own Worlds as usual. He let other group members be with their own activity. Halfway through the session he made a transition: he dug and shaped a place for a community; houses, cars, some people, a few animals and trees. His World became quiet. It became peaceful. It had an air of harmony. There had emerged a geography and a sense of connectedness. The parts were nestled into the whole. There were no major obstructions to free movement and interaction. He said nothing, so we cannot know what he was really experiencing. Yet his quiet and reflective stance marked this World as being significant in a new way. The group leader quietly watched from across the room, feeling that young man had entered a new dimension of relationship to environment and the world at large. The builder remained still and finally smiled briefly. Then he got up and began his customary walk around the room, curiously eyeing the Worlds of his peers. On this day he was more quiet and deliberate than was usual during his frequent "inspection strolls" about the room. He seemed more benignly attentive to his peers' Worlds.

He came upon the World of a fifteen-year-old who had been referred for extreme introversion, shyness, inability to take leadership, and suspected depression. This young man had set up a World of super heroes and super villains, much like we might see in the play of seven-year-olds. The two opposing sides were clearly delineated. They were frozen in their position. The builder stood in front of his World with a perplexed but intense look on his face. Each hand kept moving toward a good guy and a bad guy. Holding them tightly, it seemed like he was intent on having them engage in battle. Yet nothing happened. There was no movement. He released his hold. Then he started up again, gripping each character only to release them again and again. Our visiting spectator watched with great interest. Taking a deep breath, he expanded his chest, reached his right arm to rest on the creator's shoulder. Very gently, with heartfulness, and very much out of character, he said: "Hey, man. Go ahead. Let them do it. Get it out. You will live. Go ahead and do it." As if not having a stake in the outcome and perhaps in respect for that deep private place of truth from which we make life-changing decisions, he quietly moved on without touching the World.

The builder also took a deep breath and this next time did not let go of his grip: the forces of good and evil began to battle. It was as if he had been released from a spell. He now had an avenue of externalizing the internally held conflicts. He had begun the journey into relationship to himself and to others. He now was able to engage with duality and oppositional stances. His guide of inspiration had been a young man who had been stuck in the "battling-killing phase" for many of his latency and adolescent years and who had just discovered in his own play-world a bridge to a place of peace where community was allowed to be.

During sharing, each was quite drawn into the other's World. They had shared a mystery—they had communed together. The group as a whole initiated a discussion about the value of putting up a fight and of war, and the need for offensive and defensive strategies in their daily life. They contrasted this to the value of peace, trust, togetherness, and safety. In future groups they experimented with good and bad, pleasure and pain, and their experiences of law and justice.

Once sandplay is introduced to groups, there never seems to be a dearth of meaningful, socially poignant topics of exploration. It seems that each person, even when excessively exuberant, is able to make a meaningful contribution to the group's time together. Many initial group sessions are very dynamic and have at times a distinctly chaotic flavor at the beginning of the session, until the play itself brings the children into focus. For children in the school setting many supportive friendships blossom that continue to develop during the school hours. Between sessions children are more apt to join cooperative group efforts at school. It seems that group-effort and group-play gradually become operational mental and behavioral constructs for them, that is, they are able to convert concepts into action and experience.

Beyond Parallel Play

In time, I developed additional avenues for group play: Groups of two to four built Worlds together in the standard-sized sandtray (anywhere from twenty to twenty-six inches wide by twenty-four to twenty-eight inches long and three to five inches deep; sometimes a round sandtray, twenty-four to thirty inches in diameter, was used). This manner of playing in group marks a direct shift from parallel to joint play. Such play evokes very different interpersonal dynamics and relationship stresses. It is a more advanced form of communal play, requiring more trust, patience, faith, and interest in the other. It requires the ability and interest to create communally, that is, to pour one's individual promptings into the World of the group. This play teaches not only the ability to be open and visible but also to tolerate being sometimes irritated and sometimes positively stimulated by the sudden and unexpected contributions made by the other members of the group.

Group sandplay magnifies these reactive postures. This causes many strong feelings, opinions, and judgments to emerge readily, which are then woven into the play. As group members continue to play together a new identity, the group ego, is created. Slowly it begins to overshadow the individuals' sense of separate identity. The sandtray becomes a true mirror of the group psyche and what human community is really about. Every member of the group is responsible for this mirroring process, even though neither the process nor the product belongs to any one member of the group. Interpersonal boundaries take on a new and a healthier dimension.

Later, I used a whole-group joint sandplay format. Square group sandtray tables (between four and six feet wide) were used by groups of four to sixteen participants. Here, either all built simultaneously, or each participant took a number of turns where he or she was able to bring one to three objects at a time with verbal sharings into the sandtray. This large group joint sandplay format provided an in-vivo experience of active interpersonal, communal dynamics. These joint group plays quickly demonstrated how much impact each person's actions have. Each person's play destroys some of the integrity of play reality that has come before, while at the same instant creating new and different realities to be played with. This challenged the resources of each participant. There was no hiding or disappearing from the sandplay process, even as the numbers of building-team participants grew.

The psychological processes that are always active during interpersonal relationships were more readily experienced in a conscious manner at the moment in which they happened. They also left their traces in the sand: the slightest shift in sand and objects created a new experience for everyone in the group. Each new shift demanded a physiological, emotional, mental, and spiritual adaptive response, which eventually would be translated into the play. Even when participants did not bring characters or objects into the World, their commentary, touchings, or corrections of the World revealed their relationship to others and their purpose in that group for the day. As we learned to be conscious and to experience each newly emerging event during play time, projection, blaming, denial and other dynamics of nonresponsibility or "unconscious," automatic behavior decreased dramatically.

In group sandplay, we practice spontaneously creating and allowing ourselves to fully experience the play in present time. The group therapist interprets neither the play nor the play behavior of any one member of the group. During the early phases of the group sandplay work, the nonhidden presence of the group's process frequently creates tension, apprehension, and anxiety. The therapist encourages conscious experiencing in each group member: witnessing, reflecting, and sharing skills are learned. Participants realize the risk of participating and the risk of letting others participate. Everyone becomes visible. As witnessing and experiencing are cultivated, everyone becomes just a bit more honest. Biographical and group issues of rejection, exclusion, inclusion, and being supported almost immediately raise their shadowy heads. They tend to become the subject of experimentation in play before the group dares to discuss them verbally. It is far easier for group members to play out the process concretely than to reason or talk it out conceptually among themselves. After play, it is easier to reflect on the building process and the experiences that each member of the group had initiated and had received. With the final World in view, with the outcome clearly visible, it is possible to explore the dynamics of communal creation, cooperation, and relationship. There is no need for the therapist to offer interpretation or summary.

This process is seen in the following example. At the beginning of an adult group, one of the participants rushed to the group table. Reaching her arms as wide as she possibly could, she scooped up a central mound upon which she placed a very large Mother Goddess. In one fell swoop she had conquered the center of the World. Fifteen men and women gasped in disbelief. They had not even chosen an object yet. Here the theme had been chosen. The place had been marked. It felt like a giant provocation. No one said a word. Our conquistador stood beaming; she had claimed her stake. The group leader did not interrupt the process. For thirty minutes each member of the group slowly but surely worked the World, until a higher Mountain, upon which a Male and a Female Deity stood in embrace, emerged. Below them swelled many mounds of differing heights and valleys with rivers and lakes. The varied freedoms and possibilities of life were in clear view—particular attention was paid to the many different ways that people walk the path of life. Many critical and often extremely difficult rites of passage were shown. Life in its diverse manifestation clearly flowed from the Great Mother and the Great Father. The beautiful Mother Goddess had not been moved to the Sacred Mountain. Instead, during the group's weaving of communal story, she was seen as having descended onto Earth to be among the people. She was one of several deities who visited with the many different peoples and animals in this World. She gave the gift of "presence and being noticed" to all who came to her. She received each creature in its fullness. She was the receptive Mother. Although she had been honored by each member of the group, she was no longer the central experience. Although she had arrived with the explosion of one group member's narcissism, after group play she became that which all of us dream of: the wonderfully caring Mother who makes room for us all and who receives us just the way we are.

After building and group storytelling was completed the group used their reflective processing time to explore their initial reaction to the attempted takeover, and how they slowly recovered from it. Members were surprised to learn that during the building process of a session there are many different stages of communal work that are necessary to go through, including the following:

1. *Shyness and intimidation* about what inner play promptings to follow
2. *Shock and surprise* evoked by the often unexpected, radically different initial plays of the participants
3. *Chaos and disorganization* as each member tries to give more enthusiastic expression to their individual promptings
4. *Emerging islands of small visions and mutual intentions* as members notice how their spontaneous contributions begin to interface and overlap with those of one or two other members in the group
5. *Experimentation and increasing the scope of possible play expressions* as the group slowly begins to develop common interest, recognizing and playing with the life-questions that are posed by the group's psyche
6. *Revisioning and refinement* as the group begins to take responsibility for the created World and attends to the small details and their active relationship to the whole World
7. *Resolution or a place of rest* as the play process comes to a natural pause or conclusion for that day

During group sessions over time members of the group become more adept at cooperative communal play. They increasingly refine these phases of the creative relationship process and are able to give more attention to mythmaking and reflective processing of the significance of the completed play project.

When using this large group sandtray joint-building format, it is notable that participants' social adaptive responses increase. Territorialism and possessiveness at first increase. Later they tend to give way to a greater desire to be empathic and curious about others. Those who could not hold a place or position in the World slowly learn how to claim a space for themselves and their contribution. Some participants, often for the first time, clearly experience the laws of cause and effect, as they see their unique, undeniable impact on the communal World. This allows for the exploration of the concepts of personal and social responsibility, which have often eluded them in individual verbal therapy. Ultimately, it is not social moral pressure that confronts the builder. It is, rather, experiencing the builder's unique impact on the World—whenever anyone takes a turn, that individual's influence on the community increases.

The impact on the World recedes as subsequent members take their turn and thus gain influence. When group members eagerly participate, Worlds change and evolve dramatically and inevitably become lessons about life and community for each member of the group. Over time members become aware of group visions and group ideas—and of their increasing acceptance and support of these group forms. Repeatedly it is found that the topics of sandplays are completely germane to the participants' current life issues and that there is rarely a need to assign themes or life tasks to the group. The group psyche seems to know just what needs to be explored each day.

Perhaps most poignant is the recognition that a group's creative process is more than the sum total of the individual members' contribution. Groups can create Worlds undreamt of by individuals alone. This generates untold excitement. I believe that the creative potential of a group of individuals is the primary driving force behind positive, voluntary socialization practices. Group sandplay initiates us into the joy of interpersonal possibilities.

Such positive experiences with clinical individual and group Sandtray-Worldplay sessions led me to include filial sandplay, couple sandplay, and family sandplay sessions into my therapeutic practice. Strictly speaking whenever two or more people work in the sandtray, the group psyche is evoked. Whether we are working with teacher-student, father-child, a six-member family, or a couple who live and work together, we are dealing with interpersonal processes (De Domenico, 1988).

In 1984, I incorporated educational group sandplay into my experiential Sandtray-Worldplay training program for clinicians, educators, business consultants, creatologists, and transformational workshop leaders. In this program both directed and nondirected plays using single, dyadic, and large-group formats are used to teach the principles of Sandtray-Worldplay, the nature of the human psyche, the multidimensionality of human consciousness, and the processes by which individuation and socialization are supported by sandplay.

When using the directed group play approach, the therapist assigns themes and topics that are felt to apply to that particular group. For example, at a memorial service for a mutual friend, the therapist chose to ask each player to select one to three objects that characterized their special relationship to the deceased. They were to tell the story and memories associated with their image choices. At the end of the four-hour session, the group was amazed at how they understood the meaning of their friend's life. They were now ready to go and scatter his ashes.

Another example involves a classroom setting where the teacher asked each student to bring a number of objects that illustrated their significant experience of being an adolescent in their family. After several hours of play, students were able to speak freely about the ecstasy and the tribulations, including the unhealed wounds of childhood and the exciting possibilities that they wanted to have within their reach. Students were then assigned to journal their experiences, which eventually became essays.

A third example included a latency-aged sexual abuse group, where the therapist asked the children to show how their living conditions had changed since the disclosure of the abuse. This allowed children to get in touch with both the grief and the relief, the guilt and the many other issues that they rarely had the opportunity or the ability to express verbally.

During nondirected group sandplays, the group psyche determines the themes and the evolutions of the themes during each session. No thematic frame is given by the therapist. Members of the group are free to suggest any topics, to pose questions, or to work and play together spontaneously. These sessions require a great deal of trust on the part of the therapist, who often may not trust either the clients' individual psyches or the group psyche. Nonetheless, spontaneous play processes are often the best, the most inspired, and the most useful in present time.

For some time, I have used sandplay for verbal group closure. At the end of a conversational, therapeutic group exercise, children or adults are asked to remember what they have experienced during group that day. They are then asked to pick one to three objects, place them in a group sandtray, and very briefly share in this way what was most important to them that day, what they learned, what they disliked the most, and so on.

Students who have been trained in Sandtray-Worldplay have successfully used group sandplay with hospital and school groups, classroom educational group activities, church and business retreat groups, women's and men's groups, HIV groups, grief groups, adolescent and adult batterers groups, recovery groups, victim groups, and many other special interest groups. When group leaders are well trained in the ways of Sandtray-Worldplay, they report excellent results. They are able to use this dynamic expressive tool intelligently.

Guillermo Garcia (1994), of Monterey, Mexico, uses Sandtray-Worldplay techniques combined with transformational rituals and sound business consultations to help large corporations revise their way of visioning and defining company goals. This allows the corporations to restructure themselves so that everyone's unique talents are employed in the work community in a natural manner, without strain. He uses a combination of teaching "techniques of visioning," cooperative management skills, and individual and communal sandplay sessions. The group sandplay sessions focus primarily on visioning the corporate goals and the possible pathways to attaining those goals. Using sandplay, the group then creates transformational rituals that combine the company's visions with a sense of personal meaning for group members.

Alternative Special Sandplay Groups

At the Institute for the Study of Health and Illness in Bolinas, California, Marion Weber and Rachel Naomi Remen use the sandtray during their adult retreats for cancer patients, physicians, and community agencies. They explore special topics that are salient to the life challenges that face every member of the group. Through group sandplay rituals, participants discover and find visible, individual essence and meaning in a profoundly respectful way. They create a sacred community as each group member's inner wisdom enriches the group's knowing: participants return to their daily life able to focus on the essential in their life at home or at work.

Setting Up the Space for Communal Sandtray Therapy

To conduct group sandplay session it is essential that you provide the following setting and materials.

You need a well-lit, pleasant room that will allow for the number of participants that you anticipate. That is, the room needs sufficient space for everyone to work on their own sandtray and still have room to move about, and for everyone to access the sandtray collection easily, without disturbing others in their work and without being too crowded. This is particularly important with children, as insufficient space between their physical bodies will encourage interpersonal physical body play, rather than symbolic play in the sandtray. Therapists will focus more on behavior than sandplay and thus will undermine the process.

Supply a well-organized collection of miniature objects, including many different categories (De Domenico, 1987). The objects are a vocabulary of human and universal life experiences; they are multidimensional and interdimensional, giving the opportunity to represent concrete and abstract, fantastic and realistic experiences with equal facility. An impoverished vocabulary results in impoverished play opportunities. It creates lack of specificity and precision in the play expression.

Children and adults need the identical sandtray collections. They both will find uses for small, precious, and breakable objects, spiritual and archetypal images, as well as for plastic animals, monsters, cars, and different large-sized objects. If you have specific interest groups, such as children of addicted parents, sexual abuse survivors, and so on, make sure that you have small objects that are directly related to these experiences in your collection. Often therapists and counselors are reluctant to introduce religious objects into their collection, but it is helpful to use some objects from all religious and spiritual traditions. One standard of measurement of an adequate collection may be considered: if you and six of your colleagues can play together once weekly for a year with the collection you are offering your clients in group and you are able to express yourselves without difficulty, your collection is adequate for a group of seven children or adults, regardless of their diagnosis.

Displaying objects on shelves creates a permanent sandtray room. This is the best setup, provided that you can maintain the shelves in an orderly fashion. This is particularly important in group play, since each group creates a certain amount of chaos as part of their evolution of play. As we do not wish clients to experience the chaos of either the clinic staff or the therapeutic facility, it is essential to keep the sandplay room orderly. Children are very prone to mirror the chaos that prevails in the environment in which they are placed. The chaos that resides in each individual child and the group at large ought to manifest in the particular sandtray that is created by the group. It is certainly not necessary to model chaos.

For preschool children it is often best to store some objects of different categories in a series of small bins, so that these may be dumped into the sandtray or onto the floor and sorted out. Tactile play with grouped, clumped objects is an essential and normal aspect of cognitive play. It is not necessary for children to use the shelf display for such developmental play when small toy bins are available, so providing such bins will save the clinic staff a great deal of effort. Place the bins somewhere between the sandtrays and the shelves.

When you are forced to use a portable sandtray collection, place objects by categories into small baskets and bins. Set these up on tables or on the floor. Make sure that everyone can reach the bins without crowding into one another. Leave heavy and large items, such as rocks, driftwood, and special figures that you can readily duplicate at the facility where the group meets, while you transport the rest in a suitcase with wheels for easy transport.

If you do not have a sandtray collection but you want to conduct several sessions with groups of children, adolescents, or adults, bring as many rocks, flowers, natural objects, and miniatures as you can collect. During other group sessions, have members of your group create objects to add to your basic collection. Then ask each member of the group to bring fifteen to thirty objects in a little basket. Let these objects be the member's favorites, or request that they be related to specific topics that you may wish to explore in the group work. Make sure they are marked with a waterproof pen and have each person make a list of what items they brought. Put all objects on a communal table for everyone to use during each group sandtray session.

You want to provide individual and joint sandtray opportunities for your sandplay groups. For preschool children or groups functioning at a preschool level of development consider providing some very deep sandtrays. These lend themselves better to energetic sandplay and to the digging, burying, uncovering activities that are an essential part of the cognitive play patterns of early childhood and of those who have experienced much trauma. Do not use sandtrays that are smaller than twenty inches by twenty-four inches by three inches: it will be too difficult for the child's psyche to express itself fully in a smaller space. To create a portable group sandtray, you can stretch a heavy blue tarp over a square frame of four- to six-foot-long pieces of two-by-four boards, making a large box that can be filled with sand. This portable box works, but is somewhat fragile; it is obviously preferable to have a permanent, deep, large-group sandtray.

Although I do not partition the group sandtray into equal portions to be used by members of the group, other therapists do so at times. My perspective is that this creates paradox and is contraindicated in joint sandplay: it is like saying, "play together" but "do not play together—stay in your own space." This may be convenient for the therapist who does not have six or ten sandtrays available and who can simply divide up the large group tray into sections that can serve as individual trays. Consider that the large tray is still an invitation to do what is natural: to play together. Individual sandplay means having your own sandtray—your own space that you can access from any side of the tray, without having to be concerned about others.

The group members themselves may freely choose to divide up the tray, create barriers, make rules for territory, trespassing, and so on. As the play progresses through transgressions, wars, conflicts, peace, invitations to join, and so on, each member of the group will automatically be exposed to teachings about group creation. You will see a history of human civilization emerge before your eyes.

Eventually, each member of the group, in their own time, will be initiated into the group consciousness. Group sandplay goes beyond individual sandplay. It involves the discovery of group. Group sandplay teaches about the integrity of the group and the community. Eventually it teaches that rugged individualism, territorialism, and terrorism are harmful to the group. It teaches about the wonders of sharing individuality in a common container. Eventually, everyone learns about the "common good" and what happens when creativity is used for the greater good of all. Social responsibility and environmental responsibility are born through self-initiated group experimentations and reflections.

Therefore, when you wish to teach children about the wonders of their individual beingness, their integrity of character, and their special abilities to express and share who they are, give each child an individual sandtray. Have plenty of sandtrays on hand. Let sandplay be done as parallel play. It will serve the purpose. If, on the other hand, you cannot resist and you, the therapist, must divide the group sandtray with boundary lines or dividers, consider taking them out at the end of the session and letting participants ponder a World without divisions.

Do not substitute lentils, rice, or cornmeal for sand, even when dealing with small children. Make sure that everyone can play with the sand. Provide pitchers of water, so that the sand can be moistened and flooded, if necessary. Sandplay is elemental play, that is, it is natural play. Pay attention to how you can provide earth, air, water, and fire for safe and protected play. There are some populations where it is considered essential that you let them work with the elemental matrix of sand and water—behaviorally disordered children, those who have experienced physical, sexual, or medical trauma, or who those who exhibit autistic, withdrawn features.

It is possible to teach children not to eat sand. Simply provide food and drink during group session. During sandplay the alimentary canal is stimulated as much as the hands of the player: "eating the world" readily fuses with "playing with the world." By separating the playing consciousness from the eating consciousness, the child will slowly gain mastery over the difference between the inside and the outside of the body. Play with sand in a container regulates physiological energy. It may arouse and stimulate physical energy. It may calm physical energy. In fact, it promotes the exploration of various intensities of energies and helps the children and adults to appreciate their physical body as a source of energy and movement over which they can learn to have control.

Rather than constantly acting in reaction to outside stimuli, children and adults can learn to listen to their insides and to remember that there is an inside and an outside to their body. Play with sand helps children reorient themselves with their physical bodies, affecting their coordination. At later phases of the work it allows them to orient themselves in relationship to the external world. A sense of geography and interpersonal space develops as they are able to explore roads, topographies, cities, and various habitats.

Play with sand provides for development of a mental acuity that allows for the appreciation of wholeness and relatedness; it tends to bridge splitting and the denial of opposition and disharmony. As children dig deep into the sand, the steady-state condition created by the sandtray container quickly shows them that they are also going up: so "going deep down under" also evokes the experience of "going up high." You cannot do one without the other. Simultaneously, experiencing "inside" allows them to become conscious of "outside."

Further, play with sand allows children to feel a full range of emotions that come under their control as they manipulate the sand and the objects during sandplay. Play with sand stimulates the emotional body and encourages the physical expression of affect. Pounding, hitting, and smashing of sand is common.

Play with sand also teaches children about time and the evolution of present to past and the evolution of future into present time. Play with sand stimulates the awakening and the use of memory. As such, it allows for demonstration of and experimentation with events that took place in the past. Frequently this leads to revisionings and integration.

It is clearly quite possible to allow children to play in sand and to experiment with molding and shaping in their own sandtrays and in large-group sandtrays. It does involve making messes, but both life and sandplay are messy. Out of the mess emerges order, providing that play is allowed to happen and that time is given to experience play consciously. For best results, provide both wet and dry sand—and have a good vacuum cleaner and linoleum or tile flooring, or lay down tarps if your playroom is carpeted. Use bowls of water to wash sand off the hands and the toys. Empty these bowls into gardens, flowerbeds, driveways, or other places where sand is welcome—it will block plumbing, so keep it out of sinks and toilets.

Cleanup After Group Sandplay

There are different procedures for cleaning up after group sandplay. After the Worlds have been shared and photographed it is possible to ask each member of the group to help clean up the objects, putting them back on the shelves and into their respective baskets. If you have your collection on shelves, it may be easier for children to hand you the clean objects, so that the objects will find their correct place on the shelves.

When each person has done their own sandtray, it is vital that the builders remove the first three to five objects from their own World: this breaks the integrity and the reality of the World and dissipates the experiences that are depicted. At times, participants do not wish to dissemble their own World. They would like to leave it intact. It is important that the therapist respect these wishes. The World should then be dissembled after the person has left the sandplay facility.

Cleaning up is best done as a respectful ritual. It is not about teaching children how to clean up after themselves. It is about ending an important group ritual. It is about creating a membrane that will allow what has been born during the session to incubate in the conscious psyche of each participant.

Selection Criteria for the Sandplay Group

Group sandplay therapists have found that it is sometimes quite difficult to have children whose developmental levels are too different in the same group. If this is unavoidable make the group small, for example, have four children working together. You may match groups according to common interests and concerns, according to age, gender, or other characteristics. When you do so, be prepared that participants will respond quite differently to these common concerns, even when you direct the group process. In general, group psyche will direct the nature of the individuals' contribution to the group play. If you as the therapist are ready to receive whatever play emerges in the individual or group sandplays, the healing and learning value of the play will become obvious. Conducting groups challenges the group leader's capacity to be surprised by the unexpected.

How to Structure the Group Sandplay Session

It is generally best to allow two to four hours for a sandplay session. Adolescents and adults can often benefit from a day-long vision quest or from a weekend retreat. Each session can follow a general format:

1. Begin with a welcome circle, so that everyone may check in with the group.
2. Follow with the building of individual, dyadic, or group Worlds.
3. Give time for quiet reflection and revisions.
4. Allow members of the group to quietly sit before the Worlds created by others, so that they can become known.
5. Invite each group member to share a story or their associations to their own World or the entire Group World.
6. Give time for asking questions and initiating sharings about the group process, the impact of the Worlds on different group members, the relationship of

the issues raised in the Worlds and how they correspond to each member's concerns about daily life at home or school or in the neighborhood.

7. Finally, allow the group to reflect on the actual teachings that they received from the play with sand, water, and miniatures.

At all times discourage interpretation—neither indulge nor let others indulge in the act of telling or showing others who they are, what they think, feel, intuit, or remember, and where they are going. Group sandplay is very effective when each one gives voice to how they experience their own reality.

You may find that some groups spend most of their initial sessions in the building phase. If that is the case, see that you schedule a longer period of time or leave just enough time for personal reflection, quiet looking at everyone's creation, and a short verbal sharing and summary.

Recommended Training and Experience

It is essential that the play therapist who intends to use sandplay with groups have extensive personal experience using the sandtray in individual and in group sessions. Individual and group play therapy training does not adequately prepare the therapist for the issues that arise during individual and group sandplay. I believe that the greatest contraindication to the use of the sandtray is the therapist or facilitator who is inexperienced and lost in inappropriate countertransference responses. Such a therapist repeatedly resorts to interpretation and is fearful of the experiences depicted so vividly in the sandplay. Although limited training for group sandtray therapy is available, there are ample experiential training possibilities for individual sandplay work throughout the country, and individual work is a good beginning. Thereafter, it is recommended that one seek out experiential Sandtray-Worldplay training centers.

Conclusion

There are many ways of conducting a sandtray group. Experiment and be watchful. Allow the group to take the lead. Each session is different. Notice the evolution of the sandplay process as the group moves into attunement over time. Do not hesitate to combine group sandplay with other expressive modalities. Always support the group in its process, for it will tend to move toward equilibrium, growth, and maturity.

In a group Sandtray-Worldplay session, children and adults can tap the individual and group psyche and promote the expression of deeply felt experiences—including traumatic and inspirational events—all of which become visible within an interpersonal group context. The group is the witness, even when a nonverbal stance is taken. The sandtray itself is the evidence. It becomes simply life, consciousness, and an opportunity to learn how to create and how to be with phenomena. Sandplay becomes playing with present time. Sandplay becomes creation of history. This simple, concrete process creates honesty. Honesty promotes the expression of truth. The group may be experienced as a safe and a sacred community. Most clients have rarely experienced the safety and empowerment of a functional group either at home or in their neighborhood, their school, or their community at large. Group sandplay may arouse much joy and excitement.

Sandtray group community is neither based on coercion into sameness nor on the extinction of differentness; it is based on the loving celebration and constructive use of human diversity and individual uniqueness. Nonharmful communal experiences facilitate learning, healing, recovery, cooperation, and joyful living. It is possible to create sandtray community, no matter how young or how old participants are.

When the principles of Sandtray-Worldplay are applied in a group setting, it is possible to achieve excellent results. During sessions, members of the group break down their walls to become more open and more willing to communicate personal experiences with themselves and others. They learn new skills to express themselves and to tell their true story, and sometimes they reedit old scripts. Group members learn to face life issues among their peers, find their inner resources to solve problems, and learn from the lessons of life that others bring to group. They additionally develop the capacity to witness and to listen to others as much as they learn to tolerate being witnessed and being listened to in a space kept safe by both the group leader and the group. Participants also develop a sense of a free and respectful community as they explore a new and different practice of interpersonal communication skills. They learn how to formulate reflective language in order to create personally meaningful relationships. Relationships become interesting. Relationships become joyous.

Often narcissism, alienation, aggression, and other inappropriate defense mechanisms against communal relationship decrease as the wisdom of the personal psyche expresses itself strongly in the group. Group members, including the leaders, experience tribal consciousness and the empowerment that comes about when individual life stories and their corresponding psychospiritual wisdom and understanding are woven together in the here-and-now of group sandplay. With deceptive ease, folklore, mythology, and the scientific and spiritual traditions of humanity appear in the sandtrays of groups. Each member contributes. The

Worlds of Community become poignant teachers about self, others, and life. They answer many questions. They create much awe and wonder.

Because of combined individual and group efforts of Sandtray-Worldplay groups, there is a gradual expansion of each individual's consciousness that includes increased awareness of physical body sensation, affect, biographical, familial and archetypal memory, social and individual thinking patterns, hunches and premonitions, and universal metaphysical truths. All these avenues of awareness primarily support the individual's ability to be self, to plan, to decide, to take action, and to take responsibility for self when alone and when in the presence of others. Conscious awareness expands during the group play session. It continues to grow during the weeks, months, and sometimes years following a session. This is so whether you conduct Sandtray-Worldplay groups with children or adults.

References

De Domenico, G. (1986). *The Lowenfeld world apparatus: A methodological contribution towards study and analysis of the sandtray play process.* Unpublished doctoral dissertation, Pacific Graduate School of Psychology, Menlo Park, CA. UMI #8717059.

De Domenico, G. (1987). *The Vision Quest Into Symbolic Reality training series, Level 5.* Oakland, CA: Vision Quest Into Symbolic Reality.

De Domenico, G. (1988). *Sandtray worldplay: Comprehensive guide to the use of the sandtray in psychotherapy and transformational settings.* Oakland, CA: Vision Quest Into Symbolic Reality.

Garcia, G. (1994). *Sandtray worldplay as a multidimensional approach/process for team's vision development and transformation.* Unpublished doctoral dissertation. Pacific Graduate School of Psychology, Menlo Park, CA. UMI# LD03125.

Kalff, D. (1966). The archetype as a healing factor. *Psychologia, 9,* 177–184.

Kalff, D. (1980). *Sandplay.* Santa Monica, CA: Sigo Press.

Lowenfeld, M. (1979). *The world technique* (2nd ed.). London: Allen & Unwin.

CHAPTER THIRTEEN

RELATIONAL ACTIVITY PLAY THERAPY GROUP

A "Stopping Off Place" for Children on Their Journey to Maturity

D. Michael Smith and Nancy R. Smith

In his poem "The Death of the Hired Man," Robert Frost (1969) tells of Warren and Mary as they discuss the return of Silas, the seasonal worker on their New England farm, and his yearly trek to resume his duties of clearing and haying. Mary has noticed that Silas is decidedly different this year—he looks much older and appears fragile and finished. She believes he has come "home" to die. Even though he has a brother nearby who is a successful bank director, Mary believes Silas has returned to their farm under the guise of doing another year's farm work, though he is clearly incapable of it. As the two ponder why he has returned to them, Mary offers this: "Home is the place where, when you have to go there, they have to take you in." To which Warren replies: "I should have called it: 'Something you somehow haven't to deserve' " (p. 38).

Home—a place to go when you have no other place to go, a place where you belong and you can't earn your place. To gain entrance, you are not required to pass any kind of exam or have a net worth of certain size. Something essential of who and how you are is distinct from all others—a place where you belong and fit in and find a kind of acceptance that you don't find any other place.

Through Warren and Mary, Frost offers this as one definition of *home:* a place where, when you have no other place, you go there simply because in that place you experience a quality of acceptance and regard that you've found nowhere else. Somehow, this place, and especially what happens among the people there, embodies and conveys a quality of relationship that you, consciously or not, perceive or experience as necessary at that point in time. It is a place where, defects and all, you experience a degree of emotional safety that makes it acceptable to be who you are, as you are, without needing to offer rationale, defense, or pretense.

Naturally, Frost is not speaking of a physical home, but of a relational home—an experience in which individuals are loved, accepted, and welcomed in spite of personal deficits, complicating problems, and bothersome behaviors. Such a home is the birthright of each child, the ideal place for a child to begin life's journey toward health and wholeness. However, in light of the myriad distractions and difficulties in our society, many children either have never had such a safe haven or need an additional sense of "home" in which they can overcome behavior difficulties and discover new ways of thinking, feeling, and behaving in order to move forward toward maturity.

Because children's difficulties arise in the context of relationships with others, many of them are in need of a peer group experience in which they can resolve personal problems that, if left unattended, will dramatically impair their healthy development. Frost's metaphor can also represent the kind of "safe home" experience that is created in a Relational Activity Play Therapy (RAPT) group, providing a launching point for a presentation of the kind of "safe stopping off place" experience that children need if they are to become more fully who they are. This chapter combines the theoretical and practical aspects of such a group, illustrating them with verbatim and actual group examples. One primary goal in a RAPT group is to enable children to learn, through their experience and involvement with the other children and the leader, ways of living with others and with themselves that will make them more capable of meaning and fulfillment throughout life.

With this as a touchstone, the chapter moves on to a description of the essential elements of a Relational Activity Play Therapy Group. The authors are indebted to the pioneering work of Samuel Slavson (1945, 1948, 1952), Mortimer Schiffer (1969, 1977, 1984), Virginia Axline (1969), Haim Ginott (1961, 1968), and Garry Landreth (1991, 1993), for their contributions to the fields of play therapy, group therapy, and group play therapy with children. The Relational Activity Play Therapy group model incorporates and combines their ideas and ours, developed from experience in leading children's groups over the last fifteen years.

Presuppositions Concerning Play Therapy

By way of presuppositions and assumptions concerning play therapy in general and its importance in the growth of children, we believe, and our experience has shown, that children use play and toys to express themselves in ways that they are unable to achieve with words because play is their most natural and immediate form of communication (Landreth, 1991). If toys are not available, they will use found objects (sticks, stones, mud, for example) and play with what is available to them. We embrace what has become something of a mantra to play therapists: "play is the language; toys are the words" of children (Axline, 1969). Landreth, in Berg and Landreth (1990), puts it succinctly when he says: "Play is to children what verbalization is to adults. It is a medium for expressing feelings, exploring relationships, describing experiences, disclosing wishes, and achieving self-fulfillment" (p. 261).

We also affirm that children do not have to be taught or learn to play. Play, as the child's language, is innate and universal—and children communicate freely and openly in their "native language" (Landreth, 1991). From their first tentative stabs and grasps at the mobile hanging above their cribs or the rattle by their sides, children reach out to their world in play. Thus, for children, play is a primary means of communicating themselves to the people and world about them.

We further suggest that children appear to play without conscious intent or purpose. If you ask a child, "What are you doing?" or "Why are you playing that right now?" you will likely get little more than a mumbled "I don't know" or "It's fun"—or a puzzled look. Children aren't well known for their rational, carefully reasoned responses to adult questions about their play. Children appear to play for play's sake alone, much of the time.

They also appear to enjoy and seek out opportunities to play with other children. This need to engage other children in play seems to be innate and universal as well. It is part of the human socialization process to want to be with other children in play, even if their play skills at times are undeveloped or troublesome. The particular difficulties that bring a child into therapy also limit that child's ability to connect meaningfully with other children. This difficulty in establishing and maintaining relationships with other children is often a primary reason for referral to a play therapy group. The observational comment that a child "plays well with other children" is a standard evaluation of early childhood teachers through the years. Yet it captures the wisdom of the widely accepted notion that children who are well balanced are children who possess and exercise the ability to play with other children in ways that are mutually fulfilling and meaningful. Nurturing this quality of relationship among children is a primary goal of Relational Activity Play Therapy groups.

Rationale for Relational Activity Play Therapy Groups

To integrate the progress made in individual play therapy, some children need to be in a group setting, with many of the same toys and the relationship with the therapist still available to them, but also with other children. They need the opportunity to take what they have gotten from their relationship with the therapist in individual play therapy and use it to connect with real kids. Often children require this additional experience before they are able to form workable relationships as friends with other children. Other children need a group experience as their primary mode of therapy. These children show the traits that make them viable group candidates from the outset.

Thus several key questions pose themselves at this point: What are reasons for referral to a Relational Activity Play Therapy group? What essential characteristics and traits should be considered before placing a child in a Relational Activity Play Therapy group? What characteristics eliminate a child as a workable candidate for group? Beyond these, what types of children combine well to form a therapeutically balanced group? And what types of children should *not* be combined in the same group? These questions and others we will now consider.

Reasons for Referring to Group

In general, we concur with Landreth's criteria for referral to play groups (Berg & Landreth, 1990), indicating RAPT groups are viable for children who

- Have difficulty developing workable social and peer relationships
- Lack self-discipline in controlling their own behavior and impulses
- Suffer poor self-esteem
- Experience a general lack of motivation
- Have difficulty in developing coping behaviors that enable them to make adequate and self-enhancing adjustments in life

The child's chronological age and developmental age (level of maturation) are essential considerations when placing a child into any type of group therapy, whether a RAPT group, group play therapy, activity group play therapy, structured group counseling, or social skills group (Berg & Landreth, 1990). Landreth recommends the placement of children up to age nine in group play therapy (which is characterized by a lack of specific group goals and in which group cohesion is not considered essential to the process of change) and the placement of children nine to thirteen in activity group play therapy. However, we find that by incorporating both free play time and group activity time into the RAPT format, children ranging in age from four through preadolescence are able to make dramatic changes in RAPT groups.

In structured group counseling, which is often reserved for latency and preadolescent ages and traditional social skills groups (as distinct from group play therapy and activity group therapy), children primarily verbalize their thoughts and feelings, as opposed to playing or acting them out. In this type of group, members talk about topics selected beforehand by the group leader. Group discussion is augmented by members' participation in some aspect of structured activity that is designed specifically to meet particular identified needs of participants to assist them in managing real-life social situations. The emphasis is on furnishing group members with specific social living skills that have been identified as necessary to their healthy functioning (Ohlsen, Horne, & Lawe, cited in Berg & Landreth, 1990). RAPT groups gradually incorporate group discussion and structured activities into the group process as the members emerge into a functioning unit. An elaboration of how Relational Activity Play Therapy makes use of elements from each of these types of groups with supplemental beliefs and additions will follow later in the chapter.

An Essential Trait for Group Membership

Ginott (1961) regards "social hunger" as an essential trait a child must possess if participation in group play therapy is to be therapeutic. Social hunger is a child's "desire to gain acceptance by his peers, to act, dress, and talk as they do, and to attain and maintain status in his group" (p. 17). The child is motivated to change behavior in exchange for acceptance by the group. The presence (or absence) of social hunger is a function of the child's earlier primary attachment to parents or essential caretakers. If the child's caretakers have met "enough" of the basic needs for food, clothing, shelter, physical and emotional closeness, and protection to have awakened the child's hunger for approval and recognition by others, the child is a viable candidate for group play therapy. However, if the child did not attach to the mother or a mother figure in such a way that these primary attachment needs were met in a satisfactory manner, the child is not regarded as workable in group play therapy. Ginott believes that a child who did not bond satisfactorily may not be able to delay impulses and gratification of needs enough to manage the frustration inherent in working in a group play therapy setting and should be referred to individual play therapy instead. Ginott is also of the opinion that children who have suffered extreme emotional deprivation are not likely to succeed in a group setting: "Because their primary relationships failed them, they are suspicious of all relationships" and need individual therapy to being the slow process of building a trusting relationship with the therapist (p. 17).

We accept Ginott's premise of some emotional bonding as a prerequisite for group membership, yet we have found that while a careful consideration of each child's background and current life issues eliminates some children from placement in a RAPT group, a large percentage of children with a wide range of emotional and behavioral difficulties can and do benefit in RAPT groups. Indeed, most children can benefit from working in group. The following section lists those children who do not work well in group, and therefore, should not be included.

Children Who Should Not Be Included in RAPT Groups

Children who have not developed and do not possess Ginott's basic premise of "social hunger" may not be appropriate for RAPT groups. These children do not appear to possess enough of a need to belong to a group of peers to trade behavioral changes for group membership (Ginott, 1968). We have also noted some additional types of children who should be kept out of RAPT groups:

- Children who are not able to tolerate the degree of permissiveness necessary for the group to function effectively. For these children, their need for structure, predictability, and perfection makes them unable to manage the degree of permissiveness characteristic of RAPT groups (Berg & Landreth, 1990).
- Children who act out sexually and run the risk of exposing other children to sexualized behavior or sexual acting out in the group (DeMaria & Cowden, 1992). However, we do place children who have worked through much of the trauma in RAPT groups as a way of helping them safely reenter the world of relationships—relationships deserving of trust.
- Children who are so driven by narcissistic self-love that they are unable to give and take with others. These children appear unable to get outside of themselves enough to manage in a group setting.
- Children who have been so traumatized and abused that they are unable to establish trust with other group members. These children appear more workable in longer-term individual play therapy wherein they can take their time learning to trust and rely on an adult before they are considered for group.
- Children who are so hostile and angry that they are unable to interact without physical violence toward others.
- Children who are openly psychotic or who exhibit a marked deviation in their ability to separate fantasy from reality (Ginott, 1968).
- Children who appear to be antisocial or sociopathic in terms of their personality orientation and conduct history, and children with such severe characterological impairment that they would be likely to victimize, traumatize, or impair the growth of other group members (Slavson & Schiffer, 1975).

Facilitating Change in Relational Activity Play Therapy Group

The primary goal in creating a RAPT group is to create an emotionally secure, permissive, and accepting environment that is such an emotionally safe place that all the children cannot help but be their real selves without fear of reprisal, punishment, shame or rejection. It takes an experienced, highly skilled therapist to create a place and process so safe that each child feels truly accepted and valued all the time—whether behaving or misbehaving, participating or withdrawing, creating or destroying, helping or hurting (Slavson & Schiffer, 1975). Only in such an accepting environment can children risk being their worst selves, a vital necessity if they are to unravel their "mixed-upness" and reorganize themselves into a healthier whole (Berg & Landreth, 1990).

The RAPT group provides a cocoon-type experience in which each child's personal metamorphosis can occur. Though the process of change is individually unique, children generally follow a predictable cycle of change, observable in four distinct phases of the process: *reenactment, reexamination, redirection,* and *reintegration.* In this cycle the child will reenact problematic behaviors, reexamine self in light of unexpected responses of the children and therapist, redirect self to experiment with more positive behaviors and attitudes, and eventually reintegrate newly acquired ways of thinking, feeling, and behaving into self and relationships with others. Following a description of reenactment and reexamination, we will illustrate how children move through this cycle of change with a verbatim transcript from a RAPT group.

Phase One: Reenactment

Most often, children initially put their best foot forward in a group, but as soon as a child senses the accepting, permissive attitude of the therapist, he or she begins to reenact, or recreate, problematic behaviors. This reenactment is grist for the therapist's mill, bringing problems into the open so that the child can directly address these difficulties and begin the process of change. Sometimes there is no grace period of good behavior, and a child will display problematic behaviors in a first session. Examples of this may include a hostile outburst, haughty bossiness, silly baby talk, or other defensive, self-defeating behaviors that have brought the child to group. In the group setting, "children reveal through their conduct their basic personality traits and defenses" and will eventually "mobilize the courage to draw the curtain of concealment" and risk being vulnerable if emotional safety is adequately generated (Slavson & Schiffer, 1975, p. 39).

Phase Two: Reexamination

Following reenactment, the child has the opportunity to reexamine self in light of the responses (or lack of responses) received from group members and the therapist (Berg & Landreth, 1990). Children generally come to group expecting the same responses they receive in the world outside of group. The change process begins in earnest when the other children and leader do not respond with the familiar anticipated reactions of the child's parents, siblings, teachers, and peers.

Both reenactment and reexamination are vividly demonstrated in the following excerpt from a RAPT group made up of first- and second-grade boys. This segment is from the fourth session. The participants are Carl and Jim, plus a new boy, Eddie. Seven-year-old Eddie enters the group with a huge chip on his shoulder, conveying a sort of "I'll get you before you can get me" attitude. Halfway through his first group session, Eddie suddenly grabs Carl's freshly made clay pot and throws it into the dartboard, laughing and pointing to make sure the other boys see the pancake of clay embedded in the board's plastic prongs. What appears to have been an unprovoked hostile outburst is actually Eddie's defensive reenactment of his characteristic way of covering up hurt and rejection. Just a few moments before, eight-year-old Carl, himself immaturely self-centered and self-entitled, volunteered to teach Eddie to play the Skittles game. However, Carl, re-creating his own issues within the group, suddenly lost interest and abruptly announced "I'm quitting," leaving Eddie to fend for himself. Eddie, exquisitely sensitive to the slightest hint of rejection, immediately reacts in the only way he knows. He spies Carl's freshly molded clay pot, snatches it, and hurls it at the dartboard mounted on the wall.

Jim and Carl stop dead in their tracks, mouths agape in astonishment at this new kid whom they are disliking more and more by the minute. This just happens to be the key issue that brought Eddie to group: he has no friends because he treats them in the same manner he has just treated Carl. Carl predictably reacts in a high-pitched, keening voice: "Why did you do that? Why did you do that? That is my clay! You had no right to do that!" Eddie's one-word rejoinder—"Asshole!"—caps an all-too-familiar, unconscious reenactment of each of their issues, a dysfunctional dance in which each ends up feeling lonely, angry, rejected, and afraid, though their fear is well masked beneath Carl's persona of helplessness and Eddie's facade of aggressiveness.

All three simultaneously turn to the therapist, Jim and Carl looking for this upstart kid to be kicked out of group right now, and Eddie nonverbally threatening: "Whatcha gonna do about it?" Instead of the expected verbal tirade and punishment for Eddie, the therapist intervenes in a firm and straightforward but caring manner.

Therapist: Boys, come here and sit down. Eddie and Carl, looks like you have something to say to each other. Wait just a minute, Eddie. In group, we stop and talk about disagreements and solve problems together. *[an educative statement about what is expected in group]* Boys, put all toys aside . . . no toys or playing right now. Guys, looks like you have a problem that needs solving. *[directed to all group members, not just Carl and Eddie]*

Jim: Why me? Eddie threw it, not me. I didn't have anything to do with it!

Therapist: I know, Jim. Right now, the problem is between Eddie and Carl. But whenever there is a problem in group, we need everyone to help solve the problem. Eddie and Jim, look at Carl and listen with both your eyes and your ears. Sometimes we can hear more with our eyes than our ears. Carl, look at Eddie and tell him what you are thinking and feeling about your clay. Eddie, I want you to listen so closely you can tell Carl exactly what he says to you. OK, Carl, look at Eddie and talk to him.

Carl: *[turns toward the therapist and starts to tell about what happened]*

Therapist: Carl, talk to Eddie, not me. Tell Eddie how you felt when he threw your clay. *[taking care to keep directions simple and direct]*

Carl: I wasn't very . . . *[searching for a word]* comfortable.

Therapist: Eddie, tell Carl what you heard him say to you.

Eddie: He didn't like it.

Therapist: *[taking care to not leave out the third boy]* Jim, what did you notice about Carl and Eddie?

Jim: Eddie is making a mess in here . . . and—

Therapist: Jim, look at Eddie and tell him. *[redirecting the boys to talk directly to one another, not through the therapist]*

Jim: You're making a mess in here *[looking around at the trail of toys Eddie has strewn about the room]* and you should clean them up. And you should ask before you take something someone else is using.

Eddie: [angrily] I hate you! You're an idiot! You are also this! *[he defiantly shoots the middle finger at Jim]*

Therapist: [not commenting on the obscene gesture] Carl, tell him what you heard him say.

Carl: That I'm an idiot! And, hey, that's a nasty sign you made with your finger! I don't even want to know what it means!

Therapist: Right now, Eddie is telling you he is really angry. He used words and a sign to tell you he was really mad. And, Carl, you have told him you don't want him to take your stuff without asking.

Eddie: *[gets up and throws some pieces of a game]*

Jim: Those are not for throwing *[ironically setting the limit for a fellow group member with an educative, limit-setting statement, just as the therapist does]*

Therapist: *[sensing the main points had been communicated from all three boys]* Do you, Eddie, or do you, Carl, have anything else you want to say to one another? *[They each shake their heads, no.]* Well then, play time can begin again.

Carl: *[turning to Jim]* I hope Eddie doesn't come back to group.

Jim: *[glancing at Eddie]* Guess he's going to just ignore you, Carl.

Therapist: Sounds like, Carl, you are mad at Eddie right now. That's something you can tell him directly.

Carl: *[tossing up a ball of clay]* I'd like to make a baseball out of this and throw it at you! What would you think of that, huh?

Eddie, without making eye contact, hits a drum with a plastic musical tube. Jim reaches out and angrily flips the end of the tube back toward Eddie. Eddie lightly hits Jim on the back. This could quickly erupt into a physical scuffle.

Therapist: Eddie, people aren't for hitting. Jim, you hit the music tube that Eddie is holding. Will you put into words, rather than actions, what you have to say to Eddie?

Eddie: *[picks up a camera and looks at Jim through it—a clever way to distance himself from Jim's direct confrontation]*

Jim: I can't talk to you when you're looking in that camera.

Therapist: Eddie, Jim is going to put in words what he is thinking. Please look at him and listen with your eyes and your ears. *[Eddie reluctantly puts the camera down and glances at Jim.]*

Jim: You don't have to stare at me through that camera. If you want to talk to me, just say, "Jim" . . . Me and Carl were fine until you joined the group.

Carl: *[glancing at therapist]* Eddie has a *bad* attitude.

Therapist: *[not getting distracted by Carl's side comment]* Jim, tell Eddie, instead of me.

Jim: I don't want him, uh, you, in our group, if you don't know how to act. You hit people and mess up the stuff they make.

Therapist: So you're letting him know, if you want to be in this group . . . *[reframing Jim's statements to assist him in communicating his message, pausing, hoping Jim will complete the lead-in]*

Jim: *[picking up and continuing the lead-in]* You have to act nice, and you've got to quit doing bad signs with your finger and stop making such a mess.

Therapist: *[sensing that it would be too much to expect Eddie to respond, shifts focus to Carl, who is working to reflatten the clay that the therapist has peeled off of the dartboard]* Carl, you're sure using your muscles on that clay.

Eddie: *[quickly picking up a tool for rolling wallpaper seams, approaches Carl and says in a helpful tone]* Here. This will make it flat.

Eddie starts helping Carl flatten the same clay that only moments before he had thrown into the dartboard. The therapist sits and waits expectantly to see what will happen with Eddie's new behavior, wondering if Carl will be able to accept this apology.

Carl: Hey, thanks! *[in an accepting and cheerful tone]*
Jim: *[from across the room]* Hey, good idea, Eddie! *[reinforcing Eddie's positive shift]*
Carl: If you act like this, you maybe *can* be in our group.

In the last fifteen minutes of this session Eddie experiments more with new behaviors. He discovers plain white T-shirts on the art shelf and tubes of fabric paint. He begins to use the paints on paper. The therapist intervenes with a redirective response: "Oh, Eddie, you found the fabric paints. Those are for using on those T-shirts on the shelf." Eddie accepts the redirection, picks out a T-shirt, flops on his stomach, and begins to decorate it. Jim and Carl soon notice Eddie.

Carl: Can I make one?
Jim: Me too?
Therapist: *[holds back in answering to give the boys room to interact]*
Eddie: Sure, the shirts are over there. *[motioning to the stack of T-shirts on the shelf]*

Within moments, all three boys are sprawled out on the floor with the paints in the center, like spokes coming out from the hub of an old wagon wheel, heads facing inward. They share the paints, compliment one another on their designs, and even discuss how Jim loves this so much, he might do it as a business when he grows up.

These last few minutes made it clear that Eddie *can* make it in group. To avoid the question of whether Eddie will be coming back to group, the therapist says, "Hey, guys, have you ever used those tubes of colored icing? If you want to, you could each bring one or two tubes of icing next week. I'll bake us some brownies, and you can decorate brownies after free play time. What do you think?"

Jim, Carl, and Eddie all chime in together, "Yeah, sure! I'll bring red!" "Me, too!" "Can we eat the brownies after we decorate them?"

As they leave, all three carry their freshly painted T-shirts with them, each telling their moms they are to bring tubes of icing to group next week.

This is a dramatic example of the group serving as a dynamic catalyst for change in a first session for a new child (Berg & Landreth, 1990). Though all three boys made therapeutic gain in that session, we will focus for a moment on Eddie, the new boy. Within thirty minutes, Eddie unknowingly re-created his retaliatory reactive response to what he perceived as a major rejection when Carl abruptly quit playing with him. Though he showed no outward signs of intense listening, he truly did hear and reexamined his behavior in light of the other boys' confrontation of his out-of-control behavior—messing up the room, taking and ruining Carl's clay without asking, making a "nasty" hand gesture, gawking through the camera at Jim. The therapist's timely intervention facilitated Jim's and Carl's telling Eddie, in fair but firm terms, that his behavior was not acceptable if he wanted to be in the group. Eddie had enough social hunger (buried beneath his "I don't care" persona) that he wanted desperately to be in the group. Therefore, he made a significant midcourse correction. He reexamined his behavior and made a dramatic move to rectify it. He noticed Carl's attempt to rework the clay, still carrying the imprints of the dartboard, whereupon he offered the wallpaper seam roller as a perfect tool to help Carl. But more significantly, he used the tool as a peace offering for his mess-ups and an indicator that he indeed wanted to belong to the group.

Proof of the power of the session was reported to us by Eddie's mother. That night as the family gathered at the dinner table, Eddie announced to his dad and brothers, "Hey, I'm getting better. I get to be in a group. And I don't have to go see that asshole Dr. [so-and-so] anymore!" (meaning he accurately interpreted his movement from individual play therapy to a play group as an indicator that he was improving). In his bedtime prayers that night he said, "God, help the bad Eddie to get smaller, and the good Eddie to get bigger, every day." The next day Eddie wore to school the T-shirt he made in group.

Phase Three: Redirection

When handled effectively by the therapist, a child's reenactment of his problems fortunately opens the door for self-examination. Reexamination of self naturally leads the child into phase three, in which the child decides, consciously or unconsciously, to redirect self into experimenting with new and hopefully more productive behaviors. Experience has taught that lasting internal change comes when the child senses, for himself or herself, a readiness to try new behaviors, rather than when the child merely adapts to suggestions or pressure from a directing adult. Children generally begin, ever so timidly, to experiment with different behaviors, often trying out behaviors they have learned vicariously through observing other children in the group (Berg & Landreth, 1990).

During the weeks following the boys' group detailed in the preceding section, Eddie's angry outbursts were as regular as clockwork. Though angry on the surface, these were actually reflections of his intense anxiety, his fear of rejection and people, and his personal shame for his inappropriate behaviors. Eddie slowly came to trust the therapist's consistently warm and caring response to him, even when his behavior was most out of control. Great care was taken to follow consistent limit setting without becoming hostile or judgmental. Eddie knew that when he broke certain limits, he was choosing to sit for ten (sometimes fifteen) minutes with his mother in the waiting room before returning to group. During these sit-outs, Eddie seemed to rethink his behavior and redirect his focus upon reentry into group.

As children begin to redirect themselves, the other children in group are often the first to notice and cheer the child on. The following is an example from several weeks later in the same group, a session in which Carl notices and affirms Eddie's efforts to change. One day, as Eddie reentered group following one of his "sit-out with Mom" times, Carl commented, "Hey, Eddie, you're getting better. Have you noticed that after your blowups, you settle down by taking things apart or hammering them together?"

Carl's observation was uncommonly astute. As he had noted, upon reentry into the playroom, Eddie would immediately begin screwing or unscrewing such items as the seat of a chair or top of an end table in an effort to redirect his out-of-control behavior. The therapist discovered that it helped Eddie to have a broken VCR, telephone, computer component, or answering machine for him to hammer and dismantle as a way of releasing his high levels of anxiety. During this cumbersome trial-and-error period of change, it is imperative that the therapist provide consistent support so that no child ever risks losing face or losing his place in the group.

Phase Four: Reintegration

Because children's characteristics are still malleable in the formative stages of development, the cumulative corrective experiences week after week are gradually integrated into the child's personality structure (Slavson & Schiffer, 1975). Children slowly assimilate the many therapeutic group experiences into new decisions about themselves, others, and how to successfully get along in the world. Eventually, the child solidifies the new decisions into lasting life patterns that form a healthier foundation for future character development (Berg & Landreth, 1990).

Though most children are in group for a few months, Eddie, because of the severity of his problems, has continued in group for two years. He has internalized so many changes that now he is the group leader, the one who often gives corrective feedback to other boys when they start to act out or misbehave. Whereas upon entering treatment, Eddie was an extremely defended, isolated, unhappy child, the healing power of the RAPT group has given him the unique opportunity to mature into a child who now likes himself, experiences a special closeness with his family, romps and plays with buddies in the neighborhood, and receives recognition for his gifted abilities at school.

Creating a Therapeutically Balanced RAPT Group

The therapist's success in putting together a therapeutically balanced group often determines the initial and eventual success of a group. In fact, Slavson and Schiffer (1975) regard group balancing as *the* most crucial factor in determining whether the group will be a therapeutic agent of change. Slavson and Schiffer, pioneers of all forms of play-based group therapy, especially view the behavioral patterns of the prospective group members as significant determiners of the emotional climate of each group.

To ensure an appropriate combination of children, we encourage a careful process of multilevel assessment that includes the following steps:

1. *Take a comprehensive history that includes identification of the child's therapeutic issues and problematic behaviors.* If possible (in some settings it may be impossible), it is desirable to assemble a comprehensive life history and consultation with parents or primary caretakers, including referring professionals and school faculty. This is extremely helpful in coming to understand and appreciate the child's basic therapeutic issues, including life adjustments, defenses, "stroke economy" (positive and negative), picture of self, other, and world, living circumstances within the family, and relevant social, school, and learning issues. Such an assessment is also crucial in coming to understand each child's symbolic play and interactional play with group members, remembering that the same play behavior may have very different meanings for different children.

2. *Make an individual play therapy assessment.* If a child is being considered for group and has never been in individual play therapy, we recommend at least one to four individual play sessions to adequately assess the child's individual needs and contribution to the therapeutic balance (or imbalance) of the group. This enables the therapist to make an initial determination as to the child's assets and struggles and allows the child to experience the therapist and the play setting itself. And, perhaps more important, it allows the therapist to "be with" the child personally, a beginning of a relationship with the child that will carry over, although in a different form, into the RAPT group setting. While the child's relationship and interactions with other group members will be primary factors in the child's growth within the group itself, the relationship with the therapist still remains crucial as the child develops a new, more workable sense of self. Without a strong sense of trust in the person of the therapist and safety of the setting, the child's opportunities for genuine growth are diminished greatly, if not altogether.

3. *Carefully consider each child's current condition.* In particular, assess the following factors:

- Primary relatedness to parents and caretakers. (Is the child's "social hunger" strong enough for group work?)
- Symptomatic behavior, including chief complaints of child and parents.
- Physical size and strength.
- Level of oppositionality and physical combativeness.
- General levels of maturity and immaturity, including areas of each.
- Typical defensive reaction and reaction to frustration.

- General capacity for impulse- and self-control.
- General adjustment to school and peers.
- General level of distractibility versus ability to focus attention when asked to do so.
- Learning differences, if any.
- Psychoactive or other regularly taken medications, if any.
- Preferences for spending leisure time and hobbies.

4. *Assemble a diverse group, avoiding the placement of polarized extremes.* Children who seem to be extremely alike or extremely opposite one another tend to get on poorly in the same group unless you can include other children who bring diversity and contrast to the very similar or very different behaviors.

5. *Look beyond the reports and records.* It is essential to pay attention to the intuitive sense a therapist develops as to how an individual child would fit with other group members.

6. *Consult with a supervisor or colleague.* Where feasible, it is useful to discuss the profile of each child and the proposed matching of children to create a therapeutically balanced group.

These criteria are meant to be suggestive rather than exhaustive. However, our experience has been that if these are considered when deciding who should be with whom, the therapist is likely to come up with a good fit for all the children involved. Such thoughtful matching will greatly enhance the likelihood of the experience being therapeutic.

As a part of the assessment process, we have also found it helpful to make use of several different roles that children assume in groups, as suggested by Slavson and Schiffer (1975). The group membership should ideally be representative of several different roles, rather than being made up of children who are primarily functioning in the exact same or exact opposite roles. Slavson and Schiffer enumerate three primary roles that children are likely to assume within the group—instigators, neutralizers, and followers (p. 113).

An *instigator* is a child who acts as a catalyst, stimulating in other children either positive or negative activity and interactions. Instigators exhibit what might be thought of as natural leadership ability. These children are able to get other children to join them in what they choose to do, whether their initiative is positive or negative. Life is never dull with these children in group!

Neutralizers are children who "counteract the effects of negative instigation by blocking destructive processes without adding to a group's tension and conflicts and who are more reasonable, have impulse control and, therefore, have a calming effect" (Slavson & Schiffer, 1975, p. 113). A neutralizer serves as a "healthy identification model" and provides a sense of individuality and independence for other group members to vicariously ponder (p. 113). Neutralizers are able to stand their own ground enough to offer a counterbalancing effect to the positive and negative stimulus of instigators and have enough inner identity and strength to do their own thing in group when they so decide. They are able to function without always having to have the instigator's approval, and they thereby provide security and insight during tumultuous times in group.

Followers, on the other hand, are those children who go in the direction of the instigator's leading or suggesting or withdraw in the opposite direction to avoid interaction and potential conflict. Children functioning in the follower role are not yet strong enough within themselves either to know independently what they want to do or to gather the courage to do so; neither are they able to actively oppose the instigator if they think the proposed course is not appropriate for them. They tend to "easily succumb to the influence of stronger personalities," but they are capable of growing to the point that they will at some point assume the role of an instigator or neutralizer themselves (Slavson & Schiffer, 1975, p. 113).

Of course, the same child may assume different roles, depending on the circumstances and situation. However, it seems safe to say that, at least on first entering group, children are likely to be most comfortable with one of the three roles and will function in that role as stress increases within the group. Over time children expand their repertoire and become able to function as instigator, neutralizer, and follower according to individual choice or the needs of the group.

Still, in terms of various roles within the group, it is important that the therapist be aware of and consciously attempt to effect a balance among the different roles when putting the group together. Obviously, it would be apt to reinforce tug-of-war behavior to put three strong-willed negative instigators together in a group, or support shyness to put three extremely withdrawn children together whose natural bent is to stay to themselves. The therapist's challenge is to use the roles as guides for thinking in terms of the different children, picturing how they are likely to interact if placed in group together.

We have also found it helpful to think in terms of different types of children according to their position on a developmental continuum. If carried to an extreme, it can be demeaning to children's individuality to apply a personality type label, and that is obviously not our intent. Our aim is to furnish guidelines for group placement rather than discount or limit any child with an observational label. Imagine children on a developmental continuum like the ones depicted in Figure 13.1, beginning with the extremely withdrawn child on one side and progressing to the extremely aggressive child on the opposite end of the continuum, adding different types of children who are being considered for group to create a picture of the group as a whole.

FIGURE 13.1. DEVELOPMENTAL CONTINUUM.

Withdrawn child	Compliant child	Well-adjusted child	Manipulative child	Aggressive child

Inhibited child	Perfect child	Independent child	Whiny child	Defiant child

Anxious child	Compulsive child	Self-assured child	Bossy child	Acting-out child

Envisioning children in this way is another guide for the therapist to use in confirming or reconsidering which children should be placed together so as to enhance and hasten the change process.

A Trio of Time Constructs

As we have developed and modified our model over the past fifteen years, we now work within three distinctively different time constructs: Free Play Time, Group Activity Time, and Snack 'n Talk Time. These time constructs provide an overall structure for the group but are not rigidly followed in any one group session. The following is a description of each time construct with accompanying examples that identify the therapist's unique functioning within the various time constructs.

Free Play Time

Most children enter group somewhat wary, anxious, and curious. The therapist begins with the same directions given to children in a beginning play therapy session, "Kids, you can play with any of the toys and materials in here in most of the ways you want to." The therapist's initial job is to maintain emotional contact with each child, calling them by name while making occasional reflective comments in response to each child, yet being careful to not be too verbally active. In fact, from the outset, the therapist is less active verbally than in individual play therapy, leaving plenty of space, including awkward pauses, for children to ponder one another. It is especially important that during the Free Play Time children be allowed to find their own way with one another. The therapist turns down requests to play with individual children, so that children will be more likely to venture connecting with one another.

During free play, the therapist notices each child's emotional state and idiosyncratic behaviors, yet often refrains from commenting on abreaction-type, regressive behaviors (Slavson & Schiffer, 1975). During the formative period of the group, the therapist demonstrates an attitude of relentless acceptance and appreciation for each child even as the child recreates familiar dysfunctional behaviors (Slavson, 1952). Also, the therapist must create a permissive atmosphere, otherwise children will not feel safe enough to reenact their problem behaviors.

The importance of the Free Play Time was recently underscored by an insightful third-grade girl. During a moment of quiet when each girl in her group was absorbed in her own play, Natasha said to the therapist, "You're tricky. . . . You just let us come in here and play and then we get into our problems with each other and have to learn how to solve them ourselves."

It is possible that for weeks, a new group may spend all of its time in free play, except for the closing ritual of the Snack 'n Talk Time. The therapist trusts the wisdom of the children to pace themselves as they explore relationships with one another.

Group Activity Time

As used in this chapter, the term *activity* carries both a broader and a more specific definition than is generally used in everyday conversation. In a RAPT group, activity "includes all human processes: physical, intellectual, and emotional" (Slavson & Schiffer, 1975, p. 30). Slavson and Schiffer are adamant that "activity that is designed, imposed or directed, robs the child of the opportunity to realize and expand potential capabilities" (p. 30).

We agree that activities are not to be employed as a medium to "get the child to talk" or conducted in such a way as to require or direct children's involvement (Slavson & Schiffer, 1975). However, we have discovered amazing results when we creatively enlarge a child's comment or actions into a possible group activity or project. Also, in response to a child's impasse, we often experience amazing results by designing a group activity to facilitate movement for a particular child or for progression of the group process.

Think back to the group including Carl, Jim, and Eddie. Carl woefully lacks confidence in himself, his ideas, and his ability to accomplish much of anything. He comes from an extremely wealthy family in which little is expected of him. As a result, he has developed a sense of learned helplessness suffused with an inflated sense of self-entitlement. During one of the group's Snack 'n Talk times, the following conversation unfolds naturally, with no preplanning or suggestion from the therapist.

Jim has been complaining that he is tired of popcorn for snack. Carl, who seldom contributes to the group's conversations, suddenly perks up.

Carl: I know a really good dessert made with graham crackers and pudding.
Therapist: [*encouragingly, after waiting awhile for either of the other boys to respond*] Mmm, sounds good, Carl. What kind of pudding?
Carl: Oh, vanilla, chocolate, strawberry . . . whatever kind you want.
Jim: [*the pudding flavors having captured his interest*] Hey you guys, I like vanilla!
Eddie: [*jumping in, assuming his familiar oppositional stance in the group*] No, I want chocolate!
Carl: [*buoyed by the other boys' interest*] Well, we could use both, and maybe strawberry, too!
Therapist: [wanting to affirm Carl for taking the initiative and suggesting they do something, new behavior for him] Well guys, no more boring popcorn next week! Carl, tell us the recipe. We'll divide up what each person should bring and make the dessert ourselves next week.

As might be expected, the next week was a turning point for Carl. During Group Activity Time, he beamed with delight as he directed the group in smashing graham crackers and mixing pudding with Cool Whip. By the therapist's picking up on Carl's initially timid suggestion and turning it into a group project, Carl was able to experience a few moments of leadership, a new beginning in his emerging as an important, contributing member of the group.

During Group Activity Time, the therapist continues to protect the children's need to be self-directive and to participate as they choose, be that enthusiastic involvement or no involvement at all. In the example just cited, the pudding project evolved out of Carl's suggestion for a new snack. However, the children were free to choose whether to join in or not participate in the project. Had the group members shown no interest in Carl's suggestion, the therapist would have commented on their lack of interest and Carl's disappointment over their ignoring his suggestion. The therapist's nonjudgmental yet empathic response might have gone something like this: "Looks like you guys are deciding to stay with popcorn, your usual group snack. Carl, it seems like you are feeling kind of sad. You think it would be fun to make your dessert as a group."

RAPT group activities fall into three major categories:

- *Spontaneous activities* (either child or therapist suggested)
- *Preplanned activities* (either child or therapist suggested and preplanned by group)
- *Designated activities* (therapist designed for a specific purpose)

An example of a designated activity for a specific purpose involves the case of Sam, an extremely shy kindergartner, who, week after week, turned down other group members' invitations to join them in play. Sam, an extremely creative and resourceful child, appeared perfectly content to entertain himself with the elaborate wooden structures he created by himself in group. However, an occasional glance at the other children as they frolicked and played clearly indicated that he was simultaneously longing to be involved with the other boys in group. It was as though the two conflicting parts of Sam were at war within him. At times this inner conflict seemed to spill over into his play in the group. On several occasions, Sam moved his solitary play activity close to the center of activity where he would continue to play separately but near the others, demonstrating his desire to join them and his hesitancy to join them. Despite his interest, Sam appeared unable to accept their invitations to play and certainly was not ready to insert himself into their play. He showed no movement toward addressing his inability to play with other children within the group or at school. Even during group problem-solving times, though physically near the other children on the "talk rug," he chose not to talk and distanced himself by displaying little or no emotion.

Concerned about his lack of movement within the group, the therapist decided to create a group project that might facilitate Sam's involvement. It was the week before Easter, and since all group members happened to come from Christian families, the therapist made a quick run for plastic eggs and chocolate Easter candy. As group started, the therapist announced, "Today is going to be a little different. We will have thirty minutes of free play, and then we are going to do an activity together." At the appointed time, the boys were gathered on the talk rug. "Guys, here are some plastic eggs and candies. I'd like you, as a group, to decide on an activity using these Easter eggs and candies. After you come up with your plan, you can begin your activity." The therapist then sat back and reflected their planning process.

As things worked out, it was Sam who shyly suggested that they put the candy in the eggs and have an Easter egg hunt. They then decided to work in pairs, two hiding eggs while two hid their eyes. Sam got so excited hunting eggs that he momentarily lost his shyness. This suggested activity began to bring Sam into the group. As the boys discussed the game during Snack 'n Talk Time, Sam ventured another idea. He brought up doing something with Beanie Babies. To this the therapist replied, "Hey, next week would you like us to have a 'Beanie Baby Day?'" "Yeah . . . yeah . . . that'd be fun," they replied. "Well, everybody re-member to bring your Beanie Babies next week." The next week, Sam was the only one who remembered to bring his Beanie Babies—all eight of them. Because they were his Beanie Babies, the therapist asked Sam to tell the other children what his rules were for playing with them. He firmly said, "Be sure and don't throw them or hurt them and be sure and don't get them dirty."

Again Sam took giant leaps as group made up a "Hide the Beanie Babies" game. In just two weeks, Sam began to move past his fear of joining the other children. Though there was no guarantee that this or any planned group activity would work, the Easter Egg and Beanie Baby hunts became the vehicles that eased the way for Sam to do what he so desperately wanted and needed to do—to take the leap and join the group, no longer frozen by his fear and shyness.

It may be helpful to note that both activities were presented by the therapist in an open-ended manner: "Here are some eggs and candy that you can use in a way that you all agree on." While the therapist added: "I'd like you, as a group, to decide on an activity," the children were still free to take part or not. Each could still choose whether to join in our sit out. The therapist's decision to suggest this group activity grew out of her careful observation and awareness of Sam's inner struggle and wish to join the others, and also the fact that he was stuck and was not being able to move forward by himself. The suggestion of using the eggs and candies furnished enough of an opportunity, as well as enough of a plausible means for movement, that Sam was able to make the choice to risk joining the others.

Following and building on the therapist's suggestion, the boys came up with how they would play with the eggs, candy, and Beanie Babies. They worked out their own rules and decided how the game would be played. In fact, Sam stepped out of his shyness and negotiated the idea that no matter how many eggs each boy found, they should divide the candy evenly at the end of the game. What a delightful ending (and therapeutic beginning), as all of the boys carefully counted out the candy, making sure no one got less than his fair share.

Snack 'n Talk Time

Group members take turns bringing a simple, nonsugar snack and drink for the weekly closing ritual called Snack 'n Talk Time. For the final ten to fifteen min-utes of group, the entire group gathers around a table for a snack, sharing a few moments to be together without the interplay or distraction of toys or activities. The therapist is firm that this is a "time for talking, not playing or being silly." In these closing moments, the therapist guides all group members to process what happened in group that day, which may lead to discussions of previous group experiences and related social skills; create an open forum for children to bring up what is going on in their lives outside of group (home, school, friends, personal problems, and so on); initiate evaluative comments among the group members as to how each group member is changing; and provide time for the group to plan special projects or field trips in which the group delegates responsibilities related to the upcoming event (for example, birthday snack, items for a game, decorations, or birthday surprise).

The closing ritual helps children step back from their active experiences in group and view themselves and others with added objectivity and sensitivity. Without assuming a traditional teaching role, the skilled therapist guides the conversation so as to highlight not only personal awareness but interpersonal communication and social skills that are pertinent for individual children or the group as a whole. These brief talk times allow children to cognitively integrate the corrective experiences of group, following the axiom that "teaching is not telling, it is learning through experience."

As an example, consider the following portion of a Snack 'n Talk Time in which four kindergarten boys are sharing their final snack as they terminate a group after being together for nearly a year. The verbatim account of their conversation demonstrates the poignancy and depth of awareness they realized while in a RAPT group.

Therapist: Well, boys, this is your last group and your last Snack 'n Talk Time. Let's think back how everybody was when they first started in group. Take a minute and see if you can remember how you were when you came to group.

Sam: I remember . . . I was too scared to go to anybody's house to play. I was shy.

Walter: Hey, Sam. You buried your shyness!

Sam: I know. I'm not very shy anymore.

Walter: You know what, Sam? I like you better without your shyness.

Sam: Me, too.

Walter: Hey, my turn . . . I noticed Al's not mean any more.

Al: Yeah, I used to hit and kick people all the time. I haven't been to the principal's office for a long time.

Therapist: Hey, guys, can anyone tell Al some of the friend-making things he did in group today? You did a bunch of friend-making things, today, Al.

    Al: I did? Oh, yeah, I picked up those cardboard blocks for you.

Therapist: I noticed you did that just to help me—that was a friend-making thing, for sure.

  Walter: And you don't call us names like you used to. Hey, Ricardo! Are you going to keep coming to group after we leave?

 Ricardo: Won't be much fun without you.

  Walter: Ricardo, why are you coming to group anyway?

 Ricardo: Oh, I get in trouble at school all the time. Kids beat me up and I just hit them back.

  Walter: Well, let me tell you how it works, Ricardo. If you will just keep coming to group, you'll have so much fun you won't even know you're getting gooder. And then one day you'll find out you're not a bad boy anymore.

Advanced RAPT Group Activities

As the group matures, the cooperative planning of involved projects and field trip excursions (a trip to the creek, to each member's home, to the sand lot on the corner) enables the group to become self-managing with the ability to direct and correct itself. Thus the group becomes its own therapeutic agent, having taken the role of therapist upon itself (Berg & Landreth, 1990). At this point, the therapist often feels like a spare tire, along for ride just in case the unexpected happens. Slavson and Schiffer (1975) noted that the "details of planning and the management of these enterprises . . . generate an awareness of the supra-individual existence: that is, the group as an entity becomes involved in their lives . . . and the group enters into the children's psyches to serve as a socially therapeutic force that enriches each child's ability to cope with daily living" (p. 52). The group emerges into a "miniature society that offers motivation and support for change as well as safe arena for testing new modes of behavior" (Ginott, 1961, p. 13).

  Such was the case with three third-grade girls, for whom a twenty-pound lump of clay became a visual representation of the therapeutic change in each girl and in the progression of the group as a whole. One girl was the self-appointed boss, with two very obedient followers. The therapist decided to use a group project to make the inequality of the group self-evident. Very quickly, the group dynamics became glaringly self-evident, particularly to the group's two acquiescent members. The therapist's directions were: "Girls, here is a lump of clay for you to use for a group project. You can do whatever you decide as a group so long as all of you participate." Within minutes, the bossy one had decided they would make an animal, and the animal would be an elephant. As they began to mold the clay, she announced that the other two girls were to make the elephant's legs. One of the followers timidly asked, "Well, who is making the head?"—to which she replied, "Me." Another ventured, "Well, I'd like to make the trunk," to which the leader replied, "Nope, that's my job." The first girl volunteered, "Oh, I'll make the ears," to which the reply was, "No, no, no . . . you are only to make the legs." The two followers never made a verbal protest, but they began to make protesting glances to one another, gaining strength from each other's presence.

Finally, a week later, the self-appointed boss directed each girl to attach the legs they had sculpted to the body, and finally, the elephant was set out to dry. To everyone's chagrin, when they returned the next week and uncovered their clay elephant, the overly heavy head and trunk had broken off during the drying process. The bossy leader was beside herself and lobbied to throw the broken elephant away, but neither of the other group members would hear of it. In fact, the shyest one immediately began repairing the elephant. She not only patched the clay, she made an elaborate brace to hold the trunk and head in place while drying. How pleased she was with herself when, a week later, the elephant had all of its major parts securely attached and was ready for painting. The tide had turned, and the two followers began to insist on having a voice in making decisions where "their elephant" was concerned.

Ownership in the elephant paralleled their sense of ownership in the group. There were so many decisions to make in the weeks ahead. What colors should they paint the head, trunk, ears, body, legs, and tail? Who should paint what part? By this time, all three girls had an equal voice in the color choices and the actual painting. Next came other important decisions. Was their elephant going to be a "he" or a "she"? What should they name him? Where would he be kept between group sessions? Their final group decision was to choose a permanent home for "Ed, Our Beloved Elephant," because it was time for the group to terminate. Their work was complete. Having come so far from their unequal beginning, they made a unanimous decision that Ed should live "forever" at the counseling center. They went as a group and asked the office manager if she would become Ed's keeper and let him live on the top of her file cabinet, a prominent place in view of all who entered, yet a safe place out of the reach of small children. With joy and sadness, they shared a common bond of ownership as they placed Ed in his new home, gave each other a good-bye hug, and left the center much more ready for life than when they entered. In birthing Ed, the girls birthed a new part of themselves that had been waiting to be born.

As suggested by Ginott (1961), the group experience provided these girls a "new quality of intimate relationships" and a place in which they each could "shed defenses and yet remain protected" while getting close to other children and an adult without getting hurt. This is yet another example that the cooperative living that emerges in the miniature society called *group* prepares children for the larger society called *life* (p. 13).

Problem-Solving Interventions

At any time during the group session, whether Free Play Time, Group Activity Time, or closing Snack 'n Talk Time, the therapist is available to skillfully intervene to facilitate on-the-spot problem solving and interpersonal communication between children. The problem-solving discussion involves the entire group, those children actively embroiled in the conflict at hand and all other group members, even if they are not directly involved in the current problem. When a conflict begins to escalate, the therapist may let the interaction play itself out or may deem it advantageous to call everyone together. The children are directed to sit down wherever they are (if they are in close proximity to one another) or to come to a neutral area such as the talk rug. The talk rug is a colorful four-by-six-foot throw rug that is in a less-busy area of the room. During this time, the children do not continue to use toys or play materials. The therapist refrains from solving the conflict, avoiding such directions as, "Johnny, you can use the ball for five minutes, and then, Sally, you can use the ball for five minutes." Instead, the therapist acts as a communication facilitator for the children, enabling them to come up with a workable solution before play can resume. The therapist involves the whole group in the discussion. Oftentimes the group members not directly in the midst of the conflict can contribute a more objective, less emotional perspective than those who are directly involved with the argument or disagreement at hand. All the children are asked to "listen with their eyes and their ears," looking at the person who is speaking. (Refer to the transcript presented earlier in the chapter as an actual example of a communication and problem-solving intervention.) Nothing resumes until there is a workable solution or at least a clarification of differences between the individuals involved.

A recent example of such an intervention involved a group of five ADHD fifth-graders in which one boy was hogging the ball, refusing to let another boy use it. Because of the size of the group and the easy distractibility of all five boys, the therapist shifted the group to an adjoining adult therapy office. Even though several reasonable solutions were suggested by different group members, the boys who were warring with one another were not willing to agree on a solution. After fifteen minutes of dialogue, the therapist said, "Boys, you have five minutes to come up with a solution. If you have not agreed upon a solution in five minutes, you will have chosen for no one to use the basketball for the remainder of today's play time." Within moments, Bob, the ball-hog, said, "OK, you can have the ball."

The therapist replied, "So you'd rather give in than do without the basketball the rest of today's session." Though he did not give in out of fairness and concern for the other boy, he did shift his position, which was a beginning step in the right direction for him.

Opportune Comments, Reflections, and Observational Statements

With experience, the therapist develops an intuitive sense as to what comments and reflections would be helpful for a particular child and what observations would best be left unsaid for fear of hurting a child who is not yet ready to handle such candid information.

Slavson and Schiffer modified their original model, coming to recognize the importance of the therapist's making opportune comments, reflections, and observational statements when "underlying meanings of manifest behavior, attitudes, and feelings are brought to light" (Schiffer, 1977, p. 379). When offering explanations and interpretations to a child, the therapist must be especially sensitive and extremely careful to make sure that the child is ready to handle the interpretation offered. We concur that "it is unwise in the beginning to pursue any child's disclosure in depth" and that at "all times the therapist must be sensitive to children's feelings and their tolerance limits, which is possible only when the therapist possesses comprehensive knowledge of each child's total problem and can correctly assess the nature and adequacies of each child's defenses" (p. 379). We believe it is better to err by lagging a step or two behind a child's readiness, rather than running the risk of rushing the process, thereby hindering the child's healthy movement in group.

Logistics

Based upon our experience with RAPT groups, we have several recommendations for the basic setup and logistics of the process.

Group Size

RAPT groups vary in size from two to five children. The size of the group is based primarily on the right match of children available to come at the same time. Consider the scheduling difficulties of three children: Each individual child's activity schedule (soccer, tutoring, music lessons) and the schedules of two parents or caregivers times three equals nine schedules to consider, plus the therapist's schedule. Many therapists do not do play-based groups, despite the advantages such groups offer, because of unfortunate scheduling difficulties and because of inadequate room size.

Open-Ended or Time-Limited Groups

RAPT groups are generally not time limited from a clinical standpoint, yet the requirements of schools and agencies may impose an external time limit on the group. If at all possible, we ask parents to commit to their child's participation for twelve weekly sessions. We have seen dramatic change in children who may have had only eight to ten weeks in group, and we have had extremely disturbed children who have been in the same group for as long as two and a half years with a gradual turnover of children in the group. A most crucial part of the therapeutic process is how the therapist handles a child's leaving group and the entry of new children into an existing group.

When a child is ready to graduate from the group, the group needs two to four weeks to plan its own way of saying good-bye. Sometimes that may take the form of making a special dessert together during the last group session or going on a special field trip excursion. Some groups want the last group to be as routine as possible, a time to do for one last time the activities that have become so special to them. Some groups will plan a special craft activity as a remembrance of their times together, such as plaster masks, a card, a final dismantling of a broken VCR for souvenirs for each group member.

Regardless of the free play or structured activity planned for a good-bye session, the therapist sensitively guides the discussion so as to bring a healthy sense of closure for the child leaving group and the children who will remain in group. Recall the previous account of the closing conversation of a group of kindergarten and first-grade boys in which they verbalized for themselves *why* they had come to group (because I was shy, because I hit and kicked kids, because I go to the principal's office every day) and *how* they had changed—"If you will just keep coming to group, you'll have so much fun you won't even know you're getting gooder."

During the final Snack 'n Talk Time, the therapist may use some questions like these to facilitate saying good-bye:

"Will each one of you share with Greg a special memory that you have of being in group with him?"

"Let's go around the circle and each person tell Greg one thing about him that you really like——and, Greg, that includes you saying something you like about yourself."

"Does anybody think of anything they wish had not happened while Greg has been in group or anything you wish had happened but never did?" (A sharing of resentments and regrets.)

"Hey, guys, let's each one think of how you were when Greg joined group. Let's each one say one change you've seen Greg make and one change you have made since you started group together."

"Now, as we get ready to say good-bye, let's each one share one wish you have for Greg—not a wish that costs money—but a wish from you to him."

These are merely examples of how the therapist can facilitate the very important good-bye experience, a time in which the children express incredible insight into themselves and the child that is leaving. The good-byes in time-limited groups, though different, are still as important as children part from one another after having developed a very intimate, honest relationship with children whom they may never see again (unless the group is conducted at their school) but who may have had a profound impact on their life.

Fees and Payment

Concerning payment, a group fee is generally more affordable than an individual fee. When parents are dependable, some therapists do not require payment for appointments missed because of illness or a special event in the child's life; however, others find the only way to be able to financially maintain an active group practice is to charge for the child's place in group. A sliding fee scale, available through a nonprofit corporation, accommodates a wide range of socioeconomic backgrounds, which adds to the diversity of the group and allows many children to receive therapeutic help who could not afford the additional cost of individual play therapy.

RAPT Facilities

Ideally, the play-activity room should be large enough to provide all the children freedom of movement for active interaction with one another and additional space that will allow children to distance themselves from other children as they see fit. Rather than designate an ideal dimension for the room, we invite therapists to match the size of the group and the level of physical activity of the group members to the size of the room. It is important not to attempt to crowd children in a room that is snug for the size of the group. Such confinement will activate unnecessary conflict and limit independent separation from one another.

In addition to traditional play therapy toys and art media (refer to Landreth, 1991, for a listing), specific play media that invite interactional play and other more sophisticated materials are added, particularly when the room also is used for latency age and preadolescent groups. The following categories and lists of materials are presented for consideration without the expectation that any RAPT room must have all the items listed:

Construction Supplies:

- Workbench with vise
- Basic tools—saw, hammer, screwdriver
- Building supplies—lumber, nails, screws, bolts
- Glue gun
- Wood glue and tapes—masking, duct, scotch
- Nonelectric hand drill
- Woodburning set and simple wood-carving tools

Art Supplies:

- Paints—tempera, watercolors, special acrylics (for special projects)
- Large to small paint brushes, sponge brushes, and sponge pieces
- Oil pastels, colored chalk, and colored pencils
- Markers of various sizes
- Various paper suitable for various media
- Colored tissue
- Posterboard
- Glues—glue gun, Modge Podge, spray shellac, spray adhesive, fabric glue, rubber cement, white glue
- Various tapes
- Various magazines
- Potter's clay and colored clay suitable for drying for baking in regular oven
- Colored beads, feathers, glitter, scraps of felt, yarn, and fabric
- Plaster of Paris gauze strips for facial masks

Music-Making Instruments:

- Old guitar (garage sale type)
- Tambourine
- Various drums
- Battery-powered keyboard

Sandtrays and Sandtray Miniatures:

- Dry sand tray
- Wet sand tray
- Sandtray miniatures
- Micro machines and micro soldiers

Cooking Supplies and Ingredients:

- Electric skillet
- Egg beater or hand-held electric mixer
- Paper plates
- Mixing utensils and bowls
- Flour, sugar, salt, food coloring, tubes of icing, decorative sugars
- Toaster oven with temperature range (garage sale item)
- Vinyl tablecloth
- Brownie, cookie, and pancake mixes
- Small aluminum baking pans

Sports Equipment:

- Basketball goal for door
- Various balls—Nerf, volleyball, basketball, Nerf football
- Training gloves (like boxing gloves)
- Large vinyl bop bag (sand in bottom)
- Balls and catcher's mitts coated with Velcro hook-and-loop fasteners
- Home type trampoline
- Badminton rackets and birdies
- Whiffle ball and scoops

Games:

- Checkers, chess
- Deck of cards
- Labyrinth
- Pick-up sticks
- Skittles (spinning top with string)
- Small table-top pinball game (battery run)
- Foos ball, Ping-Pong, or two-by-four-foot pool table

Additional Furnishings:

- Floor pillows
- Shelf for safekeeping of unfinished projects
- Dual work and snack table
- Throw rug (for gathering)
- Old quilt or blanket

Dramatic Play:

- Hats
- Makeup
- Jewelry
- Scarves, wigs, ties, vests
- Masks
- Props—feathers, wand, baton

Unique Crafts:

- Group journal books
- Jewelry making
- Leather making
- Copper work
- Mosaic work
- Embroidery thread for sewing, bracelets, and necklaces
- T-shirt painting
- Tie dye
- Mask masking
- Papier-mâché
- Clay sculpting
- Bread dough objects

This list is provided to awaken creativity in therapists as to the wide array of activities and materials that may arise in RAPT groups.

Summary

Relational Activity Play Therapy groups represent a model of group play therapy that allows children the opportunity to reenact problematic behaviors, reexamine self in light of peer and therapist reactions, redirect self in experimenting with more functional behaviors, and reintegrate the corrective group experience into a more workable sense of self and view of others and the world of the child. RAPT groups are characterized by the unique blending of Free Play Time, Group Activity Time and a closing Snack 'n Talk Time, each of which contributes to the therapeutic value of the group experience.

The therapist seeks to respond to each child in a genuinely accepting and nurturing manner, while at the same time leaving the child to find his or her way of being in relationship to other children in the group. Conflicts between children are seen as opportunities for group members to develop problem-solving skills. The therapist senses when to let children work through their own difficulties with one another and when to interrupt the process with a problem-solving intervention that involves the whole group. The therapist weaves together the use of elementary and advanced group activities and projects according to the developmental stage of the individual children and the group as a functioning entity. Activities, projects, and excursions, when used in a timely and nondirective manner, facilitate the growth of individual children and the group as a whole.

Relational Activity Play Therapy groups provide children a "stopping off place" in their journey to maturity, an emotionally safe home of the kind described by Robert Frost, in which children are able to reactivate and cultivate the innate internal movement toward health and wholeness that resides deep within them (Landreth & Sweeney, 1997).

References

Axline, V. (1969). *Play therapy.* New York: Ballantine.

Berg, R., & Landreth, G. (1990). *Group counseling: Concepts and procedures* (2nd ed.). Muncie, IN: Accelerated Development.

DeMaria, M., & Cowden, S. (1992). The effects of child-centered group play therapy on self concept. *International Journal of Play Therapy, 1,* 53–67.

Frost, R. (1969). *The poetry of Robert Frost: Complete and unabridged.* New York: Henry Holt.

Ginott, H. (1961). *Group psychotherapy with children: The theory and practice of play therapy.* New York: McGraw-Hill.

Ginott, H. (1968). Innovations in group psychotherapy with preadolescents. In G. Gazda (Ed.), *Innovations to group psychotherapy.* Springfield, IL: Thomas.

Landreth, G. (1991). *Play therapy: The art of the relationship.* Muncie, IN: Accelerated Development.

Landreth, G. (1993). Child-centered play therapy. *Elementary School Guidance Journal, 28,* 17–28.

Landreth, G., & Sweeney, D. (1997). Child-centered play therapy. In K. O'Connor & L. Braverman (Eds.), *Play therapy: Theory and practice* (pp. 17–45). New York: Wiley.

Schiffer, M. (1969). *The therapeutic play group.* New York: Grune & Stratton.

Schiffer, M. (1977). Activity-interview group psychotherapy: Theory, principles, and practice. *International journal of group psychotherapy, 27*(3), 377–388.

Schiffer, M. (1984). *Children's group therapy: Methods and case histories.* New York: Free Press.

Slavson, S. R. (1945). Differential methods of group therapy in relation to age levels. *Nervous Child, 4,* 196–210.

Slavson, S. R. (1948). Play group therapy for young children. *Nervous Child, 7,* 318–327.

Slavson, S. R. (1952). *Child psychotherapy.* New York: Columbia University Press.

Slavson, S., & Schiffer, M. (1975). *Group psychotherapies for children.* New York: International Universities Press.

CHAPTER FOURTEEN

GROUP PUPPETRY

Sue Carlton Bratton and Dee Ray

The use of puppet shows to express human experience dates back to ancient civilization. It was not until the early 1900s, however, that puppets were employed for therapeutic purposes. Since that time puppets have been widely used diagnostically and therapeutically because they provide a nonthreatening means for clients of all ages to express themselves. Puppetry is a particularly effective therapeutic modality for working with children in small groups. Puppets offer a means for children to express their thoughts and feelings symbolically and concretely. In addition, group interaction is facilitated as group members more readily interact with each other behind the safety of the puppet characters. This chapter briefly explores the history and rationale for the therapeutic use of puppets, outlines a procedure for using puppets in group activity and play therapy, and presents a case study to illustrate the use of puppetry.

History and Rationale

The use of puppets is a form of art that can be dated back to the ancient societies of Egypt and Greece (Fletcher & Deckter, 1947), as well as the Native American cultures (Malkin, 1977). Puppet shows in seventeenth-century Europe and Asia were quite popular and well respected. However, the use of puppets as a therapeutic tool was not introduced until the twentieth century. As early as the 1920s, Melanie Klein noted that children used puppets, among other objects, to express inner feelings and personify people in their lives (Klein, 1929). By the 1930s, Bender and Woltmann were using puppet shows as a psychotherapeutic intervention with seriously ill, hospitalized children (Bender & Woltmann, 1936; Woltmann, 1967).

Puppets may serve many different therapeutic purposes. In Woltmann's (1967) work, he concluded that in structured puppet show presentations, each child in the audience identifies with characters and action. Although situations presented may be threatening, everything is still make-believe, thereby creating safety for the child. More recently, Irwin and Malloy (1994) used puppets in their work with families in order to observe the family's communication patterns, decision-making strategies, and so on. Gendler (1986) conducted group puppetry therapy with small groups of children. She proposed several therapeutic objectives in using puppetry, including Woltmann's conclusion of psychological safety in expressing denied feelings. In addition, Gendler (1986) determined that puppets provide a means of talking about unspeakable events and serve as transitional objects for younger children.

The use of puppets as transitional objects serves as a developmental tool to allow children to bridge the gap between reality and fantasy. Hence, puppetry is developmentally appropriate for young children in therapy. In enhancing the group process, puppets provide a vehicle for developing empathy and support among group members and enable the expression of deep conflicts through the pooling of unconscious needs. Children in the group serve as alter egos to each other.

Other therapists have also found therapeutic purpose in using puppets. Puppets allow children to create a separate persona through whom they express forbidden thoughts and feelings (Linn, 1982). The ability to quickly and safely express these feelings allows for effective short-term therapy. In addition, using puppets to facilitate the emergence and processing of fears and concerns allows for mastery and resolution to occur (Linn, 1982; Woltmann, 1967). Through the repetition of puppet play, solutions to problems will often develop and gain momentum.

In their review of therapeutic puppetry, Dillavou et al. (1954) determined that puppetry provides escape from frustration, identification with desired characters, development of group morale, creative projection, and reduced tension through free choices of roles. In a group, children and adolescents share common experiences through puppets that contain personal meaning. They discover that they are not alone, others have the same feelings, which leads to provocative group discussion.

Finally, puppetry is used not only for therapeutic purposes but also for diagnostic assessment (Irwin, 1985; Irwin & Shapiro, 1975). Using a highly structured process, Irwin and Shapiro developed a method of diagnosing children through their puppet play. Puppets are used in diagnosis because of their appeal and projective value. In this method, the therapist prompts the child to choose puppets and make up a story. Following the puppet show, the therapist conducts an interview with the child and the puppet characters. By looking at the length and complexity of story, images, vocabulary and sentence structure, and story content, the therapist is able to make a diagnosis.

Structured and Unstructured Use of Puppets

Although it is agreed that puppets can serve a therapeutic purpose, there is some debate about the way in which puppets should be employed toward this purpose. There appear to be two primary camps of therapeutic puppetry, structured and unstructured. In traditional structured use of puppet shows, the therapist presents a puppet show that will address issues specific to its audience (Bender & Woltmann, 1936; Spiegel, 1961; Woltmann, 1967). An example of this structured process is Cassell's (1965) presentation of puppet shows acting out the medical procedure to twenty children admitted to a children's hospital for cardiac catheterization. Of the forty children studied, the twenty who participated in the puppet shows showed less emotional disturbance during the procedure and more willingness to return to the hospital for further treatment.

The second approach to the therapeutic use of puppetry involves unstructured puppet use, which allows for more free and creative exploration by the child. Pure, unstructured puppet play generally occurs in a playroom where puppets are among the toys available for use by the child. One example is a case study presented by Burch (1980), who conducted play therapy with a thirteen-year-old boy who had been severely abused and abandoned. By the seventh play session, the boy had chosen two puppets, an aggressive-looking parrot and a red bird. He used these two puppets to play scenes of abandonment, abuse, and eventually salvation. The therapist concluded the puppets allowed the child to replay and master his childhood traumas. In a similar case, Carter (1987) described a case of a ten-year-old boy in nondirective play therapy who had witnessed his father's murder. By the third play session, he chose puppets to repeatedly play out the violent themes involving his father's death and his narrow escape. Through this repetition, the boy mastered this trauma through the acceptance of his father's death in the puppet play. Allowing children the freedom to choose puppets as a means of expression appears to therapeutically enhance the process for some children.

In addition to unstructured individual puppet play are the unstructured puppet shows usually used in the group format. Unstructured puppet shows are presented to children in terms of asking the children to each create or choose a puppet, then asking them to act out a story involving those puppets. Although this method is still somewhat structured in requesting the use of puppets, the children are allowed to create themes and content that are purely their expression of themselves. The therapist merely serves as a facilitator and observer of the process. In the unstructured use of puppets, Kors (1964) found that the goal is to achieve the utmost creative possibilities of a particular child rather than focusing on a specific neurosis. Children use the processes of group and puppetry to address therapeutic issues in the appropriate manner and time that feels safe for them.

Procedure for Introducing Puppetry

The procedure employed by the authors in their work with groups of children is based on Irwin and Malloy's (1994) Family Puppet Interview. This procedure can be used at various stages in therapy for a variety of purposes, including the assessment of individual group members' styles of interacting, coping, and so on, the facilitation of interaction between group members, and the provision of opportunities for problem solving and conflict resolution.

Materials Needed

A wide of variety of puppets is important and should include human and animal figures, combining both realistic and fantasy factors such as turtles with shells, alligators, spiders, sharks, caterpillars, birds, dragons, butterflies, witches, fairy godmothers, judges, police, reversible puppets, royalty, culturally diverse puppets, a family of puppets. There is a tendency for commercial puppets to be soft, furry, and cute, regardless of the animal or character. It is important to have a few mean, hostile puppets; several of the therapeutic catalogues have molded rubber dragons and dinosaurs with big teeth that are really scary. At least one puppet should also have a tongue that protrudes from the mouth, for use with sexually abused children. It is important to provide a puppet theater large enough for all group members to fit behind. The authors use a puppet theater, mounted on wheels, that measures five feet wide and five feet from top to bottom. The stage area is three feet off the ground and there is an eighteen-inch open area above the stage, with curtains. We find that this size of theater can accommodate children, adolescents, and families. If a large puppet theater is not available, a five-foot table turned on its side can be used.

Method

The procedure for structuring the puppet show involves four steps: selecting the puppets, planning the show, presenting the show, and processing the experience. The therapist facilitates the selection of puppets by bringing a large basket of puppets to the group. The therapist dumps the basket of puppets on the floor and introduces the activity by saying, "Here are some puppets for you to look through. Take a few minutes and choose a few that you would like to play with." Next, group members are asked to decide names for their puppets and introduce them to the group in their character voices. The therapist gives instructions for the group to tell a story with the puppets, a story that has a beginning, middle, and end. The group is given approximately fifteen minutes to plan their story. Obtaining prior consent by group members and their legal guardians to video this process would provide yet another option for therapy in allowing the group to later view the video for further therapeutic and educational benefits. Group members title their story and perform it for the therapist.

Following the performance, the therapist interacts with each puppet character portrayed in the story. Several interventions may be useful for the therapist during this processing time, such as helping create new interactions between characters, posing questions that assist group members in considering different explanations, challenging belief systems that are portrayed, and reworking the final outcome to a more positive and healthy one. The therapist then asks group members to come back from behind the puppet theater and talk about their characters, which they like most, which is most like them, and so on. Finally, the group is asked if they were to put their show on television for other kids to watch, what would they call their show and what moral or lesson would kids learn from watching it.

Case Example

The therapist formed a group of three girls to participate in activity group therapy. The therapist interviewed all three girls and their mothers or guardians prior to beginning therapy. Each girl was experiencing family and school difficulties. The following is a brief description of each girl.

Betty: Betty is an eleven-year-old girl in fifth grade who is an only child. Her parents have been divorced for five years and originally separated because her father was physically abusive to her mother. Betty lives with her mother and visits her father every other weekend. Her mother has recently become seriously involved with a man who has two sons. The five of them spend a good deal of time together on weekends and holidays. Betty consistently challenges her mother by breaking rules, not coming home after school, and speaking disrespectfully to her mother. When she visits her father, she is the center of attention and receives material goods on request. At school, Betty is unhappy and feels she has no friends. Previously an honor roll student, Betty has received failing grades in the past few months by refusing to do her homework. Her promotion to sixth grade is in jeopardy. Betty is seemingly withdrawn and distant from others.

Cathy: Cathy is an eleven-year-old girl in the sixth grade. Cathy is the first child of two from her parents' marriage. Her parents have been divorced since she was four years old. Her parents also separated due to physical abuse to her mother. She sees her father every other weekend and on holidays. She is close to her father, who meets most of her material demands. Two months ago, her father left the country for a month and returned married to a woman Cathy did not know. Cathy has one younger brother whom she claims to hate. Her mother also reports continual problems between the two siblings. Cathy is verbally abusive to her mother and refuses to follow home rules. At school, she does have a few friends but is quite upset about not being in the popular crowd. Cathy is quite outspoken and generally negative toward new situations. She does appear to show strong leadership skills.

Tina: Tina is an eleven-year-old girl in the sixth grade who is in the custody of a state home for children. She and her younger sister were removed from their home due to their mother's alcoholism and physical abuse. Even though both girls live at the state home, they reportedly physically fight often with each other and are not close. Tina has been removed from her mother several times in her life. She has experienced physical and verbal abuse from her mother and her mother's boyfriends. She has also witnessed extensive physical abuse to her mother. Tina sees her mother sporadically, close to once a month. Tina participates in physical fights at the home and at her school. She does not have friends at school and is often teased by other children. She is academically behind and often argues with her teachers. Upon meeting an unfamiliar adult, however, Tina is quite friendly and willing to please. She demonstrates a low frustration level, at which point she acts aggressively toward others.

The second session of activity therapy with this group employed the puppet technique described in this chapter. The following is a partial transcript, with commentary.

All four participants entered the activity room. The therapist dumped out a bag of puppets, approximately twenty-five, on the floor. The puppet theater was already in the room.

Therapist: *[to all girls]* I'd like for you to select a few puppets that you like to tell a story.

Tina: Which ones should we choose?

Therapist: Any ones that you like.

Cathy: *[tries out a few puppets, mostly attracted to the aggressive puppets]* This is stupid.

Therapist: Cathy, you're just not sure you want to do this.

Cathy: *[picks out a puppet with big teeth, unattractive features]* This one reminds me of my brother.

Tina: [*also picking up an unattractive, aggressive puppet*] This one looks like my dorm mother. I hate her.

As the girls continue to explore the different puppets, they pick out different ones that remind them of people in their lives. Betty remains quiet but participates in trying out the different puppets. This continues for approximately ten minutes.

Therapist: It looks like you have found a few that you like. Are there any that you like that remind you of you?
Betty: I like this butterfly. I'd love to be able to fly around. She's beautiful.
Therapist: Betty, you found one that fits what you'd like to be.
Tina: [*picking up a small witch, and a big witch*] This one [*small witch*] is just like me and this one [*big witch*] is just like my mother.
Cathy: [*holding an alligator with big teeth*] This one is just like my mother.
Tina: [*to Cathy*] But which one is like you?
Cathy: None of them. [*picking up an aggressive-looking dragon*] I guess, this one.
Therapist: I can see all of you have chosen some puppets you really like. I'd like for you to make up a story to tell me using the puppets. Not a story you already know, from a book or TV, but a story that you create.
Tina: OK, I want it to be about our moms and us. I have an idea. Let's go back here.

Tina leads the group behind the puppet theater, Cathy is also quickly coming up with ideas. Betty trails behind. There is a lot of inaudible talk and arguing. Cathy does not like Tina's idea, so she makes up her own. The group agrees to follow Cathy's idea. At that point, Betty speaks up about not wanting to choose a puppet for her mother. She quickly runs out from behind the stage and grabs a soft unicorn puppet. She announces that it is her father. The group continues to talk, and then Tina announces that they are ready.

Therapist: Do you have a title for your show? [*lots of whispering ensues*]
Betty: Yes! I'll write it. [*comes out from behind the stage and writes "Kill The Parents" on the marquee; all the girls laugh*]
Therapist: I can tell you've put some thought into this.
Tina: Scene one.

The three puppets chosen for the girls appear at the same time—Betty's butterfly, Cathy's dragon, and Tina's little witch. They enact a scene where they are all on the phone, each one has a part pretending to talk to a friend. Suddenly, an alligator appears and in an aggressive tone orders the dragon to get off the phone. The dragon attacks the alligator, beats it up, kills it, then throws it in front of the theater. The same act ensues with the little witch and big witch, then with the butterfly and unicorn. The therapist is quiet throughout the show.

> *Tina:* *[announces]* The end.

At this point the girls are laughing hysterically, with some hint of needing approval.

> *Tina:* *[to therapist]* Did you like it?
> *Therapist:* That was quite a powerful show. I'd like to talk to some of the puppets if I could.

The girls come out to get their puppets from in front of the stage. They quickly return behind the stage with each of the puppets showing. They seem quite eager to interact.

> *Therapist:* Butterfly, dragon, and little witch, it looked like you were you enjoying yourselves at first. What were you doing?
> *Dragon (Cathy):* We were just trying to talk to some friends on the phone.
> *Little Witch (Tina):* Yeah! We were just trying to have some fun.
> *Therapist:* Then what happened?
> *Dragon (Cathy):* *[sounding angry]* Then she *[pointing at the alligator]* had to come in and ruin everything.
> *Therapist:* Yeah, you got pretty mad at her. You really wanted to hurt her.
> *Dragon (Cathy):* She deserves it. She always trying to ruin my fun. I hate her.
> *Little Witch (Tina):* *[pointing at the big witch]* She never cares about what I'm doing. She only cares about herself.
> *Butterfly (Betty):* I wasn't really that mad. He *[pointing at unicorn]* just always tries to tell me what to do.
> *Therapist:* Sometimes it seems like you're just trying to have some fun, and someone comes in to stop you.
> *All three girls:* Yeah!
> *Cathy:* My mom never lets me do anything.

At this point, Cathy seems too angry to really see another perspective. The therapist chooses to talk to Tina (little witch) who is connected with both other girls and a little more expressive with her feelings.

Therapist: Little witch, do you think you could tell big witch how you feel?

Little Witch (Tina): No, she doesn't care.

Therapist: Would you be willing to try?

Little Witch (Tina): OK. You never care about what I'm doing. You only care about yourself.

Therapist: Big witch, can you tell little witch how you feel?

Big Witch (Tina): I'm sorry. I'll never do it again. I love you. *[both witches hug and kiss]*

Therapist: I'd like for all us to come out and sit in a circle together.

All the girls come out willingly. Betty heads for the art easel.

Therapist: Betty, I'd like us to talk for a few minutes. *[Betty complies]* Betty, can you tell me who your puppet represented?

Betty: Yeah, it was my dad. I don't have any problems with my mom. My dad's OK too, but I like him less than my mom.

Therapist: So, you don't see you have any big problems with your parents?

Betty: Nope!

Cathy: *[angrily]* You're lying.

Tina: Yeah, you're lying. Everybody's got problems with their mom.

Betty: I don't. My parents give me everything I want.

Cathy: Then you're lucky. I get nothing. I hate my mom.

Tina: At least you get to see your mom. *[Tina then lets the group know for the first time that she lives in a state home. She answers the girls' questions and explains her situation.]*

Cathy: I'd rather live where you do.

Tina: No, you wouldn't. It sucks there.

Betty: It sounds awful. *[The group continues the discussion with each girl participating. Session ends.]*

Commentary

As demonstrated through the transcript, the puppet show was a powerful impetus to the group process. Although reluctant at first, mostly due to their discomfort, the girls quickly joined in the activity. Choosing puppets allowed them the opportunity to concretely describe the people in their lives. The puppet show itself provided clues to how they perceive their home situations. Betty is in denial about her angry feelings, claiming she has no anger with her mother. Cathy is openly hostile, acting quite aggressive and developing the theme of "Kill The Parents." Tina, meanwhile, seems quite confused, alternating between anger and fantasy, a world where her mother would demonstrate love and affection for her. In putting together the puppet show, Betty, who had been withdrawn, became a part of the group. Tina attempted to bring all the girls together, and Cathy proved her skills as a leader. The discussion with the puppets and the girls brought the group to a deeper level, where some heavy topics were discussed. This was especially powerful considering this was the group's second session. As established in the literature, puppets in this case allowed an atmosphere of safety, a vehicle for unaccepted feelings, and a facilitation of the group process.

Conclusion

Puppetry provides a safe, enjoyable means for children to express their thoughts and feelings symbolically. As seen in the case study, puppets can quickly facilitate group interaction by allowing group members to hide behind their fantasy characters as they dramatize their own lives. By emphasizing the make-believe aspect of play, children can be helped to express themselves and work through problems in an effective yet nonthreatening way.

References

Bender, L., & Woltmann, A. (1936). The use of puppet shows as a psychotherapeutic method for behavior problems in children. *American Journal of Orthopsychiatry, 6,* 341–354.

Burch, C. (1980). Puppet play in a thirteen-year-old boy: Remembering, repeating, and working through. *Clinical Social Work Journal, 8*(2), 79–89.

Carter, S. (1987). Use of puppets to treat traumatic grief: A case study. *Elementary School Guidance and Counseling, 21*(3), 210–215.

Cassell, S. (1965). Effect of brief puppet therapy upon the emotional responses of children undergoing cardiac catheterization. *Journal of Consulting Psychology, 29*(1), 1–8.

Dillavou, J., Gahan, D., Leonhardt, W., Binkley, M., Brinkmeyer, G., & Boerio, C. (1954). Puppetry: A form of play therapy to help adolescents. *Progressive Education, 31,* 252–255.

Fletcher, H., & Deckter, J. (1947). *The puppet book.* New York: Greenberg.

Gendler, M. (1986). Group puppetry with school-age children: Rationale, procedure and therapeutic implication. *Arts in Psychotherapy, 13*(1), 45–52.

Irwin, E. (1985). Puppets in therapy: An assessment procedure. *American Journal of Psychotherapy, 39*(3), 389–400.

Irwin, E., & Malloy, E. (1994). Family puppet interview. In C. D. Schaefer & L. Carey (Eds.), *Family play therapy* (pp. 21–33). Northvale, NJ: Aronson.

Irwin, E., & Shapiro, M. (1975). Puppetry as a diagnostic and therapeutic technique. *Psychiatry and Art, 4,* 86–94.

Klein, M. (1929). Personification in the play of children. *International Journal of Psychoanalysis, 10,* 193–204.

Kors, P. (1964). Unstructured puppet shows as group procedure therapy with children. *Psychiatric Quarterly (Supplement), 38,* 56–75.

Linn, S. (1982, December). Techniques for puppet therapy. *Association for Play Therapy Newsletter, 1*(3), 1–2.

Malkin, M. (1977). *Traditional and folk puppets of the world.* New York: Barnes.

Spiegel, S. (1961). The use of puppets as a therapeutic tool with children. *Virginia Medical Monthly, 88,* 272–275.

Woltmann, A. (1967). The use of puppetry in therapy. In W. M. Long & R. N. Long (Eds.), *Conflict in the classroom: The education of emotionally disturbed children* (pp. 202–208). Belmont, CA: Wadsworth.

CHAPTER FIFTEEN

MULTICULTURAL CONSIDERATIONS IN GROUP PLAY THERAPY

Geraldine Glover

Multicultural counseling is a topic that has become popular in recent years. Many therapists feel an urgency to become more aware of their role in a relationship that involves cultures other than their own. Some of this urgency comes from the clients themselves as they demand acknowledgment of their individuality. In the United States it is particularly easy to meet and have the opportunity to work with children from cultures that would not be considered part of the mainstream. Census data as of 1992 reflect that approximately 25 percent of U.S. citizens belong to one of four major ethnic minority groups, with approximately 12 percent African American, 9 percent Hispanic and Latino, 3 percent Asian and Pacific Islander, and 1 percent Native American. Current trends indicate that the proportion of the non-Hispanic white population in the United States will drop to just over 50 percent by 2050 (U.S. Bureau of Census, 1992). Zayas and Solari (1994) state that current literature suggests that parents from ethnic and racial minorities socialize their children based on distinct beliefs and behaviors that are determined largely by their cultural and socioeconomic situation. Acceptance of differences as strengths is a common theme among therapists, but simply to accept differences leaves many therapists feeling inadequate to meet the needs of such diverse populations.

To add another dimension, such as group counseling, to multicultural counseling can in some ways complicate the situation. If the group itself is diverse, the therapist needs to be especially sensitive to the reactions, needs, and differences each child brings to the group. Not only will the therapist need to be accepting of differences as strengths, but some education may be required for other group members. Opportunities to set limits on inappropriate behavior between children because of misunderstandings due to cultural differences can only be taken advantage of if the therapist is aware of the negative impact. If the opportunity exists for a group to be formed that consists of members from a single culture, the therapist has the chance to learn from the group members.

Strupp (1973) noted that between the choices of healing through the therapeutic relationship or emphasis on technical skills and specific therapeutic techniques, those who favor transferring therapy methods from one culture to another focus heavily on the significance of the therapeutic relationship. Although there has been little research on the effectiveness of relationship-based therapies for multicultural counseling, in studies conducted by Glover (1996) and Chau (1996), parents reported positive results with their children after having been trained in child-centered play therapy techniques. These studies involved Native American families residing on the Flathead Reservation in northern Montana and Chinese families in the north Texas area. Earlier studies of child-centered group therapy revealed no differential process issues or significantly different results for minority groups (Ginsberg, Stutman, & Hummel, 1978).

As a relationship-based therapy, child-centered group play therapy is ideal for working with children who may have a different cultural background from that of the therapist. In child-centered group play therapy, opportunities for responsible self-direction are maximized. An accepting, nonevaluative relationship allows the child to explore new ways of feeling and behaving (Dorfman, 1951). The therapist actively reflects the child's thoughts and feelings, believing that when a child's feelings are expressed, identified, and accepted, the child can accept them and is then free to deal with those feelings (Landreth, 1991). The intent of child-centered group play therapy is to allow children the freedom to be who they are. The use of empathic understanding, acceptance, warmth, congruity, and behavioral limits provide an environment in which the children can move toward adaptive behaviors. When the therapist does not have a specific structure in mind, the children are allowed to explore the issues that are most significant to them. The children are relied upon to direct the process.

To prepare therapists for multicultural consideration in group play therapy, this chapter will briefly explore common values, parenting practices, and therapeutic concerns of four primary minority groups. Attention will be given to biracial or multiracial issues and the effects of acculturation level. This will be followed by sections on engaging the family and providing a culturally sensitive environment. The chapter will conclude with a short case study of two children of Hispanic descent in sibling group play therapy.

Understanding Cultures

Traditional societies have developed their own institutions and techniques for deal-ing with psychological problems (Heinrich, Corbine, & Thomas, 1990). These may include confession, suggestions, reassurance, and direct influence. Keeping this in mind, therapists are charged with the task of evaluating their own approach to counseling in relation to the client they are working with. Whenever counsel-ing is used to restrict rather than foster the well-being and development of per-sons who are culturally different, therapists are participating in overt or covert forms of prejudice and discrimination (Pedersen, 1991). It is also important to be aware that functional adaptation for one person may be maladaptive for another. Therapists must first be aware of the way in which they perceive health and ill-ness. It is essential for them to be specific about the categories of illness and dys-function and the meaning of various symptoms and feelings, so that when they are confronted with an individual who does not share these particular values and meanings, they can adjust their worldview. Sue (1981) emphasizes the need to show true concern and respect for the worth, dignity, and uniqueness of the in-dividual. Each individual's freedom must be valued. The goal of the therapist is to help the individual to attain the individual's own self-determined goals.

Choosing child-centered group play therapy as an appropriate intervention with children of cultures different from that of the therapist relies heavily on the effectiveness of the therapeutic relationship. Adequate preparation of the thera-pist and the environment becomes paramount for responsible multicultural child-centered group play therapy. Initially, therapists must develop an understanding of their own cultural backgrounds and their culturally laden beliefs, values, and as-sumptions. Therapists need to develop an understanding of a group's cultural makeup, both historical and contemporary, and a sense of the problems the group faces. To be culturally responsive, Locke (1990) identifies several guidelines. Ther-apists must be open to culturally different values and attitudes. They should learn about different cultures and their mores, yet retain the uniqueness of each child by avoiding stereotyping within cultural groups. Therapists should encourage children and their parents to be open about their cultural backgrounds. One method of learning about a culture is to participate in activities in a child's cultural commu-nity. In addition, therapists must eliminate all personal behaviors that suggest bias or prejudice and hold high expectations for all children across all cultural groups.

Certain attitudes and practices are common to various cultures. This is not to say that a specific child or family the therapist is working with will manifest all or even some of these attitudes and practices. Still, an awareness of what is common will broaden the therapist's perspective and will assist the therapist in being genuine, warm, and congruent. In addition Zayas and Solari (1994) caution that early childhood socialization may also be influenced by the interaction of education, income, acculturation, and residency between and within different minority subgroups.

The more thoroughly therapists know the symbols, meanings, and messages of a child's culture, the greater will be their ability to achieve cross-cultural identification. This requires listening carefully, asking sensitive questions about those meanings, reading and studying about the culture native to the child, and recognizing that the families are expert in their own realms of experience (Hoare, 1991). The following sections look at some common values and parent expectations of African Americans, Hispanic Americans, Asian Americans, and Native Americans.

African Americans

Values that many African American families hold dear include a strong sense of family and a positive racial identity (Forehand & Kotchick, 1996). There is a sense of great loyalty to the family that is reinforced through community pressure that everything a person does reflects on the family (Hines, Garcia-Preto, McGoldrick, Almeida, & Weltman, 1992). No person succeeds for self alone, but for family and race. At the same time, people are respected not for their successes but for their intrinsic worth.

The elderly are revered, especially women, who are looked to for wisdom and support. For many African American families there is a strong reliance on religion and church structure to provide guidance (Forehand & Kotchick, 1996). And, possibly as a result of years of oppression, great value is placed on perseverance in the face of adversity.

Parents have certain expectations for and ways of interacting with their children. Children can voice their opinions but are not to argue with adults once a decision has been made (Hines et al., 1992). Strong and sometimes seemingly harsh discipline is used to help children learn acceptable behaviors. Parents are concerned that their children obey and are respectful of adults (Forehand & Kotchick, 1996). Personal appearance and grooming are also important.

In addition, many African American parents attempt to educate their children about the duality of their existence in American society. The goal is to live as close to the mainstream culture as possible while maintaining their African cultural identity.

The challenge for the therapist is to be aware of possible differences in behaviors children might display in the child-centered play therapy group. The

African American child is often sensitive to both verbal and nonverbal forms of communication (Hines et al., 1992). Hands-on experiences are often preferred, and children can be very persistent in their efforts to complete a task (Dunn et al., 1990; Griggs & Dunn, 1989). African American children may be considered louder in their verbal interactions than other children. If a therapist is sensitive to noise, this may be an opportunity for personal growth. It is essential that the therapist communicate genuineness, familiarity, and respect for the cultural, historical, and current sociopolitical context of the African American family (Hines et al., 1992).

Hispanic Americans

It is important to remember that many generations of the Hispanic families a therapist works with may have inhabited the areas of California, Arizona, New Mexico, and Texas even prior to the establishment of those states. It is also possible that their origins may be in Mexico, Puerto Rico, Central America, South America, or Cuba, among others. This is a broad and complicated group with many idiosyncracies that can only be discovered by asking.

A primary value for many Hispanic Americans is the strength of the family (Hines et al., 1992; Westwood & Ishiyama, 1990). Strong family ties are maintained from generation to generation. This support and emotional acceptance can be healthy, nurturing, reassuring, and validating (Hines et al., 1992). Parents expect to have very close relationships with their children, especially mothers with their children. Mothers and daughters develop a reciprocal relationship in adulthood, and eldest sons are often expected to become a source of financial support for older parents. Hispanic parents prefer behaviors in children that encourage family closeness, respect for parental authority, and interpersonal relatedness (Zayas & Solari, 1994).

The challenge for the therapist is to accept that some Hispanic children may have a tendency to move about a lot and may take breaks from their play (Griggs & Dunn, 1989). It might not be uncommon for psychological problems to be described in physical terms such as nerves or a stomachache. To be more in tune with families and children, it would be helpful for the therapist to become familiar with culturally meaningful expressions (Santiago-Rivera, 1995). Religion is often a great source of strength for many Hispanic families, and the relative importance of religion should be assessed (Westwood & Ishiyama, 1990). Being aware of support systems that the family could rely on adds to the credibility of the therapist. In addition, the therapist should not be afraid to consult a Hispanic therapist for additional insight into this particular group.

Asian Americans

There is significant diversity in demographic profiles among Asian Americans. Over 40 different Asian groups currently live in the United States, including Asian Indians, Chinese, Filipinos, Japanese, Koreans, Southeast Asians, Cambodians, Laotians, Vietnamese, Pacific Islanders, Hawaiians, Guamanians, and Samoans. Even with this diversity, however, there do seem to be some common themes among these groups.

As with other groups, the individual is valued, but within the context of the family. Sandhu (1997) notes that family needs are placed above those of the individual, and bringing praise and honor to the family is a goal. It is expected that the individual will make personal sacrifices for the good of the family.

Asian Americans in general have a strong ethnic identity (Ibrahim, Ohnishi, & Sandhu, 1997). Self-respect, dignity, self-control, and humility are important qualities. Respect is given to older members of the community because they possess knowledge by virtue of their maturity. There is a belief in fatalism and that certain challenges are preordained, hence the ability to adjust to the environment is important.

Because many Asian American value systems originate with Confucian doctrine, clarification of a family's spiritual identity is helpful. With Confucian doctrine, there are clear demarcation lines defining male and female gender roles. Women receive respect as mothers through their children and are subject to their fathers, husbands, and then their sons.

Asian American parents expect their children to repress strong emotions in obedience to parental authority and family honor (Sandhu, 1997). Cooperation and obedience are valued and not necessarily considered maladaptive in the sense of being nonassertive and dependent (Landreth & Kao, 1997). Independence and self-directedness may be viewed as aggressiveness and stubbornness. There is the expectation that children will work hard and excel in academic endeavors.

Within the context of child-centered group play therapy, the therapist must be aware that shame may be sensed more intensely and for longer periods of time with Asian American children than with other children (Sandhu, 1997). These children are sensitive to nonverbal communication (Ibrahim, Ohnishi, & Sandhu, 1997). When working with families, it is important to recognize the impact of life stage, age, and gender. The therapist is in the position to educate and explore with the family their ethnic subculture, religion, values, and worldview.

Asian American children tend to be quiet and play in an absorbing mode rather than interactively (Landreth & Kao, 1997). Because of a sensitivity to mental impairment bringing shame on the family, it is generally desirable to avoid using the term *therapy*.

Giving gifts is a common way to show appreciation, and the therapist must be careful not to embarrass a family who feels compelled to follow this tradition. Some education of the family will help them to understand that gifts are not necessary; however, should a family give a gift, the therapist should accept it graciously.

Native Americans

There are over five hundred recognized tribes in the United States. Just as with other minority groups, this diversity must be acknowledged. Traditional Native American values include sharing, respect for others, independence, cooperation, and non-interference (Heinrich, Corbine, & Thomas, 1990). Elders are held in high esteem. The mind, body, spirit, and nature are considered inseparable. There is a preference for explaining natural phenomena according to the supernatural. Rituals and sacraments are of great importance, and breaking with tradition results in disharmony that may be manifested in disability, disease, or distress (Lewis & Hayes, 1991). Time is not rigidly structured but circular; there is never a lack of time.

Spiritual beliefs and practices can vary considerably between tribal peoples. Some practice more rituals than others, and this can affect how they interact with the world outside their own communities. For example, traditional Navajos have strong beliefs about death. It is taboo to discuss relatives who have passed on. Places where a dead body has been laid must be ritually cleansed with a blessing. It would be important for a therapist to know how to work with a Navajo child grieving the loss of a loved one in ways that respect this belief. Other tribal peoples who were involved with Catholic or Mormon missionaries may have converted to Christianity and practice religion in ways similar to the dominant culture. And still others may have become involved with the contemporary Native American Church.

Within the extended family, oftentimes children refer to many significant adults as auntie and uncle, not just their parents' siblings. All elders may be referred to as grandmother or grandfather. If a child is being raised by extended family members, those adults acting as parents become mother and father, and cousins may be referred to as brothers and sisters, even though no legal adoption has occurred. This could become a difficulty for therapists who are accustomed to working with a nuclear family group.

Native American parents are often considered to be permissive. Because of the value placed on independence and noninterference, children are allowed abundant opportunities to make choices without coercion, with the understanding that to make a decision for a child is to make the child weak (Brendtro &

Brokenleg, 1993). Children are not prevented from making mistakes unless the consequences would be life threatening. Native American parents hope that their children will learn to give unreservedly as the accumulation of property for its own sake is considered disgraceful.

Children are not punished often, and the form of punishment when used generally involves inductive reasoning. The consequences of the bad behaviors are put into community terms of how the behavior affects others. Embarrassment is also used to correct unacceptable behaviors (Burgess, 1980).

As with other groups, children are taught to be aware of nonverbal communication (Thomason, 1991). Long pauses and silence during play may not be unusual. The therapist may need to be aware of speaking softly. Because of the belief that time is circular, lateness and absence may be more common than with other children (Garrett, 1995). Goals for therapy may be best understood if they are short term and oriented toward the present. As with other groups, group play therapy allows for both visual and oral communication.

While interacting with parents it is important to recognize the history of very difficult cross-cultural relations between tribal and nontribal peoples. Political, territorial, and cultural sovereignty continues to be highly valued by many Native Americans (Lewis & Hayes, 1991).

Multiracial Children

A final category to look at briefly is biracial or multiracial children. Societal practice is to neatly categorize people into specific groups, and those who belong to more than one group are required to choose one or none. Although not all children of mixed races have difficulties, a certain kind of social marginality and loneliness are descriptors of biracial children who have difficulty finding a group that accepts them. Children of a white and a minority parent tend to identify with the minority parent because they think the white community will not accept them; however, an exploration of all sides of racial heritage helps children form a positive sense of identification with ethnic and cultural roots (Herring, 1992). All children need to believe that their family, whether traditional or not, is respected and validated.

Herring (1992) suggests that the therapist needs to examine the biracial circumstances as a possible influencing factor, being alert to possibilities that the biracial child's presenting problem may—but does not necessarily—shield a deeper problem of ethnic identity confusion. This child may need to ventilate feelings about biracial identity and its meaning in society. Therapists must be sensitive to possible mistrust and hostility based on ethnic factors.

Acculturation

Acculturation is a natural process. The level of acculturation depends on the strength of the group's support systems and the members' own determination to maintain their traditions. When a group enters the dominant culture, members necessarily make adjustments in their behavior to fit into their new community. There may be less acculturation within some pockets, for example, some isolated Indian reservations, Hispanic communities of northern New Mexico, or San Francisco's Chinatown. However, even these communities have incorporated much of the dominant culture while maintaining their own traditions.

Garrett (1995) describes four levels of acculturation. At the traditional level a person holds only traditional beliefs and values. At the transitional level, a person holds both traditional beliefs and values and those of the dominant culture, possibly without accepting all of either culture. The third level is to be bicultural—accepted by the dominant culture while also knowing and practicing traditional ways. The fourth level of acculturation is to become assimilated—that is, to embrace only dominant cultural beliefs and values.

For recent immigrant families, the acculturation process has only just begun. The children of new immigrants are in an especially awkward position. They are continually confronted with new and different things with which their parents are not familiar. This can cause distress. The more familiar the therapist can be with the family's traditional culture, the more able the therapist will be in assisting the child and family through the transition.

Immigrant families live with a variety of sources of stress to a greater or lesser extent. Some may still be suffering as a result of the circumstances under which they left their home country. They may be grieving over loss of friends and family in the home country, and dealing with poverty, lack of acceptance by peers, and the negative perception of their minority group held by the dominant culture. The discrepancies between minority and dominant culture may be more or less problematic, and in any case the family members are finding it necessary to learn a new language, new culture, new geographic area, and new ways of accomplishing tasks of daily living (Kopala, Esquivel, & Baptiste, 1994). Children may manifest stress reactions by developmental arrest, anxiety, transitional psychosis, health problems, withdrawal, low self-esteem, aggression, academic problems, masked depression, isolation, and posttraumatic stress.

Clients whose first language is not English require special sensitivity from the therapist. Although it may not be possible, combining children of similar cultural backgrounds provides a familiarity and strength within the group that may not be attainable in a diverse group. This is essential with children whose first language may not be that of the therapist. If the intent is for the children to express them-selves and explore their feelings and practice new responses, it is best done in their first language. An interpreter may be necessary for the therapist to interact on a significant level. Child-centered group play therapy provides ample opportunities for children to express themselves in ways other than by language—dramatic play, art, music, storytelling, and making collages. The therapist can also encourage children to speak in their own language (words and phrases) to best illustrate feel-ings at the moment for ease of expression. The therapist can observe and sense what the children are trying to express while providing an opportunity for cathar-sis. The therapist must continuously check the accuracy of interpretation of non-verbal signals and be ready to solicit the assistance of a well-trained bilingual interpreter (Westwood & Ishiyama, 1990).

Diversity Within a Child-Centered Play Therapy Group

A group comprising traditionally raised children from each of the cultural groups described in this chapter might emphasize the differences. While Native Ameri-can and Asian American children may both prefer a quiet environment, the Asian American child might be more task-oriented while the Native American child may wish for more interaction. This interaction would be possible with the African American child, although the latter's preference for loud interplay may be un-comfortable for the Native American child.

The parents of the African American, Hispanic American, and Asian Amer-ican children may have difficulty with the nondirective nature of the group. While family is highly valued in each group, the expectations for how a member of the family is to behave vary greatly.

Stereotypes can interfere with interactions between children and families of various groups. Therapists must be aware that children, especially those from the dominant culture, are often unaccustomed to differences and may make embar-rassing statements or ask difficult questions about other members of the group. Young children at the concrete stage of development may find it difficult to ac-cept new information and insist that what they have believed in the past is the truth. The therapist must be sensitive to these attitudes and help broaden the child's perspective, at the same time being aware of the impact such beliefs have on the children of various minority groups.

Children may come to the group with preconceived ideas about people who are different from them, especially if they have not interacted with diverse groups in the past (York, 1991). Young children might believe that Africans live in huts in the jungle with wild animals and do not wear much clothing. They might think that African Americans have funny hair, get into a lot of fights, and all look alike. Children might think that Asian Americans all look alike, and have yellow skin and slanty eyes with which they can not see very well. Asian Americans may be viewed by children as very polite people who bow when they greet people, practice karate, and celebrate exotic festivals. Children may think that Hispanic Americans all have only brown hair and brown eyes, are greasy and unclean, and have piñatas at all their parties. Children also have misconceptions about Native Americans. Children think that Native Americans take scalps, have red skin, use tepees as houses, speak in grunts, wear feathers and costumes, ride horses, and do not live now.

On the other hand, children from minority cultures, from the time they enter school if not earlier, are continually exposed to images of the dominant culture and are less likely to formulate unrealistic stereotypes. In fact, children from minority cultures may ascribe advantages to being from the dominant culture and may try to become as much like those from the dominant culture as possible.

Engaging the Family in the Therapeutic Process

Children between the ages of three and ten do not come to therapy in isolation. They are most certainly accompanied by parents or guardians. They are at a susceptible period in their lives and are just beginning to learn the common practices and beliefs of their culture and family systems. It is not the therapist's place to shift the child toward the therapist's viewpoint. Child-centered group play therapy provides a strong basis for keeping the therapist's priorities clear. It is essential to encourage the parents to educate the therapist about cultural and personal systems of language, metaphors, worldviews, and meanings just as it is essential for the therapist to be accepting of this new information (Westwood & Ishiyama, 1990). The therapist must recognize that families are experts in their own realm of experience and that what is functionally adaptive for one person may not be so for another (Hoare, 1991).

Because of the impossibility of knowing exactly how important certain aspects of a culture can be, a therapist is advised to develop a relationship with the family of the child. It is important for the therapist to be aware of the parents' concerns and what they consider to be developmentally appropriate for their child within their culture. This knowledge can only be captured by personal research and high involvement with the parents of the child.

York (1991) identifies certain aspects of raising children that may be culturally related. Different cultures have different age-related expectations of children, including an interest in and concern over children acquiring skills such as toileting by a certain age. Sleep patterns and bedtime routines vary between cultures, as does the acceptance, meaning of, and response to crying. Children of different cultures show different levels of attachment to adults. A child's role and responsibility in the family can also be culturally determined. In addition, diet and mealtime behavior, dress and hair care, discipline and child guidance methods, and the importance of gender identity and traditional sex roles are all influenced by culture. Parents of different cultures may have different ways of talking to their children and different ways of showing affection. The use of medicine or folk cures and remedies for illness may be frequent in minority families.

Parents are an invaluable source of information. To discover the aspects of a culture that may be unfamiliar to a therapist, questions can be interspersed in the intake interview and at follow-up conferences that reveal much information that could be inadvertently taken for granted. York (1991) and Forehand and Kotchick (1996) suggest the following questions for gathering useful information from parents:

- What is your ethnic or cultural background? How do you identify yourself?
- What languages are spoken in your home? With your extended family?
- What traditions, objects, or foods symbolize your family? Why are these things important? What values or history do they represent?
- What are your child's favorite foods? What are your child's favorite objects, toys, things to talk about?
- What is your church affiliation or religious background?
- What is your child's preferred way of expressing self and comforting self?
- What values are important for your children to learn?
- What child behaviors are most appreciated by you as a parent?
- What child behaviors are most difficult for you as a parent?
- What heroes, celebrations, songs, and stories represent and support your cultural heritage?
- What are the most important characteristics you would like in a professional who helps you deal with your child's problems?

The Environment

It is the therapist who has control over the environment in which the group functions. In child-centered group play therapy, a variety of toys and materials are provided from which the children choose in order to work through the issues that may be significant to them. Sensitivity to the images available in the playroom is paramount. Ideally, every playroom would be fully equipped with a variety of materials that would reflect the multitude of cultures existing in the United States. This is a noble goal, but may be unfeasible for most play therapists. The alternative is to be fully aware of the particular groups that the therapist encounters and create a playroom that reflects this diversity.

Not only should the playroom reflect this diversity, the waiting area or school corridors should also make children, parents, and guardians feel welcome. Derman-Sparks (1992), York (1991), and Allen, McNeill, and Schmidt (1992) all contribute suggestions for creating an environment that is culturally sensitive to the young child. There should be images in abundance of all children, including children and adults from major racial and ethnic groups. These images should accurately reflect people's current daily lives at work and with their families. A numerical balance should be maintained among different groups, making sure that people of color are not represented as a token one or two. There should be a fair balance of images of women and men, elderly people of various backgrounds, handicapped people of various backgrounds, and diversity in family styles (two mothers or fathers, extended families, interracial and multiethnic families, and families including people with handicaps).

The therapist can select artwork, prints, sculpture, and textiles by artists of various backgrounds that reflect the aesthetic environment and the cultures of the families represented in the local community. Rather than dolls in ethnic costumes, artwork and artifacts can be displayed—fabric, paintings, beadwork, rugs, wall hangings, musical instruments, sculpture, windsocks, wind chimes, and photos.

Within the playroom itself, the various areas provide the opportunity to acknowledge diversity. The art area can provide colors, patterns, and textures from multiple cultures. Additional materials include origami paper for folding, rice paper for painting, and red clay for modeling. Various scraps of imported cloth, leather scraps, and beads and feathers are appropriate for creating collages. It is important to provide skin-colored crayons, markers, paint, paper, and modeling clay so that children can accurately portray themselves and their families.

The dramatic play area should include multiethnic dolls in contemporary clothing. Nurturing themes are often recreated in the playroom. Providing familiar materials in the kitchen area supports this activity. Items that reflect diverse cultures include tea boxes, tea tins, canned foods, cardboard food containers, plastic bottles, and plastic play food. Rice, flour, and potato bags can be stuffed with batting and sewn closed. Baskets, gourds, mesh bags, and pottery are all used as storage containers by various cultures. Different cultures use different cooking utensils—a tortilla press, molinillos, tea ball, rolling pin, strainer, ladles, wok, steamer, food grinder, mortar and pestle, cutting board, frying pan, kettle. The playroom can supply a variety of kitchen accessories—silverware, wooden spoons, spatulas, graters, eggbeaters, whisk, rice bowl, wooden bowls and plates, tin plates, plastic plates, teacups, chopsticks, tea and coffee pots.

Traditional costumes might be useful, but the typical daily wear of various cultures is less specific in supporting dramatic play. Clothing can be provided such as dresses, skirts, jackets, and large pieces of fabric in squares, rectangles, and triangles. Fabric can be of different patterns such as batik, tie-dyed, and madras prints.

As was mentioned earlier, to equip a playroom with this entire list would not be cost-effective for most play therapists. Instead, it is suggested that the therapist concentrate on selecting items that reflect the families of the community in which the therapist works.

Case Study

Teresa (age seven) and Juan (age six) were a sibling pair of Hispanic descent referred for therapy as part of requirements of a parenting plan established by family court. An initial intake conference was held with the custodial parent, in this case the father, to determine family support systems and the nature of any problems the children might be encountering or negative behaviors they might be manifesting. According to the father, the parents became separated just before Christmas in 1995. From this time until the final divorce in February 1997, the children's residence shifted sporadically back and forth between the parents. In February an official visitation schedule was designed giving physical custody to the father three-quarters of the time and to the mother one-quarter of the time. The mother stopped her visitations in mid-March, and the children had not seen her in over four months.

The therapist in this case was not Hispanic, resulting in a multicultural counseling situation. Special attention was made to gather specific information about the children and the family. This was supplemented with general knowledge of Hispanic culture and values so the therapist could prepare adequately to meet the needs of this particular family.

The father said that a large extended family was available to assist him with the raising of the children. The children were very close to these relatives and spent much time with them, in particular with the father's sister, who was the primary caregiver in the father's absence. Grandparents and father spoke Spanish in the home, but the children were primarily English speakers. The family members were practicing Catholics. The father described a great deal of guilt in regard to the divorce and was genuinely concerned about its impact on his children.

The father wanted his children to be happy and to behave properly and respectfully toward adults.

Child-centered group play therapy was selected as the mode of therapeutic intervention for these children. The children were close in age and were experiencing the same family disruption. Their parents' divorce had resulted in separation from their mother, and they had become close and dependent upon each other for emotional support during the past year. There was no sign of intense sibling rivalry, and the father felt that the children would feel more comfortable together.

The playroom was equipped for child-centered group play therapy, providing opportunities for creative arts and aggressive, nurturing, construction, and fantasy play. Because of the large Hispanic population in the community, many of the dolls and dollhouse figures were Hispanic characters. Art materials included skin-colored crayons, markers, paint, paper, and modeling clay. Also available were replicas of traditional foods, cooking utensils, and food containers commonly found in Hispanic homes.

The process and stages of therapy for this sibling group were not dissimilar to those of other child-centered play therapy groups. However, two specific interactions might be considered atypical by the dominant culture and could have been misinterpreted by the therapist.

In the first group play therapy session with the siblings, they both remained motionless in front of the sandtray miniatures for the first forty-five minutes of the session. They were very polite and touched nothing although the therapist had introduced the playroom with the statement that they could use the toys in many of the ways they would like. It was apparent that the younger sibling was waiting for his older sister to make the first move. During the last ten minutes of the session, each chose a couple of items and placed them in the sandtray, Teresa choosing first. Very little was verbalized during the entire session.

In psychotherapy with Hispanic children, consideration must be given to the influence of parents' stated desires about how they want their children to behave. The Hispanic child is better served, at least until more data are gathered that point to specific issues, if the psychologist can view acquiescence in play or verbal therapy as a result of socialization for *good*—that is, respectful and conforming—behavior (Zayas & Solari, 1994).

Throughout the first few sessions both children stayed physically close to the therapist, sometimes leaning up against the therapist while they worked at an activity. Oftentimes, this type of behavior displayed by a child toward an unfamiliar adult would be considered abnormal and cause for concern. Reactive attachment disorder might be demonstrated by excessive familiarity to relative strangers. It is typical for children of the dominant culture and other cultures as well to be somewhat selective about when they will approach the therapist. In large extended families, however, children may learn that adults are generally trustworthy. In addition, physical contact between adults and children is especially common in Hispanic culture.

Throughout the sessions, the play of both children was age-appropriate and typical. Teresa's play included more creative and nurturing activities with painting and family doll play. Juan shifted toward competence and aggressive play using the army figures as targets and shooting them with the dart gun. Occasionally the play activity would become cooperative; however, Teresa's overdirection seemed to become tiring for Juan, and he would return to a self-selected activity. During the course of the play therapy group, the children—who had initially started out almost inseparable—began to play somewhat independently.

These children had endured much loss and shifting of home arrangements during the past year; however, they both seemed well adjusted and closely bonded with their father. The continued support of the extended family seems to have added stability to an otherwise chaotic situation. The determination was made by the therapist that the termination process could begin. Group play therapy sessions were reduced to monthly and then to on-call. At that point, visitations with the mother were expected to resume. The father was cautioned that this might cause some anxiety for the children, and the option to resume therapy for either child or again in a group format was left to the father's discretion.

Conclusion

The goal of counseling is to help the client resolve the problem to the client's satisfaction (Coleman, 1995). This may require that the therapist make suggestions rather than impose solutions. The therapist must be clear at all times whose interests are being served.

Ford and Harris (1995) caution therapists to assess the impact of race on the relationship and assess the impact of prejudice on the client. It is helpful to be open and honest with the client by asking a few relevant questions, rather than avoiding the obvious issue that the therapist is of a different culture. This is especially important for the parent of a child client as a way of showing respect. The assessment is ongoing and not always achieved through direct questioning. The therapist must be sensitive to cues from the child and the child's parent that obstacles may have arisen that are relevant to culture.

Upon learning of the many ways in which parents interact with their children and understanding that these ways have been successful for generations, the therapist must remain open and accepting. The act of disparaging child-rearing preferences of a cultural group strikes at the group's sense of esteem and indirectly challenges its right to exist, because a society perpetuates itself by the way it socializes its children (Sprott, 1994). Child-centered group play therapy respects individuality; in combination with extensive interaction with families, it gives therapists who work with children from cultures other than their own the tools they need to be effective.

References

Allen, J., McNeill, E., & Schmidt, V. (1992). *Cultural awareness for children*. Menlo Park, CA: Addison-Wesley.

Brendtro, L. K., & Brokenleg, M. (1993). Beyond the curriculum of control. *Journal of Emotional and Behavioral Problems, 1*, 511.

Burgess, B. J. (1980). Parenting in the Native American community. In M. D. Fantini & R. Cárdenas, *Parenting in a multicultural society* (pp. 63–73). New York: Longman.

Chau, I. (1996). Filial therapy with Chinese parents. Unpublished doctoral dissertation, University of North Texas, Denton.

Coleman, H. L. K. (1995). Cultural factors and the counseling process: Implications for school counselors. *School Counselor, 42*, 180–185.

Derman-Sparks, L. (1992). *Anti-bias curriculum: Tools for empowering young children*. Washington, DC: National Association for the Education of Young Children.

Dorfman, E. (1951). Play therapy. In C. R. Rogers (Ed.), *Client-centered therapy: Its current practice* (pp. 235–277). Boston: Houghton Mifflin.

Dunn, R., Gemake, J., Jalali, F., Zenhausern, R., Quinn, P., & Spiridakis, J. (1990). Cross-cultural differences in learning styles of elementary-age students from four ethnic backgrounds. *Journal of Multicultural Counseling and Development, 8*, 68–93.

Ford, D. Y., & Harris, J. J. (1995). Underachievement among gifted African American students: Implications for school counselors. *School Counselor, 42*, 196–203.

Forehand, R., & Kotchick, B. A. (1996). Cultural diversity: A wake-up call for parent training. *Behavior Therapy, 27*, 187–206.

Garrett, M. W. (1995). Between two worlds: Cultural discontinuity in the dropout of Native American youth. *School Counselor, 42*, 186–195.

Ginsberg, B., Stutman, J., & Hummel, J. (1978). Notes for practice: Group filial therapy. *Social Work, 23*, 154–156.

Glover, G. J. (1996). Filial therapy with Native Americans on the Flathead Reservation. Unpublished doctoral dissertation, University of North Texas, Denton.

Griggs, S. A., & Dunn, R. (1989). The learning styles of multicultural groups and counseling implications. *Journal of Multicultural Counseling and Development, 17*, 146–155.

Heinrich, R. K., Corbine, J. L., & Thomas, K. R. (1990). Counseling Native Americans. *Journal of Counseling and Development, 69*, 128–133.

Herring, R. D. (1992). Biracial children: An increasing concern for elementary and middle school counselors. *Elementary School Guidance and Counseling, 27*, 123–130.

Hines, P. M., Garcia-Preto, N., McGoldrick, M., Almeida, R., & Weltman, S. (1992). Intergenerational relationships across cultures. Special issue: Multicultural practice. *Families in Society: The Journal of Contemporary Human Services, 73*, 323–338.

Hoare, C. H. (1991). Psychosocial identity development and cultural others. *Journal of Counseling and Development, 40,* 45–53.

Ibrahim, F., Ohnishi, H., & Sandhu, D. S. (1997). Asian American identity development: A culture-specific model for South Asian Americans. *Journal of Multicultural Counseling and Development, 25,* 34–50.

Kopala, M., Esquivel, G., & Baptiste, L. (1994). Counseling approaches for immigrant children: Facilitating the acculturative process. *School Counselor, 41,* 352–359.

Landreth, G. (1991). *Play therapy: The art of the relationship.* Muncie, IN: Accelerated Development.

Landreth, G., & Kao, S. C. (1997). Play therapy with Chinese Children. Unpublished manuscript, University of North Texas, Denton.

Lewis, A. C., & Hayes, S. (1991). Multiculturalism and the school counseling curriculum. *Journal of Counseling and Development, 70,* 119–125.

Locke, D. (1990). Fostering the self-esteem of African American children. In E. R. Gerler, J. C. Ciechalaski, & L. D. Parker (Eds.), *Elementary school counseling in a changing world* (pp. 12–18). Alexandria, VA: American School Counselor Association.

Pedersen, P. (1991). Multiculturalism as a generic approach to counseling. *Journal of Counseling and Development, 70,* 6–12.

Sandhu, D. S. (1997). Psychocultural profiles of Asian and Pacific Islander Americans: Implications for counseling and psychotherapy. *Journal of Multicultural Counseling and Development, 25,* 7–22

Santiago-Rivera, A. L. (1995). Developing a culturally sensitive treatment modality for bilingual Spanish-speaking clients: Incorporating language and culture in counseling. *Journal of Counseling and Development, 74,* 12–17.

Sprott, J. E. (1994). One person's spoiling is another's freedom to become: Overcoming ethnocentric views about parental control. *Social Science Medicine, 38,* 1111–1124.

Strupp, H. H. (1973). *Psychotherapy: clinical, research, and theoretical issues.* New York: Aronson.

Sue, D. (1981). *Counseling the culturally different: Theory and practice.* New York: Wiley.

Thomason, T. C. (1991). Counseling Native Americans: An introduction for non–Native American counselors. *Journal of Counseling and Development, 69,* 321–327.

U.S. Bureau of Census (1992). *Current population reports, P-251092, Population projections of the United States by age, sex, race, and Hispanic origin: 1992–2050.* Washington, DC: U.S. Government Printing Office

Westwood, M. J., & Ishiyama, F. I. (1990). The communication process as a critical intervention for client change in cross-cultural counseling. *Journal of Multicultural Counseling and Development, 18,* 163–171.

York, S. (1991). *Roots and wings: Affirming culture in early childhood programs.* St. Paul, MN: Redleaf Press.

Zayas, L. H., & Solari, F. (1994). Early childhood socialization in Hispanic families: Context, culture, and practice implications. *Professional Psychology: Research and Practice, 25,* 200–206.

PART FOUR

SPECIAL POPULATIONS IN GROUP PLAY THERAPY

CHAPTER SIXTEEN

GROUP PLAY THERAPY WITH SEXUALLY ABUSED CHILDREN

Linda E. Homeyer

Play therapy is a primary, and usually the most appropriate, intervention for children. To be an effective play therapist for young children, one must be at ease in the presence of a wide variety of play, from nurturing, caring play to the reenactment of traumatic experiences. This is especially the case in group play therapy, where the presence of other children can accelerate the play behaviors.

Play is a natural expressive language of children. Much as if they were learning a foreign language, play therapists must become adept at attending to and understanding what children *do* so as to understand what they are communicating. The play therapist must be able to hear the language of play,[1] understand the language of play, and reflect this understanding back to the child. Not only is the language of play the most developmentally appropriate communication for children, but it also allows the expression of experiences, feelings, and beliefs that are too frightening or too overwhelming or too complex (or abstract) for words. Or, especially for the sexually abused child, play provides the opportunity to communicate that which simply cannot be articulated because of a lack of a cognitive framework for understanding experiences appropriate for a later developmental stage, adulthood.

In group play therapy the play therapist must be able to carry on multiple conversations simultaneously as the children participate in a variety of parallel,

[1]Garry L. Landreth teaches that play therapists "hear with the eyes."

associative, or cooperative play. Additionally, the play therapist is also aware of the interaction between group members and reflects the meaning of relationship activities back to the children. This indicates the ability to enter the idiosyncratic world of each child while reflecting feelings, intent, and reactions of all the children present.

A General Understanding of Sexual Abuse

Sexual abuse of children is a complex phenomenon. It is beyond the scope of this chapter to review the multiple dynamics and effects of sexual abuse, the variables of sexual abuse (types of sexually abusive behavior, duration, frequency of abusive incidents, relationship to the abuser, level of threats), cognitive reactions (distractibility, splitting, dissociation), and emotional responses (anger, fear, guilt, shame). There are many comprehensive books regarding abuse with which one can explore these issues.[2] However, the play therapist should be knowledgeable of these issues and dynamics as this is key to providing the most appropriate and powerful therapeutic responses possible. More on this later in the chapter.

While it is vital that play therapists understand the dynamics of sexual abuse and how children typically respond to such abuse in general, it is also important to view children as individuals. Each child deserves to be seen as a unique person who has had a particular experience, with idiosyncratic responses to that experience (Gil, 1991; Kelly, 1995). An example is a three-year-old boy who had been molested by a teenage male cousin. The molestation, as commonly happens with this age child, was an activity that occurred within the context of other appropriate attention. During frequent gatherings of the extended family, the three-year-old would spend the majority of the time with the older male cousin. During the time together, the two boys would play a variety of appropriate games and enjoyed each other's company. However, at some point during the time they spent together, the older boy taught the three-year-old a "special game." This game, named the "rocket game," was having the younger boy masturbate the older boy to the point of ejaculation. This "rocket game" had been played many times over the period of several months. Yet the three-year-old's initial and most enduring issue in play therapy was his anger resulting from his lack of continued contact with this favorite person.

---

[2]There is a wealth of material that will educate regarding sexual abuse. Some the author finds helpful: Finkelhor, 1984, Gil, 1991, and Sgroi, 1982.

Importance of Therapeutic Intervention

It is all too common for parents of children who have been sexually abused to want to forget about it and believe their child will forget it as well (DeFrancis, 1969; Everstine & Everstine, 1989; Finkelhor, 1984). On this basis, many parents turn down recommendations for counseling intervention for themselves and their child. While working as a caseworker for child protective services, this author frequently encountered this reaction on the part of parents of her own clients. Terr states that "trauma begins with events outside the child. Once the events take place, a number of internal changes occur in the child. *These changes last*" [italics added] (1991, p. 11). The sooner the intervention occurs the better (Gil, 1991) for, as Terr points out, except for the mildest of traumas the effects may last many years or a lifetime. Young children in particular are generally able to quickly engage in the therapeutic process of play therapy if the intervention begins soon after disclosure. The child has had less time to develop multiple defenses and thus is more easily able to express the experience in play.

For example, the duration of the abuse and the closeness of the relationship with the abuser both directly affect the length of treatment. The child who has experienced sexual abuse over a period of time has typically engaged defensive techniques such as numbing, splitting, repression, and dissociating. These defensive techniques are more firmly entrenched if the child is being abused in the home, thus denying the child a safe place away from the abuser during vulnerable situations, such as bath time and sleep time. In every case, the sooner disclosure occurs and intervention can begin, the easier it is for the child to engage in the intervention process.

Even after intervention has begun, as Porter (1986) warns, "always present is the danger that . . . [the parents'] need to deny their own fears will result in a decision to 'forget about' what has happened and overtly or covertly sabotage the treatment" (p. 42). Clearly, developing an alliance with the parents is key to continued work with the child. Engaging parents in a therapeutic setting of their own frequently assists in the children's remaining in theirs.

Rationale for a Group Format

Group play therapy, as with forms of adult, adolescent, and child group psychotherapy, provides a setting where the group members can learn more about themselves through relationship with other group members (Ginott, 1961; Landreth,

1991; Slavson, 1948). Slavson states that "relationships with others and actual situations constitute true reality to the child. They are more real to him than are ideas and words" (p. 321). This experience of interactions with others is readily available in group play therapy. For the child who has been sexually abused, the opportunity to establish relationships with other peers of the same age remediates several of the results of the sexual abuse.

Universality, the discovery that one's own experience has been shared with others, is an important therapeutic factor (Yalom, 1995). Porter (1986) and Grayson (1989) indicate that this factor is of key importance, particularly for boys. Group allows for countering the elements of secrecy, isolation, and "being different." Additionally, the other group members serve as "buffers and protection against the leaders, who are often perceived as feared authority figures" (Porter, p. 41).

Vicarious learning, the learning that results from observation of other group members, identified by Yalom (1995), also occurs in group play therapy (Landreth, 1991). Group cohesiveness, however, so vitally important in adult groups (Yalom), is not essential to group play therapy (Landreth). Indeed, for young children, group cohesiveness may be a developmental impossibility.

Differences in the goals and structure of the group vary. Group intervention is more frequently psychoeducational in nature. These groups are usually structured around specific topics using a variety of activities. These groups cover topics such as victimization, setting appropriate boundaries, healthy and normal sexuality, and self-protection skills. It is important that developmental age be carefully assessed when placing children in these groups. Cognitive developmental levels are crucial given the goals to teach skills and explore the child's view of self resulting from the abusive activity. Placing four-year-olds with eight-year-olds in the same psychoeducational group results in an ineffective experience for everyone. The purpose of nondirective psychotherapy through group play therapy, in contrast to a psychoeducational group, is to allow each child the opportunity to deal with and work through the child's individual response to the sexual abuse experience and the results of that disclosure. The children in the group are allowed to direct their play, be it individual play or interactive play. Knowing that children will deal with issues in the order of importance to them, and trusting that each child will do so, is a foundational belief of the child-centered play therapist. Everstine and Everstine state that the "therapy hour is basically his or her time to say, or expressively play, whatever he or she wishes" (1989, p. 46). Providing children with the setting to deal with their reaction to the abuse must have a high priority in the overall plan of intervention.

Perez (as cited in Landreth, Homeyer, Glover, & Sweeney, 1996) conducted research comparing individual play therapy and group play therapy for the treatment of sexually abused children. Fifty-five children, four to nine years old, who had experienced sexual abuse participated in this study. These children had no previous therapeutic intervention, and there had been no more than six months since their disclosure. The type of sexual abuse included both incestual and extrafamilial; most of the abusers were men. The children were divided into three groups: individual play therapy, group play therapy, and control. Each therapeutic group received sixty-minute sessions once a week for twelve weeks. The control group, of course, received no intervention. The results of the research indicated that play therapy did result in statistically significant changes between the children who received either form of intervention and the control group. These changes were in the areas of self-concept and self-mastery. There was no statistical significance between the results of either type of intervention, individual or group play therapy. Perez suggests that the group experience provides children with the opportunity to identify with other children who have been sexually abused, thus reducing a child's sense of isolation. Perez also indicates that "group acts as a pseudofamily and allows the child to experience parental and sibling relationship in which sexual abuse does not occur" (p. 11).

Special Considerations for Selection of Group Members

Selection and screening of members for a group experience for sexually abused children should follow the general guidelines provided in Chapter One. This would include balancing the group for internalizing versus externalizing behaviors (Gil, 1991; McFadden, 1987); similar developmental age (McFadden; Ginott, 1961; Landreth, 1991); similar physical size (Landreth); and of the same gender (Ginott).

However, there are issues regarding sexually abused children that should also be considered. Group play therapy is contraindicated if a child has serious psychiatric disturbances (such as suicidal behavior), is involved in nonsuicidal self-mutilation, is experiencing a severe mood or thought disturbance, or was sexually abused in a group (Porter, 1986). O'Connor (1993) alerts the play therapist not to include those children who may be able to hurt others without remorse. He also suggests that children who have recently experienced trauma (whatever the source) will be better served if initially seen in individual therapy, indicating "that these children will need a high level of nurturance and support from the play therapy that is not available in a group setting" (p. 254).

While group play therapy may be the modality of choice, the play therapist needs to be aware that some children, even if appropriately screened and selected, may not engage in therapy in the group setting. Roesler, Savin, and Grosz (1993) present a case of a five-year-old male victim who makes very little progress in group. Only after group is terminated and the child begins individual play therapy, to which family therapy is later added, does progress occur. The family later terminated after experiencing successful intervention. In this case the group setting appeared appropriate: the group was led by cotherapists, sessions averaged three children, the group consisted of the same gender, aged three to six years, and had experienced extrafamilial sexual abuse.

No matter how closely the therapist follows the guidelines of group composition, once the group begins to meet, there may occasionally be a need to make changes. All changes need to be carried out with extreme care. The sexually abused child already has low self-esteem and feelings of powerlessness, victimization, and guilt. To experience what seems like failure in the group setting can reinforce such feelings. This experience additionally magnifies the reality that adults in authority positions, like the abuser, control the child's very world. If the child is in an out-of-home placement, this perception is even more intensified. Thus it is vital to take the time to carefully and thoughtfully put together a group.

Many social service agencies simply group together all available children. This often results in groups with too many children and too wide a range of age and developmental levels. Additionally, little thought is given the importance of balancing the group for internalizing and externalizing behaviors. This practice often results in problems within the sessions and exacerbates problems outside the sessions. Unfortunately, this practice also reduces the effectiveness of the therapeutic process and progress for the individual children. Group leaders in such a setting are often frustrated with the children's behavior during sessions, the lack of therapeutic progress, and the sense that group is not as facilitative as it should be, but are unaware of the reasons why.

While social service agency administrators have explanations at the ready (staffing problems, limited space, need for increased "client-service hours" for grant reporting, and so on) play therapists must advocate for effective and appropriate therapeutic settings for their child clients. A case in point was a situation posed by a supervisee who worked at a child advocacy center. She and a cotherapist had a play therapy group consisting of two boys, aged seven and eight, and a girl, aged three. The supervisee sought input on how to encourage the girl, who always played alone while in group, to interact with the boys. It is worth noting that the boys often made fun of the girl, thereby revictimizing her during the therapy hour. My suggestion that one of the cotherapists take the girl to another room and have a concurrent individual session, until another age- and gender-appropriate child could be found, was met with resistance. It seems the director of the agency insisted that this wasn't possible due to the need of increased group client hours. In reality, this so-called group experience was counterproductive. The girl was being revictimized, and the boys were misusing their power and being victimizers! While the cotherapists attempted to deal with the relationship issue (victim-victimizer) the dynamics of the composition of the group continued to exacerbate this issue.

The Process of Group Play Therapy with Sexually Abused Children

The purpose of therapeutic intervention for children who have experienced sexual abuse is to "help the child understand the trauma in such a way that is not incorporated into his or her construct of self or view of reality" (Everstine & Everstine, 1989, p. 34). The play therapist takes into account the developmental level of the child, the child's perception of the abuse, and the need of the child to work at his or her own pace (Axline, 1947; Everstine & Everstine; Hall, 1996).

Sexual Abuse Issues in Group Play Therapy

Finkelhor and Browne (1985) organized the dynamics of sexual abuse that "alter children's cognitive and emotional orientation to the world, and create trauma by distorting children's self-concept, world view, and affective capacities" (p. 531) into four traumagenic dynamics. These dynamics are traumatic sexualization, stigmatization, betrayal, and powerlessness. This model will be used to organize and conceptualize the thematic play of the child who has been sexually abused (see Table 16.1).

Traumatic Sexualization. Traumatic sexualization refers to the impact of sexual abuse on a child's developing sexuality and perception of and attitude toward sexual activity. Behavior in play therapy may include masturbation; self-stimulating behavior using toys, other children, or the play therapist; sexualized play with other children; sex-role confusion; and dissociation. Children may use toys to reenact the sexual abuse and act out sexual activity based on sexual knowledge inappropriate to their developmental level.

Terr (1991) suggests that a common characteristic of children with childhood disorders[3] is the revisualization of the trauma, either through play or drawings. This includes children who were too young to store verbal memories of their experiences. She gives several examples of this, including a child who had been "sexually misused" at the age of fifteen to eighteen months. Pornographic photographs

---

[3]Childhood disorders may have many causes, including but not limited to sexual abuse. The author recommends Lenore Terr's article, "Childhood Trauma: An Outline and Overview," and her book, *Too Scared to Cry,* for additional information regarding trauma in children.

TABLE 16.1. DYNAMICS OF CHILDHOOD SEXUAL ABUSE.

Traumagenic Dynamic	Sexual Abuse Experiences	Psychological Consequences	Resulting Behavior by Child
Traumatic sexualization	• developmentally inappropriate sexual activity • repeatedly rewarded for sexual activity • exchange of affection, attention, privileges, and gifts for sexual behavior • parts of child's body fetishized; given distorted importance and meaning • use of force or threats	• confusion and misconceptions regarding sexual behavior and morality • confusion between sexual intimacy and emotional intimacy • frightening memories and events are associated with sexual activity • unusual emotional associations to sexual activities	• preoccupation with sex • repetitive sexual behavior • compulsive sexual behavior • advanced sexual knowledge • use of sexual behavior to manipulate others • forcing sexual activity with peers or younger children • promiscuousness • aversion to age-appropriate sexual activity • flashbacks • negative body image • negative attitude toward sexuality • higher risk of further sexual abuse • inappropriate sexualization of their own children • sexual identity confusion (particularly with boys)
Stigmatization	• abuser blames child for sexual activity • pressure for secrecy • negative attitudes reinforced by family or community • blaming the child for the abuse	child incorporates negative connotations into self-image: • blame • shame • guilt • loose morals • "spoiled goods" • "damaged goods" • sense of being different	• gravitation toward others who feel stigmatized to reduce feelings of isolation, leading to criminal activity, prostitution, drug or alcohol abuse • self-destructive behavior, suicide

Betrayal	a person: • upon whom the child is dependent caused harm • manipulated or lied about moral standards • who is loved treated them with callous disregard • who should have protected and believed them did not • distances self from child after disclosure	• inability to trust others • inability to feel safe in a relationship • negative self-image • reduced level of self-worth	• depression and grief reactions resulting from loss of trusted figures • extreme dependency and clinginess (especially for young children) • impaired judgment in trustworthiness of adults (especially in teenagers and adults) • placing self in relationships that are physically, psychologically, and sexually abusive (especially for female incest victims) • as adults, failing to recognize partners who are sexually abusive to their children • aversion to intimate relationships • hostility, anger, and mistrust • antisocial behavior, delinquency
Powerlessness (disempowerment)	• violation of physical boundaries • violation of emotional boundaries • child's will, desires, and sense of efficacy are repeatedly ignored • impact of level of threat or manipulation • attempts to stop abuse are ineffective • inability to make other adults believe them	fear, anxiety: • impaired coping skills • impaired sense of control of one's self and world • inability to cope with environment • need to compensate for pain of powerlessness	• nightmares, phobias, hypervigilance, clinging behavior, somatic complaints • revictimization • despair, depression, suicidal behavior • learning problems • running away • unusually high need to control or dominate (especially for males) • aggressive, delinquent behavior • bullying behavior, revictimizing others • employment problems

Source: Adapted from Finkelhor and Browne, 1985.

had been discovered that revealed her abuse at a day-care home. The parents reported that once the child learned to draw, she drew hundreds of pictures of nude adults and babies. Additionally, in therapy she recreated drawings of those nonverbal experiences.

Understanding play therapy behaviors that may possibly express traumatic sexualization will assist the play therapist in forming more powerful therapeutic responses. For example, for the child who looks at the play therapist while reenacting sexually abusive behavior:

"You're wanting me to see what happened to you."

Or for the child who continues to masturbate:

"It's hard to stop rubbing yourself. It feels good."

Or for the child who abruptly leaves an intensive sequence of play:

"That got really scary and you decided to stop."

These types of responses communicate to the child a deep understanding of the child. While still very here-and-now reflections, the responses additionally communicate an understanding of the reason for the behavior, thus putting words to their experience.

Stigmatization. A negative view of self is a common result for children who have been sexually abused. This includes negative beliefs based on the attitudes of the abuser, family, and community. As a result, many children who have been sexually abused suffer from self- and other-imposed isolation (Goodwin & Talwar, 1989). Group play therapy by its very nature reduces the child's sense of isolation. Through interaction in the group setting children learn about others as well as themselves (Landreth, 1991). Also, children are enabled to regain self-respect from the acceptance that is experienced within the group therapy setting (Axline, 1955). This is a result of the group therapeutic factor, universality, mentioned earlier.

Play therapy behavior that may be used to communicate the sense of stigmatization might include the child's role-playing blaming and shaming behavior; selecting a toy that, in various play scenarios, is always isolated, different, or "bad"; repeatedly washing toys or self; playing out scenes of destruction. For example, for the child playing in the dollhouse, the following dialogue might take place:

> *Child:* This kid is bad, very bad. . . . *[while separating a child-doll from the rest of the doll family]*
>
> *Therapist:* So, you think that kid has done something bad.
>
> *Child:* Yup, everybody knows . . . the kid is bad. *[continues to move child-doll into a room where there are no other dolls]*
>
> *Therapist:* That kid has been so bad, she has to be all alone.

Child: [*in sad tone of voice*] Nobody will play with her.
Therapist: She must feel very sad . . . she's lonely.

The play therapist continues to follow the child's lead and responds in a manner that allows the child to feel understood. When a child feels and believes the play therapist is connected to the play, then the inherent trust and safety allows the child to go further:

Child: She told a secret . . . now everybody's mad at her. . . .
Therapist: She must have been very brave to tell her secret.

Note that the play therapist stays within the drama that is being acted out by the child. This distancing is crucial to the child's ability to express herself in play. However, the play therapist injects into the last response important information for the child to hear: breaking the silence regarding a secret about sexual abuse activity is a brave thing to do. Thus the child hears she was brave, implying she did the right thing, and this positive statement begins to ameliorate her negative self-talk. This is a small but clear example of how understanding the connection between children's sexual abuse and their resulting behavior can assist the play therapist in making powerful facilitative responses. In group play therapy, the other children in the group become vicarious learners by observing the sequence of play and verbal statements. Then they, too, feel the impact of a challenge to their cognitive distortion, "I'm bad."

Betrayal. Children who have been sexually abused experience a deep sense of betrayal. This sense of betrayal will vary in intensity given other factors such as the relationship to the abuser and the reaction of others in the child's world once the abuse is disclosed. This betrayal is often expressed by a child's reluctance to develop a therapeutic alliance with the play therapist or by the child's insistence on playing on the opposite side of the playroom, as far as possible from the play therapist. For this type of child the play therapist must earn the child's trust. Therefore, the play therapist must understand the extreme importance of staying in one chair and not intruding into the child's space. The mistrustful child may additionally appear to be angry with the play therapist and will test limits directly involving the play therapist, such as shooting the dart gun or throwing sand. Other children may be very clingy or even demonstrate a lack of appropriate boundaries with the play therapist.

Other play therapy behaviors in this category involve a "good" character doing "bad" things, such as a doctor who causes a patient to die or turns people into vampires, or a policeman who shoots innocent people rather than those breaking the law. For example:

Child: [*to the play therapist, after draping snakes around the therapist's neck, positioning alligators, spiders, and other bugs so they appear to be biting the therapist, and riding around the playroom on a wheeled toy*] Call me on the phone.

Therapist: Ring ring, ring ring—

Child: Hello.

Therapist: [*in a stage whisper*] What should I say?

Child: Keep saying, "Ouch, ouch, it hurts."

Therapist: Ouch, ouch, it hurts.

Child: Then say, "Come and help me, mommy."

Therapist: Come and help me, mommy.

Child: Sorry, daughter . . . I'm too busy. . . . [*in her own stage whisper*] Keep saying it!

Therapist: Come and help me, mommy.

Child: I'm too busy . . . gotta buy groceries.

Therapist: Mommy, come help me. Mommies are supposed to help kids.

Child: Sorry, too busy!

The play therapist still remains within the context of the play. In this instance, both the child and the play therapist are actors on the stage of the child's design and direction. However, the play therapist enlarges the meaning so that the child hears the meaning of the story she is producing: My mother was supposed to protect me, not leave me to be sexually abused while she went and bought groceries. The child hears a verbal validation of her belief—parents should be protectors, and she was betrayed. In group play therapy, this type of play will often result in other children joining in. They, too, resonate with this theme of betrayal. While their protector may not have been shopping for groceries during their abuse, they understand and act out the betrayal.

Powerlessness. Powerlessness results from having physical and emotional boundaries violated. This sense of powerlessness is compounded when the child is unable to make the abuse stop, either by not being able to keep the abuser away or by not being believed when the abuse is disclosed. Anger, a common reaction to feeling powerless, is expressed by children in play therapy by punching Bobo (a sock'em bag); symbolically cutting body parts off of dolls; and being extremely controlling in interactions with other children, the play therapist, and the toys. Kelly (1995) indicates progress is seen when a child can move "in the direction of respecting and directing her anger rather than feeling overwhelmed by it" (p. 7). Guilt and fear, additional reactions to powerlessness, are often difficult for boys to express (Porter, 1986). Porter indicates that boys often use anger as a cover for these "soft" emotions.

Cycles in the Intervention Process

It is useful to view the therapeutic work of children who have been sexually abused as a matter of cycles rather than stages. Kelly (1995) proposes that children who have experienced severe trauma such as ritualistic abuse move through cycles rather than a more typical, linear view of intervention. Each cycle has three components: testing the therapeutic relationship, readdressing the trauma, and protective distancing and denial. Early in the course of treatment, the cycles can be seen within a single session; later the cycle may be seen over four or more sessions. Testing the therapeutic relationship is clearly related to the child's sense of betrayal. Kelly also states that this testing the integrity of the therapeutic relationship must be successfully completed if the child is to move on to the next phase of the cycle. In group play therapy, assessing the children's ability to connect with the therapist is important. Individual sessions are useful as part of this process. The child with severe inability to trust the play therapist may benefit from observing other children's ability to do so and may also see the presence of other children as a source of safety. The group play therapist would find a session difficult to manage constructively if it included too many children who were exhibiting a severe inability to trust.

Once the testing phase is accomplished, the next phase occurs: readdressing the trauma through playing out the trauma and concerns regarding that trauma (Kelly, 1995). In this phase the child replays the abuse in the attempt to resolve it. This would include playing out new coping strategies. When the child reaches the limit of ability to deal emotionally and psychologically with the trauma play, the cycle will move to the phase of protective distancing and denial. According to Kelly, this denial phase may present as a form of indifference and aimless play, or the child may deny established facts of the trauma. In Kelly's experience it is the continued trust and respect between the child and therapist that motivates the child to begin the cycle again. Thus the cycling continues until the children conclude dealing with their issues resulting from the abuse.

Limit Setting of Sexualized Behavior

Limit setting is as important in group play therapy for children who have been sexually abused as it is in individual play therapy. The purposes are the same: to protect the child, to protect the play therapist, to protect toys and room, and to protect the therapeutic relationship (Bixler, 1982; Ginott, 1982; Landreth, 1991). As Bixler points out, the limits themselves are therapeutic. The therapist uses a nonpunitive tone and accepts and acknowledges the child's feelings, needs, or intentions. Thus limits allow the child to trust the safety of the therapeutic environment. Additionally, consistent limits communicate that the play therapist will keep the child safe and will not betray that trust. For example, consistent limits can assist children by providing a "solid and reliable anchor in reality" (p. 9), by providing the safety and security abused children have lost, and by helping them contain and redirect anger (Kelly, 1995).

Van de Putte (1995) provides a valuable review and perspective of the limit setting of sexualized behavior in play therapy. As he indicates, little has been written to identify various categories of sexualized behavior and to link this behavior with specific therapeutic stages. He identifies three categories of sexualized behavior: abuse-reactive behavior, sexual intimacy, and reenactment of the abuse. The first category occurs in the initial phase of intervention, and the second and third occur during the middle stage of intervention.

Abuse-Reactive Behavior. Van de Putte (1995) defines abuse-reactive play as the acting out of sexual behavior similar to that experienced by the child. This is seen as a response to anxiety and confusion over the new relationship with the play therapist:

Does this adult expect me to interact sexually as well? Other adults, in positions of control and power, inevitably want some kind of sexual activity.

Possibly the sexual reactive behavior may also be a defensive activity in an attempt to cope with feelings of helplessness and vulnerability. In group play therapy the sexual reactive behavior most typically would not be seen in this manner. The presence of other group members reduces the abuse-reactive play because the child perceives the other group members as allies and possible protectors.

Sexual Intimacy. As trust and the therapeutic alliance develop children may struggle with the confusion between emotional intimacy and sexual intimacy (Van de Putte, 1995; Porter, 1986). In an attempt to show affection and caring the child may attempt to engage the play therapist or another child in the group in some form of sexual contact such as rubbing their genitalia against the play therapist's leg. The child's motivation needs to be seen for what it is and appropriately reflected. Examples of the child-to-therapist limit setting may be:

"I know you want to be close to me, but I'm not for rubbing on. You can stand close to me without rubbing on me."

Or,

"I know some grown-ups asked you to do that. But you don't have to do that with me. I like you without your doing that."

Or, for a child-to-child limit:

"Amy, I know you want to let Sally know you like her, but Sally's not for rubbing on. You can tell her you like her or you can sit close without touching."

Or,

"Lauren, I know you want Megan to know that you like her. But Megan is not for rubbing on. You can ask Megan if you can give her a good touch, like a hug."

Van de Putte (1995) indicates this category of sexualized behavior is seen in the middle phase of intervention.

It is also important for the play therapist to remember to be careful in touches. Because of the child's confusion regarding intimate and sexual boundaries, the child may interpret the adult's touch as the first move toward further, and more sexual, touches (Everstine & Everstine, 1989).

Reenactment of the Abuse. The third category of sexualized play also occurs in the middle phase of intervention (Van de Putte, 1995). This play is the re-enactment of the abuse through the use of toys or other play materials. This re-creation and reexperiencing takes place in the presence of the play therapist and group members. When this occurs, clearly a strong therapeutic alliance built on trust has been developed between the children and the play therapist. It is important to reflect an understanding of the abusive behavior, that such activity was the responsibility of the abuser, and the child is not responsible for its occurrence. This author believes it is important to stay within the child's play metaphor. This allows for the continued playing-through of the experience. For example, if the play occurs in the doll house with the doll family, a play therapist's tracking response might be:

"That grown-up is doing secret touches with the girl. . . . It's not her fault that it's happening."

Or, if the child states, *"That's what happened to me,"* thereby taking the play out of the metaphor, the play therapist might respond,

"You're letting me know what happened to you. That grown-up was wrong to do that to you. It wasn't your fault."

Masturbation

Children let down their defenses in order to work through their issues in play. When these self-protective defenses are lowered emotions such as anxiety begin to be experienced. As the anxiety builds, children who have been sexually abused often use masturbation as a self-comforting behavior. The play therapist's reflection should contain this understanding:

"When things get scary, you rub yourself to feel better. Rubbing yourself feels good, but it is something to do in private."

This type of response allows the child to feel understood and develop cognitive self-awareness of the behavior, while it also sets appropriate boundaries for socially acceptable behavior.

Cautions for Play Therapists

It is important to allow the child to decide when to deal with issues. Given a safe therapeutic environment and relationship children will deal with those issues in the order most important to them. Children can respond anxiously to the over-eager play therapist and the play therapist who has a predetermined agenda. Once the limits of the child's tolerance for specific issues have been identified, those limits should be respected (Ciottone and Madonna, 1993).

Termination Issues

As abused children grow to adulthood, they will probably need subsequent or periodic sessions of therapy, and this issue must be addressed with their parents. Gil (1991) refers to allowing for and encouraging this as "discontinuous therapy" (p. 39). Issues regarding sexuality will affect the child's retrospective view of the abuse experience. This can typically be expected as the child moves through various developmental stages. How a child views self and others at different developmental ages will clearly differ. To a three-year-old male, playing the rocket game with his older male cousin is simply a game; to a prepubescent, sexual identity may become a concern. These later concerns cannot be dealt with earlier because of the changing views of self that are tied to the various developmental stages. However, without this advance warning, parents may come to believe that earlier therapy had not been successful and thus not seek intervention for their child at a later stage (Gil; Porter, 1986).

Various Therapeutic Configurations

It is typical for children who have been sexually abused to be involved in more than one form of therapy. In addition to group play therapy and psychoeducational groups, a child may participate in individual play therapy, sibling group therapy, and family therapy. These formats may vary depending on the availability of services and the needs of the individual case. Thus a child may begin with individual play therapy while the parents and siblings are involved in their own therapeutic settings. Parents may also participate in couples or marriage counseling, parenting classes, or support groups for parents of children who have been sexually abused.

Individual Play Therapy

In some cases, individual play therapy may be recommended before adding the group play therapy. There may be several reasons for a child to receive individual sessions prior to beginning group. Individual play therapy sessions may be easier to begin immediately after the child discloses the abuse, or the therapist may want a few individual sessions as part of the screening process to place the child in the appropriate group. Sometimes the child's reaction to the sexual abuse and the disclosure may result in behavior that makes group contraindicated. Or there may simply not be a group available. In other cases, the abused child may begin both individual and group interventions simultaneously.

Parental and Family Therapy

Where does family therapy fit in? The results of sexual abuse and its disclosure affect the entire family unit. This is the case whether the abuse is intrafamilial or extrafamilial. If the child begins in individual play therapy, an effective segue to family therapy is to have the parents join in the sessions. Axline (1955) notes that adding the parents to the child's play therapy session allows for each family member to "re-examine their own concepts, values and experiences" (p. 154). The opportunity to work through the impact of the sexual abuse, and resulting consequences in the family, is an important task of intervention for the entire family (Goodwin & Talwar, 1989).

Mann and McDermott (1983), however, warn that family therapy alone, with the goal of bringing about change in the family environment, is not enough to relieve the child's emotional response to the abuse.

Research suggests most young male victims are sexually abused by persons outside the family (Abel, Mittelman, & Becker, 1983). This occurs with eleven times greater frequency than abuse against young female victims outside the home, five times greater than young male children in the home, and more than three times greater than young female children inside the home (Abel et al.). In these cases, where the father is not the abuser, Porter (1986) highlights the importance of having the father of the sexually abused male child involved in the family therapy. Porter also indicates that the father-son relationship is often distant or severely conflicted and often represents same-sex role issues.

Sibling Groups

Siblings of the child who has been sexually abused frequently participate in support groups. These sibling groups often meet concurrently with the parents' support groups and the groups for the sexually abused children. Frequently these groups, psychoeducational in nature, deal with the same themes at the same time, varying activities according to age and perspective.

Another form of sibling group is made up of all the children in the sexually abused child's family, including that child. This group format is useful to normalize sibling interactions as a final step prior to termination. This is particularly true if the nonabused siblings have not had an opportunity for other intervention of their own.

Sibling groups for children in foster care placements are also important. This is especially the case if the siblings are in separate foster care homes or in other out-of-home placements. As indicated by Emily Oe in Chapter Seventeen, the sibling subsystem of a family is the longest-lasting and perhaps most important set of relationships an individual may have. A sibling play therapy group provides the setting for the continuing maintenance and growth of these relationships. It can be difficult to coordinate the logistics of such a group, but it is extremely important. It is recommended that siblings participate in this group in addition to the intervention planned to deal with abuse issues.

Conclusion

Group play therapy is an effective therapeutic intervention for children who have been sexually abused. It provides each child the opportunity to deal with the abuse in an idiosyncratic manner while also benefiting from the dynamics of a group setting. To be as effective as possible, the play therapist is aware of the many dynamics and effects of sexual abuse. This allows the play therapist to enlarge the meaning of the children's play and interactions.

As a trained mental health professional, the play therapist is able to advocate for appropriate therapeutic interventions for children. This may include educating others regarding the importance of group play therapy as a primary therapeutic intervention for the emotional and psychological response to abuse as well as a more educative, cognitive intervention, such as psychoeducational groups.

Sexual abuse affects the entire family. Therefore, additional therapeutic configurations are appropriate and may occur concurrently or sequentially to the group play therapy. The impact of the sexual abuse and its disclosure for the individual child and his or her family must be taken into account while making the comprehensive intervention plan.

References

Abel, G. G., Mittelman, M. S., & Becker, J. V. (1983). *Sexual offenders: Results of assessment and recommendations for treatment.* Presentation to the World Congress of Behavior Therapy, Washington, DC.

Axline, V. (1947). *Play therapy: The inner dynamics of childhood.* Boston: Houghton Mifflin.

Axline, V. (1955). Group therapy as a means of self discovery for parents and children. *Group Psychotherapy, 8,* 152–160.

Bixler, R. (1982). Limits are therapy. In G. L. Landreth (Ed.), *Play therapy: Dynamics of the process of counseling with children* (pp. 160–172). Springfield, IL: Thomas.

Ciottone, R., & Madonna, J. (1993). Crucial issues in the treatment of a sexually abused latency-aged boy. *Issues in Comprehensive Nursing, 16,* 31–40.

DeFrancis, V. (1969). *Protecting the child victim of sex crimes committed by adults: Final report.* Denver: American Humane Society.

Everstine, D. S., & Everstine, L. (1989). *Sexual trauma in children and adolescents: Dynamics and treatment.* New York: Brunner/Mazel.

Finkelhor, D. (1984). *A sourcebook on child sexual abuse.* Thousand Oaks, CA: Sage.

Finkelhor, D., & Browne, A. (1985). The traumatic impact of child sexual abuse: A conceptualization. *American Journal of Orthopsychiatry, 55,* 530–541.

Gil, E. (1991). *The healing power of play: Working with abused children.* New York: Guilford Press.

Ginott, H. (1961). *Group psychotherapy with children: The theory and practice of play therapy.* New York: McGraw-Hill.

Ginott, H. (1982). Therapeutic intervention in child treatment. In G. L. Landreth (Ed.), *Play therapy: Dynamics of the process of counseling with children* (pp. 160–172). Springfield, IL: Thomas.

Goodwin, J., & Talwar, N. (1989). Group psychotherapy for victims of incest. *Psychiatric Clinics of North America, 12,* 279–293.

Grayson, J. (1989). Sexually victimized boys. *Virginia Child Protective Newsletter, 29,* 1–6.

Hall, P. (1996). Play therapy with sexually abused children. In H. Kaduson, D. Cangelosi, & C. Schaefer (Eds.), *The playing cure* (pp. 171–196). Northvale NJ: Aronson.

Kelly, M. M. (1995). Play therapy with sexually traumatized children: Factors that promote healing. *Journal of Child Sexual Abuse, 4,* 1–11.

Landreth, G. (1991). *Play therapy: The art of the relationship.* Muncie, IN: Accelerated Development.

Landreth, G., Homeyer, L., Glover, G., & Sweeney, D. (1996). *Play therapy interventions with children's problems.* Northvale, NJ: Aronson.

Mann, E., & McDermott, J. F. (1983). Play therapy for victims of child abuse and neglect. In C. E. Schaefer & K. J. O'Connor (Eds.), *Handbook of play therapy* (pp. 283–307). New York: Wiley.

McFadden, E. J. (1987). *Counseling abused children.* Ann Arbor, MI: ERIC/CAPS.

O'Connor, K. (1993). Child, protector, confidant: Structure group ecosystemic play therapy. In T. Kottman & C. Schaefer (Eds.), *Play therapy in action: A casebook for practitioners* (pp. 245–280). Northvale, NJ: Aronson.

Porter, E. (1986). *Treating the young male victim of sexual assault: Issues and intervention strategies.* Orwell, VT: Safer Society Press.

Roesler, T. A., Savin, D., & Grosz, C. (1993). Family therapy of extrafamilial sexual abuse. *Journal of the American Academy of Child and Adolescent Psychiatry, 32,* 967–970.

Sgroi, S. (1982). *Handbook of clinical intervention in child sexual abuse.* Lexington, MA: Lexington Books.

Slavson, S. R. (1948). Play group therapy with young children. *Nervous Child, 7,* 318–327.

Terr, L. C. (1990). *Too scared to cry: Psychic traumas in childhood.* New York: Basic Books.

Terr, L. C. (1991). Childhood trauma: An outline and overview. *American Journal of Psychiatry, 148,* 10–20.

Van de Putte, S. J. (1995). A paradigm for working with child survivors of sexual abuse who exhibited sexualized behaviors during play therapy. *International Journal of Play Therapy, 4,* 27–49.

Yalom, I. (1995). *The theory and practice of group psychotherapy* (4th ed.). New York: HarperCollins.

CHAPTER SEVENTEEN

SIBLING GROUP PLAY THERAPY

Emily Oe

Sibling group play therapy involves the unique and effective opportunity to combine several elements for maximum therapeutic benefit. The efficacy of both group counseling and play therapy are combined and made available to the already existing subsystem of siblings within a family or blended system.

Group Work with Children

The importance of play in children's development, the viability of play therapy for facilitating developmental adjustment, and a group context for counseling children have been documented extensively, but *group play therapy* has received far less attention in the literature. Most early proponents referenced their work as *therapeutic play groups* (for example, Ginott, 1958; Rothenberg, 1966; Schiffer, 1969; Slavson, 1948). However, Gibbs (1945) and Axline (1947) used *group play therapy* in their writings, and that is the term used most often in current literature (for example, Benedek, 1982; Ginott, 1982; Landreth, 1991; Wakaba, 1983). Both terms indicate a therapeutic environment established to create an intermediate area of experience where group members can comfortably move between and intertwine the private internal world and the external reality (Lewis, J., 1993).

In the early 1960s, Haim Ginott (1961) noted some of the rationale for group therapy with children in contrast to individual therapy: more ease and speed in establishing the relationship between the therapist and each child; more safety with less direct therapist-individual contact; opportunity to give and receive help; opportunity for vicarious and induced catharsis through more sources of stimulation; vicarious and direct learning; more child insight into relationship issues; more therapist insight into the "real world" of each child; potential for more reality testing and limit setting; and more probabilities for practicing, developing, and mastering effective relationship skills. Berg and Landreth (1990), in writing about group therapy with children, adolescents, and adults, placed the emphasis on self-discovery, discovery of others, redefining of self, developing interpersonal awareness, reality testing, learning to help, and dynamic group pressure for growth in a supportive environment.

Consequently, group therapy can facilitate identification of personal strengths and limitations within the group as well as of group strengths and limitations. It provides a setting for free expression of thoughts, feelings, needs, and desires between and among group members through a variety of communication modalities. As a testing laboratory for new behaviors, group therapy can provide opportunities for redefinition and modification of role and social relationships (Hamlin & Timberlake, 1981). It is an environment intended to promote increased individual self-esteem, improvement of interpersonal skills, and restoration of relatedness (Hunter, 1993).

Sibling Group Therapy

There is a glaring paucity of literature on *sibling* group therapy itself and even less mention of *sibling group play therapy*. Hamlin and Timberlake (1981) appropriately asserted: "The sibling group is rarely considered as a viable treatment entity" (p. 101). Rather than providing therapy for the siblings in their own group context, the most common therapeutic modalities for siblings are within family therapy or siblings in concurrent individual therapy. Rather than recognizing the rich resources already extant in the sibling group, therapists most often look to other family members as the primary resource or consider many sibling issues as pertinent only to individual siblings. Unfortunately, this may be a pervasive deficiency, as suggested by Bank and Kahn (1976): "The general under-emphasis of sibling status is common to our entire culture" (p. 494), and others (Markowitz, Harrigan, Koontz, & Klagsbrun, 1994; Nichols, 1986) make similar points. The sibling relationship is one that exists separate from, and sometimes unknown to or misunderstood by, other family relationships (Eno, 1985; Marty, 1994). Potentially, it is the longest-lasting relationship of any family subsystem—a lifelong, highly influential process played out as an adolescent, an adult, and a parent (Bank & Kahn; Crispell, 1996; Fraiberg, 1987; Jones, 1995; Lewis, K., 1990; Norris-Shortle, Colletta, Cohen, & McCombs, 1995; Sachs, 1993).

Consequently, it is important to understand how sibling interactions affect daily and lifelong functioning (Jones, 1995; Sachs, 1993). Interactions between and among siblings become internalized images carried into adulthood. These images can empower siblings in accepting and nurturing each other to counteract isolation and interrupt destructive intergenerational social and psychological needs (Hunter, 1993). On the other hand, "these images, idealized or maligned, can become legacies, touchstones, or mooring points which some adults use to forget their own identities and to determine how they will carry out their own values, behaviors, or ideals" (Kahn & Bank, 1980, p. 156).

Sibling Subsystem

The sibling relationship is a natural microcosm of family, community, and individual well-being in that the context of the sibling world reflects learning and development. "Siblings have a complex relationship that varies in degrees of intensity throughout life" (Lewis, K., 1988, p. 187). Children have their own unique perspectives on their phenomenological worlds, and the framework of a sibling relationship provides a socialization structure for learning to face, analyze, and cope with the developmental issues of growing up.

Several developmental functions of the sibling group have been enumerated (Bank & Kahn, 1976; Floyd, 1995; Hamlin & Timberlake, 1981; Hunter, 1993; Kahn & Bank, 1980; Norris-Shortle et al., 1995; Rosenberg, 1980). Here is a brief summary of the primary issues:

• Sibling identification and differentiation as a group and as individuals within the group are developed through reflected self-appraisal in looking to one another for interpretation of and, if necessary, protection from other siblings, parents, and the larger community as well as resolution of individual and shared conflicts. It is in the sibling relationship that children first experience the costs and rewards of interacting with peers in learning how to negotiate, communicate, and follow group rules.

• Mutual regulation occurs as the siblings serve as sounding boards for one another in testing out ideas and behaviors. The sibling context helps children "learn how to fight, compete, win, lose, attack, and protect each other" (Hamlin & Timberlake, 1981, p. 103); they learn the importance of "fair play, self-control, sharing, and being able to listen as well as talk" (Bank & Kahn, 1976, p. 498) and define boundaries for the group and individuals. Siblings "offer each other emotional support, intellectual stimulation, and a proving ground for later relationships in the give-and-take of life" (Norris-Shortle et al., 1995, p. 253).

• Siblings have at hand sources for direct services, both explicit and implicit—making life easy or hard for one another, being neat or sloppy, quiet or noisy, oppositional or cooperative. There is someone readily available for a "deal" to exchange skills, lend money, withhold and reward, protect and reject. All in all, spontaneous and empathic reciprocation often occurs more than withholding when the siblings are not in the presence of possible parental intervention or distraction.

• Sibling coalitions offer options in dealing with parents:

A "protect-and-rescue" means of balancing the power of parents and looking to one another for nurturing, support, and understanding

Joining with or against one another in supporting or opposing parents

Keeping secrets or tattling in guarding each of their private worlds

Serving as go-betweens in translating parental behaviors

Pioneering new behaviors implying permission for other siblings to follow accordingly

• The sibling group offers dependability as an existing subsystem when other systems appear to be in chaos.

Therefore, siblings are a naturally occurring group of two or more individuals whose functioning is to some extent interdependent (Hamlin & Timberlake, 1981). Sibling group therapy can thus provide a thread of consistency and predictability in regard to immediate adjustment problems as well as build a trust bank for future relationships among the siblings and with others (Lewis, K., 1988). Sibling group therapy simulates a natural, familiar, and nonthreatening group experience wherein the group members share a common social network of home, school, and neighborhood friends and acquaintances (Hamlin & Timberlake) and wherein change is not so threatening when the siblings can be together in experiencing difficult behaviors and ideas (Frey-Angel, 1989). The most natural and effective way to expose children with common concerns to different behaviors or ideas is in a group setting with their siblings—the people with whom they can have some level of trust because of their shared experiences (Frey-Angel). Because the siblings know what to expect from each other, it is safe to progress relatively fast. Therefore, therapeutic intervention with the sibling group can enhance the supportive and minimize the destructive elements of sibling interactions, resulting in long-term as well as immediate benefits (Hunter, 1993; Kahn & Bank, 1980).

Sibling Group Play Therapy

In three of the four families of one study (Eno, 1985), "play was the dominant mode of interaction between siblings; it was play that most often brought the children together and was the principal means by which they belonged to each other" (p. 143). As play is the natural and appropriate medium of self-expression for children (Axline, 1947; Landreth, 1991, 1997) and a central, all-encompassing characteristic of children's development (Hughes, F., 1991), Eno's findings are not surprising. The play medium is an emergent phenomenon that constructs its own contexts for establishing and exploring relationships creatively (Lewis, J., 1993; Lynch, 1982). In play, children can make a world where roles can be changed, feelings can be expressed, dreams can be dreamed, ideas can be tested, and problems can be resolved.

However, emotional trauma may hinder the use of play as a natural means of dealing with the trauma. For example, "in clinical practice, it is not unusual to hear parents report that their children's play diminished or increased following their separation" (Eno, 1985, p. 143). As play is the active pursuit of self-understanding as well as understanding of one's social and physical needs (Sleet, 1974), incorporating play into sibling group therapy can restore that common framework for resolving conflicts and removing interferences to mutually supportive relationships (Rosenberg, 1980).

Child-centered play therapy assumes that the potential for change and self-actualization already exists within each person (Axline, 1947; Landreth, 1991). The play therapist attempts to provide an atmosphere of acceptance and trust in each child's own strength to move forward personally and to build strong personal relationships with others. In the therapeutic context, it is important that a significant adult, the play therapist, provide adequate protection and nurturing to give the children "the experience of being completely accepted as they freely play in any way they choose" (Hunter, 1993, p. 68), consequently allowing them to have "experimental dialogues with the environment" (Eibesbeldt, as cited in McNamee, 1983).

Special Considerations

Therapeutic Focus. The outcome goals for sibling group play therapy are relevant to individual issues within a group context rather than to group issues in themselves. The choice for the group context centers on facilitating personal growth that is unlikely or slow to occur in an individual therapy context. The focus is on taking advantage of the unique opportunities of the group atmosphere for individual development rather than on meeting problem-oriented, prescribed goals for the group as a whole (Ginott, 1982).

Group Composition. Assuming that children will modify behavior in exchange for acceptance and belonging (Ginott, 1982), group membership is "never a random assembly. It requires planned design and complex construction. The final composition—including consideration of populations/referral issues, birth relationships, age, and number in the group—is a group in which children can exert a remedial impact on each other" (pp. 327–328).

To maximize the prospects of developing a more effective level of functioning among all sibling group members, children should be placed in sibling therapy for specific reasons. A family issue about which there are some misunderstandings or misconceptions, such as divorce, death of family member, or abuse (Hughes, H., 1982; Schibuk, 1989) is a strong indication for sibling therapy. Siblings socially and emotionally affected by circumstances surrounding a sibling being emotionally disturbed, handicapped, chronically ill, or otherwise traumatized (for example, sexual abuse) are also well served by sibling therapy, as are siblings separated from parents by foster care, residential treatment, or hospitalization. The process is also useful before, during, and after major family transitions (for example, residential move, new sibling, blended family) (Hamlin & Timberlake, 1981); when there are problems between siblings, family crises, and unstable family structure (Lewis, K., 1988); or when parenting is unavailable or inadequate (Rosenberg, 1980).

Homeless children and children in foster care are two populations for which this treatment modality is rarely made available. Very often, homeless children in family violence shelters or other temporary living conditions look on themselves and the world as being shaped by insecurity, fear, and isolation, so the use of play in the context of the sibling group can help these children restore relatedness, familial security, and self-esteem. Empowering them to accept and nurture each other can help them counteract isolation (Hunter, 1993).

Foster care placement for siblings necessitates severe changes—loss of the biological family system, neighborhood, school, and friends in exchange for a new foster family system, neighborhood, school, and friends (Johnson, Yoken, & Voss, 1995). Children in foster care exhibit problems in relationships and find it difficult to make healthy decisions, deal with loss, and maintain school performance and behavior and general self-esteem (Gunston & Sable House Team of Foster Care Specialists, 1995). Understandably, a sense of family connectedness is of utmost importance (Begun, 1995; Hegar, 1988; Kegerreis, 1993; Norris-Shortle et al., 1995). Continuity as a sibling group may provide a stabilizing influence as the children struggle with sharing their inner world because they fear being punished for talking, fear being disloyal to their parents, idealize their parents to hold on to positive memories, lack understanding of the ambiguity of their situation, and fear further rejection by current caretakers (McFadden, 1992). So abuse, neglect, insecure early attachments, and inconsistent caregiving often result in inability to tolerate intimacy as well as in impulsivity, fear of rejection, aggression, and lowered self-esteem (Dore & Eisner, 1993). Consequently, whenever possible, it is important that siblings be placed together in foster homes—and at the very least, supported in their right to associate with one another even when placed in separate foster homes (Hegar, 1988). Whether together in a foster home or in separate foster homes, play therapy groups provide a setting where siblings can provide each other a stable emotional bond (Norris-Shortle et al., 1995) that can facilitate the sharing of sad, angry, and confused feelings (Palmer, 1990). James (1989) contends that, initially, traumatized siblings should usually have the same therapist and engage in joint sessions for some time so they can have a sense of familiarity, security, and consistency.

Sibling group therapy is contraindicated for siblings with strong animosity and hostility (Gazda, 1984; Ginott, 1982; Nichols, 1986) or when one sibling functions ineffectively due to mental illness (Nichols). Parenting factors also may deem sibling group play therapy as inappropriate, such as when parenting is adequate enough to allow for problems to be handled within the family or when parents may retaliate due to fear of losing parental control, breach of family confidentiality, or collusion against them (Nichols; Rosenberg, 1980).

The structure of the therapeutic relationship differs between nonsibling and sibling groups. Nonsiblings are constantly building a relationship with one another and the therapist. On the other hand, siblings come into the setting with a relationship already established with one another; "the process of the siblings—what recurs all the time with brothers and sisters—is now happening in the therapy room" (Lewis, K., 1988, p. 192). The majority of the sibling energy goes into maintaining or repairing the existing relationship; together or separately, relationship building with the therapist is secondary to living out the sibling relationship. As the customary sibling interactions are often subtle or covert, the therapist sometimes is the "third wheel" or lags behind in understanding the group dynamics.

It is the established relationship that allows for a wide age variance and mixed genders for siblings together in group therapy, whereas neither is recommended in placing nonsiblings in group therapy. The sibling relationship already includes age variances and mixed genders whereas the building of the nonsibling relationship is highly dependent on the commonality of minimal age difference and same-gender experience. However, developmental life tasks can present an exception for sibling groups. For example, a five-year-old and a nine-year-old may have similar developmental reactions to the parents' divorce; however, the reactions may be extremely different for a five-year-old and a thirteen-year-old because their developmental life views of relationships and divorce can be very different. Consequently, it is less probable that sibling group therapy would be effective with the five-year-old and the thirteen-year-old together.

Although there may be several siblings, it is recommended that the therapeutic group have no more than three siblings, preferably two. The number must be such that the therapist can attend with acceptance to everything that is going on as much as possible. For therapeutic effectiveness, four or more siblings together would necessitate cotherapists. If a choice of siblings is to be made, a basic consideration is a group in which the siblings can exert a remedial impact on one another (Ginott, 1982).

Confidentiality. Confidentiality in sibling groups is largely governed by the existing subsystem boundaries on keeping secrets, tattling, dyads, and triads. This established familiarity with one another often facilitates early disclosure of who can be trusted and to what extent. Likewise, it is easier to deal with breach of confidentiality in sibling groups than in nonsibling groups for two reasons: disclosures are not going to be shared with complete strangers outside the group, and the breach cannot be overlooked because siblings form a lifetime group that, in essence, cannot be disbanded by removing a member.

Facility and Materials. The facility must be large enough to accommodate the children, therapist (or cotherapists), and play materials. There must be enough space for children to move without stumbling over others or materials. Those play materials used for individual play therapy are also appropriate for sibling group play therapy.

Length and Duration of Sessions. It is not necessary to modify the session length or the number of sessions. The quality of the facilitation in each session seems to be more important than time or number. Because the number of children often accelerates the process, it is possible that fewer sessions will be necessary than in individual therapy.

Limits. Increased activity, more verbalization, and greater probability of personal harm (physical or emotional) created by the presence of more than one child may necessitate a need for the therapist to have preconceived ideas of limits that may be more necessary in the sibling group situation than in an individual session. Use of paint, possibility of sexual activity, increased sound level, and speed of the children's movements are pertinent examples. For example, several children who are all allowed to paint their faces and arms at the same time are apt to egg each other on, splashing so much paint around that the floor gets dangerously slippery.

Redirecting sexual behavior with the therapist to an inanimate object is not permissible in the group because such sublimation serves as a model for the other children who have no need for that information. Office neighbors may tolerate high decibels of sound by one child, but they are less likely to smile and walk on when two or more children are performing at the same level. One child running around the playroom or swinging the rope can be easily monitored by the therapist, but such speed can be potentially dangerous when multiple children are present.

Therapist's Role. The role of the therapist may vary, as "the direction and therapeutic interventions within sibling group treatment are based upon the problems, strengths, and deficits confronting a particular sibling subsystem" (Hamlin & Timberlake, 1981, p. 105). The special needs of the subsystem can be met by examination and modification of the critical sibling relationship issues relative to the referral concerns, and by focusing on strengthening and supporting the subsystem—using the natural sibling ecology to help siblings function more effectively as individuals within the subsystem and as a group (Barlow, Strother, & Landreth, 1986; Nichols, 1986). Although most attention is given to the group dynamics, the therapist is also constantly attentive to the uniqueness of each individual (Lewis, K., 1988).

The therapist's main objective is to decrease his or her involvement as the siblings become more available to each other and more interdependent without the therapist as intermediary. The therapist provides conditions that facilitate more effective interpersonal interactions, rather than emphasizing intrapersonal issues (Lewis, K., 1988).

Process: Case Example

K. Lewis (1988) noted three major components of the shift in communication patterns from intrapersonal functioning to interpersonal problem solving, shifting from handling the world by oneself to engaging others in the process. When analyzing the process of sibling group play therapy, it can be very helpful to consider

- The struggle siblings have in maintaining individuality while being inevitably bound by blood boundaries, emotional boundaries developed over the years of being siblings whether living together or not, and the contract making that goes on to establish, reconstruct, and uphold individual selfhood and the sibling bond at the same time
- The dynamics involved in the determination of interaction norms, leadership positions and responsibilities, the hierarchy of roles and responsibilities, division of labor, and the rules and modalities of conflict resolution
- The themes of effective or ineffective communication as reflected in the degree of cohesion, affection, and approval

Siblings test the waters, struggle for leadership, and immerse themselves in involvement as they seek inclusion, control, and affection both individually and as a group. Consequently, facilitating more sibling cohesiveness, closeness, and confidence in each other can provide support both for the sibling subsystem and for an individual child (Hughes, H., 1982).

The case of Chelsea (age four) and Amber (age five) exemplifies the unique expression of the therapeutic process with a sibling play therapy group. Once Amber started kindergarten, Chelsea spent most of the after-school hours interfering with Amber's activities by trailing her, demanding her attention, taking her toys, and verbally and physically berating her. They were placed in sibling group play therapy because the problem appeared to be pertinent to their relationship; Chelsea had behaved appropriately with Amber before the latter started kindergarten and was still behaving appropriately while Amber was away at school each day, both on her own and with the other children in her mother's home day care. Initially, the mother resisted including Amber in therapy because she perceived the problem as being Chelsea's rather than that of "always well-behaved" Amber. However, she agreed to the group situation when the therapist pointed out the probable relationship issue and the potential benefits of group play therapy for both girls.

Sessions 1 Through 4. Chelsea watched Amber and "copycatted" Amber's activities after Amber had moved on to something else. Neither girl directly acknowledged the therapist's presence.

Sessions 5 and 6. Chelsea started interrupting Amber's activities with requests for particular items or to do what Amber was doing, sometimes soliciting the therapist's assistance. With neutral affect, Amber gave Chelsea whatever she wanted. Although the therapist's assistance was requested by Chelsea, the therapist's focus was on noting the dynamics of the interactions and leaving the problem-solving responsibility to the girls. The therapist's comments included statements like these: "Even though you had it first, Amber, you just let Chelsea have it." "Chelsea, seems like when Amber has something, you want it." "Doesn't seem to matter to you, Amber. You just give Chelsea whatever she wants."

Session 7. In this session, the pattern changed. As usual, Chelsea wanted the Barbie doll that Amber had.

Chelsea: I want that.
Amber: I'm playing with it.

Therapist: Chelsea, it sounds like you really want that, but you aren't finished with it, Amber.

Chelsea: *[after walking around room]* You can have this one *[holding out the Ken doll]*, and I'll take that one.

Amber: I'm playing with it.

Therapist: Amber, seems like you still want that one, but you want to trade, Chelsea.

Chelsea: *[stomps around the room, then sits on floor with arms folded and pout on face]*

Therapist: Chelsea, you seem really upset, but you don't seem to care, Amber.

Chelsea: *[tries to kick Amber]*

Therapist: Chelsea, I know you are really angry, but Amber's not for hurting. You can pretend that *[pointing to nearby puppet]* is Amber and hit that.

Chelsea continued to sit and pout with her arms folded. Amber played with the doll for seven minutes and then put it on the shelf. Chelsea immediately took the doll and played with it for the rest of the session, frequently stating what she had and what she was doing. The therapist said, "Chelsea, you really want us to pay attention to you, but you don't seem interested, Amber." Amber engaged in several other activities and gave no attention to Chelsea.

Sessions 8 Through 12. Increasingly, Chelsea used more age-appropriate words and mannerisms to ask Amber for items or to play with her, including taking refusal or delay more amiably. At the same time, Amber accepted more of Chelsea's invitations to interact and even initiated some interactive play on her own.

The therapist met with the mother every third session. After the sixth session, the mother was very discouraged and wanted to quit bringing the girls for therapy because Chelsea's inappropriate behaviors at home seemed to be intensifying. ("Just as they were in the playroom," thought the therapist.) The therapist explained that such seeming regression or intensification was not uncommon before more positive changes would take place. The mother was also frustrated because her "sweet" Amber was ignoring some of Chelsea's approaches and sometimes was talking back to Chelsea—confirmation for the therapist that Amber was becoming aware that she could stand up to Chelsea.

It was not a complete surprise to the therapist, therefore, that the scenario in Session 7 occurred. Amber finally trusted the playroom atmosphere of freedom to be herself and to express her own inner world openly, and, of course, Chelsea did not know what to do with Amber's new behavior. The next four sessions were the girls' laboratory for gaining more insight into their relationship and for practicing, developing, and mastering more effective relationship skills. It was the time for more self-discovery, gaining more knowledge about one another, each redefining her own self and using the group pressure for growth in a supportive environment (Berg & Landreth, 1990; Ginott, 1961). It was the time of identifying personal strengths and limitations in respect to each other as well as their strengths and limitations as a unified duo (Hamlin & Timberlake, 1981). It was the time of increasing individual self-esteem, improvement of interpersonal skills, and restoration of relatedness (Hunter, 1993) in the playroom and at home.

Relationship Principles. The basic relationship principles for individual child-centered play therapy (Axline, 1947; Landreth, 1991) are no different in the group context, but a broader perspective must be taken into account when facilitating the process for sibling group play therapy.

Establish Rapport. If the sibling relationship is relatively compatible, rapport between the children and the therapist may be slow in building as the siblings look to one another for their support and safety; on the other hand, that very mutual support may hasten building rapport with the therapist because the children already have a safety net. If the sibling relationship is not compatible, establishing rapport may be difficult as the therapist endeavors to facilitate rapport with each sibling as well as between and among siblings.

In the early sessions, it was important that the therapist's verbal and nonverbal responses reflected that she was accepting of the girls' interactions even though they did not directly include her. She was careful to use a warm, caring voice and to make statements that reflected the girls' activity, such as: "Amber, you seem determined to get that just right, and, Chelsea, you seem interested in what Amber's doing." And "Chelsea, you're doing just what Amber did, but you're already concentrating on that, Amber."

Later, it was equally important that the therapist reflected Chelsea's desire to have Amber's items and Amber's willingness to concede, but remained empathic with both girls and did not take sides with either by issuing no reprimands, lectures, or teaching. It was enough to say, "Chelsea, it seems like you want everything that Amber has, and you always let her have what she asks for, Amber."

Accept Each Child Completely. The therapist must be constantly alert to avoid contrasting or comparison, to give equal and direct attention to each child, to be impartial, and to reflect the group dynamics rather than the content.

The therapist was consistent in reflecting the dynamics of the girls' interactions, being sure to note the behaviors of each girl with an impartial and nonjudgmental attitude (voice tone, words, and body language). She talked to each girl instead of reporting what one or the other was doing.

Establish a Feeling of Permissiveness. An atmosphere is perceived quite rapidly in the group context as one sibling gains courage to freely express self from observing the behaviors of others and the impartial and nonjudgmental reactions of the therapist.

Although the therapist never told Amber that she could decide to refuse Chelsea's requests, the consistency and nonjudgmental nature of the therapist's responses seemingly facilitated Amber's freedom to be herself. Likewise, acceptance of both girls equally with all their feelings and desires seemed to free Chelsea to express herself as she was doing at home.

Recognize and Reflect Feelings. Because the therapeutic focus is on individual development within the sibling group context, the therapist centers attention on each child's feelings in regard to interactions with, between, and among the siblings. Consideration is given to the feelings of all siblings involved in a particular interaction, thus facilitating recognition of the effect of an individual's behaviors on self and on others. If it is necessary to give considerable attention to one child's feelings, scattered responses must be given to others, also, so as not to have the others feel neglected.

By acknowledging and accepting Chelsea's desire to engage with Amber by way of Amber's materials and activities and Amber's seeming indifference, the therapist helped both girls move toward expressing their inner feelings more openly and directly.

Maintain Respect for Each Child. Relationship problems tend to be more overt and escalate more rapidly with siblings together than when the siblings participate on an individual basis or in group play therapy with nonrelated children. Often, when conflict arises, one sibling or the other will try to engage the therapist for protection, defense, or rescue. The therapist still has the responsibility to facilitate problem solving and initiation of change on the part of the children, being careful not to give even subtle direction (especially in response to more dominant or passive behaviors).

The therapist experienced ambivalent feelings—irritation with Chelsea's demanding behavior and frustration with Amber's giving in to Chelsea and ignoring her. However, rather than describe or model different ways to interact, the therapist described the dynamics and trusted the girls to solve the conflict in a way that was meaningful and safe for them.

Allow the Children to Lead. With more than one child to lead the way, the themes, content, and direction of the process may seem chaotic and nontherapeutic at times. Again, it is important for the therapist to remember that the siblings know best who they are as a unit and what they need to do for healing.

The therapist's first impression was that Chelsea looked to her sister for modeling—imitating Amber's lead—whereas Amber independently did as she wished. In sessions five and six, it was clearer that Chelsea wanted more direct attention from Amber but did not know how to ask for it directly; likewise, Amber did not directly express her desire to be left alone. Amber made no attempt to interact with Chelsea. At first, it appeared that Amber was more than willing to cater to her sister's desires but made no attempt to interact with her; however, Amber later made it clear that she did not always want to give in but wanted to decide when she wanted to interact.

Follow the Flow of the Process. Group dynamics often accelerate the process, but the therapist needs to be cautious about getting caught up in the faster pace and hurrying it along even more. Being with one's siblings can provide mutual support, but it can also provide the possibility of retreat and regression if the boundaries of the relationship are not yet clear and safe. The siblings need to set their own pace of identification and differentiation.

In the parent-therapist meeting after the third session, the mother reported that nothing had changed at home even though the therapist was not seeing the problematic home behaviors in the playroom. Only the girls knew when it was safe to bring the home behaviors into the playroom and when it was safe to initiate change, as began occurring in Session 5.

Set Limits. Consistent, assuring, natural, and sincere limits can be therapeutic; clumsy, uncertain limit setting may incite the group to challenge the limits even more.

The therapist was alert to possible emotional distress as Chelsea demanded Amber's items. If Amber had shown discomfort, the therapist would have reflected that feeling but would not have set a limit on Chelsea's verbal language—empowering Amber to do so if she desired. However, when physical harm was imminent, a limit was set on Chelsea's behavior.

Conclusion

Understanding of the sibling subsystem structure and dynamics by the siblings and the therapist can facilitate exploration of options for change for all siblings (Bank & Kahn, 1976). Each sibling separately and all siblings together have their rules, patterns of behavior, and needs. A crucial aspect of the therapy process is exploring the extent to which the sibling subsystem has split apart or coalesced (Nichols, 1986) and then deciding what needs to be done to meet everyone's needs.

Although the blood boundaries continued to exist for Chelsea and Amber, the emotional boundaries changed when Amber went off to kindergarten. Amber's daily absence and perceived "other life" threatened Chelsea's assurance of her sister's care and love to the extent that Chelsea kept testing Amber's constancy by demanding her attention in various ways—taking Amber's things, following her around, being aggressive verbally and physically. The problem escalated as Amber handled her sister's new behaviors (smothering approaches) by passively giving things to Chelsea, allowing her to be physically close, and ignoring the aggressiveness while still separating herself from Chelsea by staying involved as much as possible in her own isolated play. It appeared that neither sister knew how to deal constructively with the changes on both sides.

Sibling group play therapy provides the opportunity for siblings to explore their relationships alone in a specially designed, developmentally appropriate environment; improve interpersonal skills that may be transferred to other relationships; make less defensive and consequently faster progress than with nonsiblings or individually because of the security of familiarity with the siblings; and clarify and express positive and negative feelings toward each other (Ranieri & Pratt, 1978). At referral time, Chelsea and Amber were each acting independently to solve their problem; throughout the course of therapy, both learned to ask more directly for what they wanted and needed, often in the context of give-and-take contract negotiation. The transition from intrapersonal functioning to interpersonal problem solving included establishing norms for communication, sharing control and leadership, and cooperatively resolving their conflicts. The demanding decreased; the avoiding and ignoring decreased; the asking and negotiation increased; the stating of personal needs and boundaries increased; and the softer tones, smiling faces, laughter, and renewed friendship prevailed.

References

Axline, V. (1947). *Play therapy: The inner dynamics of childhood.* Boston: Houghton Mifflin.

Bank, S., & Kahn, M. (1976). Sisterhood-brotherhood is powerful: Sibling sub-systems and family therapy. *Annual Progress in Child Psychiatry and Child Development,* pp. 493–519.

Barlow, K., Strother, J., & Landreth, G. (1986). Sibling group play therapy: An effective alternative with an elective mute child. *School Counselor, 34*(1), 44–50.

Begun, A. (1995). Sibling relationships and foster care placements for young children. Special issue: Social work practice with children. *Early Child Development and Care, 106,* 237–250.

Benedek, L. (1982). Group play therapy. *Magyar Pszichologiai Szemle, 39*(3), 290–300.

Berg, R., & Landreth, G. (1990). *Group counseling: Concepts and procedures* (2nd ed.). Muncie, IN: Accelerated Development.

Crispell, D. (1996). The sibling syndrome. *American Demographics, 18*(8), 24–30.

Dore, M., & Eisner, E. (1993). Child-related dimensions of placement stability in treatment foster care. *Child and Adolescent Social Work Journal, 10*(4), 301–317.

Eno, M. (1985). Sibling relationships in families of divorce. *Journal of Psychotherapy and the Family, 1*(3), 139–156.

Floyd, K. (1995). Gender and closeness among friends and siblings. *Journal of Psychology, 129*(2), 193–202.

Fraiberg, S. (1987). The adolescent mother and her infant. In L. Fraiberg (Ed.), *Selected writings of Selma Fraiberg* (pp. 166–182). Columbus: Ohio State University Press.

Frey-Angel, J. (1989). Treating children of violent families: A sibling group approach. *Social Work with Groups, 12*(1), 95–107.

Gazda, G. (1984). *Group counseling: A developmental approach* (3rd ed.). Boston: Allyn & Bacon.

Gibbs, J. (1945). Group play therapy. *British Journal of Medical Psychology, 20,* 244–254.

Ginott, H. (1958). Play group therapy: A theoretical framework. *International Journal of Psychotherapy, 8,* 410–418.

Ginott, H. (1961). *Group psychotherapy with children: The theory and practice of play therapy.* New York: McGraw-Hill.

Ginott, H. (1982). Group play therapy with children. In G. L. Landreth (Ed.), *Play therapy: Dynamics of the process of counseling with children* (pp. 327–341). Springfield, IL: Thomas.

Gunston, T., & Sable House Team of Foster Care Specialists. (1995). A model of foster care services for South Africa. *Community Alternatives International Journal of Family Care, 7*(1), 107–125.

Hamlin, E., & Timberlake, E. (1981). Sibling group treatment. *Clinical Social Work Journal, 9*(2), 101–110.

Hegar, R. (1988). Legal and social work approaches to sibling separation in foster care. *Child Welfare, 67*(2), 113–121.

Hughes, F. (1991). *Children, play, and development.* Boston: Allyn & Bacon.

Hughes, H. (1982). Brief interventions with children in battered women's shelter: A model preventive program. *Family Relations Journal of Applied Family and Child Study, 31*(4), 495–502.

Hunter, L. (1993). Sibling play therapy with homeless children: An opportunity in the crisis. *Child Welfare, 72*(1), 65–75.

James, B. (1989). *Treating traumatized children: New insights and creative interventions.* Lexington, MA: Lexington Books.

Johnson, P., Yoken, C., & Voss, R. (1995). Family foster care placement: The child's perspective. *Child Welfare, 74*(5), 858–874.

Jones, L. (1995). The sibling connection: The most crucial link of all? *Cosmopolitan, 218*(4), 200–203.

Kahn, M., & Bank, S. (1980). Discussion: Therapy with siblings in reorganizing families. *International Journal of Family Therapy, 2*(3), 155–158.

Kegerreis, S. (1993). From a gang of two back to the family. *Psychoanalytic Psychotherapy, 7*(1), 69–83.

Landreth, G. (1991). *Play therapy: The art of the relationship.* Muncie, IN: Accelerated Development.

Landreth, G. (1997). Play therapy: Facilitative use of child's play in elementary school counseling. Special issue: Counseling with expressive arts. *Elementary School Guidance and Counseling, 21*(4), 253–261.

Lewis, J. (1993). Childhood play in normality, pathology, and therapy. *American Journal of Orthopsychiatry, 63*(1), 6–15.

Lewis, K. (1988). Sibling therapy: A blend of family and group therapy. *Journal for Specialists in Group Work, 12*(4), 186–193.

Lewis, K. (1990). Siblings: A hidden resource in therapy. *Journal of Strategic and Systemic Therapies, 9*(1), 39–49.

Lynch, R. (1982). Play, creativity, and emotion. *Studies in Symbolic Interaction, 4,* 45–62.

Markowitz, L., Harrigan, S., Koontz, K., & Klagsbrun, F. (1994). Sibling connections. *Utne Reader, 63,* 50–62.

Marty, M. (1994). Siblings. *Christian Century, 111*(20), 663.

McFadden, E. (1992). The inner world of children and youth in care. *Community Alternatives International Journal of Family Care, 4*(1), 1–17.

McNamee, G. (1983, March). *The meaning and function of early childhood play.* Paper presented at the conference "Being with Children: A Psychoanalytic Perspective" sponsored by the Psychoanalytic Foundation of Minneapolis, Inc., Minneapolis, MN.

Nichols, W. (1986). Sibling subsystem therapy in family system reorganization. *Journal of Divorce, 9*(3), 13–31.

Norris-Shortle, C., Colletta, N., Cohen, M., & McCombs, R. (1995). Sibling therapy with children under three. *Child and Adolescent Social Work Journal, 12*(4), 251–261.

Palmer, S. (1990). Group treatment of foster children to reduce separation conflicts associated with placement breakdown. *Child Welfare, 69*(3), 227–238.

Ranieri, R., & Pratt, T. (1978). Sibling therapy. *Social Work, 23*(5), 418–419.

Rosenberg, E. (1980). Therapy with siblings in reorganizing families. *International Journal of Family Therapy, 2*(3), 139–150.

Rothenberg, L. (1966). The therapeutic play group: A case study. *Exceptional Children, 32,* 483–486.

Sachs, J. (1993). Sibling rivalry: The adult aftermath. *New Woman, 23*(8), 138.

Schibuk, M. (1989). Treating the sibling subsystem: An adjunct of divorce therapy. *American Journal Of Orthopsychiatry, 34*(6), 581–588.

Schiffer, M. (1969). *The therapeutic play group.* New York: Grune & Stratton.

Slavson, S. R. (1948). Play group therapy with young children. *Nervous Child, 7,* 318–327.

Sleet, D. (1974). Play: In all seriousness. *Society and Leisure, 6*(3), 143–145.

Wakaba, Y. (1983). Group play therapy for Japanese children who stutter. *Journal of Fluency Disorders, 8*(2), 93–118.

CHAPTER EIGHTEEN

PLAY GROUPS IN ELEMENTARY SCHOOL

JoAnna White and Mary Flynt

Elementary school counselors fill a unique role. They are among the few groups of helping professionals who work from a preventive model as well as providing remedial services to children. Perhaps no other professional counselor uses the group approach more than an elementary school counselor. Not only is group counseling the most time efficient and parsimonious means of providing counseling in the school, it is more effective than individual counseling for many children (Brigman & Earley, 1991; Morganett, 1994).

An ideal elementary school counseling program provides for the needs of all students. This program is based on the philosophy that if school counselors help children at an early age to socialize appropriately and develop a positive attitude toward learning, they will become productive, well-adjusted students. Therefore, prevention is a large component of the elementary counseling program.

Preventive counseling and guidance services are typically provided in large group classroom guidance activities and in small counseling groups. Topics for these large and small groups would be directly related to the age and developmental needs of the children. For example, a first-grade classroom guidance activity might center on following the class rules and respecting one another. A typical fifth-grade classroom guidance activity might involve preparation for middle school. The elementary school counselor provides developmentally appropriate learning experiences for all children in the school through the group format (Gysbers & Henderson, 1988; Myrick, 1987; Wittmer, 1993).

Elementary counselors work from a holistic perspective in order to understand their students; therefore, they value consultation with teachers and parents. They provide group training for teachers in classroom management skills and models for understanding children. They also provide parent education through individual and group consultation and classes. This consultation with teachers and parents also prevents difficulties for students because both groups become more adept at helping children adjust to the learning environment.

Elementary counselors are involved in the delivery of remedial counseling services as well as in preventive work. They provide individual counseling and small group counseling for students experiencing academic and social difficulties. The types of small groups in elementary settings are as varied as the problems of society in general. For example, a typical remedial small group for third graders might focus on family adjustment issues such as divorce or other types of loss. Fourth or fifth graders might be involved in a remedial small group experience related to living in an alcoholic family.

Elementary counselors are well aware of the developmental needs of their students. They know that play is a natural activity of children, and that through play the child "communicates, tests, incorporates, and masters his external realities" (Gazda, 1973, p. 123). Because elementary school counselors understand the developmental needs of children and the effectiveness of groups with children, they employ play and play media in a variety of group experiences for children. This approach illustrates adult responsibility to provide appropriate counseling services for children at their unique stage of development rather than expecting children to comply with adult demands (Vriend & Dyer, 1973).

The use of play groups is not a new approach. Slavson (1947) and Ginott (1961) were pioneers in group activity therapy and group play therapy respectively. As elementary counseling began in the 1960s and 1970s, professionals advocated for play groups for children in schools as well (Bosdell, 1973; Gazda, 1973). In addition to the therapeutic benefits for children, the play group experience is a valuable observational tool for school counselors who are called upon to help with a child that other professionals are having difficulty understanding. As a result of the growing attention given to play counseling in elementary schools, the journal *Elementary School Guidance & Counseling* dedicated an entire special issue to counseling and children's play (Gerler, 1993). However, this special issue contained no play therapy group articles.

Although there is an abundance of literature to support the use of group counseling in elementary schools and the importance of play as a natural means of expression for children, there is a lack of literature related to play therapy groups in the schools. The authors have found the play therapy approach to be so effective and useful that we encourage others in schools to adopt it as a regular component of their developmental guidance programs.

School counselors struggle under the restriction that their work with students is not to be considered therapy. Nonetheless, children experience a variety of traumas, and the school counselor may be the only professional providing mental health services to a child. There is a fine line between therapy and counseling. It is difficult to know when one ends and the other begins. The present educational, political mood demands the application of strict boundaries to the school counselor's work. Therefore, school counselors who are providing therapy choose to label it counseling to comply with outside demands.

Rationale for Play Groups in the School

Theorists and researchers agree that children must learn to socialize appropriately if they are to develop in a healthy manner. Adler (Dinkmeyer, Dinkmeyer, & Sperry, 1987) believed that we are all primarily social beings, and our behavior can only be understood within our social context.

As Harris (1995) stated, "Children learn how to behave outside the home by becoming members of, and identifying with, a social group" (p. 482). In her review of the literature of the effects of various environments on children, she concluded that socialization outside the home may have an even greater effect than parents' efforts. If so, play groups would provide an opportunity for children to begin the socialization process. The group is a microcosm of society in which children can practice new behaviors, reality test, and learn to sublimate behaviors inappropriate for the group (Ginott, 1982).

While some experts propose that play therapy groups should focus on individual, not group, issues (Ginott, 1982), school counselors will focus on both individual and group issues. Their goals are to help the individual child with intrapersonal issues as well as creating a group environment where children can expand their socialization skills. In this way children can learn to be socially interested and develop a concern for the welfare of the group as well as for themselves. This concept of "social interest," first identified by Alfred Adler, is the basic indicator of good mental health. School counselors can easily get a picture of a child's level of social interest by observing that child with other children in a play group.

Ginott's (1961) and Axline's (1947) support of play therapy groups, based on their observations and research, provides strong rationale for play group counseling in elementary schools. Ginott's thinking about children in distress was that they are usually reacting to stressful situations in their lives but still have a "social hunger." This is true of most children in elementary school. They do not suffer from severe personality disorders that would prevent them from the social benefits of a play group experience.

Ginott (1982) discussed advantages to play group therapy. The following is a discussion of these advantages and how they relate to the elementary school setting. Subsequently, the chapter case study will highlight these advantages.

Developmental Appropriateness

As noted at many points in this volume, "Play is the child's natural medium of self-expression" (Axline, 1947). Ideally, school counselors help children identify and name their feelings and ask for their needs to be met in appropriate ways. However, this is a process, and children cannot participate and benefit from talk counseling exclusively. Bosdell (1973) agreed with Axline that play is the natural medium of expression but added that it does not replace verbalization. She believed that it may serve as preverbalization. She described the play counseling experience as "a living segment of life where play and words coexist for a totality of meaning that neither could achieve alone" (p. 29). This is a critical concept for school counselors to incorporate into their group work with children. School counselors facilitate cognitive development and school success as well as emotional adjustment, and they do this by combining verbal and nonverbal play experiences in developmentally appropriate counseling experiences for children. The children in the case study presented in this chapter were able to access their feelings and therapeutic issues because of the concrete nature of the play group experience.

Preventive, Remedial, and Crisis Intervention Counseling

Play groups are effective whether the school counselor is working on a preventive, crisis, or remedial situation. For example, a counselor might take a group of children in kindergarten into the playroom to help them adjust to school before issues develop (preventive), to help them with classroom behavior problems (remedial), or to help them deal with the illness of a classmate (crisis). The group approach is one of the most beneficial counseling tools available to the school counselor. Additionally, the group approach affords the school counselor the opportunity to reach more students in a shorter period of time.

Vicarious Learning and the Catalytic Effect

Ginott (1982) proposed that "group therapy is based on the assumption that children will modify behavior in exchange for acceptance" (p. 327). Through the play group experience with other children, a child can benefit from the appropriate behaviors that others model, have a chance to try new behaviors in a social setting, and learn that inappropriate behaviors do not get desired results (Axline, 1947). For example, in one group a boy named Steven was testing limits with the Bobo punching bag. He pushed the limits to the point that the school counselor stated (as she was taking the Bobo away from Steven), "I see that you have chosen not to play with Bobo today." Bobby was playing with blocks and invited Steven to join him. Steven was able to make the transition quicker than usual and joined Bobby in the block play. In this way the two boys were affecting each other's behavior in ways that would not have been possible in individual play therapy.

Slavson (1948) emphasized the catalytic effect that each child can have on the others. In the play group environment it is easier for each child to act out and bring forth anxieties. Slavson believed that the individual child tends to repeat the same activity whereas the group experiences encourage the child to try new behaviors. He called this the "growth-producing environment" (p. 320). This would be especially helpful in a school setting where a great deal of emphasis is placed on growth through learning. This expanded interpersonal growth can lead to new ways of thinking, new options, and problem solving. This will then transfer to the classroom.

Positive Socialization

Elementary school counselors are especially interested in the positive socialization of children. Their work is based on the belief that a child who has a sense of belonging in his or her social group will be open to learning experiences as well as to developing positive relationships with others. Elementary school children spend their entire day at school in groups. Part of their survival is to learn group skills in order to achieve a sense of belonging.

The group setting provides children with a tangible social matrix in which they can test reality (Ginott, 1982). The child will test the reaction of the counselor and the other children as well as the applicability of the materials to play themes. Related to appropriate socialization, Ginott (1961) believed that group play activities provide children with a rich experience in which they can begin to sublimate inappropriate urges and substitute more appropriate behaviors. This ability to sublimate and delay gratification is the key to the socialization process.

Growth Through Insight

Groups are more conducive to insight than individual work because they provide experiences through relationships. Elementary school–aged children's cognitive development is in the preoperational stage (two to seven years) or concrete operations stage (seven to twelve years) (Myrick, 1987). Therefore, they access information by doing. As a play therapist, the school counselor can use the group interactions to point out self-defeating behaviors and also positive behaviors and progress. Ginott (1982) describes the complex issue of insight as usually occurring after improvement has been made. As group members progress, they can begin to have more awareness of themselves and others by gaining insight into their behaviors.

Recommended Practice

There are many behaviors and verbalizations to pay attention to during the sessions. It is good if one can videotape the sessions and review them later. It is also important to make one's own comments as neutral as possible so that a child does not feel singled out or embarrassed (Axline, 1947).

The basic principle is, *Do not lead the sessions.* Be tentative with goal disclosure and guesses so that children can feel safe to say no. Be particularly careful not to align with one child. This is not uncommon, especially when you have seen one child in the group individually and you have a big investment in this child's progress.

Be aware of ethical issues such as what to relate to parents so that the child's confidentiality is protected, whether or not to tape the sessions, and how to work within your level of training. Play therapy techniques are useful within the framework of a school counseling program provided the counselor has had the appropriate training in play therapy and group counseling. At the university where both authors are affiliated, play therapy and group counseling are required courses for everyone who is studying elementary and middle school counseling.

Be aware of the importance of screening for age (no more than one year apart), sex (mixed groups are fine with K–3 students, but same-sex groups are preferable after third grade), and presenting issues. Even though it is ideal to screen and plan for the play groups, school counselors do not always have that luxury. However, bear in mind that children with serious emotional issues, developmental delays, aggressive issues, or sexual acting out issues would not be appropriate for group play counseling (Ginott, 1961).

Case Study

In this example, a school counselor worked with kindergarten students in a play counseling group setting for twelve sessions. Their kindergarten teacher referred three for group counseling services, and the counselor added a fourth child from the same class. The group consisted of three girls (Nancy, Sherry, and Kahja) and one boy (Richard).

Nancy, who was placed in this group by the counselor, was a puzzle to teachers and paraprofessionals. She appeared noncommunicative, she masturbated in class, and she ate glue and crayons. At the beginning of the school year the teachers described her as autistic or mentally retarded. She was taking part in other service programs, such as speech therapy, throughout the year and continued to see the school counselor for individual play counseling until the holiday break at midyear.

Nancy's mother suspected abuse and neglect during Nancy's first two years of life. As a young mother lacking family and financial resources, she left her infant with unscrupulous caretakers. She later found that Nancy had been exposed to drug abuse and violence at the baby-sitter's home. Nancy's mother and stepfather were open to consultation and counseling but were put on a waiting list at the local mental health center. The school counselor worked with the parents on appropriate expectations for Nancy at home and the use of encouragement and logical consequences.

Throughout this period of individual play counseling, the teacher reported that negative behaviors had decreased significantly. Nancy was also communicating more with teachers and other students. Her play themes centered on nurturance issues (feeding the baby, preparing food, house chores) and sand work (burial of miniature families who at times would come back out and at other times could not get out).

Sherry transferred into the school three months into the school year after being homeless for six months. Her parents and their three children lived in their car and then in a shelter. They presently live in government housing, and both parents are employed. Sherry was withdrawn and gave up easily when asked to participate in classroom activities. The counselor saw Sherry individually in the playroom twice before the group began. The two individual sessions were characterized by safety issues such as finding safe places to hide the miniature people.

Kahja speaks Urdu and English. She has an older sister and brother who both excel in school. Her teacher describes her as bossy, monopolizing class discussions, and having difficulty with relationships. She is a successful student who often uses her need for power in positive ways, taking a constructive leadership role among her peers.

Richard's teachers described him as bright and extremely shy. His first language is Spanish, but he had two years of preschool in which he learned English. Richard is the middle child of three young children. In consultation with the school counselor, his parents shared their frustrations about their own struggle to survive in a foreign country and Richard's "lack of initiative." They were receptive to the counselor's recommendations and seemed encouraged concerning Richard's participation in group counseling.

Kahja and Richard knew the counselor through their participation in group classroom guidance activities. They had not been in individual play counseling.

Formative Stage

Gladding (1995) describes the formative stage of a group as that time when the members feel the initial caution of a new situation, attempt to avoid being rejected by others, and limits are usually set.

First Group Meeting. The first meeting took place in the counselor's group area in her office. The children and the counselor sat around a table with a large piece of drawing paper and several crayon boxes and pencils. To begin the group experience the counselor introduced the purpose of the meetings by saying that this was a opportunity to learn about each other. The counselor introduced the importance of cooperation (socialization) by asking the children to draw a house together in any way that they wished. The counselor said: "If you could live together in a house, what would the house look like?" They approached the art materials with enthusiasm:

> *Kahja:* Just the children live here, yeah.
>
> *Richard, Nancy, and Sherry:* Yeah!
>
> *Counselor:* You can all decide that, if that's the way you want it. You would like for only the children to live in that house and no one else.
>
> *All children:* Yeah! Yeah! That's the way we want it!!!

Nancy and Sherry began to draw the outside grass, trees, flowers, and sky. Kahja and Richard got busy with the actual construction of the house. There was an unspoken understanding among the children concerning the job assignments. They worked in silence. When they finished, the counselor asked them to tell a story about the children who lived in the house.

> *Kahja:* *[laughing]* They play all day and night, and they have lots of toys.
>
> *Counselor:* They are going to play all day long and all night with lots of toys.
>
> *Nancy:* They eat candy anytime they want.
>
> *Counselor:* There is going to be candy to eat at all times.

Richard: *[in low tones]* If a robber comes the children will hide.

Counselor: If a robber comes the children know where to go so the robber won't find them.

Sherry: If they play inside the house, the robber won't get them.

Counselor: You think that to be safe from the robber all the children need to play inside.

Kahja: I am going to play outside sometimes.

Counselor: Even if all the others choose to play inside, you have decided that sometimes you are going to be outside playing.

Kahja: Yeah!

Counselor: I wonder what the other children will do about where to play?

Nancy: I go play with Kahja. *[catalytic effect]*

Counselor: Nancy, you are going to play with Kahja anywhere she plays.

Nancy: *[nods. Sherry and Richard never answered. Group time ended.]*

This initial exchange begins to show the differences among the children. The counselor learned a great deal about each child. As was stated earlier, play therapy groups offer a rich opportunity to observe children and get a sense of who they are. Kahja, the leader, and Nancy, the follower and pleaser, connected. They needed each other to maintain their behaviors successfully. In later groups, Nancy began to try new behaviors, and that change affected Kahja's bossiness and appeared to promote insight for her.

Play Groups in the School's Playroom. After the first meeting in the school counselor's office, the group began its regular sessions in the school's playroom. This initial exchange in the playroom begins to show the differences among the children. Once again, Kahja and Nancy connect and reinforce each other's respective roles as leader and follower. Sherry and Richard are cautious and noncommittal. To some extent this pattern remained the same throughout the group experience.

Counselor: Pretty fancy footwork, Richard. You can hit that Bobo hard and you can hit him right on the face . . . and even with one finger you can push him down.

Nancy: *[joins in by punching Bobo.]*

Counselor: Nancy, you know how to join with Richard and punch Bobo.

Counselor: Sherry and Nancy are dressing up and playing with the sand.

Richard: *[escalates the beating of the Bobo.]*

Counselor: You beat him down every time, Richard. You can hit him in all kinds of different ways.

The three girls:	*[gather in the dress-up area and help each other with jewelry and clothing items]*
Counselor:	You have decided to help each other by dressing up and putting on necklaces and earrings. *[socialization]*
Kahja:	*[breaks away and goes over to one of the shelves]*
Richard:	*[continues to look around the room]*
Counselor:	Kahja, you found something new.
Nancy:	*[walking over and speaking to Kahja]* Let's get the baby, let's play baby.
Kahja:	I don't want to do that.
Nancy:	*[lowers her head, collects the baby, and takes it to another corner in the room]*
Counselor:	She is not sure she wants to do that.

Here the counselor failed to track clearly, adding vagueness to the situation. A better response could have been, "Kahja, you don't want to play with the baby, and Nancy, you seemed disappointed because Kahja told you no." Maybe the counselor was trying to soften the blow of rejection. This is an example of overprotecting a child that the counselor has seen in individual play counseling.

At the beginning of the next exchange, Kahja, Richard, and Sherry were trying to get up on a chair to get some plastic straws from a high shelf. Nancy continued to rock the baby while standing at the opposite corner of the room.

Kahja:	I want to get up there. *[elbowing her way up and raising her voice]* No me.
Counselor:	It is important that you get up there first and that you get what you want.
Kahja:	Can I play with these sticks? *[catalytic effect]*
Counselor:	In here you can choose. It looks like you have an idea.
Kahja:	*[grabs the straws and shows them to the others; Nancy comes close and is joined by the others]* OK. Here is the sticks, see. Wait, I am going to get something. [The others follow Kahja intently doing what she tells them to do. Kahja begins to place the straws in the sand and the others do the same.]*
Counselor:	Kahja gets an idea and everyone else follows her. *[counselor's attempt to promote insight]*
Sherry:	Can I have that hat?
Counselor:	You wish you could have that hat. Things in the playroom stay in the playroom.
Nancy:	*[engages with Richard in a pretend sword fight and chase around the playroom.]*
Counselor:	Nancy, you are trying to get Richard.
The three girls:	*[giggle and run around Richard laughing and pretending to be scared]*
Counselor:	Richard is attacking all the girls.
Kahja:	Stop, stop.
Counselor:	Kahja, you are saying, Don't do that anymore. I don't want to be bothered.

The children tried different activities alone and with each other. Individual themes emerged out of their brief encounters. Richard settled with the task of building and sculpting. Kahja played house with Nancy, always being the mother. Nancy played the daughter with a baby sibling while longing for the mother role. Sherry concentrated on dressing up and wearing jewelry, always looking for counselor approval. She later switched to mastery themes during the working stage, and this is attributed to vicarious learning by watching the other children engage in more purposeful play.

Storming Stage

Gladding (1995) describes this stage in group development as a time when members struggle over power issues that may result in anxiety, resistance, and conflict. The following are excerpts from session five.

Sherry:	*[trying to open the cap of a fancy marker]* It doesn't open. *[signals the counselor to help her open it]*
Counselor:	It doesn't open. You would like for me to help you open it. You have tried and tried and it doesn't open.
Sherry:	Can you open it?
Counselor:	I bet you'll try some more and you will get it done. I have seen you do things like that before.
Sherry:	*[gets the cap off]*
Counselor:	You did it! You got it done. *[reinforcing Sherry's sense of her own abilities]*
Kahja:	*[looking at the marker]* I think that's beautiful.
Richard and Nancy:	*[trying to look closer]* What is it?
Counselor:	You think that what Sherry found is pretty neat. Everybody wants to look at it.
Richard:	*[announcing in an excited voice]* Is a marker!! Is a marker!!
Richard and Kahja:	*[grab the marker away from Sherry and begin to pull at it, trying to gain control]*
Kahja:	*[yelling]* Give me it!!! Give me it!!!
Richard:	*[gives in]*
Counselor:	Everybody wants the marker, and Richard, you went ahead and gave the marker to Kahja. Even though Sherry found the marker, Kahja has it now. *[attempting to encourage insight]*

The counselor applied the concept of goal disclosure in the playroom as a mild confrontation by naming the observed behaviors in a neutral way. This is a nonthreatening way to look at the behaviors, allowing the power-oriented child to learn without a heightened feeling of opposition toward the counselor. The following are excerpts from session six. Just before the dialogue begins, Sherry and Richard were working on pictures for the baby. Kahja grabbed a crayon and began to color on Sherry's picture.

Sherry:	*[angrily]* I don't want you to paint!! I don't want you to paint!! *[pushing Kahja's hand out of the way]*
Counselor:	Sherry, that is your picture and you don't want Kahja to do anything on your picture. You are telling her you don't want her to do that.
Kahja:	*[insight: acting confused and looking around avoiding eye contact with everyone in the room]* Is it for the baby? Is it for Ms. Floyd?
Richard:	*[appearing annoyed]* Is for the baby!!
Counselor:	Is for the baby. Richard and Sherry are both doing pictures for the baby.

Kajha's recognition of her goal for power and control was seen in the form of questions and confusion. As play sessions continued, Kajha's recognition reflex was observed every time the counselor tracked her controlling behaviors.

The following are excerpts from session seven. In this session, there was a lot of activity and negotiating. The individual play themes started to merge into the framework of a birthday party for the baby. Kahja and Nancy had been working hard with sand and plates preparing food for a celebration. Nancy fed and rocked the baby several times during the food preparation. The other children seldom engaged in this type of interaction with the baby. Sherry hesitated in and out of the "house play" with Nancy and Kahja.

Nancy:	I am going to be the mother.
Kahja:	I can be the sister. OK, mom? *[in a baby tone]*
Sherry:	*[brings the jewelry box and all three girls begin to put on earrings and necklaces]*
Nancy and Kahja:	We are having a party for the baby! *[singing]*
Counselor:	All you girls are getting ready for the party putting on all different kinds of things.
Nancy:	*[to Kahja]* Daughter, you need to get ready!!
Counselor:	Nancy, it feels good to be the mom! You can be in charge and tell daughter what she needs to do. *[promoting insight]*
The three girls:	*[quietly try to match earrings and necklaces]*
Kahja:	*[suddenly]* Sherry needs to be the mother because she has not gotten to ever do it, and we *[Kahja and Nancy]* can be the sisters getting a surprise for the mom. OK, Sherry? Please be the mother. *[again demonstrating her need for power by directing the outcome of the play]*

Counselor: You have decided that Sherry should be the mother, and you and Nancy will be the daughters.

Sherry: *[walks away twirling around the room and ignoring Kahja's comment]*

Nancy: *[dejectedly walks away following Sherry, comes up behind her, and whispers]* Say no. Say no.

Sherry: *[laughs without answering]*

The counselor should have tracked this moment by saying, "Nancy, you really want to be the mother this time. Kahja wants Sherry to be the mother. You would like for Sherry to say no." It is not uncommon for therapists to miss this type of interaction because of the intense activity of all group members at one time. The counselor only became aware of this exchange after viewing the video of the play session. It was very brief, and all three girls soon resumed going through the jewelry box in silence.

Kahja: *[looking at the necklace Nancy is wearing]* I like that necklace. Please give me the necklace.

Nancy: No, I had it first. *[initial assertiveness as a result of catalytic effect of the play]*

Kahja: *[pouting and walking away]* Well, I am not going to play anymore.

Nancy: *[turns to the mirror and begins to comb her hair and put on lipstick]*

Counselor: Kahja, it's hard when you don't get what you want. You have decided not to play. *[attempting to promote insight]*

Kahja: *[continues to explore away from other group members for a few minutes, then returns and stands by Nancy, joining in by putting on makeup for the celebration]*

Counselor: You decided to come back and play with Nancy.

During all this time Richard was totally absorbed in building with blocks and had managed to construct an intricate design. The counselor commented throughout the play session on the different arrangements of blocks and his knowledge of creating all kinds of designs.

Richard: *[standing up proudly, showing his block design]* For the baby. *[catalytic effect]*

Kahja: For the baby . . . a present for the baby.

Richard: *[smiles broadly]*

Nancy and Sherry: *[clapping and jumping]* Yeah, Yeah, for the baby.

Counselor: Everyone is excited because the design that Richard made will be the present for the baby.

Kahja: *[pushing Sherry out of the way]* Go. Go mom. You are the mom this is a surprise for you.

Sherry: [*insists on coming back into the house area*]
Kahja: [*screaming and pushing Sherry away*] It has to be a surprise. Go. Go.
Counselor: [*to Kahja*] You want Sherry not to see what you are doing, but she does not want to do what you want.

Meanwhile, Nancy rocked and held the baby tight. Richard grabbed the baby from Nancy, who screamed in frustration, "stop it, stop it!" Nancy stomped her feet and continued her screaming while Kahja and Sherry laughed as they pushed each other, and Richard ran around with the baby.

Counselor: Nancy, things are not turning out the way you want. You don't like it when Richard takes the baby away from you.
Nancy: [*continues to scream and stomp her feet*]
Counselor: Nancy, it seems frustrating to you right now because no one is listening to you.
Counselor: There are five more minutes left in the playroom.

Grabbing the baby, Kahja went over to the plate of sand they'd set up as a birthday cake and started putting in a straw to serve as a candle. She began to sing "Happy Birthday." Sherry came and took the plate away laughing and running.

Counselor: Sherry, you don't want Kahja to celebrate the party. You figured out how to stop her. [*attempting to promote insight*]
Nancy: [*spanks Sherry, trying to make her stop laughing and running around*]

The catalytic effect of the upheaval that the other children created resulted in Nancy's outburst. This intense behavior was uncharacteristic for Nancy.

Counselor: You want Sherry to stop all that running around.

The counselor should have set limits on the spanking behavior. An example could have been: "Sherry is not for hitting. You may hit the Bobo instead."

In this session, Richard and Sherry—who usually stayed in the periphery of Nancy's and Kahja's play—intervened in a disruptive, passive-aggressive manner and dominated the turn of events. Nancy had a lot invested in the party celebration and her role as a mother. Her frustration peaked as she realized that the party was being terminated by the others' behaviors. This session clearly served as an opportunity to ease the underlying tension, paving the way to more coherent, cooperative play. Axline (1947) refers to the importance of the storming as a catalyst to change the dynamics of conflict and struggle into something resembling a state of equilibrium.

Working Stage

Gladding (1995) describes this stage as characterized by achievement of individual and group goals as the group becomes more unified and productive. Members are able to confront one another appropriately.

After the struggle in the seventh session, the birthday party was enacted at the five remaining sessions. Richard would make the baby a block design. Sherry would draw a picture. Kahja and Nancy would make the preparations in the kitchen area. They would all come together toward the end of each session to sing "Happy Birthday" and present the gifts to the baby. The following are excerpts from sessions nine and ten. At the beginning of the first excerpt, Kahja, Nancy, and Richard are working with clay, cutting it with plastic knives.

> *Kahja:* Can you give me that knife?
> *Nancy:* I still need to cut this. No.
> *Kahja:* Please, you need to share.
> *Counselor:* Kahja, you think that Nancy needs to help you when you ask for help.

To support Nancy in her efforts to assert herself, the counselor should have added: "Nancy, you decided to say no because you were still using the knife. Sometimes you can say yes to friends and sometimes you can say no."

> *Kahja:* She does not want to.
> *Nancy:* You can get a new knife.
> *Counselor:* You think she can solve her problem by getting a new knife.
> *Richard:* [hands Kahja a new knife from kitchen area]
> *Counselor:* You found a knife for Kahja. Now she can cut the clay. I wonder what would happen if Kahja could not have gotten a new knife?
> *Nancy:* Share.
> *Counselor:* Then you would share.
> *Nancy:* If she did not know where it was, I share.
> *Counselor:* In that case you would share.

At this time the counselor needed to be cognizant of balancing Nancy's therapeutic goal of risking assertiveness with Kahja against the group goal of cooperation. Nancy progressed from inappropriate aggression in the previous session to assertiveness. In the next excerpt, the group is exploring a shelf containing some games. Richard finds one he knows. Nancy leaves the area and goes to rock the baby. Sherry also leaves to try on hats.

Richard: I know this game.

Kahja: I want to play too. *[both children settle on the floor to play]*

Counselor: Richard, you and Kahja are going to give that game a try. Nancy, you are taking care of the baby. Sherry, you are trying different things on, over there.

Kahja: Oh, this is fun!! *[as Richard opens the game]*

Richard: That's what I told you.

Counselor: Kahja, you think you are going to enjoy that game. It looks like you guys are going to figure out how to play it. *[socialization]*

Nancy: *[continues feeding and rocking the baby]*

Sherry: *[tries on a hat and looks at the counselor]*

Counselor: Nancy, you are giving that baby all your attention. It looks like you know a lot about babies. Sherry, you are trying all kinds of different looks.

Richard: If you roll red you can't move . . . if you roll green you can move.

Counselor: So you think you figured out the rules for that game.

Richard: I know what to do. No, Kahja, you can only get one card, and you have to shake these first, like this. *[showing Kahja how to take her turn]*

Counselor: Richard, you are teaching how to play the game. Kahja you are doing it just like Richard told you. *[insight for Kahja]*

As counseling sessions progressed, Richard showed his ability to seek out the activities that captured his interest. He engaged effectively and with self-assurance when he chose to interact with others. Parents and teachers saw him as withdrawn and insecure prior to the play group intervention. Many times when children's style of interacting with the outside world is characterized by quiet introversion, significant adults interpret their behavior as deficient. These adults unintentionally make matters worse by trying to alter the child's natural way of managing the environment. At a later consultation, the counselor helped Richard's parents and teacher begin to view him as capable and self-confident.

Termination Stage

Gladding (1995) believes that termination is as important as the other stages of group, and that it is often overlooked. It is a transition event that leads to a new set of experiences in the group as members begin to practice new behaviors outside the group.

The following are excerpts from sessions eleven and twelve. As the first begins, Sherry has taken some traffic signs from the shelf and held them out for the counselor to see.

Counselor: You found something and you want me to see it.

Sherry: You walk around and I hold up signs and I'll tell you to stop.

Counselor: So you want me to walk around and you give me the signal to tell me to stop. *[socially acceptable way of being in control]*

Sherry: Around the table. *[pointing to a small round play table in the middle of the playroom]*

Counselor: OK, you tell me.

Sherry: Now go. *[holding up the green sign that said Go]* Now walk around and go over there. *[smiling and giggling]*

Counselor: It is fun when you tell me where to go and when I do exactly as you say. *[promoting insight]*

Kahja: *[placing herself in front of counselor, holds up a big dog puppet]* This is a doggy.

Counselor: You want me to see it.

Sherry: *[alternates stop signs and go signs]*

Counselor: You like for me to walk and tell me stop with your signs. It's kind of fun to give me directions and see me do as you tell me.

Sherry: *[grins with mischief and hides under the easel, just showing her hand holding the signs]*

Counselor: You are making it even harder. I've got to look under the easel so I won't miss the sign.

Sherry: *[laughs out loud with pleasure]*

Counselor: *[laughing also]* You think this is a lot of fun!!

During this time the others watched from their individual play areas. Sherry showed signs of self-confidence as well as trust in the counselor and other group members by controlling the play situation in an amusing and clever manner.

Sherry: *[putting the signs back on the shelf]* You can go now.

Counselor: You are through playing that game so I don't have to walk around anymore.

Sherry began to explore another shelf and carefully choose some figures. She brought them to the floor and began to place them in some type of order. Richard created another structure with blocks.

Counselor: Sherry, you seem to have another idea about what you are going to do next. Richard, you are getting ready to work on another creation.

> *Sherry:* I did a pattern—ladies/men/ladies/men/ladies/men. . . .
>
> *Counselor:* You did a pattern with ladies and men in a row.
>
> *Kahja:* That is so good, Sherry!!! *[in an excited, "grown-up" voice]*
>
> *Nancy and Richard:* *[clapping]* Yeah!! Yeah!!
>
> *Counselor:* All of you like what Sherry made.
>
> *Sherry:* *[gives them a big smile]*

The preceding excerpt shows that Sherry found the playroom a comfortable place to take risks with mastery issues. The other group members spontaneously gave her much-needed encouragement. The teacher reported that Sherry increasingly attempted new concepts taught in kindergarten. As the next excerpt begins, Richard is building. Sherry is writing letters on the board. Nancy and Kahja are "cooking" with sand.

> *Counselor:* Richard, you are carefully placing those blocks in a certain way to stop them from falling. You know a lot about creating with blocks. Sherry, you can write many different kinds of letters on the board.
>
> *Nancy:* This is a cake. This is a cake. Right?? *[asking Kahja]*
>
> *Kahja:* Is going to be a pie.
>
> *Counselor:* Nancy, you ask for Kahja's permission to name what you are making, and then you go along with her idea, not your idea.
>
> *Kahja:* *[looking at the counselor and showing the sand cake or pie]* Is this good?
>
> *Counselor:* You would like for me to tell you whether I like that or not.
>
> *Kahja:* That's good?
>
> *Counselor:* You really want to know what I think.
>
> *Kahja:* I think this is good.

The counselor refrained from answering, thus facilitating Kahja's positive response toward her own creation. Later the girls turned to each other for encouragement, adding cohesion to their relationship. Landreth (1991) and Axline (1947) both discuss the importance of not taking responsibility away from the child.

> *Counselor:* Kahja, you decided it is really good. You like what you have made. Richard, it looks like you were able to mix all different kinds of blocks together.
>
> *Richard:* Is a ship for the baby. *[raising it up from the floor]*
>
> *Counselor:* You are giving the baby the ship that you made. You worked at it and is finally done.
>
> *Nancy:* *[showing her sand creation to Kahja]* You like mine?
>
> *Kahja:* *[looking up and smiling]* Yes.

Counselor: Kahja, you also like what Nancy made.

Nancy: I like yours better. *[in a playful tone]*

Kahja: No I like yours better. *[imitating playful tone]*

Counselor: You like to encourage each other. You like what the other has made. You like to help each other feel good. *[socialization]*

Nancy: This is a cake.

Counselor: You decided that this is going to be a cake, not a pie. *[This time Kahja did not try to rename Nancy's cake.]*

Nancy: *[goes over to the baby and picks her up from the baby bed]*

Kahja: *[to Nancy]* You wake up her. I am your mom.

Nancy: *[ignores Kahja and walks around the room lovingly holding the baby]*

Counselor: You still like to be the mom, Kahja. That's the part you like the best. That's your favorite.

Kahja: *[smiling and following Nancy with a spoon full of sand]* Taste this. Just pretend.

Nancy: *[shaking her head]* No.

Counselor: Nancy, you don't want to do that.

Nancy: *[pretends to taste, without letting her mouth touch the spoon]* As long as is pretend is OK?

Kahja: These are not for real. *[showing her plate full of sand]*

Counselor: Both of you know that for real you are not supposed to eat that.

Nancy felt comfortable ignoring Kahja's request not to wake up the baby. At the same time, Kahja was able to accept Nancy's noncompliance. Nancy's odd behaviors of eating glue and crayons in the classroom had disappeared at the end of individual counseling. It was reassuring to see that after several weeks she continued to have no interest in placing nonedible objects in her mouth. This segment of play illustrates the strength gained by Nancy from the previous confrontation with other group members and from the feelings of safety and acceptance offered by the counselor in the playroom setting.

Counselor: *[looks at her watch to announce remaining time]*

Children: Oh no no!!

Counselor: You know what I am going to say. Five minutes left.

Nancy: No, six minutes.

Counselor: You wish you could stay longer in the playroom.

Kahja: *[beginning to sing]* Happy Birthday to you . . . *[bringing the sand cake that Nancy worked on]*

Nancy: *[joins in singing and picks up the baby from the bed]*

Richard: *[brings his block creation and joins in the singing]*

Sherry: [*hurries to finish a picture started earlier in the session and brings it to Nancy and the baby*] This is for you.

Counselor: Everyone has done something for the party. Nancy and Kahja have cooked and taken care of the baby, and Richard and Sherry made presents for the baby.

The birthday party took place as an unspoken union of the group members' individual play. It developed during each of the last four sessions with equal excitement and pleasure among the children. The individual themes were like parts of a puzzle that blended perfectly into the group effort signified by the party. This ritual seemed to serve as the binding force to accomplish the group goal of cooperation.

Consistent Issues Throughout the Twelve Group Meetings

During the initial stages of group work, the children would briefly join in exploration together and then quickly break apart for their individual play. As time went on, they settled into their individual themes for longer periods of time.

After the storming period they were able to fit their individual play into a group play theme of a birthday party for the baby doll. Preparing for and having the party was a part of every session after the storming period until the final group session.

Kahja's power behaviors were always present, but she did learn from Nancy's eventual assertiveness. Nancy began the group as passive, and as a result of playing with Kahja, she was able to be angry and then assertive.

Richard was an introvert who chose what he liked and felt comfortable with his block play, building, and hitting the Bobo. Unlike Nancy, who was struggling with her self-concept and relationships with others, Richard seemed comfortable to engage or disengage in play with the others.

Sherry's play centered on approval from the school counselor and wanting to be noticed. Her play in the group progressed to mastery issues. Kahja, with her need to be in charge, recognized Sherry's accomplishments many times, and the others joined in to give her recognition of her accomplishments in the play group.

This case study serves as an example of the value of the group process for children. Through interaction with fellow group members each child received feedback related to current socialization skills. Through vicarious learning experiences, all the children were able to make positive changes that will enable them to cooperate more fully in their classroom and approach learning experiences with more confidence. This group served both a remedial and preventive purpose. Each child came to the group with individual needs and addressed them through the play process.

Other Play Group Applications for Elementary School Counselors

In addition to conducting play group counseling in a traditional playroom setting, elementary school counselors use play in other ways. Depending on their goals with particular children they provide play experiences in their offices that may be structured through the use of games or toys or unstructured through the use of sand or art materials.

Initial Observation Group

The elementary school counselor's multifaceted role involves many time constraints in the educational setting. Often a school counselor does not have the opportunity to interview individual group members prior to the formation of the group. In this case the counselor can structure the first meeting as a diagnostic and observational tool. The play atmosphere provides fertile ground for learning about the lifestyles of the different members. As illustrated in this chapter, the use of art materials "to build or draw a house where all group members live" provides information about leadership, cooperation, negotiations, and verbal and nonverbal communications and alliances among members.

Therapeutic Board Games

School counselors employ therapeutic board games in play groups to help children learn ways to cope with specific, stressful issues in their lives. These cooperative, noncompetitive games have the potential to help children work cooperatively while still learning new information and strategies related to their presenting problems such as divorce, stepfamily living, impulsiveness, or friendship difficulties (Brigman & Earley, 1991).

Sandplay and Art

Sandplay and art play groups are valuable tools for the school counselor. Children, for the most part, tend to be drawn to sand and art play activities. The authors have used these play media in the following ways:

- Have the group draw a mural
- Have the group tell a story in the sand
- Have each member draw a self-portrait and tell about it
- Have the members draw what they like best about themselves

With art and sandplay, the possibilities are endless.

Structured Games with Toys

One of the authors has conducted group sessions in the counselor's office with fourth and fifth graders, structuring different games using wooden blocks of various shapes. The group members were dealing with anger control, nonassertiveness, and impulsivity. At times, the group was instructed to build a free-standing structure with the blocks. The counselor distributed the blocks, and members took turns placing their blocks in the middle of the floor. In this exercise, the members were not allowed to communicate verbally, or to move someone else's block. If the structure fell, the group started over again. Variations of this game can be employed in the following types of play sessions: adding verbal communication, allowing negotiations among players, planning the structure first, and letting members decide the rules of the game. The counselor is able to facilitate issues of tolerance, group goals versus individual needs, assertiveness, conflict resolution, and interdependence.

Summary

School counselors use play groups in a variety of ways in the school setting. Play groups are a natural, developmentally appropriate way for children to socialize, learn from one another, face emotional issues, and gain insight. These play groups range from preventive classroom guidance group activities to remedial play groups—that is, from educational counseling to activities that can be called *therapy* wherever the school environment doesn't contraindicate use of the word. The use of play groups is one of the most effective strategies available to the elementary school counselor.

References

Axline, V. M. (1947). *Play therapy: The inner dynamics of childhood.* Boston: Houghton Mifflin.

Bosdell, B. J. (1973). Counseling children with play media. In M. M. Ohlsen (Ed.), *Counseling children in groups: A forum* (pp. 27–45). Austin, TX: Holt, Rinehart and Winston.

Brigman, G., & Earley, B. (1991). *Group counseling for school counselors: A practical guide.* Portland, ME: Walch.

Dinkmeyer, D. C., Dinkmeyer, D. C., Jr., & Sperry, L. (1987). *Adlerian counseling and psychotherapy* (2nd ed.). Columbus, OH: Merrill.

Gazda, G. M. (1973). Group procedures with children: A developmental approach. In M. M. Ohlsen (Ed.), *Counseling children in groups: A forum* (pp. 118–145). Austin, TX: Holt, Rinehart and Winston.

Gerler, E. R., Jr. (Ed.). (1993). Counseling and children's play [Special issue]. *Elementary School Guidance & Counseling, 28*(3).

Ginott, H. (1961). *Group psychotherapy with children: The theory and practice of play therapy.* New York: McGraw-Hill.

Ginott, H. G. (1982). Group play therapy with children. In G. L. Landreth (Ed.), *Play therapy: Dynamics of the process of counseling with children* (pp. 327–341). Springfield, IL: Thomas.

Gladding, S. T. (1995). *Group work: A counseling specialty* (2nd ed.). Englewood Cliffs, NJ: Merrill.

Gysbers, N. C., & Henderson, P. (1988). *Developing and managing your school guidance program.* Alexandria, VA: American Counseling Association.

Harris, J. R. (1995). Where is the child's environment? A group socialization theory of development. *Psychological Review, 102,* 458–489.

Landreth, G. (1991). *Play therapy: The art of the relationship.* Muncie, IN: Accelerated Development.

Morganett, R. S. (1994). *Skills for living: Group counseling activities for elementary students.* Champaign, IL: Research Press.

Myrick, R. D. (1987). *Developmental guidance and counseling: A practical approach.* Minneapolis, MN: Educational Media Corporation.

Slavson, S. R. (Ed.). (1947). *The practice of group therapy.* New York: International Universities Press.

Slavson, S. R. (1948). Play group therapy for young children. *Nervous Child, 7,* 318–327.

Vriend, J., & Dyer, W. W. (1973). *Counseling effectively in groups.* Englewood Cliffs, NJ: Educational Technology.

Wittmer, J. (Ed.). (1993). *Managing your school counseling program: K–12 developmental strategies.* Minneapolis, MN: Educational Media Corporation.

CHAPTER NINETEEN

GROUP PLAY

Wholeness and Healing
for the Hospitalized Child

Lesley Lingnell and Lori Dunn

Hospitalization for most children is an extremely traumatic, emotional, and stressful experience. Depending on their level of development, children often experience separation, a loss of autonomy and control, fear of mutilation, guilt, pain, and rage (Adams, 1976; Alger, Linn, & Beardslee, 1985; Clatworthy, 1981; Cooper & Blitz, 1985; Golden, 1983).

Children's concept of self and self in relation to others is jeopardized as they encounter novel experiences that may involve pain and a lack of predictability. At the core of these experiences is the child's sense of loss of control. The sick child is frequently required to accept a passive role during hospitalization, and, as a result, experiences a loss of autonomy and control. In an attempt to regain control, hospitalized children often resort to negative behaviors such as tantrums, regression, angry outbursts, aggression, and noncompliance with medical regime.

Fear and anxiety are also associated with pediatric hospitalization. Some factors that may cause anxiety include separation from parents, an unfamiliar environment, medical procedures, fear of death and mutilation, and abstract explanations of hospital experiences (Adams, 1976; Clatworthy, 1981).

Feelings of fear, isolation, and anger are not concrete enough for some children to express with words. Children may be uncomfortable with their feelings or sense that they are unacceptable. Maladjustments may occur as the hospitalized child suppresses feelings and concerns in attempts to receive praise or attention from adult caregivers, who often overemphasize the necessity of being "good" or "brave." Another example of a common misconception of hospitalized children is that misbehavior, anger, or acting out may result in punishment by way of extra or more painful medical procedures. Misconceptions also occur because children can only filter new experiences through what they are already cognitively capable of understanding. For example, terms such as *CAT scan, dressing change, stretcher, put to sleep, ICU,* and *IV flush* may be too ambiguous. Because feelings of loss of control, fear, anxiety, and anger can be difficult for children to verbalize, play is imperative for young patients.

Table 19.1 provides a developmental perspective on children's expected responses to hospitalization, referring to Piaget's stages of cognitive development (1963).

Play Therapy in the Hospital

A child naturally expresses feelings about self and experiences through play (Landreth, 1991). Researchers have found that play therapy during hospitalization results in the reduction of maladaptive anxieties and fears (Adams, 1976; Cassell, 1965; Clatworthy, 1981; Cooper & Blitz, 1985; Golden, 1983). Cassell found the use of play therapy with puppets to role-play medical procedures lessened children's emotional disturbance during a cardiac catheterization. In another study, lower levels of anxiety were found in children who received daily thirty-minute sessions of therapeutic play during hospitalization (Clatworthy). Pediatric patients may use therapeutic play to facilitate communication and expressions of anxiety, fears, and questions regarding their illness and hospitalization (Adams; Brunskill, 1984).

Play therapy for the hospitalized child facilitates release of feelings and enables the child to communicate to parents and health care staff information otherwise not verbalized. While engaging in therapeutic play, the relationship between the therapist and hospitalized child is of utmost importance (Adams, 1976; Brunskill, 1984; Clatworthy, 1981; Golden, 1983). The development of trust, rapport, respect, and acceptance assists the child to achieve self-realization and master fears and anxieties (Golden, 1983; Gottlieb & Portnoy, 1988).

Group Play

Group play, by nature, often speeds the therapeutic process as children interact with each other, simulating more of a real-world situation, through facilitating expressions of feelings and anchoring the experience to the here-and-now (Berg & Landreth, 1990). Cooper and Blitz (1985) outline several benefits of play groups

TABLE 19.1. COMMON DEVELOPMENTAL RESPONSES TO HOSPITALIZATION.

Age	Developmental Tasks	Expected Responses
0–2	• Trust in caregivers • Attachment to primary caregivers • Maturation of sensory and motor functions • Object permanence	• Fussiness and irritability due to disruption of routines • Immediate response to pain—needs and seeks comfort • Stranger anxiety (beginning at about six months)
2–3	• Growing independence • Learning self-control • Language development • Limit testing • Fantasy-based play and thought processes	• Separation anxiety • Fear of strangers • Regression in skills (motor, language, toilet) • Immediate physical response to pain and unfamiliarity
4–6	• Preoperational thinking • Early moral development • Increasing independence • Awareness of sex role	• Separation anxiety • Fear of body mutilation • Anxieties resulting from ego-centric thought, fantasies, and magical thinking • Interpreting medical experiences as punishment (intense guilt feelings)
7–12	• Concrete operations • Social cooperation • Need to be creative • Increasing independence • Growing problem-solving skills	• Fear of pain • Fear or loss of control, respect, or love • Concerns about separation from peers • Modesty concerns • Fear of never being well again
13–18	• Formal operational thinking • Need for social acceptance • Identity development • Sexual maturation • Struggle between dependence and independence	• Anxiety related to long-term implications of illness or injury • Concerns about separation from peers • Anxiety related to body injury and pain • Concern for body image and changes in physical appearance • Need for privacy • Desire to be active in treatment and medical decisions

in the hospital setting. One advantage of the group play scenario is relief from social isolation by providing opportunity for interaction with peers. This interaction expedites relationship building and the development of trust within the group. Once children identify with a group, separation from parents may be easier.

Another benefit to the group setting is that reciprocal relationships among the children foster feelings of empathy, accomplishment, and self-esteem. Once children have observed peers openly expressing feelings of anger, hostility, and fear, they are more comfortable expressing their own negative feelings. Children feel more free to express such negative feelings when they observe the therapist's unconditional acceptance of behaviors and feelings of other group members (Ginott, 1958).

Personality dynamics within a group also enable children to identify with one another's strengths and needs. For example, a shy child may model the behaviors of an outgoing child, while an overactive child may develop increased self-control through identification with more reserved group members (Ginott, 1961). The group also encourages children to try out new roles that may benefit other group members. An emotionally needy child who plays caretaker for a more independent child feels more capable of caring for self. The passive child who contributes to a solution within the group gains confidence in his or her own problem-solving skills.

Group Play in the Hospital

In the hospital setting, two types of group play can be employed: therapeutic group play and group play therapy. The goal of *therapeutic group play* activities is to address the ongoing developmental, emotional, cognitive, and social needs of the child during hospitalization. By contrast, the goal of *group play therapy* (which will be addressed in more detail later in the chapter) is to address the ongoing emotional issues for the chronically ill child in an outpatient setting. Inpatient therapeutic play groups are scheduled for specific time periods during the day or evening and remain open to children of various ages and diagnoses. Because of the impact of their medical conditions, children may only be able to tolerate participating in activities for short periods of time, thus group dynamics are ever changing. This open group format also allows for parents and siblings to participate as patient needs dictate.

Leader Qualities

For children to fully experience the benefits of group play in the hospital, a well-trained leader is essential. The leader must possess the ability to accept, respect, and empathize with children (Ginott, 1982; Landreth, 1991). The group leader in the hospital setting must maintain awareness of medical equipment such as IV poles, chest tubes, wheelchairs, traction beds, and oxygen tanks, without allowing it to become a barrier in the play process. Often, the leader advocates for medical treatments and procedures to be scheduled around group play times so a child is able to benefit fully from the group process. The leader uses an understanding of play behaviors typical for hospitalized children to make developmental assessments of children's coping with their medical experiences. In accordance with the philosophy of child-centered play therapy (Axline, 1969), the group leader employs communication skills that return control, promote independence, recognize feelings, and encourage self-acceptance.

Child Life Specialists

Child life specialists are specially trained professionals who provide therapeutic group play activities in the hospital. Child life specialists may receive training in various fields of study, including child development, psychology, counseling, and education. Regardless of the specific degree emphasis, a thorough knowledge of child development and of the impact of hospitalization and illness on development is essential. Child life specialists should complete an internship under the supervision of a certified child life specialist before being considered for employment. The child life specialist makes ongoing assessments of the ill child's coping with hospitalization through interaction with the child on an individual basis and in the group play setting. These assessments become the basis for treatment plans that address the developmental and emotional needs of the hospitalized child. Child life specialists firmly believe that play is children's primary modality of communication, expression, and healing (Child Life Council, 1995). In some health care institutions, other professionals such as social workers, pediatric counselors, and psychologists may also provide such services.

Playroom Environment

The playroom environment must be inviting and warm, conveying a message to the ill child that this place is safe and familiar (Golden, 1983; Landreth, 1991). No medical procedures are permitted in the playroom, and medical staff are invited into the playroom with the understanding that they are present only to talk or play. This stipulation promotes emotional safety and predictability for the children, controls for disruptions in the children's play processes, and facilitates freedom of expression. For example, if a child were to receive an injection in the playroom, this would incite fear not only in that child but also in other group members, who might fear they would be next to receive an injection. Allowing interruptions of this type inhibits patients from fully immersing in their play because their environment is not consistent or predictable. The playroom is often the one place in the hospital where a child can make choices and experience control.

As Berg and Landreth (1990) suggest, a large room that allows for privacy and freedom within limits, with toys openly displayed, is recommended for groups in the hospital. Adequate playroom space is essential to allow for wheelchairs, wagons, traction beds, and IV poles. Toys available to the children should be suitable for all ages and developmental levels and represent three broad groups: real-life toys, toys that release aggression and allow for acting out, and toys for creative expression and enhancement of self-concept (Berg & Landreth). Hospital-related toys and medical equipment are essential for the hospital playroom. These items allow children to safely explore new or threatening experiences and provide opportunities for children to feel control over the health care environment.

Infection control is an important consideration in the hospital environment. The hospital therapist must remember that many children with ongoing medical problems are more susceptible to infection than is usual outside a hospital practice. Toys need to be cleaned after each play session in accordance with the hospital's infection control standards. The playroom itself should also be meticulously cleaned and disinfected on a regular basis.

The following list includes suggestions for the hospital playroom.

Medical Items (use real equipment when possible, and when working with a group of children with the same diagnosis, use more diagnosis-specific medical items):

Cotton balls	Syringes
Alcohol wipes	Tourniquet
Blood pressure cuff	IV tubing and bag
Pulse oximeter probe	Oxygen mask
Anesthesia mask	Cardiac leads
Specimen bottle	Blood collection tubes
Medicine bottles	Medicine cups
Tongue depressors	Bandages and Band-Aids
Gauze	Tape and scissors
Stethoscope	Surgical hats, masks, and gloves
Hospital ID bands	Thermometer

Medical Toys:

Ambulance	Helicopter	Toy medical kit
Police car	Fire truck	

Hospital room and operating room play sets, such as Playmobile

Stuffed animals, dolls, or medical teaching dolls to serve as "patients"

Sibling Participation

Research highlights the psychosocial needs of siblings of hospitalized children. Common emotional responses of healthy brothers and sisters may include guilt about being healthy or that they did something to cause their sibling's illness; fear about their own health or about their sibling's possible death; anger over the extra attention their sibling receives because of the illness and disappointment about having to be separated from their parents for lengthy periods of time; and increased anxiety due to misconceptions about the hospital environment and medical treatments (Craft, 1993; Sieman, 1984; Swain, Sexson, Brown, & Ragab, 1993). Involving siblings in the therapeutic group play activities not only promotes continuation of their relationship with the ill child, but also facilitates recognition and acceptance of their feelings and unique issues related to their sibling's hospitalization. Participation in group play also increases their understanding of and empathy for what their sibling is experiencing and encourages them to play an active role during their ill brother or sister's hospitalization.

Parent Participation

Parents of hospitalized children find their role as primary caretakers is no longer possible and must be shared with or taken over by health care personnel (Knox & Hayes, 1983). This intensifies their feelings of helplessness over the illness and not being able to help their child. An ongoing model program designed to decrease the negative impact of frequent hospitalizations found parents in need of a focus on parent-child interactions (Brill et al., 1987). By being present during group play, parents have the opportunity to engage in normal play routines with their child. Parents benefit from observation of and instruction by the child life specialist in the areas of limit setting, recognizing feelings, and returning control. Parents may use these skills outside of the playroom to enhance their relationship with their child and to gain insight into their child's feelings and behaviors. During a time when parents feel out of control and vulnerable, these play interactions increase parents' feelings of competence as they do something positive with their ill child.

Group Play Process

The child life specialist invites all children who are medically able to attend scheduled play activities. The child life specialist greets the children as they enter the playroom and introduces the playroom as a place where children can choose to do many of the things they would like to do (Landreth, 1991). This introduction emphasizes to children and any accompanying adults that children direct their play. Based on assessments of predicted group dynamics and needs of individual patients, the child life specialist plans an unstructured group activity. Activities that are open-ended and directed solely by the children encourage creativity, feelings of control, and expression of feelings related to self and hospitalization. Landreth also notes that the child life specialist enhances the therapeutic process through facilitative comments that free children from adult expectation and convey acceptance of the children and of their feelings and experiences. These facilitative responses create group cohesion and contribute to each child's identification with other group members.

Case Example

After undergoing an IV start (an invasive medical procedure in which a catheter is inserted into a vein using a needle), José entered the playroom and decided to sit at the activity table with the group. Using the materials provided, José completed a medical collage and then proceeded to cover it in black paint.

> *José:* I hate this place.
>
> *Child life specialist:* *[recognizing and accepting José's feelings]* You hate a lot of the things you have to do here, and you've decided to cover that up.

Following José's lead the other children in the group also covered their pictures in paint and began to discuss things they did not like about the hospital.

> *Child life specialist:* *[facilitating group identification]* Sounds like some of you feel the same as José.
>
> *Lisa:* *[hospitalized for asthma]* I hate when I have to get breathing treatments.
>
> *Sam:* *[speaking directly to José]* I didn't like getting that *[the IV]* either, but I'd rather have that than get a shot.
>
> *Child life specialist:* *[validating Sam's knowledge and positive focus]* You can think of something the IV is good for.

> *José:* At least we can come to the playroom.
>
> *Child life specialist:* *[acknowledging José's coping strategy]* You've figured out something that helps when you're in the hospital.

The group then moved into painting the activity table together, laughing and sharing medical experiences. The child life specialist continued to recognize feelings and the hard work involved in complying with medical procedures.

This example shows that José was able to enter the unstructured activity and take it in the direction he needed to go. Other group members were able to identify with and support José's feelings, and the activity ended up being cathartic for all involved. The child life specialist had not planned for the children to paint the table, yet by allowing the group to lead the therapeutic process, the child life specialist enabled the children to engage in decision making and control their activity, and also enabled each individual child to find personal meaning within the activity.

Group Medical Play

Medical play is another therapeutic technique used by the child life specialist to inform children about the plans and purposes of medical events, to provide children with an expressive outlet, to relieve misconceptions, and to gain insight into children's coping and understanding. In group medical play, children experience the same therapeutic benefits as previously mentioned for group play. Medical play is the process by which medical items (listed earlier) are provided for children to manipulate and to experiment with on an inanimate object, such as a stuffed animal or doll. Medical items are only to be used on fantasy objects rather than people to maintain emotional safety and to minimize potential guilt feelings in the children who are participating. Medical play allows children to rehearse coping strategies, act out the role of a doctor or nurse, experience catharsis, explore unfamiliar medical equipment, and gain understanding of the purposes of various medical items.

Group medical play may take place during scheduled group play activities where the ages and diagnoses of patients are varied. Medical play in this setting can occur spontaneously as directed by the participants. For example, during one hospital group play time, a patient with a broken leg in a traction bed noticed several of the other children in the playroom had an IV just like her. The child also commented on another patient's chest tube and asked what it was for. This child's questions stimulated conversation among several of the other patients, including a surgery patient, a child with cancer, and a child with pneumonia. To facilitate further group conversation, as well as to promote understanding of each child's different medical equipment, the child life specialist brought out several dolls and the medical play supplies for the children to explore. The children started IVs, gave shots, administered medicine, checked temperature and blood pressure, and sent blood samples to the lab. At one point in their play, one child stated, "If you are bad, you are going to get a shot!" Another child quickly responded, "You don't get shots because you are bad." The child life specialist added, "In the hospital, you only get a shot if your doctor says you need one to help you get better." Through the medical play experience, the children experimented with different roles of medical staff, explored real medical equipment in a nonthreatening environment, and expressed curiosity about things they had observed or experienced. A specific misconception was alleviated and replaced with a more realistic understanding.

Group medical play can also be used with a selected population of patients as identified by the child life specialist. Children who have diagnosis-specific concerns, feel isolated because of illness or treatments, or have not displayed development of specific coping strategies ideally should be included in group medical play sessions.

Case Example

Jessica, age eight, newly diagnosed with diabetes, was referred to the child life specialist by her nurse, who reported Jessica was having difficulty complying with daily medical routine, including finger sticks and insulin injections. The child life specialist's intervention was to create a group medical play scenario involving Jessica and Kendra, a seven-year-old, who was regularly hospitalized for cystic fibrosis and had established effective coping techniques for her many medical procedures. During the medical play session, Kendra led the girls into initiating a blood draw on a stuffed bear. She was purposeful in carrying out the procedure and began to wipe the bear's arm with an alcohol swab.

Child life specialist: *[indicating the girls' choice in coping strategy]* Does the bear want to watch or look away?

Kendra: He wants to watch. I watch when I get mine done.

Jessica: Ohhhh. I can't stand to watch.

Kendra: That's your choice.

Child life specialist: *[emphasizing that Jessica still has other choices]* You each know what works best for you. Kendra, what are some other things the bear wants to do when he has to have this done?

Kendra: He can tell the doctor to count to three, so he'll know just when the poke will happen.

Jessica: He could ask his mom to hold his hand.

Child life specialist: It helps to have support when you are scared.

Kendra finishes the procedure, then Jessica picks up the medical items.

Jessica: Now, let's do it my way.

Kendra and the child life specialist follow Jessica's lead and validate her choices of coping techniques for the bear. After completing the blood draw, Jessica appeared confident and stated, "Next time, I'm going to ask my mom to hold my hand."

Through identifying with a same-age peer, Jessica quickly moved from a passive to a more active role in coping with her medical regime. The group setting offered her support and validation and gave her an opportunity to try out alternative behaviors. Kendra took on a leadership role and experienced a sense of mastery over the medical procedure. Group medical play helped the girls recognize their strengths and develop confidence in their own abilities to comply with future procedures.

Group Play Therapy in the Hospital

Therapists are becoming increasingly aware of the benefits of outpatient play therapy in the hospital setting, particularly of group play therapy as an intervention to address the emotional needs of children with chronic medical issues. Children with chronic disease or prolonged acute illness such as cancer, cystic fibrosis, asthma, sickle cell anemia, or HIV, or needing long-term medical follow-up of the type required by burn victims or victims of a traumatic injury, benefit from on-site group play therapy services.

Parents have reported that children often dread regular outpatient hospital visits and may demonstrate emotional and behavioral difficulties prior to, during, and after these visits. A child's experience of loss of control may begin before leaving home when anticipating going to the hospital. Group play therapy in conjunction with regularly scheduled hospital visits promotes predictability, returns control, facilitates peer identification, and provides a safe and trusting relationship with an adult in the hospital setting. A child's comment while en route to the hospital best illustrates this benefit: "I know I have to go to that scary room, but then I get to go to the playroom."

Outpatient play therapy services in the hospital are convenient for parents, who usually have a hectic schedule and have difficulty keeping medical appointments.

Parents are forced to juggle the ill child's medication schedule and hospital appointments along with usual family routines. Busy parents of children with medical needs, unfortunately, may not place a high priority on emotional needs, so they may not take advantage of counseling services at another location outside the hospital.

The hospital play therapist is able to work closely with a multidisciplinary medical team to provide insight into a child's emotional needs and coping issues. Therefore, when comprehensive care plans that incorporate psychosocial and medical needs are developed, the ongoing input of the play therapist is valuable to the medical staff. Additionally, providing group play therapy services in the hospital setting maximizes therapy time and allows the therapist to provide counseling services to more children.

The goal of group play therapy in the hospital setting builds on the theoretical basis for group psychotherapy with children. Group counseling for children provides opportunities for a child to gain insight into self and others, experience catharsis, experiment with new feelings and behaviors in a safe environment, identify with same-age peers, and explore consequences of behavior in relation to others (Ginott, 1961).

Since children's developmental understanding of their illness has great impact on their coping, it is crucial when working with groups that the children are all functioning at the same developmental level. Many authors agree that children in group counseling should not differ in age by more than one year (Dinkmeyer & Muro, 1971; Ginott, 1982; Gumaer, 1984). The size of the group is an important consideration when attempting to provide for an atmosphere that is safe as well as therapeutic. Groups of no more than four children seem to be most effective in the hospital setting. It is important that each child receive individual reflection of feelings and acceptance of behavior and feelings. Play therapy groups in the hospital are closed in that children start at about the same time and no new members are added during the course of therapy.

Special Considerations

When selecting children for a play therapy group, consideration is given to a child's diagnosis, coping, understanding of illness, and support system. Children with various diagnoses can be selected for a group, since children tend to relate based on experiences more than on diagnosis. With a diagnosis such as HIV, for example, children who know their diagnosis should not be included in groups with children who do not know their diagnosis. For obvious reasons, information may be shared in the group that could cause confusion for a child who has been assessed as not yet ready for disclosure of his or her illness and its implications.

Placing children who employ negative coping behaviors such as noncompliance, aggressive and angry outbursts, and withdrawal in groups with children who have well-developed positive coping skills can promote behavioral modeling, learning of new skills, and peer support that individual play therapy can not provide. During group play therapy, children gain insight into their own coping abilities (Ginott, 1961). For the child who has already demonstrated positive coping, the group process can recognize and validate these effective coping skills.

The group format facilitates informal comments and discussions about children's diagnoses and home care issues. Children often learn more easily from other children than they do from the medical jargon and complicated explanations offered by adults. The group play therapy process naturally increases a child's understanding of his or her illness and encourages the child to accept the illness as a part of life through interaction and identification with the experiences of same-age peers.

Incorporating children with minimal family or peer support into a play therapy group offers a support system within the group that can be extended into other medical situations. For example, a child whose parent is unable to be present during weekly injections can be supported by members of his or her play therapy group during these injections. Children also use the support available within the play therapy group to vent feelings of disappointment or anger about the lack of family support and to express fears and anxieties related to medical experiences.

The hospital play therapist must possess the same skills and training as the child life specialist with additional training in counseling and specific coursework and supervision in play therapy. Ideally, this would include a graduate degree and meeting the criteria of a Registered Play Therapist as outlined by the Association for Play Therapy (1996).

Group Play Therapy Issues

After forming a play therapy group using the criteria discussed in the preceding section, the hospital play therapist schedules either weekly or bimonthly group meetings that may be coordinated with the children's outpatient appointments. During the group session, the play therapist places emphasis on reflecting individual feelings and behaviors of each child as well as interpersonal dynamics and interactions among group members. According to child-centered play therapy (Axline, 1969), children who are given unconditional positive acceptance in a relationship that brings warmth and trust as well as understanding and permissiveness can fully reach their potential. When abiding by this theory, the therapist's objective is the relationship with each individual child rather than group cohesion. No group goals exist, and limits are only set as children test them in order to ensure the safety of group members, therapist, and playroom property (Berg & Landreth, 1990; Ginott, 1961).

There are several play themes typical of children with medical issues seen in the group play therapy setting. Children's developmental responses to hospitalization and illness are reflected in their play themes. The most common theme demonstrated by children of all ages with medical issues in play therapy is the attempt to gain control. Children experience loss of control in that medical treatments are not a choice, medical treatments infringe on daily childhood activities, and unwanted side effects cannot be controlled. A child may attempt to control behaviors of other group members, frequently test limits, or select toys that put them in charge, such as handcuffing the therapist or other children or pointing the dart gun at them. Associated with the need to experience control is the need to feel powerful. Experiences such as being held down by adults for medical procedures or having to take medicine or come to the hospital against their will increase children's feelings of powerlessness. Children use aggressive play to feel in control or powerful. Examples of children's play may include being a super hero, beating on the punching bag, and playing out good versus evil scenarios with dinosaurs or army figures. Opportunities to release aggressive feelings in play therapy help children feel more in control of their anger outside the play therapy room and validate feelings that are typically viewed as inappropriate.

Another prevalent theme among chronically ill children in group play therapy is the need to experience freedom. Children experience freedom when they are able to give other children permission to do those things that can only be done in the play therapy room, such as being messy or noisy. While experiencing this freedom within a group play therapy session, one child repeatedly spit water around the room while another child went to the sink and refilled his cup.

Children with ongoing medical issues encounter multiple constraints on their normal growth and development. Having to comply with doctor appointments, medications and treatments, and sometimes activity or diet restrictions as well can rob children of valued childhood experiences. Children use group play therapy to engage in normal developmental play and to enjoy "just being a kid."

Similarly, children often respond to parents' overprotectiveness by using the play therapy setting to engage in caretaking behaviors, such as adopting a parental role in playing house with the other children or in caring for the dolls. Children may also reverse roles and dictate how they want to be cared for by other group members. For children who have difficulty separating from their parents, it is easier to leave their parent's side when joining a group of other children to go to the play therapy room (Ginott, 1961). Establishing relationships of trust with the group members and with the therapist promotes an overall sense of trust in other hospital staff.

It is important for the play therapist to remember that a child with a medical diagnosis not only deals with issues surrounding that diagnosis, but also with many of the same adjustment issues typical for a child of that age. These adjustment issues may include divorce, sibling rivalry, moving to a new school, house, or city, school-related problems, difficulty getting along with peers, abuse, recent death in the family, or trauma. When a child becomes more focused on working through one of these issues, the therapist may want to consider seeing that child in individual play therapy. The therapist should maintain a broad perspective when assessing children's play themes so as to avoid becoming too focused on medical issues. Of paramount importance is the relationship with each child and allowing the children to take therapy in the direction in which they need it to go.

Conclusion

It is evident that therapeutic group play is beneficial to children during hospitalization in helping them cope effectively with the experience. Group play therapy is an effective tool in supporting patients with ongoing medical issues. Although therapeutic group play and group play therapy may differ in structure, leadership, and group composition, the group format itself provides children with a means to endure the stress involved with hospitalization and ongoing medical issues.

References

Adams, M. (1976). A hospital play program: Helping children with serious illness. *American Journal of Orthopsychiatry, 45*(3), 416–424.

Alger, I., Linn, S., & Beardslee, W. (1985). Puppetry as a therapeutic tool for hospitalized children. *Hospital and Community Psychiatry, 36,* 129–130.

Association for Play Therapy. (1996). Registered Play Therapist Application. Fresno, CA: Author.

Axline, V. (1969). *Play therapy.* New York: Ballantine.

Berg, R., & Landreth, G. (1990). *Group counseling: Concepts and procedures* (2nd ed.). Muncie, IN: Accelerated Development.

Brill, N., Cohen, S., Fauvre, M., Klein, N., Clark, S., & Garcia, L. (1987). Caring for chronically ill children: An innovative approach to care. *Children's Health Care, 164*(2), 105–113.

Brunskill, S. (1984). Play therapy for the hospitalized child. *American Urology Association Journal, 54*(2), 17–18.

Cassell, S. (1965). Effect of brief puppet therapy upon the emotional responses of children undergoing cardiac catheterization. *Journal of Consulting Psychology, 29*(1), 1–8.

Child Life Council. (1995). *Child Life Council position statement.* Rockville, MD: Author.

Clatworthy, S. (1981). Therapeutic play: Effects on hospitalized children. *Journal of the Association for the Care of Children's Health, 9*(4), 108–113.

Cooper, S., & Blitz J. (1985). A therapeutic play group for hospitalized children with cancer. *Journal of Psychosocial Oncology, 3*(2), 23–37.

Craft, M. (1993). Siblings of hospitalized children: Assessment and intervention. *Journal of Pediatric Nursing, 8*(5), 289–297.

Dinkmeyer, D., & Muro, J. (1971). *Group counseling: theory and practice.* Itasca, IL: Peacock.

Ginott, H. (1958). Play group therapy: A theoretical framework. *International Journal of Psychotherapy, 8,* 410–418.

Ginott, H. (1961). *Group psychotherapy with children: The theory and practice of play therapy.* New York: McGraw-Hill.

Ginott, H. (1982). Group play therapy with children. In G. L. Landreth (Ed.), *Play therapy: Dynamics of the process of counseling with children* (pp. 327–341). Springfield, IL: Thomas.

Golden, B. (1983). Play therapy for hospitalized children. In C. D. Schaefer & K. J. O'Connor (Eds.), *Handbook of play therapy* (pp. 213–233). New York: Wiley.

Gottlieb, S., & Portnoy, S. (1988). The role of play in a pediatric bone marrow transplantation unit. *Children's Health Care, 16*(3), 177–181.

Gumaer, J. (1984). *Counseling and therapy for children.* New York: Free Press.

Knox, J., & Hayes, V. (1983). Hospitalization of a chronically ill child: A stressful time for parents. *Issues in Comprehensive Pediatric Nursing, 6,* 217–226.

Landreth, G. (1991). *Play therapy: The art of the relationship.* Muncie, IN: Accelerated Development.

Piaget, J. (1963). *The origins of intelligence in children.* New York: Norton.

Sieman, M. (1984). Siblings of the chronically ill or disabled child. *Nursing Clinics of North America, 19*(2), 295–307.

Swain, A., Sexson, S., Brown, T., & Ragab, A. (1993). Family adaptation and coping among siblings of cancer patients, their brothers and sisters, and nonclinical controls. *American Journal of Family Therapy, 21*(1), 60–70.

CHAPTER TWENTY

GROUP PLAY THERAPY WITH GRIEVING CHILDREN

Jane Le Vieux

Miss Jane, you mean I'm not the only one. . .
—MARK, AGE SIX

Play is the child's language. It is the most natural source of self-expression for children between the ages of three and eight. It can be used in many ways, shapes, and forms. Play therapy allows the therapist to establish a relationship with the child, to find out more about the child's world, and to uncover the child's fears, anxieties, and defenses. Through play therapy the child's unconscious and conscious material is acted out, often alleviating the pain and turmoil that exists in the child's life (LeVieux, 1993).

Group play therapy is the approach often used for children between the ages of four and eight (Ginott, 1961; Kottman, 1995; Landreth, 1991). Children are often a part of many and various types of groups throughout their early learning experiences. Children are often taught in groups, they live in groups, and almost always play in groups. There is opportunity for learning that cannot always be provided in one-to-one relationships with an adult. It is here in the group setting that children can learn to master such qualities as empathy, concern, cooperation, jealousy, anger, and even joy. Young children are often more comfortable in a group setting rather than individually.

Some research indicates that children who have experienced severe trauma, such as the death of someone close to them, are not acceptable candidates for group therapy (Terr, 1991). It has been assumed that these children would fare better in individual therapy. However, in my own practice, I have come to value and respect the ability of children to deal with death and its effects on their lives over the years. In a group setting, these bereaved children can find comfort and relief in the positive influence of a peer group.

Children dealing with the loss of a significant other often experience isolation from their peers because of the impact death has played in their lives. The world that once felt so safe and secure now feels strange and unbelievable. Everything in the child's life appears to have changed overnight. "My friends don't know what it's like!" is a common refrain. The group setting provides children a safe place to know they are not alone (Ginott, 1961). Death, the common denominator, makes them all similar in some shape, form, or fashion. The group setting provides the children a shelter where behaviors can be explored. A grief play therapy group can provide the child with peers to normalize emotions and changes, removing the feelings of isolation that death often brings to children, and can help them discover ways to remember the deceased loved one. The group becomes a safe haven where all feeling can be expressed and understood and where participants can learn new ways to express feelings.

Parents, significant others, or the surviving caregiver are often unable to support the grieving child because they are dealing with their own grief issues. In many cases, children are shielded from grief. My encounters over the years have taught me that the ability of children to cope depends on the important adults in their lives sharing and expressing their own grief and concerns to the child (LeVieux, 1993). Children learn by example and learn much from the adults they look up to in their life. Unfortunately, even the best of parents may feel helpless to guide their child during this difficult time.

Children may even attempt to protect their parents by refraining from expressing their own grief. Group play therapy for grieving children may inspire children to express their feelings at home once they have left the group setting. Groups help children explore their thoughts and feelings about death and dying while finding meaning in life and living.

Composition of the Group

Play therapy groups for bereaved children should be carefully thought out and planned. The children in these groups are often exposed to a variety of circumstances related to the cause of their bereavement. Early on you will decide what works best for your group makeup. Depending on the area in which you live, you may or may not want your group to be homogeneous. In my practice, I find it useful to combine children coping with homicide, terminal illness, sudden death, and even suicide in the same group. When questioned about my rationale for this type of grouping, I explain to parents and other therapists that it is an unfortunate fact that children today are exposed to violent deaths in many shapes and forms. Children know that people die senselessly. They know that people kill other people as well as themselves. Children can learn from each other about the uniqueness of their grief and appropriate ways to express themselves. The diversity in the group offers the children new opportunities to respond to their peers. I have observed children in these groups learn to trust again, especially when the world seems like a scary, unpredictable, and frightening place.

It is important for therapists to be aware of the different emotions that may be expressed depending on the type of death. Children who have experienced a murder in their family may feel vulnerable and a need to place blame. Knowing that the special person in their life died through a senseless act can add overwhelming feelings of unrest, suspicion, violation, and defenselessness. Survivors of murder victims can feel misplaced in a society that does not understand. Placement in this group allows the children to support one another as well as learn sensitivity to different situations. This allows the children to be exposed to other children not only with behaviors similar to theirs but also with issues that are complementary to their own.

In the process of group selection, the developmental level of the child is more important than age. I usually try to group children who are within a year of each other's age. For example, six- and seven-year-olds would be grouped together. Same-sex groups appear to work well with children of school age. Selection for grief play therapy groups requires the therapist to select children who seem likeliest to be helped. I make a note of how recently the loss occurred. In my practice, I have found that the family system is very chaotic during the first three months following a death. There is much to be done during this period—not to mention the variety of feelings each family member is experiencing. It is difficult for caregivers to make sure that children attend sessions with the reliable consistency needed for therapeutic progress if the death is too recent. Nevertheless, I will accept children into the group regardless of the time period providing the caregiver understands the need for consistency of attendance.

Caregiver Interview

Prior to accepting a child into the group, I interview the family member seeking participation for the child, whether a parent or other caregiver. I gather as much information as I can about the child, including information about behaviors exhibited before and after the death. The caregiver's physical and emotional accessibility to the child can pose several types of problems for the child. Often, the parents or other caregivers are lacking in emotional availability, dealing with grief reactions of their own so strong that they cannot be emotionally available to the child.

Throughout the therapy process, I maintain communication with the caregivers. I have found this to be a crucial element in group retention. The objectives of the group and its process and routines are explained so that the adults feel involved and invested in the process. At the end of each session, I explain to the caregivers what the topic of the session has been. This helps them to be prepared for any related questions and thoughts that may be explored by the child during the week.

Factors Influencing Children's Grief Responses

Children react to death in many different ways, which differ both by age and by individual temperament. Their grief is often expressed in ways unlike those employed by adults. To summarize briefly, between the ages of two and five, many grieving children become clinging to primary caregivers. They are often afraid to be alone or away from home. Their repetitive requests for answers to the same questions may become tedious for the primary caregiver. Because of these children's egocentric nature, they may believe that they caused the death. They also tend to believe that death is reversible and to engage in magical thinking: "If I am very good, mom will come back." Their play behaviors often exhibit re-enactment of events as well as being reunited with the deceased. Children between the ages of six and nine do understand that death is irreversible. They become concerned that those they love may also die. These children may show an increased interest in staying home or become overly concerned about the primary caregiver's health and well-being. At the same time, they tend to avoid emotional pain at all costs, which leads them to play wildly, act silly, and become easily distracted when the deceased is spoken of. They desperately want to be like their peers and often express their feelings by acting out rather than talking. Between the ages of nine and twelve, many children tend to keep emotions inside. They may become self-conscious about expressing their emotions, feelings, and thoughts. Some may ask for help. They are apt to be confused about what to say or how to act. As a result, many become withdrawn, quiet, and irritable.

Trying to grasp the various meanings and concepts of death is a difficult task for children of all ages. It is important to recognize that children do grieve. When a parent or sibling dies, it is often speculated that because children are young, they are oblivious and not affected or changed by the death. As play therapists and adults, we need to recognize and fully accept that children do have feelings. Informing the surviving parent or caregiver of this crucial issue is essential to the growth of the child throughout the grief process.

Preschoolers

Preschool children do not have the cognitive ability to verbalize what is happening in their minds and bodies. These feelings of being scared, lonely, and unsure of life are all very new to them, especially in times of loss. Often the preschooler sees death as temporary and reversible (Webb, 1993; Weber & Fournier, 1985; Wolfelt, 1993). This inability to see death as irreversible may result in the child asking the same questions over and over. They do not understand that when someone dies that person can no longer eat, sleep, or get hungry. The preschooler often thinks that the person who died chose to leave or go away. In the child's mind, if they chose to leave they can certainly decide when to come back. Preschool children are self-referential and concrete in their understanding of death.

Preschool children have an unsophisticated sense of causality (Webb, 1993). Often they are likely to credit factors related to the death to elements related in time and space. For example, if a mother and child get into a fight shortly before the mother's death, the child may believe that the death was caused by the fight. Seemingly unrelated events are causally related if children perceive them together. This "transductive reasoning" leads to images of particular events that often catch adults off guard.

Children of this age can often scare themselves with the power of their own creations (Speece & Brent, 1996; Webb, 1993). Their thinking remains concrete and is governed by fantasy and imagination. If they do not quite understand what has happened, they will try to make sense of it in their own world. Sometimes their thoughts are even more frightening than the truth.

Preschool children generally see all natural events as occurring with themselves at the center. Piaget (1954) described the thinking of children in this preconceptual stage as egocentric, animistic, and artificialistic. They have difficulty seeing any other point of view but their own. Adults can explore children's understanding of events and offer explanations that may fuel a reorganization in the child's thinking, but should not be surprised if the child's logic persists (Piaget & Inhelder, 1969).

For preschool children, exploration of death and grief requires an abundant amount of tolerance on the part of families because of their own emotional pain. It is often difficult for parents to deal with their own grief, much less with their child's pain. Children are sensitive to a parent's needs for emotional stability and safety in their lives. You may see them suppress their own feelings in an effort to adapt to the adult world.

School-Aged Children

Children in the concrete operational stage of development, roughly seven to ten years of age, are able to understand the concept of death and its finality in more logical and less magical—though still concrete—ways. Children in this age group also correspond to the psychoanalytic stage of latency (Webb, 1993). They will typically appear to the outside observer to be the least affected by the death of a close family member. In comparison to preschoolers, who are creative and expressive, school-aged children want nothing more than to draw accurate observations of what is reality. This age group typically tends to be more avoidant of speaking about their grief (LeVieux, 1993). School-aged children are especially vulnerable to fears that the death was somehow caused by something they said, did, or thought. It is, however, unlikely that they will verbalize these fears.

Children this age are also often misunderstood. Their vulnerability differs from that of preschool children, whose cognitive distortion is more obvious. School-aged children, with their more sophisticated capacities to repress or avoid overwhelming emotional information, want more than anything to be ordinary, just like their peers. To be asked questions about their parent's death is difficult and often marks them as being outside the norm. They believe that if things are not spoken, then they can act as if everything is just as it was before the death. School-aged children continue to demonstrate many of the preconceptual qualities of thinking typical of preschoolers. The ways in which children think and obtain knowledge as they develop into middle childhood are apparently less rigid than the Piagetian cognitive stage was once thought to be (Hobbs, Perrin, & Ireys, 1985).

The cognitive-emotional transition in school-aged children, and its implications for understanding bereavement, is important in observing children referred for problems in the classroom and at home. While their symptoms may look like Attention Deficit Hyperactivity Disorder (ADHD), it is important to look at the child's behavior before and after the death (Wolfelt, 1993). Normal bereavement and ADHD have a common factor—acting out. Many bereaved children express their pain of grief by wandering around the classroom. Some have a difficulty staying on task, while others express their anger on the playground. A swift diagnosis of a disruptive behavior disorder may overlook an important grief issue.

School-aged children also have a new capacity to repress, an unfortunate byproduct of maturation. They are able to simplify the complete self through more elaborate categorizations and stereotyping of their experiences (Piaget, 1954). They understand the finality of death, but their misunderstandings of the cause of death can be confusing to them. The fear of losing another loved one, especially the remaining parent, can produce considerable anxiety. Anxiety can also be associated with children fearing for their own safety.

Children grieve! Unlike adults, their grief responses are many and varied. Each age group has its own grief responses, which will be discussed further. Guidelines and suggestions for therapists and adults should be reviewed often.

It is important to note that a diagnosis of depression is not valid within two months following the death of a loved one unless there is marked impairment. Deciding whether a child is depressed or experiencing a normal grief reaction is a difficult assignment for the therapist. In a study by Weller, Weller, Fristad, and Bowes (1991), bereaved children were compared with inpatient depressed children and displayed several significant differences that aid in the diagnosis process. Bereaved children often report similar symptoms to those reported by depressed children—loss of interest, increase or decrease in appetite, sleep disturbances, guilt, agitation, and suicidal thoughts. It is important to note, however, that bereaved children reported fewer symptoms than depressed children. There were large differences between the groups on sleep disturbance (29 percent of bereaved versus 74 percent of depressed), fatigue (8 percent of bereaved versus 76 percent of depressed), inability to stay focused (5 percent of bereaved versus 47 percent of depressed), and guilty feelings (21 percent of bereaved versus 76 percent of depressed). While there is some overlap between bereavement and depression that the therapist should keep in mind, differential diagnosis becomes an important issue in terms of treatment.

Behavioral Responses

Most adults do not understand the process of childhood grief because they are not aware of the variety of characteristics of grief that arise from the child's cognitive and affective development. Children generally do not understand the finality of death and, before the age of six, tend to view it as reversible (Corr & Corr, 1996; Furman, 1974; Koocher, 1974, 1986; Webb, 1993).

Even preschool children can have an understanding of much about death and grief. A child's understanding of death and the circumstances that caused the death consists of information that is concrete and may lead to confusion. The egocentricity of the child who has experienced the death of a parent often leads to asking questions such as: Will someone else that I love leave? Was it something that I did or said that made them die? Who is going to take care of me now? There is often extreme confusion and fear in these children. They will need accurate information and a significant amount of support.

When an event becomes so overwhelming for children, they often attempt to blame themselves and feel responsible for the event in an effort to deny that bad things can happen indiscriminately (Terr, 1991; Webb, 1993). Children, unlike adults, are unable to clarify their distortions on their own. Because of this, the adults involved need to give the child accurate and concrete information regarding the death and its circumstances. Suicide and trauma often leave the young child feeling bewildered and perplexed. When protecting the child from information regarding the trauma, adults unintentionally jeopardize the child's ability to integrate the experience (Bluebond-Langner, 1978; Bowlby, 1980; Webb, 1993). Even when a death has been anticipated, the family needs to deal with information and emotions in an honest and forthright manner.

Cultural, Ethnic, and Religious Backgrounds

It is additionally important for the therapist to be aware of how the child's response to death is affected by his or her cultural, ethnic, or religious background. Knowing how different cultures express or repress their grief is key to a successful group. There is simply no "normal" or "appropriate" way to grieve. Anne Brener (1993) has written a very detailed book on the Jewish mourning rituals and practice. It is insightful as well as appropriate for groups with or without religious upbringing.

The Grief Group

The grief group meets for ten weekly one-hour sessions. I generally divide the sessions into four areas: a ten-minute beginning discussion, followed by thirty minutes of child-centered play therapy and ten minutes of role-playing, art, puppet shows, and therapeutic storytelling, and winding up with a final five minutes of discussion and closure to end the session.

The beginning of each session has a pattern that has become a weekly ritual that the children look forward to and expect. Each child is given the opportunity to talk. A magic talking stick is passed from child to child. Only the child who is holding the stick is allowed to talk. During this time the child describes what has occurred in the past week. Sometimes the children bring pictures of the deceased or something special from home. Each week the therapist should remind the children how many sessions are left. This is important in terms of termination, which must not come as a surprise. On the wall there are squares that are from the previous sessions. On this session's square each child adds a symbol or picture. At the end of the tenth session, we will have made a paper quilt that signifies our group.

The thirty-minute child-centered play therapy session allows the children the opportunity to play out their feelings. Some of the children play with the doctor kit or the dollhouse, others play in the sand or engage in some other activity. The purpose of group play therapy is to allow the children to learn not only about themselves but also about each other. The play therapist has the unique ability to watch, observe, and participate with the children. It is an opportunity to observe children as they help each other, cooperate, and attempt to work out their relationships with one another. This type of group play therapy has no goals or objectives. Each child is allowed to participate, watch, and join in, if he or she chooses. This process allows children to assimilate these experiences and apply them to other settings outside of the group.

Themes in Play Sessions

The play therapist watches the children as they explore feelings of hopelessness, fear, powerlessness, anger, guilt, and even joy. Common themes appear to arise during this time period. Deep feelings of sadness and longing for the deceased loved one are often expressed.

"It's OK to be sad and cry," said Sarah as she gently stroked Timmy's head. He looked up at her as he was burying the dad doll in the sand. "I don't like to cry because it hurts," Timmy replied. From across the room, Tom said, "Well, I sure cried a lot and then I felt good." The look on Timmy's face was one of relief as the tears welled in his eyes. Suddenly the four other children simply sat down beside him. As he cried, they sat in silence. I remember watching this powerful moment knowing that the group knew what to do. I was merely an observer, there if they needed me. This time they had each other.

Another theme that often appears is the excessive worry about the chance that other family members will die. After all, if Dad could die, so could Mom. "Who will take care of me?"

During one play session, Sarah could not find the mom doll. She had a small female doll figure going from room to room in the dollhouse. "Where are you, mommy?" "Please, mommy don't leave like daddy!" "Mommy, mommy, where are you?" Meanwhile, Mark was playing nearby with Timmy. He got up, found a doll that could represent Mom. He picked it up and walked the doll around outside the doll house. "Here I am. I was outside. Why are you crying?" Sarah's doll said, "I got scared you left me, too." The mommy doll went over to the daughter doll and said, "I'll be here for you." It was at that point I said, "Sometimes you worry that the person who loves you and takes care of you will die, too." Both children nodded their heads "yes." I usually tell the children that the surviving parent will do everything he or she can to take care of them.

This heightened fear of abandonment and separation can often cause children to regress. Parents often comment that the grieving child is wanting to be held a lot, sucks his thumb, talks baby talk, or even reverts to bed wetting. It is important for these children to receive reassurance that they are loved and will be cared for.

Guilty feelings over whether the children caused the death are often explored in the play sessions. Children often remember a time when they were so angry they may have wished their parent, brother, or sister were dead. Perhaps a parent said something like, "Oh, my, you scared me to death." Comments and thoughts such as these are often made without realizing the impact it may have on children. Guilt reactions often lie underneath the surface in the unconscious of children, because to express these feelings could be too overwhelming for them.

A theme that frequently comes up involves various questions about death and dying. I feel it is important for the play therapist to be comfortable with his or her own mortality. An understanding of the types of questions that may arise is important. Young children may want to know if the deceased person gets cold in the winter. The questions will also be a reflection of the child's cognitive and emotional developmental level.

Winding Up the Group

Termination for any group is often a perplexing process. Ending a group brings up the issues of abandonment and separation. Even when special relationships have been made the child finds that life has beginnings and endings. I like to read *Lifetimes* (Mellonie, 1991) to the group. This delightful book explains life and death in concrete ways that are easy for children to grasp. Just as all living things have their own lifetimes . . . so do groups. This metaphor helps the children who may be having a difficult time saying good-bye when the group disbands. Sensitivity and concern on the part of the therapist is essential. I always end the group by giving each child my business card. I show them where my phone number is and let them know they can call anytime. I also present them each with a white snowflake. This is to remind them that they are each unique. It is something that they can remember the group by.

The ending of a therapeutic relationship can be difficult for children. Advance preparation is essential. Children should be given the opportunity to express their feelings, such as sadness and anger.

"Are you going to make us leave?" asked Mark. "Yeah, it's just like when my dad died," replied Timmy. Sarah sat outside the circle looking forlorn. I made the comment: "Saying good-bye is never easy. I'm thinking each of you has many different feelings right now. I wonder if anyone would like to share." Almost all at once the group began to chatter. It is important to validate and allow the children to know that they are heard. I try to review what we have covered over the weeks, mention how they can use the things they have learned, and how I see how they have grown. I offer the children the opportunity to participate in a ceremony for our last session. What is amazing to me is the variety and differences each group can design into such a ceremony. It becomes unique and their very own.

Activities for Grief Groups: A Rationale for Interventions

I have found that the children's grief play therapy groups are groups that include many activities. This allows children the opportunity to do more than just talk. Through art, music, dance, puppet shows, plays, and storytelling the children can address their emotions. Powerful feelings can be expressed through the play that may feel overwhelming to a child who simply tries to talk. Activities often decrease the anxiety, tension, and fear that may be felt when sharing emotions. Through group activities the child often feels the support, encouragement, and sense of being heard by the group members. For some children, crying may be a sign of weakness. Children do not need to be stoic and strong. They need permission to cry, to know that it really is acceptable to start feeling. Knowing that the group will be there to support them offers children the opportunity to be vulnerable and to grieve.

Children in my grief groups enjoy art and play activities, which allow them to express themselves freely without worrying about getting into trouble. The structure that a group provides helps children work through their issues and investigate hopes, fears, dreams, and wishes. The following sections describe some of the activities that I have found useful.

Bubbles. A play therapist can never invest in enough bubbles! There is something unique about the use of bubbles. One exercise I have used is having children blow a bubble and as it floats off into the breeze outside to say "good-bye" to their special someone. I have found many different uses for them. Children seem to gravitate to bubbles and enjoy their beauty and symbolic power. I often have the children sit in a circle. We pass one bottle of bubble fluid around. Each child takes the wand and states a feeling, then blows a bubble. At times there is a quiet presence in the group as the bubbles float off and pop.

Treasure Boxes. Use an empty shoe box, cigar box, or any container that the child feels comfortable with. The children can decorate their individual boxes in any way that they choose. Fabric, paint, collage, words, or pictures can be used. The children will have collected things at home prior to this session that they consider remembrances of their loved one. Inside the box, objects such as pictures, shells, rocks, or gifts can be placed. It becomes a special memory box for children that they can revisit from time to time.

For some, these treasure boxes may be a symbolic type of casket or coffin. It is common in Western culture to bury the dead in often very special coffins made out of precious woods or metals, often to "protect" the deceased.

Shields of Armor. Collect large cardboard squares that can be obtained from packing stores, pizza restaurants, or cut out from packing boxes. The children can display on their shield of armor symbols, pictures, or designs. These designs may include things that protect the child, make them feel safe, powerful, and secure. A handle can be added in the back so the children are able to hold onto it.

Memory Quilts. Sometimes the children have access to the deceased's clothing and items that were made of cloth. One family I worked with cut up old T-shirts, blue jeans, blankets, and so on that belonged to their son and had them made into quilts. Designs can be cut to express feelings. Some examples include hearts, sad faces, happy faces, even thunderbolts.

Walking Sticks. I often collect sticks that can be sanded down and made into a walking stick for the child. On the stick can be placed yarn, ribbons, feathers, and even designs to represent the person they loved. Whenever they go for a walk, they can keep it close by, as a remembrance and celebration of the lost loved one.

The Therapist's Journey: Self-Reflection

Working with children who are bereaved requires an awareness of who you are and your own personal issues. Be mindful of how you conduct therapy and how you interact with clients, especially children. I have found that with children, issues related to death and dying are often emotionally charged. The child's issues and fears often touch us at the core of our own soul. On a daily basis you may be faced with your own mortality as well as your own fears about death and dying. If you are not truly in touch with your own issues in this aspect of your life, your ability to be with your clients will be jeopardized.

Take the time to explore your own background related to death, your personal issues related to grief and loss, and what motivates you to pursue this area of play therapy. Find a therapist peer group, a personal growth group, or even invest in working with another therapist on these issues. Your work in this area will be greatly enhanced by your own level of personal and psychological growth.

There will be times when you will need to draw on your own inner resources to work through some of the stories you may hear. Real life hurts and disappoints. Learning to appreciate all of life, you can view the children's painful events as opportunities for growth. Sometimes those dark moments allow us to stretch, grow, and deepen beyond who we think ourselves to be.

If you choose to work in the area of grief and loss with children, you will find that over the years you will change in both subtle and very dramatic ways. I have gained a deeper appreciation for life and living. On a daily basis, I am reminded of how fragile and precious life is. I have learned that there are many personal tragedies, each unique to the individual. I now see clearly that many of my own losses and painful experiences have been gifts, for each gave me the chance to grow, practice compassion, and learn to be at peace. I am grateful to my child clients for trusting me enough to share their pain and sorrow as well as their joy in healing.

References

Bluebond-Langner, M. (1978). *The private worlds of dying children.* Princeton, NJ: Princeton University Press.

Bowlby, J. (1980). *Attachment and loss: Vol. 3. Loss: Sadness and depression.* New York: Basic Books.

Brener, A. (1993). *Mourning and mitzvah: A guided journal for walking the mourner's path through grief to healing.* Woodstock, VT: Jewish Lights.

Corr, C., & Corr, D. (1996). *Handbook of childhood death and bereavement.* New York: Springer.

Furman, E. (1974). *A child's parent dies: Studies in childhood bereavement.* New Haven, CT: Yale University Press.

Ginott, H. (1961). *Group psychotherapy with children: The theory and practice of play therapy.* New York: McGraw-Hill.

Hobbs, N., Perrin, J., & Ireys, H. (1985). *Chronically ill children and their families: Problems, prospects, and proposals from the Vanderbilt study.* San Francisco: Jossey-Bass.

Koocher, G. P. (1974). Talking with children about death. *American Journal of Orthopsychiatry, 44,* 404–411.

Koocher, G. (1986). Coping with a death from cancer. *Journal of Consulting and Clinical Psychology, 54,* 623–631.

Kottman, T. (1995). *Partners in play: An Adlerian approach to play therapy.* Alexandria, VA: American Counseling Association.

Landreth, G. (1991). *Play therapy: The art of the relationship.* Muncie, IN: Accelerated Development.

LeVieux, J. (1993). Death of a father: The case of Celeste. In N. B. Webb (Ed.), *Helping bereaved children: A handbook for practitioners* (pp. 81–95). New York: Guilford Press.

Mellonie, B. (1991). *Lifetimes.* Suva, Fiji: Institute of Pacific Studies.

Piaget, J. (1954). *The construction of reality in the child.* New York: Basic Books.

Piaget, J., & Inhelder, B. (1969). *The psychology of the child.* New York: Basic Books.

Speece, M. W., & Brent, S. B. (1996). The development of children's understanding of death. In C. Corr & D. Corr (Eds.), *Handbook of childhood death and bereavement* (pp. 29–50) . New York: Springer.

Terr, L. C. (1991). Childhood trauma: An outline and overview. *American Journal of Psychiatry, 148,* 10–20.

Webb, N. B. (1993). Assessment of the bereaved child. In N. B. Webb (Ed.), *Helping bereaved children: A handbook for practitioners* (pp. 19–42). New York: Guilford Press.

Weber, J., & Fournier, D. (1985). Family support and a child's adjustment to death. *Family Relations Journal of Applied Family and Child Studies, 34*(1), 43–49.

Weller, R. A., Weller, E. B., Fristad, M. A., & Bowes, J. M. (1991). Depression in recently bereaved prepubertal children. *Journal of Psychiatry, 148,* 1536–1540.

Wolfelt, A. (1993). The misdiagnosis of ADHD in bereaved children. *The Forum Newsletter, 19,* 9–10.

SUGGESTED READING

Allan, J., & Bertoia, J. (1982). *Written paths to healing: Education and Jungian child counseling.* Dallas, TX: Spring.

Axline, V. (1969). *Play therapy.* New York: Ballantine.

Berg, R., & Landreth, G., & Fall, K. (1998). *Group counseling: Concepts and procedures* (3rd ed.). Muncie, IN: Accelerated Development.

Brody, V. A. (1997). *The dialogue of touch: Developmental play therapy.* Northvale, NJ: Aronson.

Gil, E. (1994). *Play in family therapy.* New York: Guilford Press.

Ginott, H. (1961). *Group psychotherapy with children: The theory and practice of play therapy.* New York: McGraw-Hill.

James, O. (1997). *Play therapy: A comprehensive guide.* Northvale, NJ: Aronson.

Kottman, T. (1995). *Partners in play: An Adlerian approach to play therapy.* Alexandria, VA: American Counseling Association.

Kottman, T., & Schaefer, C. (1993). *Play therapy in action.* Northvale, NJ: Aronson.

Landreth, G. (1991). *Play therapy: The art of the relationship.* Muncie, IN: Accelerated Development.

Landreth, G., Homeyer, L., Glover, G., & Sweeney, D. (1996). *Play therapy interventions with children's problems.* Northvale, NJ: Aronson.

Moustakas, C. (1959). *Psychotherapy with children: The living relationship.* New York: HarperCollins.

Moustakas, C. (1997). *Relationship play therapy.* Northvale, NJ: Aronson.

Oaklander, V. (1988). *Windows to our children: A Gestalt therapy approach to children and adolescents.* New York: Gestalt Journal Press.

O'Connor, K. (1991). *The play therapy primer.* New York: Wiley.

O'Connor, K., & Braverman, L. (1997). *Play therapy: Theory and practice.* New York: Wiley.

O'Connor, K., & Schaefer, C. (1995). *Handbook of play therapy* (Vol. 2). New York: Wiley.

Schaefer, C. (1993). *The therapeutic powers of play.* Northvale, NJ: Aronson.

Schaefer, C., & Carey, L. (1994). *Family play therapy.* Northvale, NJ: Aronson.

Schaefer, C., & O'Connor, K. (1983). *Handbook of play therapy.* New York: Wiley.

Slavson, S. (1950). *Analytic group therapy with children, adolescents, and adults.* New York: Columbia University Press.

Sweeney, D. (1997). *Counseling children through the world of play.* Wheaton, IL: Tyndale House.

CONTRIBUTORS

Valerie Appleton, Ed.D., MFCC, ATR. Valerie Appleton is an associate professor and director of counselor education at Eastern Washington University. She worked for ten years as art therapist to the intensive care burn unit at Saint Francis Memorial Hospital in San Francisco. While there she developed a unique program to provide art and play therapy to trauma patients and their families. Under a federal grant she was the principal investigator of Project Success, directed at at-risk secondary students. Project Success implemented a program of creative arts and skills-based learning in seven rural county school districts and Indian reservations. Currently, she is conducting cross-cultural research on the artwork of children from indigenous cultures. Dr. Appleton is president of the Washington Counselor Educators and Supervisors Division of the American Counseling Association. She is chair of the Education and Program Approval Board of the American Art Therapy Association and president of the Evergreen Art Therapy Association state chapter.

Judi Bertoia, Ph.D., RPT. Judi Bertoia is a registered play therapist and registered clinical counselor in Delta, British Columbia, where she works with adults and children in her private practice. Internationally known as a lecturer, researcher, and writer, Dr. Bertoia also supervises counselors and offers workshops for professional development. Her special interest is in-depth and expressive therapies centered on drawing, writing, and sandplay. She has written numerous articles and book chapters, has coauthored *Written Paths to Healing: Education and Jungian Child Counseling*, and has authored *Drawings from a Dying Child: Insights into Death from a Jungian Perspective.*

Sue Carlton Bratton, Ph.D., LPC, RPT-S. Sue Bratton is an assistant professor in the Department of Counseling, Development and Higher Education and director of counseling services at the Child and Family Resource Clinic at the University of North Texas. Sue is a respected lecturer, author, and clinician with extensive experience in individual and group play therapy, as well as filial and family play therapy. She has presented extensively in the United States and South Africa. Dr. Bratton also serves as a consultant to school districts in Texas, Oklahoma, Wyoming, and Tennessee, and is a guest lecturer at various Texas universities. She has written several articles, is coauthor of *The World of Play Therapy Literature,* and is currently coauthoring a book on the ten-week model of filial family play therapy.

Viola Brody, Ph.D. Viola Brody is the originator of the Developmental Play Therapy approach. Former chief psychologist of the Child Guidance Clinic in St. Petersburg, Florida, she has been an adjunct professor at the University of South Florida and at Eckerd College of St. Petersburg. She has presented workshops in Developmental Play Therapy throughout the United States and in Canada, Ireland, and London. In 1995, Dr. Brody initiated a program to provide training for the pre-K division of the Orlando, Florida, public schools and was the keynote speaker for the 1996 Association for Play Therapy International Conference. Her current interest is in the study of how touch and the child's use of his or her body provides the foundation for everything the child does. She is author of *The Dialogue of Touch: Developmental Play Therapy* and is working on a second book, *The Magic of Touch.*

Linda Chapman, ATR-BC, RPT. Linda Chapman is a board-certified art therapist and registered play therapist. She currently directs the Art Therapy Institute of the Redwoods, which provides training in art therapy and play therapy for children in crisis. She created the San Francisco General Hospital Pediatric Play Therapy Program, which she directed for eight years, and is a nationally known expert in child art therapy and play therapy with children who are victims of violence and trauma. She served as an assistant clinical professor in the Department of Psychiatry at the University of California San Francisco School of Medicine and is currently conducting research with the University of California Injury Prevention Center. Ms. Chapman has held several board positions in art therapy and play therapy associations, and has received awards for her contributions to the field of medical art therapy, her clinical work with medically ill children, and for her contributions to the field of art therapy. She coauthored and authored chapters in *California Art Therapy Trends*.

Gisela Schubach De Domenico, Ph.D., MFCC, RPT-S. Gisela De Domenico holds a Ph.D. in clinical psychology from Pacific Graduate School of Psychology in Palo Alto, California. She has researched children's and adults' use of the sandtray resulting in the creation of the Vision Quest Into Symbolic Training Series in 1984. Dr. De Domenico developed the innovative and dynamic techniques of Sandtray-Worldplay Therapeutic Communication that go beyond Lowenfeld, Jung, and Kalff. Dr. De Domenico is a founding member of the Sandtray Network and author of several articles and book chapters, as well as several self-published training manuals, including the *Sandtray-Worldplay Manual*. She has provided training in sandplay at various local, regional and national conferences. Additionally, she regularly offers six levels of Sandtray-Worldplay training in Oakland, California.

Lori Dunn, M.S., CCLS. Lori Dunn received her master's degree in counseling, with an emphasis in play therapy, from the University of North Texas in 1994. She is currently a certified child life specialist with Children's Medical Center of Dallas. She has extensive experience working with children hospitalized for surgery, liver transplant, intensive care, and trauma. She provides individual and group play therapy for patients and siblings, and filial therapy training for parents, and has made several presentations on hospitalized children, play therapy, and filial therapy.

Kelly Webb Ferebee, M.Ed., LPC, NCC. Kelly Webb Ferebee has worked with children, parents, and other adults for twenty-five years in education, mental health clinics, and through volunteer work. She received her master's degree from the University of North Texas in 1993 with an emphasis in play therapy. She is currently a doctoral student at the University of North Texas, specializing in group counseling and play therapy. Her dissertation research is in the use of expressive arts therapy with bereaved families. She is currently a teaching assistant at the University of North Texas, where she supervises students at the Child and Family Resource Clinic in play therapy, group play therapy, expressive arts therapy, and filial therapy. She is also an adjunct faculty member at North Lake Community College, where she is teaching a course in exploring spirituality through art.

Mary Flynt, Ed.S., LPC. Mary Flynt has worked for twenty-five years in the field of education as a counselor and teacher. She has been the recipient of school counseling awards at the state and national levels. Her many presentations and active participation in the counseling profession include publications on child abuse and play techniques in the school setting. Mary is one of the co-creators of Kinder Therapy, an intervention that applies filial therapy techniques and Adlerian principles to the process of counselor-teacher education and student-teacher relationships. She is an elementary school counselor at Nesbit Elementary School in Gwinnett County, Georgia.

Haim G. Ginott, Ed.D. Haim Ginott, child psychologist, was a proponent and developer of group play therapy and activity group therapy. He saw the need for the development of new techniques and tools, not simply the modification of previous applications. As a result he worked in child guidance clinics and wrote many articles regarding play therapy and parent training groups. Dr. Ginott also taught teachers and parents how to enter a child's world by using a language of compassion and concern. He is perhaps best known for his book *Between Parent and Child,* written in 1956, which is still in print and recommended reading for parents. His book *Group Psychotherapy with Children: The Theory and Practice of Play Therapy,* originally published in 1961 by McGraw-Hill, was reprinted in 1994 by Aronson. A contemporary of S. R. Slavson, Dr. Ginott was an equal contributor to the field of group play therapy and dedicated one of his books to S. R. Slavson. Dr. Ginott wrote a weekly column titled "Between Us" and was a resident psychologist on the *Today Show.*

Geraldine Glover, Ph.D., LPCC, RPT-S. Geraldine Glover has been working with children, their parents, and other adults for over twelve years in education, day treatment programs, and mental health clinics. She completed research in filial therapy with Native Americans residing on the Flathead Reservation in northern Montana in honor of her Salish ancestry. She is a strong advocate of multicultural awareness and provides training workshops regarding its importance in the therapeutic relationship. She currently has a small private practice in Santa Fe, New Mexico, specializing in play therapy, individual counseling, and parent-child relationship enhancement (filial training). She also teaches as adjunct faculty at both the College of Santa Fe and Santa Fe Community College. Dr. Glover is coauthor of *Play Therapy Interventions with Children's Problems* and is a contributing author to *Working with Native Americans in Education and Residential Care.*

Linda E. Homeyer, Ph.D., LPC, RPT-S. Linda Homeyer is an assistant professor in the Counseling Program of the Department of Educational Administration and Psychological Services at Southwest Texas State University (SWT). She has developed a play therapy training program at SWT including the first play therapy course available by distance learning. Dr. Homeyer is a frequent presenter at professional conferences and training throughout the United States. As an active advocate for children and play therapy, she helped organize the first state branch of the Association for Play Therapy (Texas) and has served on the state board in various positions since the Texas Association for Play Therapy was chartered. She has coauthored *Play Therapy with Children's Problems* and *The World of Play Therapy Literature*, as well as various chapters and journal articles. She continues to research in the areas of play therapy and children who have been sexually abused, and maintains a small but active private practice in San Marcos, Texas.

Terry Kottman, Ph.D., LMHC, RPT-S. Terry Kottman is an associate professor of counselor education in the Department of Educational Leadership, Counseling, and Postsecondary Education at the University of Northern Iowa. She is a registered play therapist-supervisor and has a small private practice. Dr. Kottman developed Adlerian play therapy, a technique that combines the ideas and techniques of Individual Psychology and play therapy. She regularly presents workshops in play therapy, activity-based therapy, and school counseling. Dr. Kottman is the author of *Partners in Play: An Adlerian Approach to Play Therapy* and *Play Therapy: Basic and Beyond*, coauthor of *Guidance and Counseling in the Elementary and Middle Schools*, and coeditor of *Play Therapy in Action: A Casebook for Practitioners*. She is the current editor of the *International Journal of Play Therapy*.

Garry L. Landreth, Ed.D., LPC, RPT-S. Garry Landreth, internationally known for his writings and work promoting the development of play therapy, is a Regents Professor in the Counselor Education Department at the University of North Texas. He is the founder and director of the Center for Play Therapy, the largest play therapy training program in the nation, and has conducted training workshops focusing on child-centered play therapy worldwide. Dr. Landreth's more than seventy publications include his award-winning book *Play Therapy: The Art of the Relationship*, which has been translated into Chinese, Russian, and Korean, and his most recent books, *Play Therapy Interventions with Children's Problems* and *Parents as Therapeutic Partners: Listening to Your Child's Play*. He is a licensed counselor, licensed psychologist, member of the Board of Directors of the Association for Play Therapy, and registered play therapy supervisor. Dr. Landreth has received numerous professional honors from the university as well as state and national organizations.

Jane Le Vieux, M.S., M.Ed., RN, LPC. Jane Le Vieux received her master's degree in counseling and her master's degree in child and family studies from the University of North Texas. She has worked with children and families for over fifteen years as a nurse, child life specialist, and child and family therapist. In addition, she has published in professional journals as well as authored a chapter in *Helping*

Bereaved Children. Her areas of interest include children's responses to grief and loss as well as families' responses to chronic illness. She is listed in *Who's Who in American Nursing* as well as *Who's Who in American Women,* and has presented at state and national conferences on the topics of grief and loss with children and other play therapy issues.

Lesley Lingnell, M.S., M.Ed., CCLS. Lesley Lingnell has a master's degree in human development and family studies and a second in counseling with an emphasis in play therapy from The University of North Texas. She is a certified child life specialist currently employed at Children's Medical Center of Dallas and works in the Center For Cancer and Blood Disorders. She has extensive experience working with children and their families who suffer from chronic and terminal illness, as well as acute illness and hospitalization. She has initiated a play therapy program at the hospital and provides individual and group play therapy for patients and siblings, as well as filial therapy training for parents. She has presented at the state and local level on the subject of supporting and providing interventions for children and families with medical needs.

Kevin O'Connor, Ph.D., RPT-S. Kevin O'Connor is professor and director of ecosystemic clinical child psychology at the California School of Professional Psychology–Fresno. He is a licensed psychologist and a registered play therapist-supervisor. He developed ecosystemic play therapy, which promotes active, developmentally focused interventions that engage children in working to solve their problems. Dr. O'Connor was a cofounder of the Association for Play Therapy (with Dr. Charles Schaefer). He also maintains a small independent practice in Fresno, California, and travels extensively lecturing on play therapy. His presentations focus on the ecosystemic approach and the value of incorporating a cognitive approach into play therapy by using interpretation to promote problem solving. Dr. O'Connor is author of *The Play Therapy Primer* and coeditor of *The Handbook of Play Therapy,* Volumes I and II.

Violet Oaklander, Ph.D., RPT-S. Violet Oaklander has a Ph.D. in clinical psychology, an M.S. in special education, and has been a certified Gestalt therapist since 1973. Dr. Oaklander travels extensively throughout the world giving training seminars on her approach to working with children and adolescents. She currently lives in Santa Barbara, California, where she maintains a private practice and directs the Violet Oaklander Institute. The institute is devoted to the supervision and training of professionals who work with children. Her unique approach to working with children, which combines Gestalt therapy theory, philosophy, and practice with a variety of expressive techniques, has won international recognition. Dr. Oaklander authored the book *Windows to our Children: A Gestalt Therapy Approach to Children and Adolescents* and several articles, videotapes, and audiotapes on psychotherapeutic work with children.

Emily Oe, Ph.D., LPC, RPT-S. Emily Oe is nationally known for her promotion of play therapy as a mode of therapeutic intervention with individuals across the life span. She developed the play therapy training program at Sam Houston State University, the second largest program of its kind. She has done extensive training both at Sam Houston State University and is a frequent workshop presenter, emphasizing not only basic training but also advanced play therapy intervention with sibling groups, adults, mentally limited individuals, and the elderly. She is on the Board of Directors for the Association for Play Therapy and has been board secretary since 1989. She also organized the Sam Houston Association for Play Therapy, the first chapter of a state play therapy association. Dr. Oe currently maintains a private practice in Houston, Texas, and continues to provide play therapy training throughout the world. She is the coauthor of *Kaleidoscope of Play Therapy Stories.*

Dee Ray, Ph.D., LPC, NCC. Dee Ray received her Ph.D. degree from the University of North Texas with a specialty in child counseling and play therapy. She received her M.Ed. and B.S. degrees from Vanderbilt University, focusing on developmental theory of counseling. She has extensive experience working with emotionally disturbed children and adolescents. Her publication areas include political advocacy of counselors, extending the use of filial therapy, and play therapy research. She has also worked in the field enacting play therapy techniques as an elementary school counselor. Dr. Ray is currently assistant professor of counseling at Texas A&M University, Commerce and conducts her research on play therapy, school counseling, and counselor supervision.

Samuel R. Slavson, Founder of Activity Group Therapy. S. R. Slavson worked in the field of psychotherapy for over fifty years, authored over thirty books, and introduced innovations in the areas of education, group work, recreation, family consultation, reeducation of delinquents, and psychotherapy. However, he is known in the play therapy field for his pioneering work in group psychotherapy with children and adolescents. He researched the application of a variety of types of group treatment and guidance with preschool children, predelinquent adolescents in the community, and with delinquent boys in residential treatment. Mr. Slavson's numerous publications include such classics as *The Practice of Group Therapy; Analytic Group Therapy with Children, Adolescents and Adults; Child Psychotherapy;* and *A Textbook in Analytic Group Psychotherapy.* Mr. Slavson was a founder of the

American Group Psychotherapy Association and founder and editor of the *International Journal of Group Psychotherapy*.

D. Michael Smith, M.Div., LMFT, RPT-S. Michael Smith cofounded and codirects the Center for Family Care in Dallas, Texas, with his wife and partner, Nancy Smith. He has over twenty years of clinical expertise in individual and family therapy, specializing in play therapy and filial therapy. In addition to the clinical practice, he teaches courses in play therapy, filial therapy, and group play therapy to professionals and provides beginning and advanced supervision to developing play therapists and filial therapy instructors. He travels extensively conducting play therapy, filial therapy, and Relational Activity Play Therapy Group workshops. He and his wife produced a video instructional series, *Entering the World of Play, Tapes 1 and 2*. The Smiths are frequent presenters at state and national play therapy conferences.

Nancy R. Smith, M.A., LMFT, RPT-S. Nancy Smith cofounded and codirects the Center for Family Care with her husband and partner, Michael Smith. For over twenty years, she has provided play therapy and filial therapy to families. In addition to her clinical practice, she teaches courses in play therapy, filial therapy, and group play therapy to professionals and provides beginning and advanced supervision to developing play therapists and filial therapy instructors. She travels extensively conducting play therapy, filial therapy, and Relational Activity Play Therapy Group workshops, and is a regular presenter at regional, state, and national play therapy conferences.

Daniel S. Sweeney, Ph.D., LPC, MFCC, RPT-S. Daniel Sweeney is an assistant professor of counseling at George Fox University in Portland, Oregon. He is also an adjunct professor at Portland State University, a licensed counselor in several states and a registered play therapist and supervisor, and has a small private practice. He was formerly assistant director of the Center for Play Therapy at the University of North Texas. Dr. Sweeney has extensive experience in working with children and families in a variety of settings, including therapeutic foster care, community mental health, and pastoral counseling. He has presented at numerous state and national conferences on the topics of play therapy, filial therapy, and sandplay. He has authored several book chapters and articles on child counseling, play therapy issues, and families and parenting. He is coauthor of *Play Therapy Interventions with Children's Problems* and *Sandtray: A Practical Manual,* and author of *Counseling Children Through the World of Play*. He lives with his wife Marla and their four children in Newberg, Oregon.

JoAnna White, Ed.D., LPC, RPT-S. JoAnna White is an associate professor in the Department of Counseling and Psychological Services at Georgia State University in Atlanta, Georgia, where she coordinates the school counseling, play therapy, and group programs. She is a member of the editorial board of the *International Journal of Play Therapy* and recently completed a term of eight years on the editorial board of the *Journal for Specialists in Group Work.* Dr. White has made more than a hundred presentations at professional meetings, and she has more than forty publications, many in the field of play therapy. She is currently involved in research related to training teachers in play therapy skills (Kinder Therapy) to enhance student-teacher relationships and student success.

NAME INDEX

A

Abel, G. G., 315
Abelson, C., 198
Adams, M., 359, 360
Adler, A., 65, 67, 68, 338
Albert, L., 71
Alger, I., 359
Allan, J., 89, 97, 99, 102, 202, 208
Allen, J., 290
Allen, P., 179
Almeida, R., 281, 282
Anderson, F., 179
Ansbacher, H., 66, 67, 68, 69
Ansbacher, R., 66, 67, 68, 69
Appleton, V. E., 179
Axline, V. M., 39, 40, 46, 48, 51,
    53, 56–57, 58, 102, 235, 236,
    305, 308, 315, 319, 323, 330,
    338, 339, 340, 341, 349, 353,
    363, 371

B

Bank, S., 320, 321, 322, 332
Baptiste, L., 286
Barlow, K., 327

Beardslee, W., 359
Becker, J. V., 315
Begun, A., 324
Bender, L., 179, 268, 269
Benedek, L., 319
Berg, R., 4, 236, 237, 238, 239,
    240, 244, 245, 246, 256, 320,
    330, 360, 364, 372
Bertoia, J., 89, 97, 99, 100, 102
Bettner, B. L., 65, 66, 69, 71, 79
Beyer, B., 70, 71, 76
Binkley, M., 268
Bixler, R., 51, 311–312
Blitz, J., 359, 360
Blom, G., 106
Bluebond-Langner, M., 382
Boerio, C., 268
Bosdell, B. J., 337, 339
Bowes, J. M., 381
Bowlby, J., 382
Boy, A., 43, 45
Bozarth, J., 45
Brendtro, L. K., 284–285
Brener, A., 382
Brent, S. B., 379
Brett, D., 82
Briend, J., 337

Brigman, G., 336, 356
Brill, N., 365
Brinkmeyer, G., 268
Brodley, B., 45
Brody, V. A., 139, 142, 143, 153,
    159, 160, 161
Brokenleg, M., 285
Brown, G., 168
Brown, T., 365
Browne, A., 305
Brunskill, S., 360
Buber, M., 162
Burch, C., 269
Burgess, B. J., 285

C

Camp, B., 106
Caplan, E., 5
Caplan, T., 5
Carey, L., 208
Carter, S., 269
Cassell, S., 269, 360
Celano, M., 194, 198
Cermak, S., 198
Chapman, L., 179
Chau, I., 279

SUBJECT INDEX

A

Acculturation, 286–287

A.C.T. model of limit setting, 61

Acting out: bereavement behavior as, 380; as catharsis, 18; value of, 25; by young children in groups, 24–26, 32

Active Parenting Today (Popkin), 71

Active Teaching (Popkin), 71

Activities: for expressive art activity group therapy, 199–213; for Gestalt group play therapy, 173–174; for grief play therapy groups, 385–386; for Relational Activity Play Therapy groups, 251–254, 256–258; in structured group play therapy, 108–109, 112

Activity group therapy: with older children and adolescents, 11; with preadolescents, 194–199, 237; with very young children, 24. *See also* Expressive art activity group therapy; Group puppetry

Adlerian group play therapy, 65–84; Crucial Cs in, 65–66, 69; exam-
ple of, 72–84; format for, 71–72; Individual Psychology theory as basis of, 66, 67–69; limit setting in, 77–78; parent and teacher involvement in, 70–71; phases of counseling in, 65, 66, 76–83; selecting children for, 70

Adolescents, activity groups with, 11. *See also* Preadolescents

Adults, as Partners in Developmental Play Therapy, 139, 159

African Americans, 278; cultural values and expectations of, 281–282

Age of children: for activity group play therapy, 195, 237; in child-centered play therapy groups, 55; in elementary school play groups, 341; in grief play therapy groups, 377; for group play therapy, 9–10, 237; length of group sessions and, 11; in Relational Activity Play Therapy (RAPT) groups, 237; in sibling play therapy groups, 325–326; in structured play therapy groups, 113, 114. *See also* Development

Aggression, sublimated in play groups, 29

American Psychiatric Association, 6

Anger: acting out, 32; Gestalt therapy techniques with, 174; in sexually abused children, 310; sublimated in play groups, 29

Archetypes, Jungian concept of, 87–88

Art media: for art therapy, 182–183; continuum of, 180, 182–183; defined, 180; for expressive art group activity therapy, 197

Art therapy groups, 179–190; components of activities of, 184; examples of, 185–188; initial considerations with, 180–183; introducing activities to, 183–184; led by elementary school counselors, 356; literature on, 179; recommendations on, 188–190; selecting children for, 180–181; terms used with, 180. *See also* Expressive art activity group therapy

Asian Americans, 278; cultural values and expectations of, 283–284

Printed in the United Kingdom
by Lightning Source UK Ltd.
134938UK00002B/261-270/A